Four Pillars of Destiny
Exploring Metal Charts

Dr. Jin Peh

Edited by
Miranda van Gaalen

Disclaimer:

The information presented in this book should not be considered a substitute for a professional Chinese astrology reading.

ISBN-10: 1979352259
ISBN-13: 978-1979352253
Library of Congress Control Number: 2016919966
CreateSpace Independent Publishing Platform,
North Charleston, SC

Foreword

Welcome to the second book of the five part series where we look at different types of Four Pillars charts. The first book in the series analyzed Water charts. Please note that the series of Four Pillars book is not suitable for beginners. The books provide an overview of the techniques used in analyzing and interpreting Four Pillars charts and is recommended for those who are familiar with how to construct a Four Pillars chart and the corresponding Luck Cycles from a *Ten Thousand Year Almanac*.

I was first introduced to the subject of Four Pillars in Perth, Western Australia when I attended a course in the Australian summer of 1999 taught by a visiting Chinese professor. I eventually became the de facto interpreter between him and the rest of the students as I understood English and Mandarin. I left Singapore for Australia at the age of 14 so my Mandarin was elementary. Ironically, this rudimentary Mandarin gave me a foot in the door when it came to Chinese Metaphysics compared to my Western classmates. I remembered how flustered the Professor was by some of the questions the Australian students asked him. I didn't think it was a good idea to translate into English some of his incredulous responses so I stuck with the diplomatic chestnut "The Professor says it is not important".

What is more important is that the serious student needs to recognize patterns from Four Pillars charts, observe and verify the conclusions and apply them to future cases. Each person's chart is unique and examined on a case-by-case basis and the approach requires logical and rational application. After all, Chinese Metaphysics is a science that has survived centuries.

As mentioned in the Water book, I started studying with my Four Pillars teacher and mentor Lily Chung in San Francisco back in the autumn of 2009. Like almost every other student that I have come across, I committed the cardinal mistake of the novice. I wanted to study the charts of my family and friends first. While the charts of the people that are important in our lives spur us on to study and understand the subject, it is not the ideal way to learn as the approach is unstructured. After all, most of the people in our lives tend not to have extremely well delineated patterns like the ones covered in this book. And of course, when I first started, I had not arrived at the place of objectivity that comes only with experience when looking at family and friends' charts. This required a few more years to cultivate. Emotional involvement when looking at the charts of people in our lives prevents us from observing the patterns logically and rationally. It is human nature to look for auspicious configurations that are not necessarily there or attempt to manipulate the theories that are presented in the classics. After all, it is understandable that we all want to find something positive to say about the charts of our loved ones, or worse, to deny or ignore the issues that are present. That is why in order to read charts of the people in your life accurately, the first step is to be objective and approach it as you would a mathematical question.

In the classes that I teach, I always try to include course material that is relevant to the students who are attending. The first step is to classify their charts and then identify the favourable elements. I then use a celebrity's chart to draw parallels with the student's chart and illustrate to them the principles. As in other fields and disciplines of life, the person needs to see how the theory applies to their chart first. If they are convinced of its accuracy and validity, then it increases their enthusiasm to study the subject further. If they struggle to apply the principles to their own charts or fail to see their own patterns, then enthusiasm is lost and studies abandoned.

I recalled that when I studied charts of celebrities with Lily, we both realized how clear and straightforward the patterns were. This was a contrast to the charts of family and friends, where the directions were often unclear and confusing. I came to the realization that for such a vast subject, it is important for the student to build confidence in interpreting and analysing the straightforward charts first. When they can identify more than half of the charts that they come across, they can start to use the same principles to analyse the charts when the patterns are not clearly defined.

It is the usual approach that we write about what we know, so I apologize in advance if you find some of the celebrity examples here uninteresting or irrelevant. I have always been a big fan of film, music and books so my choice of examples reflects my interest. The sport that I have been most interested in has been tennis, so I hope that explains why I have included the charts of several tennis players here. Growing up in Australia, my brother was a cricket fanatic so I have also included two cricketers here with distinct charts.

So what were the steps involved in choosing the 108 Metal examples that are included in this book? First and foremost, from a Four Pillars perspective, they had charts where Metal is the most prominent element. For instance, there would be different combinations of the Partial Three Harmony Metal Combination (e.g. Snake and Rooster, Rooster and Ox or Snake and Ox). There may also be a Full Three Harmony Metal Combination or Seasonal Metal Combination in the birth chart. I have also included charts where there may not be any Combinations but rather two or more Rooster Branches that allow Metal to be the most prominent element.

Secondly, the celebrities also needed to have a large enough body of work that allowed me to observe their personal and career developments over different years or Luck Cycles. It also helped if the celebrities were able to transcend their achievements in their field and became known in popular culture, such as the cricket player Shane Warne. While the majority of celebrity examples here are American, I have also included British, European, Australian and some Asian examples to encompass a wider range of cultures.

Another new development in this book is to compare and contrast the charts of celebrities who are born on the same day, month and year, such as Examples 5.6 and 5.7, Helena Bonham Carter and Zola Budd Pieterse. The Four Pillars chart is not the be all and end all of a person's life, otherwise those who share the same birthday would share the same expiry date as well.

I have also included more information on the Special Stars in this book. In the Water book, the additional information on Special Stars was stripped down to the two most important, i.e. the Special Stars that bring success and the Mentor or Nobleman Stars as determined by the Day Master. In this book, you will also be introduced to the Academic Stars and the Red Light Pillars, as well as the days that are Sitting on their Nobleman or Academic Stars, the Six Intelligent Days and the Two Strategist Days. This information on Special Stars and days will be expanded on further in subsequent books.

In each chapter, I include celebrities who have passed away as well as celebrities with just a few Luck Cycles of success behind them. Why? For the deceased celebrities, we can identify the negative developments and elements present in the Luck Cycle, day, month and year of death and then formulate our own theories. For the younger celebrities, we can use our observations and principles to predict how their future Luck Cycles will pan out. This is similar to doing a reading for a person in their teens or 20s, when there are a lot more Luck Cycles to follow.

Finally, the most important principle that I would like you to apply after reading this book is to look at the bigger picture. From my days in medical school, I was taught to see the wood from the trees, not to get lost in the minute details and lose sight of what is important. So the key to identifying the patterns of Four Pillars charts is to look for any Combinations within the Branches that can then help you identify the most prominent element. A fundamental error is to hone in on the season of birth or the Day Master and then build a picture or reading from there. Rather, after identifying the most prominent element within the chart, you relate it back to the Day Master to classify the chart and list the favourable elements. This is why the student needs to be familiar with the Five Relationships between Elements (Resource, Output, Wealth, Power, Self).

Once again, my apologies if your chart does not have a Water or Metal Combination within its Branches. There are three more elements to go: Wood, Fire and Earth, so I hope that by the time all five books in the series have been published, they should cover the majority of charts that you have observed in your studies thus far.

As usual, this book would not have been possible without the contribution of the individuals whom I have to thank.

Lily Chung, my teacher. I thank you for your patience and generosity in sharing your years of experience and knowledge with me every time I come to see you in San Francisco. I am very grateful for the opportunities that you have given me.

Miranda van Gaalen, my excellent editor. Words cannot express my gratitude for the detail and enthusiasm that you bring to this book. You have brought it to a totally different level and I cannot thank you enough. I always look forward to seeing you in Arnhem.

Karen Yu, my San Francisco hostess. Thank you for always making my visits to the Bay Area special and memorable. This whole series of books would not have possible without your hospitality.

Crystal al Shatti, my Gulf patroness. Thank you for your support and for organizing my workbooks. Your passion and interest in the subject is inspiring.

Anna Cheung Abbott, my Dubai hostess. Thank you for your contribution to this project. I am always happy to have another class in your lovely home.

Janene Laird, my Australian patroness. Thank you to Bruce and you for your hospitality in Noosa and Melbourne and for all the laughter and good times that we share down under.

Josephine Wong, my designer. Thank you for your contribution to the book cover and for the overall layout of the book. Hard to believe that it's been several decades since we first met. It feels like yesterday.

Irina Anfinogenova and Anatoly Sokolov, my Russian organizers. Thank you for bringing me to Moscow and for making my classes in Russia a big success.

Vicki Sauvage, my Australian ami and editor. It is my pleasure and honour to share this with you. Ever since the day we met at Hobart Airport, it's been a wonderful ride. Thank you for everything.

Sylvia, Linda and Ghee, my siblings. Thank you for your unwavering support and belief in me over the years.

My parents. I am thankful every day to you for making me who I am today.

Table of Contents

List of Tables and Examples

Chapter One Introduction

Table 1.1	The Four Pillars Indicating Different Life Stages and Approximate Age
Table 1.2	The Luck Cycle and Corresponding Age
Table 1.3	The Family Members as Seen in the Four Pillars
Table 1.4	The Self, Resource and Output Elements
Table 1.5	The Self, Power and Wealth Elements
Table 1.6	The Five Relationships between the Five Elements
Table 1.7	The Five Relationships as per the Day Master
Table 1.8	The Stems in their Sequence
Table 1.9	Stem Combinations
Table 1.10	The 12 Branches and their Hidden Stems
Table 1.11	Full and Partial Three Harmony Combinations and Associated Element
Table 1.12	Seasonal Combinations with Associated Element and Season
Table 1.13	Six Harmony Combinations
Table 1.14	The Clash Animals
Table 1.15	The Special Stems as determined by the Day Master
Table 1.16	Mentor Stars as determined by the Day Master
Table 1.17	The Four Sitting on Nobleman Days
Table 1.18	The Academic Stars and the Day Masters
Table 1.19	The Six Sitting on the Academic Star Days
Table 1.20	The Two Sitting on the Nobleman and Academic Star Days
Table 1.21	The Six Intelligent Days
Table 1.22	The Two Strategist Days
Table 1.23	The Eight Red Light Pillars

Chapter Two Follow the Resource (Water) Charts

Example 2.1	Dolly Parton	American Country Music Singer
Example 2.2	Madeline Albright	American Secretary of State
Example 2.3	Shonda Rhimes	American Television Producer and Screenwriter
Example 2.4	Bill O'Reilly	American Journalist and Television Host
Example 2.5	Jennifer Hudson	American Singer
Example 2.6	Andrew Lincoln	British Actor
Example 2.7	Anita Baker	American Singer
Example 2.8	Lleyton Hewitt	Australian Tennis Player
Example 2.9	Jim Jarmusch	American Film Director
Example 2.10	Edison Chen	Hong Kong-Canadian Singer
Example 2.11	Tori Spelling	American Actress
Example 2.12	Jose Feliciano	Puerto Rican Singer
Example 2.13	Prince Christian	Second in Line to the Danish Throne
Example 2.14	Nicolae Ceaucescu	General Secretary of the Romanian Communist Party 1965 to 1989
Example 2.15	Hank Williams	American Singer
Example 2.16	Donny Hathaway	American Singer
Example 2.17	Hansie Cronje	South African Cricket Team Captain
Example 2.18	Zayn Malik	British Singer

Chapter Three Follow the Output (Metal) Charts

Example 3.1	Justin Timberlake	American Singer
Example 3.2	Dame Joan Collins	British Actress
Example 3.3	Eddie Redmayne	British Actor
Example 3.4	Frank Oz	American Puppeteer and Film Director
Example 3.5	Marc Anthony	American Singer-Songwriter
Example 3.6	Lara Fabian	Belgian-Canadian Singer
Example 3.7	Tippi Hedren	American Actress
Example 3.8	Heather Graham	American Actress
Example 3.9	Tony Leung Ka Fai	Hong Kong Actor
Example 3.10	James Cromwell	American Actor
Example 3.11	Alicia Silverstone	American Actress
Example 3.12	Nina Dobrev	Bulgarian-Canadian Actress
Example 3.13	Riley Keough	American Actress
Example 3.14	Zach Galifianakis	American Actor
Example 3.15	Jim Henson	American Puppeteer
Example 3.16	Colleen McCullough	Australian Novelist and Neuroscientist
Example 3.17	Michael Hutchence	Australian Rock Singer
Example 3.18	Harry Styles	British Singer

Chapter 4 Follow the Wealth (Metal) Charts

Example 4.1	Bruce Springsteen	American Singer-Songwriter
Example 4.2	Kate Moss	British Model
Example 4.3	Steve Winwood	Birtish Singer
Example 4.4	Mark Owen	British Singer
Example 4.5	Armistead Maupin	American Author
Example 4.6	Brian de Palma	American Film Director
Example 4.7	Clive James	Australian Broadcaster and Author
Example 4.8	Al Stewart	British Singer-Songwriter
Example 4.9	Viola Davis	American Actress
Example 4.10	Kareena Kapoor	Indian Actress
Example 4.11	Alexis Bledel	American Actress
Example 4.12	Steven Soderbergh	American Film Director
Example 4.13	Vanessa Redgrave	British Actress
Example 4.14	Joan Lunden	American Television Journalist
Example 4.15	Lindsey Buckingham	American Singer
Example 4.16	David Copperfield	American Illusionist
Example 4.17	Carolyn Bessette	American Publicist and wife of John F. Kennedy Jr.
Example 4.18	Sarah McLachlan	Canadian Singer

Chapter Five Follow the Power (Metal) Charts

Example 5.1	Anne Rice	American Author
Example 5.2	Julia Gillard	Australian Prime Minister 2010 to 2013
Example 5.3	Jana Novotna	Czech Tennis Champion
Example 5.4	Jay Chou	Taiwanese Singer and Actor
Example 5.5	Alan Ball	American Television Writer and Producer
Example 5.6	Helena Bonham Carter	British Actress
Example 5.7	Zola Budd Pieterse	South African-American Runner
Example 5.8	Elisabeth Hasselbeck	American Television Personality
Example 5.9	Bill Medley	American Singer
Example 5.10	Michelle Williams	American Actress
Example 5.11	Fran Drescher	American Actress Comedienne
Example 5.12	Andy Roddick	American Tennis Player
Example 5.13	Rick Springfield	Prime Minister of India 1984 to 1988
Example 5.14	James Gandolfini	American Actor
Example 5.15	Joan Rivers	American Comedienne
Example 5.16	Allan Carr	American Producer
Example 5.17	Cilla Black	British Singer
Example 5.18	Jason Derulo	American Singer

Chapter Six Dominant Metal Charts

Example 6.1	Mary Pierce	French Tennis Player
Example 6.2	Collette Dinnigan	Australian Fashion Designer
Example 6.3	Alan Cumming	Scottish Actor
Example 6.4	Amy Schumer	American Comedienne and Actress
Example 6.5	Enya	Irish Singer
Example 6.6	Markus Feehily	Irish Singer
Example 6.7	Richard Roxburgh	Australian Actor
Example 6.8	Joanna Newsom	American Cellist and Singer
Example 6.9	Jools Holland	British Musician and Television Presenter
Example 6.10	Paul Keating	Australian Prime Minister 1991 to 1996
Example 6.11	Avicii	Swedish Musician
Example 6.12	Josh Hutcherson	American Actor
Example 6.13	Rainer Werner Fassbinder	German Film Director
Example 6.14	Nicole Brown Simpson	American Actress
Example 6.15	Marilyn Monroe	American Actress
Example 6.16	Katharine Hepburn	American Actress
Example 6.17	Sylvia Plath	American Author
Example 6.18	Azealia Banks	American Rapper

Chapter Seven Competitive Water Charts

Example 7.1	Kelly Rowland	American Singer
Example 7.2	Mardy Fish	American Tennis Player
Example 7.3	Kevin Scott Richardson	American Singer
Example 7.4	Nancy Kerrigan	American Ice Skater
Example 7.5	Shane Warne	Australian Cricketer
Example 7.6	Ben Carson	American Neurosurgeon and Politician
Example 7.7	Vanna White	American Television Personality
Example 7.8	John Lithgow	American Actor
Example 7.9	Anastacia	American Singer
Example 7.10	Sergio Mendes	Brazilian Musician
Example 7.11	Wyclef Jean	Haitian Rapper and Singer
Example 7.12	Tarkan	Turkish Singer
Example 7.13	Jacqueline McKenzie	Australian Actress
Example 7.14	Toni Tennille	American Singer
Example 7.15	Gwen Stefani	American Singer
Example 7.16	Richard Dreyfuss	American Actor
Example 7.17	Peter Benchley	American Author
Example 7.18	Alicia Vikander	Swedish Actress

Chapter One Introductory Concepts

You know how to derive a Four Pillars chart and plot the Luck Cycles, so the next step would be to interpret and classify the chart. Before being able to analyze the Four Pillars chart, you need to be familiar with the following concepts involving the Pillars, Stems, Branches and some of the Stars. The first step would be to understand the significance of the Four Pillars.

1.1 The Four Pillars and the Signifiers

The Four Pillars are derived from the Hour, Day, Month and Year of birth. Each Pillar consists of a Stem (top row) and a Branch (bottom row). The Four Pillars can also be divided into the different stages of life, as seen in Table 1.1.

	Hour Pillar	Day Pillar	Month Pillar	Year Pillar
Stage of Life	Later Years	Middle Age	Young Adulthood	Childhood
Approximate Age	46 to 60	31 to 45	16 to 30	0 to 15

Table 1.1 The Four Pillars Indicating Different Life Stages and Approximate Age

Looking at this table, it can be deduced that the Year Pillar provides an indication of a person's family background and early childhood. If a person's Luck Cycle starts at the age of 10, then the Year Pillar will indicate the person's fortune prior to the commencement of the first Luck Cycle. The Stem will indicate the influence from birth up to and including age 4 and the Branch indicates the period from the age of 5 to and including age 9.

With this table in mind, you can see that the Day, Month and Year Pillars indicate the first half of life (until age 45). For those who are still in their twenties and thirties, the Hour Pillar has yet to exert its effects. The Year Pillar's influence will wane by the time a person reaches their mid-forties.

In the second half of life, the Hour, Day and Month Pillars take over. At this stage, the Year Pillar won't be able to exert much effect, especially by the time the person reaches the age of 60.

So for American singer Gwen Stefani (Example 7.15), the classification of her chart for the first half of life is based on the first three Pillars (Day, Month and Year). Now that she is in her forties, the last three Pillars (Hour, Day and Month) are considered. Note that the Day and Month Pillars influence a person throughout their life.

In the past when the Four Pillars system was first established, a person would have led a full life if they reached the age of 60. There are a total of 60 Stem-Branch Pairs or Combinations. Each Stem is paired with a corresponding Yang or Yin Branch. There are 10 Stems and 12 Branches. This adds up to 60 possible Combinations. So if you are born in the Yang Wood Rat year (which is the first Stem Branch Pair), by the time the next Yang Wood Rat year reappears, you would have lived through all 60 Stem Branch Combinations through those 60 years and will then start the next cycle. Every year after 60 was then considered a bonus. Even in today's age with improvements in people's health, it is extremely rare for a person to live to 120 years or two cycles of 60 years. Frenchwoman Jeanne Calment was the only person with a valid birth certificate so far documented to have lived beyond 120 years (she lived to be 122).

1.2 The Luck Cycles

Table 1.2 looks at how to interpret the Luck Cycle.

Year in which Luck Cycle Starts	Age 6	Age 16	Age 26
First half of 10 year Luck Cycle governed by the Stem	6 through 10	16 through 20	26 through 30
Second half of 10 year Luck Cycle governed by the Branch	11 through 15	21 through 25	31 through 35

Table 1.2 The Luck Cycle and Corresponding Age

A Luck Cycle indicates the influence that is present at any time in a person's life. It progresses in increments of 10. In Table 1.2, this person's Luck Cycle starts at age 6. The first Stem indicates the first half of the first Luck Cycle, which is a period of five years, from the age of 6 to 10. The next half of the first Luck Cycle is indicated by the first Branch, and governs the age of 11 to 15. The next Stem indicates the five-year period from the age of 16 to 20 and the next Branch governs the subsequent five-year period from the age of 21 to 25. These five-year periods continue on, until the end of life. As previously mentioned, the Year Pillar (Stem and Branch) indicates the influence in a person's life prior to the commencement of the Luck Cycle.

1.3 Family Relationships

A Four Pillars chart also indicates the relationship of the individual to various family members, as seen in Table 1.3.

Table 1.3 The Family Members as Seen in the Four Pillars

	Hour Pillar	Day Pillar	Month Pillar	Year Pillar
Stem	Son	Self	Father	Grandfather
Branch	Daughter	Spouse	Mother	Grandmother

Table 1.3 The Family Members as seen in the Four Pillars

The Day Stem indicates the Self. The Self is taken as the point of interpretation. It is referred to as the Day Master. The Day Branch indicates a person's life partner or Spouse, so the sector occupied by the Day Branch is also known as the House of Spouse. For a man, the Spouse would be the wife and for a woman, the husband. For gays and lesbians, the Spouse would refer to the life partner regardless of the person's gender. For someone who is not married, the House of Spouse indicates the significant other.

The Month Stem indicates the Father and the Month Branch the Mother. As the chart is derived from the moment a person is born, it represents the birth parents, rather than adoptive parents.

The Hour Stem represents the Son and the Hour Branch the Daughter. If a person has several sons, then the Hour Stem provides general information of the relationship that a person has with the sons. For a comparison of the relationship with each son, the Four Pillars chart of each son needs to be analyzed and interpreted in terms of its elemental relationships and roles. Note that the Stems always indicate male family members regardless of a person's gender. Thus, for a woman, the Month Stem represents the Father and the Month Branch the Mother independent of the person's gender.

The Four Pillars system was devised in a patriarchal society with emphasis placed on male ancestors and descendants. With this frame of reference, the Year Pillar will indicate the relationship with the paternal grandparents.

When there are any Stem Combinations (see point 3.1) involving the family members (e.g. the Self and the Father or Son), it can represent a close bond with that family member. However, if there is a Stem Combination that does not involve the Self (e.g. the Grandfather and the Father), it suggests that the Father may have been absent or taken away from the individual early in life. In the 108 examples in this book, there are several examples where the Stem Combinations represent these types of relationships.

2. The Relationships between the Elements

To interpret a chart effectively, you need to understand the relationship of the other elements as seen from the Birth and Control Cycles of the five Elements.

The Birth Cycle
The element which produces the Self is the Resource element. The element that the Self produces is the Output element or the Child element. For brevity, it will be referred to as the Output element in Tables 1.4 to 1.7.

Water produces Wood.
Water is the Resource of Wood.
Wood is the Output or Child of Water.

Wood produces Fire.
Wood is the Resource of Fire.
Fire is the Output or Child of Wood.

Fire produces Earth.

Fire is the Resource of Earth.
Earth is the Output or Child of Fire.

Earth produces Metal.
Earth is the Resource of Metal.
Metal is the Output or Child of Earth.

Metal produces Water.
Metal is the Resource of Water.
Water is the Output or Child of Metal.

Table 1.4 lists the Self, Resource and Output Elements.

Self Element	Resource Element Produces the Self	Output Element Produced by the Self
Water	Metal	Wood
Wood	Water	Fire
Fire	Wood	Earth
Earth	Fire	Metal
Metal	Earth	Water

Table 1.4 The Self, Resource and Output Elements

The Control Cycle

With regard to the cycle of control, the element that is controlled by the Self is the Wealth element. For men, the Wealth element also represents the wife.

The element that controls the Self is the Power element. For women, the Power element also indicates the husband.

Wood breaks up Earth.
Wood is the Power element of Earth.
Earth is the Wealth element for Wood.

Earth controls the flow of Water.
Earth is the Power element of Water.
Water is the Wealth element for Earth.

Water extinguishes Fire.
Water is the Power element of Fire.
Fire is the Wealth element for Water.

Fire melts Metal.
Fire is the Power element of Metal.
Metal is the Wealth element for Fire.

Metal chops Wood.
Metal is the Power element of Wood.
Wood is the Wealth element for Metal.

Table 1.5 lists the Self, Power and Wealth Elements.

Self Element	Power Element Controls the Self	Wealth Element Controlled by the Self
Water	Earth	Fire
Wood	Metal	Earth
Fire	Water	Metal
Earth	Wood	Water
Metal	Fire	Wood

Table 1.5 The Self, Power and Wealth Elements

The interaction between the five elements is known as the five relationships. It is recommended that you familiarize yourself with the different relationships in order to classify and interpret all charts. At this stage, as you are starting to interpret, no distinction is made between Yang and Yin elements. There is an approach to Four Pillars that makes the distinction between Yang and Yin, known as the Ten Gods approach. This is not covered in this book. Table 1.6 indicates these five relationships.

Table 1.6 The Five Relationships between the Five Elements

Element	Self Element or Rival	Output	Wealth	Power	Resource
Water	Water	Wood	Fire	Earth	Metal
Wood	Wood	Fire	Earth	Metal	Water
Fire	Fire	Earth	Metal	Water	Wood
Earth	Earth	Metal	Water	Wood	Fire
Metal	Metal	Water	Wood	Fire	Earth

Table 1.6 The Five Relationships between the Elements

Table 1.7 shows the five relationships between the Day Master and the five elements

Day Master	Water	Wood	Fire	Earth	Metal
Water	Self	Output	Wealth	Power	Resource
Wood	Resource	Self	Output	Wealth	Power
Fire	Power	Resource	Self	Output	Wealth
Earth	Wealth	Power	Resource	Self	Output
Metal	Output	Wealth	Power	Resource	Self

Table 1.7 The Five Relationships as per the Day Master

You need to know these relationships in order to interpret Four Pillars charts.

3. Stem Interactions

There are ten Stems. After one sequence of ten is completed, the sequence starts again. Table 1.8 below lists the Stems and their number in the series. You need to be familiar with the Series Number as this allows you to identify the auspicious Sequence of 4 Stems in a Row.

Table 1.8 The Stems in their Sequence

Stem	Series Number
甲 Yang Wood	1
乙 Yin Wood	2
丙 Yang Fire	3
丁 Yin Fire	4
戊 Yang Earth	5
己 Yin Earth	6
庚 Yang Metal	7
辛 Yin Metal	8
壬 Yang Water	9
癸 Yin Water	10

Table 1.8 The Stems and their Series

3.1 Stem Combinations

There are five different Stem Combinations involving a Yang Stem and a Yin Stem. Each Stem combines with the corresponding Stem that is five Stems away. For example, Yang Wood, the first Stem combines with Yin Earth, which is the sixth Stem in the series. Table 1.9 shows the five Stem Combinations.

Stem Combinations
甲 Yang Wood 己 Yin Earth
乙 Yin Wood 庚 Yang Metal
丙 Yang Fire 辛 Yin Metal
丁 Yin Fire 壬 Yang Water
戊 Yang Earth 癸 Yin Water

Table 1.9 Stem Combinations

Note that the Stem Combinations can only occur when the Stems are next to each other in the chart. This means that there are only three possibilities:

1) The Day Master with the Month Stem.
2) The Day Master with the Hour Stem.
3) The Month Stem with the Year Stem.

These three possiblilites DO NOT form Stem Combinations:
1) The Day Master with the Year Stem.
2) The Month Stem with the Hour Stem.
3) The Hour Stem with the Year Stem.

The Yang Stems combine with the Wealth element, while the Yin Stems combine with the Power element. A Stem Combination involving the Wealth element indicates opportunities to generate Wealth, regardless of the gender. For a man, this can also indicate the possibility of marriage or romance, as the Wealth element also represents the wife. This will *only* apply to men who are Yang Day Masters.

A Stem Combination involving the Power element indicates professional recognition or success, regardless of gender. For a woman, this can also indicate the possibility of marriage or romance, as the Power element also signifies the husband. This will *only* apply to women who are Yin Day Masters.

The Stem Combinations can also occur between the Day Master and the year or Luck Cycle. They are usually favourable and are independent of the ranking of the favourable elements.

For the purposes of interpretation, the Stem Combinations indicate generating income, professional success, romance and marriage.

4. Branch Interactions

The 12 Branches also progress in a definitive sequence, like the animals of the Chinese Zodiac years that you may be familiar with. The sequence is as follows: Rat, Ox, Tiger, Rabbit, Dragon, Snake, Horse, Sheep, Monkey, Rooster, Dog and Pig before commencing with the Rat again. Every 12 years, the Branch will be repeated. You also need to be familiar with the sequence of the Stems, as this will allow you to identify the auspicious Sequence of 4 Branches in a Row.

4.1 The Hidden Stems

The Branches also contain Hidden Stems, which indicate the mix of energies that is present in them. Table 1.10 lists the Branches in sequence with their Hidden Stems for reference. The main energy is listed first.

No.	Branch	Hidden Stems
1	子 Rat	癸 Yin Water
2	丑 Ox	己 Yin Earth, 辛 Yin Metal, 癸 Yin Water
3	寅 Tiger	丙 Yang Fire, 甲 Yang Wood, 戊 Yang Earth
4	卯 Rabbit	乙 Yin Wood
5	辰 Dragon	戊 Yang Earth, 癸 Yin Water, 乙 Yin Wood
6	巳 Snake	庚 Yang Metal, 丙 Yang Fire, 戊 Yang Earth
7	午 Horse	丁 Yin Fire, 己 Yin Earth
8	未 Sheep	己 Yin Earth, 乙 Yin Wood, 丁 Yin Fire
9	申 Monkey	壬 Yang Water, 庚 Yang Metal, 戊 Yang Earth
10	酉 Rooster	辛 Yin Metal
11	戌 Dog	戊 Yang Earth, 丁 Yin Fire, 辛 Yin Metal
12	亥 Pig	甲 Yang Wood, 壬 Yang Water

Table 1.10 The 12 Branches and their Hidden Stems

In order to interpret the Four Pillars charts, you need to be familiar with the Branch Combinations so that you can identify them and the prevalent energy within the chart.

4.2 Three Harmony Combinations

The Full Three Harmony Combination requires all three Branches to be present in the chart. However, two out of three Branches may form a Partial Three Harmony Combination. With the Three Harmony system, the 12 Branches for the Seasonal elements (e.g. Water, Wood, Fire and Metal) are assigned each to the 12 Life Stages. For the purpose of this book, you need to be familiar with the three Life Stages that constitute the Full Three Harmony Combination (e.g. Birth, Peak and Grave). It is beyond the scope of this book to discuss the remaining nine Life Stages of the Three Harmony system.

A Combination can be any two out of the three, such as the Birth and Peak, Peak and Grave or Birth and Grave Branch. The Peak Branch does not need to be present for the Partial Three Harmony Combination to occur. Within the chart, the Three Harmony Combination can still occur if there is a Branch in between. For example, the Day Branch can still combine with the Year Branch and the Hour Branch with the Month Branch. However, if there are two Branches in between, then there is no Three Harmony Combination. For instance, the Hour Branch CANNOT combine with the Year Branch. The Three Harmony Combination can also occur between one of the Branches in the chart and the year (Annual Branch) or Luck Cycle.

The Full Three Harmony Combination is more versatile. Even if one of the Branches is clashed away by the Annual Branch or Luck Cycle, the Combination will still occur. The Three Harmony Combination also has an additive effect. For instance, two Tigers will combine with a Horse to form Fire. There is no Competition for Combination.

20

Table 1.11 shows the Full and Partial Three Harmony Combinations with the associated element.

Full Three Harmony Combination Birth – Peak – Grave	Partial Three Harmony Combination	Element
申 Monkey 子 Rat 辰 Dragon	申 Monkey 子 Rat 子 Rat 辰 Dragon 申 Monkey 辰 Dragon	Water
寅 Tiger 午 Horse 戌 Dog	寅 Tiger 午 Horse 午 Horse 戌 Dog 寅 Tiger 戌 Dog	Fire
亥 Pig 卯 Rabbit 未 Sheep	亥 Pig 卯 Rabbit 卯 Rabbit 未 Sheep 亥 Pig 未 Sheep	Wood
巳 Snake 酉 Rooster 丑 Ox	巳 Snake 酉 Rooster 酉 Rooster 丑 Ox 巳 Snake 丑 Ox	Metal

Table 1.11 Full and Partial Three Harmony Combinations and Associated Element

4.3 Seasonal Combinations

For the Seasonal Combination to occur, all three Branches have to be adjacent to each other in the Four Pillars chart, i.e. in the Year, Month and Day Pillars or the Month, Day and Hour Pillars. The Three Harmony Combination is therefore more versatile, as it can occur when only two out of three Branches are present.

The Year, Month and Day Pillars govern the first half of life, while the last three Pillars rule the second half of life. The Seasonal Combination is also known as the Directional Combination. Table 1.12 lists the Seasonal Combination Branches, the Element produced and the Season.

Note that there is *no* Partial Seasonal Combination. For example, looking at the Seasonal Metal Combination, having the Monkey and Rooster, Monkey and Dog or Rooster and Dog will not form Metal. However, if the missing Branch comes in the year or Luck Cycle, then the Seasonal Combination will occur during that specific year or Luck Cycle.

Seasonal Combination	Element	Season
亥 Pig 子 Rat 丑 Ox	Water	Winter
寅 Tiger 卯 Rabbit 辰 Dragon	Wood	Spring
巳 Snake 午 Horse 未 Sheep	Fire	Summer
申 Monkey 酉 Rooster 戌 Dog	Metal	Autumn

Table 1.12 Seasonal Combinations with Element and Season

4.4 Six Harmony Combinations

A Six Harmony Combination indicates the presence of mentors or helpful individuals. This applies if there are no Three Harmony or Seasonal Combinations in the chart. However, if there is a Three Harmony or Seasonal Combination, then the presence of a Six Harmony Combination (within the Four Pillars chart, in the year or Luck Cycle) *will* create Competition for Combination.

A Six Harmony Combination has the potential to mitigate a Clash of Branches by combining with the Branch that causes the Clash. Note that the Six Harmony Combinations do not form a resultant element, they only indicate the presence of mentors or helpful individuals.

Table 1.13 lists the Six Harmony Combinations.

Six Harmony Combinations
子 Rat 丑 Ox
寅 Tiger 亥 Pig
卯 Rabbit 戌 Dog
辰 Dragon 酉 Rooster
巳 Snake 申 Monkey
午 Horse 未 Sheep

Table 1.13 Six Harmony Combinations

Clash

A Clash occurs between two Branches that are six Branches apart from each other. For example, the first Branch Rat, clashes with the seventh Branch Horse, the second Branch Ox, clashes with the eighth Branch Sheep. Table 1.14 lists the Clash Branches.

Clash
子 Rat with 午 Horse
丑 Ox with 未 Sheep
寅 Tiger with 申 Monkey
卯 Rabbit with 酉 Rooster
辰 Dragon with 戌 Dog
巳 Snake with 亥 Pig

Table 1.14 The Clash Animals

5. Stars derived from the Day Master

There are many Stars associated with each Day Master, for example, the Academic Star or the Red Light Romance Star. They are all Branches. Some are only found on the Day Pillar. For the purpose of our discussion, we focus on the following Stars:

1) The Special Stars.
2) The Mentor or Nobleman Stars. This helps us determine the Sitting on the Nobleman or Mentor Days.
3) The Academic Stars. This allows us to determine the Sitting on the Academic Star Days.
4) The Six Intelligent Days, including the two Strategist Days.
5) The Red Light Pillars.

Note that the Configurations Sitting on the Nobleman or Mentor, Sitting on the Academic Star and the Six Intelligent Days refer only to the Day Pillar. The Red Light Pillars can be found in the Hour, Day, Month or Year Pillars.

5.1 The Special Stars

The Special Stars are a pair of Stars which work in conjunction with the Day Master to bring success. They can be present in the chart, or there could be one in the chart and the other can arrive in the Luck Cycle or year (Annual Branch). In this instance, success will last for five years or only one year. Both the Special Stars need to be present for success to occur. If there is only one, there are no benefits. The Special Stars are independent of favourable elements. Even if the Special Stars do not contain the favourable elements, the individual will still experience their benefits.

Table 1.15 lists the Special Stars for the 10 Day Masters. Note that some Day Masters share the same Special Stars.

Table 1.15 The Special Stems as determined by the Day Master

Day Master	Special Stars
甲 Yang Wood 戊 Yang Earth 庚 Yang Metal	子 Rat 丑 Ox
乙 Yin Wood 己 Yin Earth	丑 Ox 申 Monkey
丙 Yang Fire 丁 Yin Fire	寅 Tiger 辰 Dragon
辛 Yin Metal	未 Sheep 亥 Pig
壬 Yang Water 癸 Yin Water	申 Monkey 戌 Dog

Table 1.15 The Special Stars and the Day Masters

5.2 The Mentor or Nobleman Stars

The Mentor or Nobleman Stars indicate the presence of helpful individuals. They can be present within the Four Pillars chart, year (Annual Branch) or Luck Cycle. Unlike the Special Stars, the Mentor Stars need to *contain favourable elements* for the individual to enjoy the positive effects. For example, if a Yang Fire Day Master's favourable element is Wood, benefits can be derived from the Pig (which contains Wood) but not the Rooster (which contains Metal which attacks the Day Master's favourable element Wood).

Table 1.16 Mentor Stars as determined by the Day Master

Day Master	Mentor Stars
甲 Yang Wood 戊 Yang Earth 庚 Yang Metal	丑 Ox 未 Sheep
乙 Yin Wood 己 Yin Earth	子 Rat 申 Monkey
丙 Yang Fire 丁 Yin Fire	酉 Rooster 亥 Pig
辛 Yin Metal	寅 Tiger 午 Horse
壬 Yang Water 癸 Yin Water	卯 Rabbit 巳 Snake

Table 1.16 Mentor Stars and the Day Masters

From Table 1.16, we can then deduce that of the 60 Stem Branch Combinations, there are four days where the Day Master is sitting on the Mentor or Nobleman. Table 1.17 lists the Four Day Pillars that are Sitting on their Nobleman.

丁	丁	癸	癸
Yin Fire	Yin Fire	Yin Water	Yin Water
酉	亥	卯	巳
Rooster	Pig	Rabbit	Snake

Table 1.17 The Four Sitting on Nobleman Days

Those who are born on the one of these four days will have helpful and supportive Spouses.

5.3 The Academic Stars

The Academic Stars represent intellect and the ability to study. They are derived from the Day Masters.

Day Master	Academic Star
甲 Yang Wood	巳 Snake
乙 Yin Wood	午 Horse
丙 Yang Fire	申 Monkey
丁 Yin Fire	酉 Rooster
戊 Yang Earth	申 Monkey
己 Yin Earth	酉 Rooster
庚 Yang Metal	亥 Pig
辛 Yin Metal	子 Rat
壬 Yang Water	寅 Tiger
癸 Yin Water	卯 Rabbit

Table 1.18 The Academic Stars and the Day Masters

From Table 1.18, we can deduce that out of the 60 Stem Branch Combinations, there are six days where the Day Master is sitting on the Academic Star. Table 1.19 lists the Six Day Pillars that are Sitting on their Academic Star.

丙 Yang Fire	丁 Yin Fire	戊 Yang Earth	己 Yin Earth	壬 Yang Water	癸 Yin Water
申 Monkey	酉 Rooster	申 Monkey	酉 Rooster	寅 Tiger	卯 Rabbit

Table 1.19 The Six Sitting on the Academic Star Days

Those born on one of the Six Sitting on the Academic Star days are extremely talented and intelligent. They have the potential to do well academically. They will also attract Spouses who stimulate their intelligence and motivate them. However, some women who are born on one of these days may have difficulties finding fulfilling personal relationships as men may feel threatened by their talent and intelligence.

Note that there are two days that sit on both the Nobleman and the Academic Stars. Those born on these two days will have talented Spouses who assist them in life. Table 1.20 lists the two days that sit on the Nobleman and Mentor Stars.

丁 Yin Fire	癸 Yin Water
酉 Rooster	卯 Rabbit

Table 1.20 The Two Sitting on the Nobleman and
Academic Star Days

5.4 The Six Intelligent Days

Those born on one of these Six days will also be noted for their intelligence, talent and charisma. This only applies to the Day Pillar and not the Hour, Month or Year Pillars.

Table 1.21 lists the Six Intelligent Days.

丙 Yang Fire	丁 Yin Fire	己 Yin Earth	己 Yin Earth	戊 Yang Earth	辛 Yin Metal
午 Horse	未 Sheep	未 Sheep	丑 Ox	子 Rat	巳 Snake

Table 1.21 The Six Intelligent Days

Within the Six Intelligent Days, there are two Strategist days. Those who are born on one of these two days are not only extremely intelligent, they are skilled in strategic planning and are often found in politics or the military. Table 1.22 lists the two Strategist days.

戊 Yang Earth	辛 Yin Metal
子 Rat	巳 Snake

Table 1.22 The Two Strategist Days

5.5 The Red Light Pillars

The Red Light Pillars indicate problematic personal relationships that can be very draining or exhausting for the individual. The effects will be more pronounced if they are in the Day Pillar, followed by the Month Pillar, Hour Pillar and lastly, the Year Pillar. We cannot generalize and say that everyone born in a Red Light Pillar Year will have difficult relationships.

The more Red Light Pillars that are present in a chart, the more problematic the personal relationships. If there are Red Light Pillars in your chart, its effects will be magnified if the same Red Light Pillar is found in one of the pillars within the Spouse's or partner's chart (note that this does not apply if both persons are born in the same Red Light Pillar year).

Table 1.23 lists the Eight Red Light Pillars.

甲 Yang Wood	甲 Yang Wood	乙 Yin Wood	丙 Yang Fire	丁 Yin Fire	庚 Yang Metal	辛 Yin Metal	癸 Yin Water
午 Horse	戌 Dog	未 Sheep	寅 Tiger	未 Sheep	戌 Dog	未 Sheep	未 Sheep

Table 1.23 The Eight Red Light Pillars

Chapter Two Follow the Resource (Metal) Charts

Follow the Resource charts are those in which the Resource is the most prominent element. Yang Water or Yin Water Day Masters have Metal as their Resource element. Individuals with Follow the Resource charts are provided with opportunities throughout their life, be it from family members, spouses or mentors. These individuals are highly intelligent and talented, and will perform well in their chosen field. They enjoy intellectual and mental challenges and dislike work that is repetitive or menial. They also enjoy comfortable surroundings and the finer things in life.

The biggest issue for Follow the Resource charts is the challenge from Rivals or Competitors. For instance, if there can only be one heir to the title, having one or more siblings creates conflict as there will now be more Rivals to share the benefits. For example, one child inherits everything, several siblings means they have to share.

For a Follow the Resource chart, the list of favourable elements is as follows:

1) Metal, the Resource element.
2) Earth, the Power element. Earth produces Metal and also controls the Water Rivals and Competitors.
3) Wood, the Output element. Wood reduces the strength of the Water Rivals and Competitors.
4) Fire, the Wealth element. Fire controls the favourable element Metal.
5) Water, the Self element. Water also represents Rivals and Competitors.

Example 2.1 Dolly Parton, American Country Music Singer (born January 19, 1946, 20:25 hours)

Hour	Day	Month	Year
壬	癸	己	乙
Yang Water	Yin Water	Yin Earth	Yin Wood
戌	巳	丑	酉
Dog	Snake	Ox	Rooster

5	15	25	35
庚	辛	壬	癸
Yang Metal	Yin Metal	Yang Water	Yin Water
寅	卯	辰	巳
Tiger	Rabbit	Dragon	Snake

45	55	65	75
甲	乙	丙	丁
Yang Wood	Yin Wood	Yang Fire	Yin Fire
午	未	申	酉
Horse	Sheep	Monkey	Rooster

There is a Full Three Harmony Metal Combination in Parton's birth chart. Her Snake Day Master, Ox Month Branch and Rooster Year Branch all combine to form Metal. The Yin Earth Month Stem and the Dog Hour Branch further support the Metal. There are no other Combinations present within the chart. Metal is the prevalent element in Parton's chart. As a Yin Water Day Master, Metal represents her Resource. Parton has a Follow the Resource (Metal) chart.

Parton is born on one of the six days where the Day Master is sitting on the Academic Star. In this case, it is Yin Water sitting on top of the Snake. This indicates that she is highly intelligent and good at writing. Parton first became noted in the country music industry for her song writing before she scored her own hits. She is also born on one of the four days that sits on their Nobleman Star. This suggests that her Spouse is extremely helpful and provides assistance to her. In 2016 (Yang Fire Monkey year), Parton celebrated 50 years of marriage to Carl Dean, whom she married when she was 20 years old.

She first achieved success in the Yin Metal Luck Cycle (age 15 to 19). In 1964 (Yang Wood Dragon year) with the favourable Earth element, Parton moved to Nashville from Sevier County, Tennessee after graduating high school. In 1965 (Yin Wood Snake year), she signed with Monument Records. The Snake that year combined with the Full Three Harmony Metal Combination already present within her chart to reinforce her most favourable element Metal.

The Rabbit Luck Cycle (age 20 to 24) clashed with Parton's Rooster Year Branch. However, there was still a Partial Three Harmony Metal Combination present between her Snake Day Branch and Ox Month Branch. She retained her Follow the Resource (Metal) chart. In 1968 (Yang Earth Monkey year), Parton enjoyed her first country Top 10 hit *The Last Thing on My Mind*, a duet with country music entertainer Porter Wagoner. The favourable element Earth was present that year. In 1970 (Yang Metal Dog year), with her two most favourable elements Metal and Earth, Parton scored her first solo hit, a cover of *Mule Skinner Blues*, originally recorded by Jimmie Rodgers.

The Yang Water Luck Cycle (age 25 to 29) contains the negative Self element, which indicates Rivals for a Follow the Resource chart. However, in years where the Resource element is reinforced, Parton enjoyed career success. In late 1973 (Yin Water Ox year), she scored her first big hit *Jolene*, which topped the country chart. The Ox that year reinforced her favourable element Metal by combining with the Full Three Harmony Metal Combination already present in her chart. In 1974 (Yang Wood Tiger year), the Yang Wood that year gave her the distinction of having four Stems in a Sequence: Yang Water Hour Stem, Yin Water Day Master, Annual Yang Wood Stem, Yin Wood Year Stem. Parton had the distinction of three country Number Ones: *Jolene, I Will Always Love You* and *Love Is Like a Butterfly*. In 1975 (Yin Wood Rabbit year), when both the Rabbit Luck Cycle and the Annual Rabbit Branch clashed with her Rooster Year Branch, she released her final duet album with Porter Wagoner.

The Dragon Luck Cycle (age 30 to 34) contained Parton's favourable element Earth. Although a Six Harmony Combination is formed between the Dragon and her Rooster Year Branch, it was not sufficient to disrupt her Follow the Resource chart. There is still her Snake Day Branch and Ox Month Branch forming a Partial Three Harmony Metal Combination. In 1976 (Yang Fire Dragon year), Parton scored her own syndicated television variety show *Dolly!* In 1977 (Yin Fire Snake year), the Snake combined with the Full Three Harmony Metal Combination present within her chart to reinforce the favourable element Metal. Parton enjoyed her first million selling album *Here You Come Again*. Not only did the title track top the country charts, it was also her first top 10 pop hit (number three). In 1978 (Yang Earth Horse year), there was a Stem Combination between the Annual Yang Earth Stem and Parton's Yin Water Day Master. This indicated professional success. Parton won a Grammy Award for Best Female Country Vocal Performance for the *Here You Come Again* album. In 1980 (Yang Metal Monkey year) with the favourable Metal element, Parton scored three number ones: *Starting Over Again, Old Flames Can't Hold a Candle to You* and the theme song to her hit movie *9 to 5* (which also starred Jane Fonda and Lily Tomlin).

The Yin Water Luck Cycle (age 35 to 39) indicated the presence of Water Rivals. However, in 1981 (Yin Metal Rooster year), Parton reached the top of the pop charts with *9 to 5*. She became one of the few country singers to have a number one on the pop and country charts simultaneously. *9 to 5* also received an Oscar nomination for Best Song. The Rooster that year reinforced her most favourable element by combining with the Full Three Harmony Metal Combination within her birth chart. In 1982 (Yang Water Dog year), the second favourable element Earth was present. Parton starred in *The Best Little Whorehouse in Texas* with Burt Reynolds and released a new version of *I Will Always Love You*, as sung in the movie.

Parton's success continued in the Snake Luck Cycle (age 40 to 44). The Snake combined with the Snake, Ox and Rooster present in Parton's chart to reinforce the favourable element Metal. In 1988 (Yang Earth Dragon year), there was a Stem Combination involving the Annual Yang Earth Stem and Parton's Yin Water Day Master. This indicates career success. Parton won a Grammy for Best Country Performance by a Duo or Group for the album *Trio* she recorded with Linda Ronstadt and Emmylou Harris. *Trio* sold several million copies and contained four top 10 country hits. In 1989 (Yin Earth Snake year), Parton appeared in the critically acclaimed *Steel Magnolias*, together with Julia Roberts, Sally Field and Shirley MacLaine. Not only did the Snake reinforce her favourable element Metal by combining with the Full Three Harmony Metal Combination in her chart, her second favourable element Earth was also present that year.

The Yang Wood Luck Cycle (age 45 to 49) gave Parton another sequence of Four Stems: Yang Water Hour Stem, Yin Water Day Stem, Yang Wood Luck Cycle and Yin Wood Year Stem. Parton enjoyed further acclaim in this period. In late 1992 (Yang Water Monkey year), Whitney Houston's version of *I Will Always Love You* recorded for the movie *The Bodyguard* sold 12 million copies and became the biggest hit written by a female. The Monkey that year was one of the Special Stars for a Yin Water Day Master. It worked in conjunction with her Dog Hour Branch to bring her success. In 1993 (Yin Water Rooster year), Parton's duet with James Ingram *The Day I Fall in Love*, recorded for the movie *Beethoven's 2nd* received an Oscar nomination for Best Song.

The Horse Luck Cycle (age 50 to 54) contained Parton's negative element Fire. Her albums did not sell during this period. Nevertheless, she was still able to enjoy success in the years with her favourable elements. In 1998 (Yang Earth Tiger year), when there was a Stem Combination involving her Yin Water Day Master, Parton was named the wealthiest country star in *Nashville Business*. In 1999 (Yin Earth Rabbit year), *Trio II* recorded with Ronstadt and Harris was released. Their version of Neil Young's *After the Gold Rush* won a Grammy for Best Country Collaboration with Vocals. Parton was also inducted into the Country Music Hall of Fame that year. Her second favourable element Earth was present in the Annual Stem.

In the Yin Wood Luck Cycle (age 55 to 59), Parton also fared well in years with her other favourable element Metal. In 2005 (Yin Wood Rooster year), Parton won her second Best Song Oscar nomination for *Travellin' Thru*, written specifically for the film *Transamerica*. The Rooster that year combined with the Snake, Ox and Rooster present in her chart to reinforce the favourable element Metal.

The Sheep Luck Cycle (age 60 to 64) disrupted the Full Three Harmony Combination present in her chart as it clashed with Parton's Ox Month Branch. However, it contained Parton's second favourable element Earth, which reduced any impact. Parton fared well in years with the favourable elements Metal and Earth. In 2008 (Yang Earth Rat year), there was a Stem Combination involving the Annual Yang Earth Stem and her Yin Water Day

Master. She performed a string of sell-out concerts at London's O2 arena. She also released *Backwoods Barbie*, the highest charting album on the Billboard Pop charts of her career.

The Monkey Luck Cycle (age 70 to 74) that Parton is currently in at the time of writing is extremely favourable as it contains one of her Special Stars. Together with the Dog Hour Pillar, the Monkey Luck Cycle will bring Parton further success. However, health issues may arise in the Yin Fire Luck Cycle (age 75 to 79). Fire represents Wealth for a Water Day Master and going through a Wealth Luck Cycle after retirement age (mid to late 60s) indicates a higher risk of illness.

Example 2.2 Madeleine Albright,
American Secretary of State (born May 15, 1937)

Hour	Day	Month	Year
	壬	乙	丁
	Yang Water	Yin Wood	Yin Fire
	寅	巳	丑
	Tiger	Snake	Ox

7	17	27	37
丙	丁	戊	己
Yang Fire	Yin Fire	Yang Earth	Yin Earth
午	未	申	酉
Horse	Sheep	Monkey	Rooster

47	57	67	77
庚	辛	壬	癸
Yang Metal	Yin Metal	Yang Water	Yin Water
戌	亥	子	丑
Dog	Pig	Rat	Ox

There is a Partial Three Harmony Metal Combination present in Albright's birth chart. Her Snake Month Branch combines with her Ox Year Branch to form Metal. There are no other Combinations within her chart. The predominant element in Albright's chart is Metal. For a Yang Water Day Master, Metal represents the Resource element. She has a Follow the Resource (Metal) chart.

Albright is born on a Yang Water Tiger day. This is one of six days where the Day Master sits on the Academic Star. It indicates a person who is very talented academically, and in her case, Albright achieved a Doctorate in Public Law and Governance. However, women who are sitting on their Academic Star may also experience relationship difficulties, which was the case for Albright.

The Yang Fire Luck Cycle (age 7 to 11) contained Albright's negative element Fire. During this period, her Czech diplomat father Josef Korbel was appointed Ambassador to Yugoslavia after the war. Albright was sent to finishing school in Switzerland, as her father did not want her to be indoctrinated by Marxist ideology. In 1948 (Yang Earth Rat year), her family emigrated to the United States after the Communist Party took over Czechoslovakia. Albright's most favourable element Metal was present that year.

The Yin Fire Luck Cycle (age 17 to 21) formed a Stem Combination with her Yang Water Day Master. The Combination between Albright's Day Master and the Wealth element indicated financial opportunities. She attended Wellesley College in Massachusetts on a full scholarship during this period, majoring in political science. In 1957 (Yin Fire Rooster year), there was a Full Three Harmony Metal Combination between the Annual Rooster Branch and the Ox and Snake Branches within her chart. Albright became a U.S. citizen and also joined the College Democrats of America.

In the Sheep Luck Cycle (age 22 to 26), there was a Clash between the Luck Cycle and Albright's Ox Year Branch. The Partial Three Harmony Combination that allowed her to follow the Resource was disrupted, which meant that there was more influence from the Annual Energies. In 1959 (Yin Earth Pig year), there was a Six Harmony Combination involving the Annual Pig Branch and Albright's Tiger in the House of Spouse. This indicated the possibility of romance. She married Joseph Medill Paterson Albright, whom she had met while interning for *The Denver Post* after graduating from Wellesley College.

The Yang Earth Luck Cycle (age 27 to 31) was highly favourable for Albright. In 1968 (Yang Earth Monkey year), she furthered her studies at Columbia University's Department of Public Law and Governance and gained a certificate in Russian. Her favourable element Earth was present that year.

Albright continued her studies during the Monkey Luck Cycle (age 32 to 36), which contained a Yang Water Rival. However, in 1972 (Yang Water Rat year), the Rat that year combined with the Monkey Luck Cycle to transform Albright into a Dominant Water chart. She made her debut in the political arena as legislative assistant to Democratic Senator Edmund Muskie.

The Yin Earth Luck Cycle (age 37 to 41) saw Albright enjoying career success. In 1976 (Yang Fire Dragon year), she was hired by national security adviser Zbigniew Brzezinski to work for the National Security Council following Jimmy Carter's victory in the Presidential Election. Her second favourable element Earth was present in the Dragon that year.

There was a Full Three Harmony Metal Combination during the Rooster Luck Cycle (age 42 to 46). Albright enjoyed more professional success. In 1980 (Yang Metal Monkey year) and 1981 (Yin Metal Rooster year), she travelled to Poland as part of her research project on dissident journalists involved in the Solidarity Movement. Her most favourable element Metal was present both years. However, in 1982 (Yang Water Dog year), there was the presence of a Yang Water Rival. Her husband left her for another woman, ending their marriage of 23 years. Albright recovered later that year due to the presence of her second favourable Earth in the Annual Dog Branch. She joined the academic staff at Georgetown University, Washington D.C., specializing in Eastern European studies.

The Yang Metal Luck Cycle (age 47 to 51) was also favourable for Albright. She served as the Democratic Party's foreign policy adviser to 1984 Vice Presidential candidate Geraldine Ferraro and 1988 Presidential candidate Michael Dukakis. While both campaigns ended in defeat, Albright's reputation as an expert on foreign affairs grew.

During the Dog Luck Cycle (age 52 to 56), she was appointed U.S. Ambassador to the United Nations following Bill Clinton's inauguration as President in 1993 (Yin Water Rooster year). The Rooster that year formed a Full Three Harmony Metal Combination with the Ox and Snake present in her chart. This reinforced her most favourable element Metal.

In the Yin Metal Luck Cycle (age 57 to 61), Albright became the first female U.S. Secretary of State on January 23, 1997. Although it was still the Yang Fire Rat year, it was a Yin Wood Ox day in a Yin Metal Ox month. The Ox present on the day and month of her appointment combined with the Ox and Snake in her birth chart to further reinforce her most favourable element Metal. In 1997 (Yin Fire Ox year), Albright played a major role in Middle East peace negotiations between Israel and other Middle Eastern nations. The Ox that year combined with the Snake and Ox present in her birth chart to reinforce her most favourable element Metal.

The Pig Luck Cycle (age 62 to 66) clashed with the Snake Month Branch that forms the Combination that allows Albright to follow her Resource element Metal. She became more dependent on the Annual Stems and Branches. In 2000 (Yang Metal Dragon year), Albright became the first Secretary of State to travel to North Korea. In 2001 (Yin Metal Snake year), she was elected a Fellow of the American Academy of Arts and Sciences. Albright also formed the Albright Group, an international strategy consulting firm. Her favourable element Metal was present that year.

As Albright's time of birth is not confirmed, it is not possible to analyse with absolute certainty the pattern of her chart following the Yin Metal Luck Cycle.

Example 2.3 Shonda Rhimes, American Television Producer and Screenwriter (born January 13, 1970)

Hour	Day	Month	Year
	癸	丁	己
	Yin Water	Yin Fire	Yin Earth
	巳	丑	酉
	Snake	Ox	Rooster

7	17	27	37
戊	己	庚	辛
Yang Earth	Yin Earth	Yang Metal	Yin Metal
寅	卯	辰	巳
Tiger	Rabbit	Dragon	Snake

47	57	67	77
壬	癸	甲	乙
Yang Water	Yin Water	Yang Wood	Yin Wood
午	未	申	酉
Horse	Sheep	Monkey	Rooster

There is a Full Three Harmony Metal Combination in Rhimes' chart. Her Snake Day Master combines with her Ox Month Branch and Rooster Year Branch to form Metal. There are no other Combinations present within her chart. The prevalent element is Metal. As Rhimes is a Yin Water Day Master, Metal represents her Resource element. She has a Follow the Resource (Metal) chart.

Rhimes is also born on one of four days that sits on its Nobleman Star. This means that she will have relationships with helpful partners. Note that the Snake in her House of Spouse also contributes to the Three Harmony Combination that allows Rhimes to follow her Resource element Metal.

In the Yin Earth Luck Cycle (age 17 to 21), Rhimes graduated from Dartmouth College with a Bachelor's degree in English and film studies in 1991 (Yin Metal Sheep year). Her favourable elements Metal and Earth were present in the year and the Luck Cycle.

After studying screenwriting at the University of California, Rhimes had her first major career success where she co-wrote the acclaimed Home Box Office (HBO) movie *Introducing Dorothy Dandridge* in 1999 (Yin Earth Rabbit year) during the Yang Metal Luck Cycle (age 27 to 31). The movie won numerous awards for its star, Halle Berry. The favourable element Metal was present in the Luck Cycle and the second favourable element Earth in the year. In 2001 (Yin Metal Snake year), Rhimes wrote the screenplay for the Britney Spears hit movie *Crossroads*. The Annual Snake Branch combined with the Snake, Ox and Rooster Branches present in Rhimes' chart to reinforce the favourable element Metal. *Crossroads* made more than $60 million USD at the box office.

The Dragon Luck Cycle (age 32 to 36) was also favourable for Rhimes as it contained her second favourable element Earth. In 2005 (Yin Wood Rooster year), *Grey's Anatomy*, the television series created and written by Rhimes debuted. The series focused on a group of surgical staff at a fictional Seattle hospital and became a huge hit. The Annual Rooster Branch reinforced her favourable element Metal by combining with the Full Three Harmony Metal Combination present in her chart. Rhimes also founded her own television production company ShondaLand that year. In 2006 (Yang Fire Dog year), *Grey's Anatomy* won the Producer's Guild of America Award for Best Drama Series.

Rhimes continued her success in the Yin Metal Luck Cycle (age 37 to 41). *Private Practice*, a spin off series from *Grey's Anatomy* became her second hit television series when it debuted in 2007 (Yin Fire Pig year). However, the negative element Fire was present that year. The first series of *Private Practice* consisted of only nine episodes due to the writers' strike. Both *Grey's Anatomy* and *Private Practice* maintained their high ratings throughout this period. In 2011 (Yin Metal Rabbit year), American Broadcasting Corporation (ABC) ordered Rhimes' pilot script *Scandal*, starring Kerry Washington as Washington, D.C. political fixer.

In the Snake Luck Cycle (age 42 to 46), the favourable element Metal was reinforced as the Snake combined with the Full Three Harmony Metal Combination present in Rhimes' chart. In 2012 (Yang Water Dragon year), the second favourable element Earth was present. *Scandal* debuted and became the first hit television series to feature an African American actress in the leading role. In 2013 (Yin Water Snake year), ABC ordered the pilot *How to Get Away with Murder*, starring Viola Davis as a law professor. The Snake that year reinforced the favourable element Metal.

The Yang Water Luck Cycle (age 47 to 51) is also favourable for Rhimes. The Yang Water forms a Stem Combination with the Yin Fire Month Stem, reducing its negative effect on the Metal present in her chart. The negative Wealth element has also been used to combine away a Yang Water Rival in the Luck Cycle. In 2017 (Yin Fire Rooster year), *Scandal*, *How to Get Away with Murder* and *Grey's Anatomy* were running for their sixth, third and thirteenth seasons on network television respectively.

The Horse Luck Cycle (age 52 to 56) may be problematic for Rhimes as her negative element Fire will be present. The Yin Water Luck Cycle (age 57 to 61) also contains a Water Rival, so there may also be some issues.

Example 2.4 Bill O'Reilly, American Journalist and Television Host (born September 10, 1949)

Hour	Day	Month	Year
	癸	癸	己
	Yin Water	Yin Water	Yin Earth
	卯	酉	丑
	Rabbit	Rooster	Ox

1	11	21	31
壬	辛	庚	己
Yang Water	Yin Metal	Yang Metal	Yin Earth
申	未	午	巳
Monkey	Sheep	Horse	Snake

41	51	61	71
戊	丁	丙	乙
Yang Earth	Yin Fire	Yang Fire	Yin Wood
辰	卯	寅	丑
Dragon	Rabbit	Tiger	Ox

There is a Partial Three Harmony Metal Combination in O'Reilly's chart. His Rooster Month Branch combines with his Ox Year Branch to form Metal. There are no other Combinations present in the chart. The prevalent element in O'Reilly's chart is Metal. As he is a Yin Water Day Master, Metal represents his Resource element. O'Reilly has a Follow the Resource (Metal) chart.

O'Reilly is born on a Yin Water Rabbit day. This is one of the two days where the Day Master is sitting on both the Nobleman and Academic Star. This suggests that he married an extremely intelligent spouse who was able to assist him. O'Reilly was married to public relations executive Maureen E. McPhilmy for 15 years, from 1996 (Yang Fire Rat year) to 2011 (Yin Metal Rabbit year).

During the favourable Yang Metal Luck Cycle (age 21 to 25), O'Reilly received his Bachelor of Arts degree in History from Marist College in 1971 (Yin Metal Pig year). The favourable element Metal was present in the Annual Stem. In 1973 (Yin Water Ox year), he earned a Master of Arts degree in Broadcasting Journalism from Boston University. He had returned to school after teaching English and History at a high school in Miami. The Annual Ox Branch combined with the Rooster and Ox Branches to reinforce his favourable element Metal.

The Horse Luck Cycle (age 26 to 30) contained the negative element Fire. O'Reilly embarked on his broadcasting career with stints at local stations across the USA: Dallas, Denver, Portland and Boston. It was only in the favourable Yin Earth Luck Cycle (age 31 to 35) that he started anchoring his own news program *7:30 Magazine* in New York. Although there was a Yang Water Rival present in the Annual Monkey Branch, the favourable element was present in the Annual Stem. In 1982 (Yang Water Dog year), the second favourable element Earth was present in the Annual Dog Branch. O'Reilly became a Columbia Broadcasting System (CBS) news correspondent.

The Snake Luck Cycle (age 36 to 40) combined with the Rooster and Ox Branches in his chart to form the Full Three Harmony Metal Combination. In January 1986 (still the Yin Wood Ox year), O'Reilly joined American Broadcasting Company (ABC) as a correspondent. The Annual Ox Branch combined with the Snake Luck Cycle and the Rooster and Ox Branches in his chart to reinforce the favourable element Metal. In 1989 (Yin Earth Snake year), O'Reilly became the anchor of *Inside Edition*, a syndicated tabloid-gossip television program. The Annual Snake Branch combined with the Full Three Harmony Metal Combination present in the Snake Luck Cycle and the Rooster and Ox Branches to reinforce his favourable element Metal.

The Yang Earth Luck Cycle (age 41 to 45) formed a Stem Combination with his Yin Water Day Master. The Power Combination indicates professional success and recognition. During this period, *Inside Edition* became the highest rated infotainment program in the US. O'Reilly established himself as a national media personality.

The Dragon Luck Cycle (age 46 to 50) contained the second favourable element Earth. In 1996 (Yang Fire Rat year), O'Reilly was hired by Fox News to start his own television news program *The O'Reilly Factor*. In 1997 (Yin Fire Ox year), the Annual Ox Branch combined with the Rooster and Ox Branches in his chart to reinforce the favourable element Metal. *The O'Reilly Factor* became a hit. In 1998 (Yang Earth Tiger year), there was a Stem Combination between the Annual Stem and his Yin Water Day Master. This indicated professional success and recognition. O'Reilly's first novel, *Those Who Trespass*, was released.

The Yin Fire Luck Cycle (age 51 to 55) contained the negative element. O'Reilly was able to thrive in years with his favourable elements. In 2001 (Yin Metal Snake year), *The O'Reilly Factor* became the most-watched cable news program in the US. The Annual Snake Branch formed the Full Three Harmony Metal Combination with the Rooster and Ox Branches in O'Reilly's chart. His book *The No Spin Zone* also reached Number 1 on the *New York Times* Non-Fiction Best Sellers List. However, in 2004 (Yang Wood Monkey year), there was a Yang Water Rival present in the Annual Monkey Branch. O'Reilly was embroiled in a sexual harassment suit filed by one of the female produces of *The O'Reilly Factor*. It was settled out of court.

The Rabbit Luck Cycle (age 56 to 60) clashed with O'Reilly's Rooster Month Branch, disrupting the Partial Three Harmony Metal Combination. He was no longer a Follow the Resource (Metal) chart. The presence of the Rabbit Luck Cycle and his Rabbit Day Branch transformed him into a Follow the Output (Wood) chart. His list of favourable elements became:

1) Output element Wood.
2) Wealth element Fire.
3) Power element Earth.
4) Self element Water.
5) Resource element Metal.

2008 (Yang Earth Rat year) was a mixed year for O'Reilly. There was a Stem Combination between the Annual Stem and his Yin Water Day Master, indicating professional success and recognition. He was presented with the *National Academy of Television Arts and Sciences* Governors' Award. However, an outtake of O'Reilly cursing at his co-workers because of issues with his teleprompter surfaced on YouTube and went viral. This damaged his credibility.

In the Yang Fire Luck Cycle (age 61 to 65), O'Reilly's chart was dependent on the Annual Stems and Branches as his Ox Year Branch was no longer able to exert any effects. In the Tiger Luck Cycle (age 66 to 70), O' Reilly was fired by Fox News as host of *The O'Reilly Factor* in 2017 (Yin Fire Rooster year). Advertisers had pulled out following a New York Times report that O'Reilly had reached settlements with five women in total over allegations of sexual harassment and inappropriate behaviour. The Annual Rooster Branch worked in conjunction with his Rooster Month Branch to transform him into a Follow the Resource (Metal) chart that year. However, the negative element Fire was present in the Annual Stem. There was a Fire-Metal conflict.

Example 2.5 Jennifer Hudson, American Singer
(born September 12, 1981)

Hour	Day	Month	Year
	癸	丁	辛
	Yin Water	Yin Fire	Yin Metal
	巳	酉	酉
	Snake	Rooster	Rooster

9	19	29	39
戊	己	庚	辛
Yang Earth	Yin Earth	Yang Metal	Yin Metal
戌	亥	子	丑
Dog	Pig	Rat	Ox

49	59	69	79
壬	癸	甲	乙
Yang Water	Yin Water	Yang Wood	Yin Wood
寅	卯	辰	巳
Tiger	Rabbit	Dragon	Snake

There is a Partial Three Harmony Metal Combination in Hudson's chart. Her Snake Day Branch combines with her Rooster Month and Year Branches to form Metal. There is also a Yin Metal Year Stem. The prevalent element in her chart is Metal. As Hudson is a Yin Water Day Master, Metal represents her Resource element. She has a Follow the Resource (Metal) chart.

Hudson is born on a Yin Water Snake day, one of four days where the Day Master is sitting on its Nobleman Star. This suggests that her significant other will assist her in life. She has been engaged to wrestler David Otunga since 2008 (Yang Earth Rat year). The Annual Yang Earth Stem combined with her Yin Water Day Master. A Power Combination indicates professional success. For a woman, the Power Combination also suggests the possibility of romance.

In the favourable Yin Earth Luck Cycle (age 19 to 23), Hudson signed with the independent record label Righteous Records in early 2002 (still Yin Metal Snake year). The Snake reinforced the favourable element Metal by combining with the Snake and Rooster Branches already present in her chart. In 2004 (Yang Wood Monkey year), Hudson ended up seventh on the reality show *American Idol*, even though she was extremely popular with viewers. There was a Yang Water Rival present within the Annual Monkey Branch in the Hidden Stems, indicating significant competition.

The Pig Luck Cycle (age 24 to 28) clashed with her Snake Day Branch, disrupting the Partial Three Harmony Metal Combination. However, the presence of the Rooster Month and Year Branches meant that Hudson remained a Follow the Resource (Metal) chart. The only element present within the Rooster Branches is Metal. In 2005 (Yin Wood Rooster year), Hudson was cast in the role of Effie White in the film version of the musical *Dreamgirls*,

2006 (Yang Fire Dog year), *Dreamgirls* was released to critical acclaim and became a box office hit. Hudson also signed with Arista Records. Her second favourable element Metal was present that year. She also won a Best Supporting Actress Oscar for her performance in *Dreamgirls*.

In 2008 (Yang Earth Rat year), Hudson's professional success continued. She appeared in the *Sex and the City* movie alongside Sarah Jessica Parker and *The Secret Life of Bees* with Richard Gere, Queen Latifah and Alicia Keys. She also released her self-titled debut album *Jennifer Hudson*, which debuted at number 2 on the US Album charts. However, the Rat year also contains a Yin Water Rival, the worst element for a Follow the Resource (Metal) chart. In October that year, the estranged husband of Hudson's sister murdered her mother, brother and nephew. As a result, Hudson took time off from public appearances.

In 2009 (Yin Earth Ox year), Hudson returned to the public eye by singing the National Anthem at the Super Bowl Football Finals that year. She also performed at Michael Jackson's funeral and had her own Christmas Special on television called *Jennifer Hudson: I'll Be Home for Christmas*. Hudson also gave birth to her first child David Daniel Otunga Jr. The Annual Ox Branch reinforced her favourable element by forming the Full Three Harmony Metal Combination with the Snake and Rooster Branches in her chart.

The Yang Metal Luck Cycle (age 29 to 33) contained her favourable element. In 2010 (Yang Metal Tiger year), Hudson became a spokeswoman for Weight Watchers, having lost 25 kg. In 2011 (Yin Metal Rabbit year), she released her second album *I Remember Me,* which debuted at number 2 on the US Albums chart. Once again, the favourable element Metal was present.

In 2013 (Yin Water Snake year), Hudson was awarded her star on the Hollywood Walk of Fame. The Snake that year reinforced the favourable element Metal by combining with the Snake and Rooster Branches present in her chart. In 2014 (Yang Wood Horse year), another negative element Fire was present. Her third album *JHUD* did not sell as well as the previous two and was considered a disappointment.

The Rat Luck Cycle (age 34 to 38) contains Hudson's negative element Water. As Water represents her Rival, she may not perform as well as in the previous Luck Cycle. In the first half of 2017 (Yin Fire Rooster year), her single *Remember Me* failed to crack the UK top 40 songs even though she performed it on the UK version of *The Voice*, where she served as one of the judges. However, 2018 (Yang Earth Dog year) has a Stem Combination involving the Power element with the Annual Yang Earth Stem, so there may be a degree of professional success.

The Yin Metal (age 39 to 43) and Ox (age 44 to 48) Luck Cycles will be more favourable for Hudson as they contain her favourable element Metal. The Ox will complete the Three Harmony Metal Combination with the Snake and Rooster branches in her chart. This suggests a successful and fulfilling period of her life.

The Yang Water (age 49 to 53) Luck Cycle forms a Stem Combination with Hudson's Yin Fire Month Stem. Yin Fire is damaging to Metal as the fire from a candle can melt Metal. The threat to the Metal within Hudson's chart is therefore combined away. This indicates another favourable Luck Cycle for her.

Example 2.6 Andrew Lincoln, British Actor
(born September 14, 1973)

Hour	Day	Month	Year
	癸	乙	癸
	Yin Water	Yin Metal	Yin Water
	丑	酉	丑
	Ox	Rooster	Ox

2	12	22	32
庚	己	戊	丁
Yang	Yin	Yang	Yin
Metal	Earth	Earth	Fire
申	未	午	巳
Monkey	Sheep	Horse	Snake

42	52	62	72
丙	乙	甲	癸
Yang	Yin	Yang	Yin
Fire	Wood	Wood	Water
辰	卯	寅	丑
Dragon	Rabbit	Tiger	Ox

There is a Partial Three Harmony Metal Combination in Lincoln's chart. His Ox Day and Year Branches combine with his Rooster Month Branch to form Metal. There are no other Combinations present within the chart. The prevalent element in the chart is Metal. As Lincoln is a Yin Water Day Master, Metal represents his Resource element. He has a Follow the Resource (Metal) chart.

Lincoln first achieved success in the Yang Earth Luck Cycle (age 22 to 26). The Yang Earth combines with Lincoln's Yin Water Day Master, indicating a Combination involving the Power element. This indicates professional recognition and success. In 1995 (Yin Wood Pig year), after finishing drama school, Lincoln was offered the role of Edgar "Egg" Cook, one of the major characters in the acclaimed BBC drama *This Life*. The series only became a cult hit in 1997 (Yin Fire Ox year) following a repeat of the first season. The Annual Ox Branch combined with the Rooster and Ox Branches in Lincoln's chart to reinforce the favourable element Metal.

The Horse Luck Cycle (age 27 to 31) contained Lincoln's negative element Fire. He struggled to secure memorable roles during this period. The only success Lincoln had during this period was in 2003 (Yin Water Sheep year), when he appeared alongside Keira Knightley and Chiwetel Ejiofor as the love-stricken best man in the star studded Christmas-themed romantic comedy *Love, Actually*. That same year, Lincoln also appeared in and directed two episodes of the Channel Four series *Teachers*. The Six Harmony Combination between the Annual Sheep Branch and the Horse in the Luck Cycle reduced the negative effects of Fire. A Six Harmony Combination suggests the presence of mentors or helpful individuals.

Lincoln also did not experience much success in the Yin Fire Luck Cycle (age 32 to 36). The Yin Fire produced by a candle damages Metal more so than the sunlight associated with Yang Fire. In 2009 (Yin Earth Ox year), Lincoln portrayed Edgar Linton in the Independent Television (ITV) series *Wuthering Heights*. The Ox that year reinforced the favourable element Metal by combining with the Ox and Rooster Branches present in his chart. The second favourable Earth was also present that year.

Lincoln's fortunes turned around significantly in the Snake Luck Cycle (age 37 to 41). In 2010 (Yang Metal Tiger year), he appeared in the French comedy *Heartbreakers* along with Vanessa Paradis and also the British comedy *Made in Dagenham*. Lincoln was also cast as Rick Grimes, the protagonist of the American Movie Classics (AMC) live-action adaptation of the comic book series *The Walking Dead*. The critically acclaimed series became a hit, scoring highest Nielsen ratings in cable television history. Not only was Metal present that year, the Snake in the Luck Cycle formed the Full Three Harmony Metal Combination with the Ox and Rooster Branches present in Lincoln's chart.

Lincoln's success continued in the Yang Fire Luck Cycle (age 42 to 46). Yang Fire represents the Sun, which is not as damaging to Metal as the candle represented by Yin Fire. In 2017 (Yin Fire Rooster year), The Walking Dead is in its seventh season still enjoying acclaim amongst critics and audiences. The same year, Lincoln also appeared on *Red Nose Day, Actually*, a mini sequel to *Love, Actually* shown on British television. The Annual Rooster Branch reinforced the favourable element Metal.

The Dragon Luck Cycle (age 47 to 51) will also be favourable for Lincoln as it contains the second favourable element Earth. For the Yin Wood Luck Cycle (age 52 to 56), the effects of the Annual energies will have to be taken into account. There may be issues in the Rabbit Luck Cycle (age 57 to 61) as there is a clash between the Luck Cycle and the Rooster Month Branch, disrupting the Partial Three Harmony Metal Combination that allows Lincoln to be a Follow the Resource (Metal) chart.

Example 2.7 Anita Baker, American Singer
(born January 26, 1958)

Hour	Day	Month	Year
	癸	癸	丁
	Yin Water	Yin Water	Yin Fire
	卯	丑	酉
	Rabbit	Ox	Rooster

3	13	23	33
甲	乙	丙	丁
Yang	Yin	Yang	Yin
Wood	Wood	Fire	Fire
寅	卯	辰	巳
Tiger	Rabbit	Dragon	Snake
43	53	63	73
戊	己	庚	辛
Yang	Yin	Yang	Yin
Earth	Earth	Metal	Metal
午	未	申	酉
Horse	Sheep	Monkey	Rooster

There is a Partial Three Harmony Metal Combination in Baker's chart. Her Ox Month Branch combines with the Rooster Year Branch to form Metal. There are no other Combinations in her chart. The predominant element in the chart is Metal. As Baker is a Yin Water Day Master, Metal is her Resource element. She has a Follow the Resource (Metal) chart.

Baker is born on a Yin Water Rabbit Day, one of the four days where the Day Master sits on top of the Nobleman Star. This suggests that her Spouse will be of assistance to her. However, the Rabbit in Baker's House of Spouse is under attack from the Partial Three Harmony Metal Combination between the Ox and Rooster.

Baker married Walter Bridgeforth Jr. in 1988 (Yang Earth Dragon year). The Annual Yang Earth Stem formed a Combination with her Yin Water Day Master. This not only indicated professional recognition and success, but also the possibility of marriage, which is the case for Baker. In 2005 (Yin Wood Rooster year), Baker separated from Bridgeforth. There was a clash between the Annual Rooster Branch and the Rabbit in her House of Spouse.

Towards the end of the Yang Fire Luck Cycle (age 23 to 27), Baker signed with Warner Music Group-associated Elektra group in 1985 (Yin Wood Ox year). The Annual Ox Branch combined with the Ox and Rooster Branches present in her chart to reinforce the favourable element Metal.

The Dragon Luck Cycle (age 28 to 32) saw Baker released her album *Rapture* in 1986 (Yang Fire Tiger year). The Dragon contained her second favourable element Earth. *Rapture* sold more than eight million copies worldwide, yielding four hit singles, including *Sweet Love*. Baker also won two Grammy Awards, for Best Female Rhythm and Blues Vocal Performance and Best R & B Song for *Sweet Love*.

In 1988 (Yang Earth Dragon year), there was a Combination between the Annual Yang Earth Stem and Baker's Yin Water Day Master. As previously discussed, she got married that year. She also enjoyed professional success as she released her second Elektra album *Giving You the Best That I Got*. In 1989 (Yin Earth Snake year), she won three more Grammy Awards. The Annual Snake Branch formed the Full Three Harmony Metal Combination with the Ox and Rooster present in her chart. Baker finished the Luck Cycle by releasing her third hit album *Compositions* in 1990 (Yang Metal Horse year). The favourable element Metal was present.

The Yin Fire Luck Cycle (age 33 to 37) contained Baker's negative element Fire. The fire generated by a candle is more damaging than the sunlight associated with Yang Fire. Baker took a break from recording and touring to start a family. She suffered two miscarriages before giving birth to two sons in January 1993 (still Yang Water Monkey year) and May 1994 (Yang Wood Dog year). The Annual Yang Water Stem in 1993 reduced the negative effects of Yin Fire by combining with it. In 1994, Baker also released the *Rhythm of Love* album. The Annual Dog Branch formed a Six Harmony Combination with the Rabbit in her House of Spouse, indicating the presence of mentors.

The Snake Luck Cycle (age 38 to 42) saw Baker taking a break from performing to raise her family. The Snake completed the Full Three Harmony Metal Combination with the Ox and Rooster in Baker's chart. It was a happy and fulfilling period for her as it allowed her to focus on family life.

The Yang Earth Luck Cycle (age 43 to 47) formed a Combination with Baker's Yin Water Day Master, indicating professional success. She signed with Blue Note Recordings and released *My Everything* in 2004 (Yang Wood Monkey year), which sold well in spite of her decade long absence from recording. In 2005 (Yin Wood Rooster year), Baker was awarded an Honorary Doctorate of Music from Berklee College of Music. While she enjoyed professional recognition, the Rabbit in her House of Spouse was under attack by the Metal being reinforced by the Annual Rooster Branch. Baker separated from her husband of 18 years.

The Horse Luck Cycle (age 48 to 52) contained Baker's negative element Fire. In 2007 (Yin Fire Pig year), her divorce was finalized. The negative element Fire was present in the Annual Stem. While she toured, she did not release any new music during this period.

The Yin Earth Luck Cycle (age 53 to 57) was favourable for Baker as her second favourable element was present. In 2013 (Yin Water Snake year), she returned to the spotlight singing her new single *Everything* on the *Jimmy Kimmel Show*. The Snake that year reinforced her favourable element Metal by combining with the Rooster and Ox present in her chart.

The Sheep Luck Cycle (age 58 to 62) may prove to be challenging for Baker, as the Sheep clashes with her Ox Month Branch that forms the Combination that allows her to be a Follow the Resource (Metal) chart. However, there is also a Three Harmony Combination between the Sheep and the Rabbit in her House of Spouse, indicating the possibility of romance during this period.

Example 2.8 Lleyton Hewitt, Australian Tennis Player (born February 24, 1981)

Hour	Day	Month	Year
	癸	庚	辛
	Yin Water	Yang Metal	Yin Metal
	酉	寅	酉
	Rooster	Tiger	Rooster

7	17	27	37
己	戊	丁	丙
Yin Earth	Yang Earth	Yin Fire	Yang Fire
丑	子	亥	戌
Ox	Rat	Pig	Dog

47	57	67	77
乙	甲	癸	壬
Yin Wood	Yang Wood	Yin Water	Yang Water
酉	申	未	午
Rooster	Monkey	Sheep	Horse

While there are no Branch Combinations within Hewitt's chart, he has two Rooster Branches, which contain only Metal. There is also a Yang Metal Month Stem and a Yin Metal Year Stem. The prevalent element is Metal. As Hewitt is a Yin Water Day Master, Metal represents his Resource. He has a Follow the Resource (Metal) chart.

Hewitt first achieved success during the Ox Luck Cycle (age 12 to 16). The Ox formed a Partial Three Harmony Combination with his Rooster Day and Year Branches. This reinforced his favourable element Metal. At 16 years old in January 1998 (still the Yin Fire Ox year), he won the Adelaide Open defeating Andre Agassi on his way to the title. The Annual Ox Year Stem further reinforced Metal by combining with the Ox Luck Cycle and the Rooster Day and Year Branches.

The Yang Earth Luck Cycle (age 17 to 21) was highly successful for Hewitt. The Stem Combination involving the Yin Water Day Master and the Luck Cycle involved the Power element. This signified professional recognition and success. In 2000 (Yang Metal Dragon year), Hewitt won the Men's Doubles Championships at the US Open with partner Max Mirnyi. He became the youngest men ever (19 years, 6 months) to win a doubles crown in the Open era. The favourable elements Metal and Earth were present that year.

In 2001 (Yin Metal Snake year), Hewitt won his first Grand Slam Singles Championship at the US Open when he defeated Pete Sampras in the final. The Annual Snake Branch reinforced the favourable element Metal by combining with the Rooster Branches present within his chart. He also ascended to Number 1 in the Association of Tennis Professionals (ATP) rankings after winning the year-end Tennis Masters Cup in Sydney.

In 2002 (Yang Water Horse year), Hewitt won his second Grand Slam Singles title at Wimbledon. He also defended his Tennis Masters Cup title and ended the year once again at Number 1. Although his negative element Fire was present that year, there was a favourable Stem Configuration that allowed Hewitt to enjoy success. The Annual Yang Water Stem provided him with the Configuration of Four Stems in a row: Yang Metal (Month Stem), Yin Metal (Year Stem), Yang Water (Annual Stem) and Yin Water (Day Master).

However, the Rat Luck Cycle (age 22 to 26) contained a Yin Water Rival that created issues for Hewitt. In 2003 (Yin Water Sheep year), he became the first defending champion to lose in the first round at Wimbledon. Subsequently, he lost his Number 1 ranking and fell out of the top 10. There was a Yin Water Rival present in the Annual Stem.

In 2005 (Yin Wood Rooster year), the favourable element Metal was present. Hewitt was runner-up at the Australian Open to Marat Safin and reached the Wimbledon and US Open semi-finals. On a personal note, he married Australian Bec Cartwright and welcomed their first child together. The Rooster is also the Branch present in his House of Spouse (Day Branch). When the House of Spouse Branch is present in the Annual Branch, there is an increased possibility of marriage, which was the case for Hewitt.

The Yin Fire Luck Cycle (age 27 to 31) was also difficult for Hewitt as the negative element Fire was present. In 2008 (Yang Earth Rat year), Hewitt was forced to take time off from competing after sustaining a hip injury that required surgery. Although there was a Stem Combination between the Annual Stem and his Yin Water Day Master indicating success, there was also a Yin Water Rival present within the Annual Rat Branch.

In 2009 (Yin Earth Ox year), the Annual Ox Branch combined with the Rooster Branches in his chart to reinforce the favourable element Metal. Hewitt reached the quarter-finals of Wimbledon and returned to the top 20 in the world rankings.

In 2011 (Yin Metal Rabbit year), Hewitt sustained a foot injury that forced his season to end prematurely. The Annual Rabbit Branch clashed with Rooster Day and Year Branches within his chart.

The Pig Luck Cycle (age 32 to 36) formed a Six Harmony Combination with his Tiger Month Branch. This suggested the presence of mentors or helpful individuals. In 2013 (Yin Water Snake year), Hewitt defeated five top 10 opponents and won the John Newcombe medal as the most outstanding Australian tennis player. The Annual Snake Branch reinforced the favourable element Metal by combining with the Rooster Branches in his chart.

In 2016 (Yang Fire Monkey year), Hewitt announced his retirement after playing in his 20th consecutive Australian Open Championships. There was a Yang Water Rival present within the Annual Monkey Branch.

Looking at Hewitt's future Luck Cycles, his House of Spouse animal Rooster will be present again from the age of 52 to 56. This suggests an increased possibility of another marriage during this period. Note that the House of Spouse animal Rooster is repeated in Hewitt's chart, indicating a possibility of having two marriages.

Example 2.9 Jim Jarmusch, American Film Director
(born January 22, 1953, 19:15 hours)

Hour	Day	Month	Year
壬	癸	癸	壬
Yang Water	Yin Water	Yin Water	Yang Water
戌	酉	丑	辰
Dog	Rooster	Ox	Dragon

4	14	24	34
甲	乙	丙	丁
Yang	Yin	Yang	Yin
Wood	Wood	Fire	Fire
寅	卯	辰	巳
Tiger	Rabbit	Dragon	Snake

44	54	64	74
戊	己	庚	辛
Yang	Yin	Yang	Yin
Earth	Earth	Metal	Metal
午	未	申	酉
Horse	Sheep	Monkey	Rooster

There is a Partial Three Harmony Metal Combination in Jarmusch's chart. His Rooster Day Branch and Ox Month Branch combine to form Metal. There is also Earth present in the Dragon Year Branch and Dog Hour Branch that further support the Metal formed. There are no other Combinations present in the chart. Even though there are two Yang Water Stems and a Yin Water Month Stem, the prevalent element within Jarmusch's chart remains Metal. He is a Yin Water Day Master and Metal represents his Resource. Jarmusch has a Follow the Resource (Metal) chart.

Note that with the Dragon Year Branch, Jarmusch's chart is able to transform into a Dominant Water chart when there is a Rat or Monkey Luck Cycle or year. In these instances, the list of favourable elements will be:

1) Resource element Metal.
2) Self element Water.
3) Output element Wood.
4) Wealth element Fire.
5) Power element Earth.

In the Dragon Luck Cycle (age 29 to 33), Jarmusch's first major movie *Stranger Than Paradise* was released in 1984 (Yang Wood Rat year) and received the *Camera d'Or* at the Cannes Film Festival. The Annual Rat Branch combined with his Dragon Year Branch to transform him into a Dominant Water chart. The Dragon Luck Cycle also contributed by combining with the Annual Dragon Branch and Dragon Year Branch to reinforce the Dominant Water status.

Although the Yin Fire Luck Cycle (age 34 to 38) contained Jarmusch's negative element, he was still able to thrive in years with his favourable elements. In 1989 (Yin Earth Snake year), Jarmusch released *Mystery Train* at Cannes and the movie became a critical favourite. The Annual Snake Branch completed the Full Three Harmony Metal Combination by combining with the Rooster Day Branch and the Ox Month Branch. The second favourable element Earth was also present.

In 1991 (Yin Metal Sheep year), Jarmusch followed up with *Night on Earth*, which starred Roberto Benigni, Gena Rowlands and Winona Ryder. The Annual Sheep Branch disrupted the Partial Three Harmony Metal Combination by clashing with the Ox Month Branch. Fortunately, Jarmusch's chart benefited from the influence of all four Earth Branches: the Annual Sheep Branch, Dragon Year Branch, Ox Month Branch and Dog Hour Branch. This is a highly favourable configuration and resulted in success for Jarmusch.

The Snake Luck Cycle (age 39 to 43) was also successful for Jarmusch, as the Snake formed the Full Three Harmony Metal Combination with the Rooster Day Branch and the Ox Month Branch. In 1996 (Yang Fire Rat year), the western *Dead Man* starring Johnny Depp was released to significant critical acclaim, considered one of the few films directed by a Caucasian director to authentically portray Native Americans. The Annual Rat Branch combined with his Dragon Year Branch transformed Jarmusch into a Dominant Water chart.

There is a Stem Combination between the Yang Earth Luck Cycle (age 44 to 48) and Jarmusch's Yin Water Day Master. This indicated professional recognition and success. In 1999 (Yin Earth Rabbit year), the Far East philosophical crime film *Ghost Dog: Way of the Samurai* (starring Forrest Whitaker) achieved mainstream success. Even though there was a clash between the Annual Rabbit Branch and the Rooster Day Branch disrupting the Partial Three Harmony Metal Combination, the second favourable element Earth was present.

The Horse Luck Cycle (age 49 to 53) contained the negative element Fire. Jarmusch confessed to having a crisis of confidence following the September 11 attacks and did not release any films for five years. In 2004 (Yang Wood Monkey year), he returned with *Coffee and Cigarettes*, a collection of eleven short films involving characters smoking and drinking coffee. For a Yin Water Day Master like Jarmusch, his Special Stars are the Dog and Monkey. The Monkey that year worked in conjunction with his Dog Hour Branch to bring success. By the age of 50, the effect of the Year Pillar would have waned, so it would have been difficult for Jarmusch to transform into a Dominant Water chart. In 2005 (Yin Wood Rooster year), *Broken Flowers* starring Bill Murray, Sharon Stone and Jessica Lange was released. The Annual Rooster Branch reinforced the favourable element Metal by combining with the Rooster and Ox present in Jarmusch's chart.

The Yin Earth Luck Cycle (age 54 to 58) contained the second favourable element Earth. In 2009 (Yin Earth Ox year), *The Limits of Control*, a meditative crime film set in Spain was released. The Annual Ox Branch reinforced the favourable element Metal by combining with the Rooster and Ox present in his chart. The second favourable element Earth was also present.

While the Sheep Luck Cycle (age 59 to 63) disrupted the Partial Three Harmony Metal Combination by clashing with the Ox Month Branch, it also resulted in Jarmusch's chart having the influence of all four Earth Branches again. This consisted of his Dragon Year Branch, Ox Month Branch, Dog Year Branch and the Sheep Luck Cycle. His success continued during this period. In 2013 (Yin Water Snake year), the vampire film *Only Lovers Left Alive* with Tom Hiddleston and Tilda Swinton debuted at the Cannes Film Festival. The Annual Snake Branch combined with the Rooster Day Branch to form Metal.

The current Yang Metal Luck Cycle (age 64 to 68) contains Jarmusch's favourable element. The Monkey Luck Cycle (age 69 to 73) is also favourable, as the Monkey will work in conjunction with his Dog Luck Cycle to bring him further success.

Example 2.10 Edison Chen,
Hong Kong-Canadian Singer (born October 7, 1980)

Hour	Day	Month	Year
	癸	乙	庚
	Yin Water	Yin Wood	Yang Metal
	丑	酉	申
	Ox	Rooster	Monkey

0	10	20	30
丙	丁	戊	己
Yang Fire	Yin Fire	Yang Earth	Yin Earth
戌	亥	子	丑
Dog	Pig	Rat	Ox

40	50	60	70
庚	辛	壬	癸
Yang Metal	Yin Metal	Yang Water	Yin Water
寅	卯	辰	巳
Tiger	Rabbit	Dragon	Snake

There is a Partial Three Harmony Metal Combination in Chen's chart. His Ox Day Branch combines with his Rooster Month Branch to form Metal. There are no other Branch Combinations present in the chart. Yang Metal is present in the Year Stem. The prevalent element is Metal. As Chen is a Yin Water Day Master, Metal represents his Resource Element. He has a Follow the Resource (Metal) chart.

There is also a Combination between the Yin Wood Month Stem and the Yang Metal Year Stem. As the Month Stem signifies the Father, this suggests that Chen's father may have been absent when Chen was growing up.

Chen is born in the Monkey year, so in the Rat or Dragon Luck Cycles or years, he can transform into a Dominant Water chart. During these periods, the favourable elements will be:

1) Resource element Metal.
2) Self element Water.
3) Output element Wood.
4) Wealth element Fire.
5) Power element Earth.

During the Yang Earth Luck Cycle (age 20 to 24), there was a Stem Combination between Yang Earth and the Yin Water Day Master. The Power element Combination indicates professional recognition and success. Chen became well known in the Hong Kong entertainment industry during this period. In 2000 (Yang Metal Dragon year), he made his Hong Kong movie debut in *Gen Y Cops*. Chen was a Dominant Water chart that year when the Annual Dragon Branch combined with his Monkey Year Branch. Metal was also present that year. He also signed a recording contract with the Emperor Entertainment Group, releasing several successful pop albums.

In 2004 (Yang Wood Monkey year), there was a Yang Water Rival present that year. Chen was not transformed into a Dominant Water chart as the Annual Monkey Branch does not combine with his Monkey Year Branch. That year, two teenagers assaulted Chen in Hong Kong's Central District. They had mocked his dance moves before punching him and then running off. Chen managed to chase after them as they were boarding a bus and hand them over to police. He sprained his ankle and his cheekbone and ear were injured due to the assault.

In the Rat Luck Cycle (age 25 to 29), Chen changed into a Dominant Water chart. In 2006 (Yang Fire Dog year), he made his American film debut playing a Hong Kong journalist in the horror film *The Grudge 2*. For a Yin Water Day Master, the Special Success Stars are the Monkey and Dog. The Annual Dog Branch worked in conjunction with Chen's Monkey Year Branch to bring him success that year.

2007 (Yin Fire Pig year) proved to be tumultuous for him. The Annual Pig Branch formed a Seasonal Water Combination with the Rat Luck Cycle and the Ox Day Branch. This disrupted the Partial Three Harmony Water Combination between the Monkey Year Branch and the Rat Luck Cycle. This is known as Competition for Combination and the instability manifested in negative developments for Chen. In March that year, police charged Chen after he kicked and dented a taxi and broke its windows after an argument with the driver. He was convicted and placed on a one year good behaviour bond.

In January 2008 (still the Yin Fire Pig year), Chen was embroiled in a major sex scandal after explicit personal pictures of him with other female Hong Kong celebrities were posted on the Internet. As a result, Chen had to take an "indefinite" leave of absence from the entertainment industry. His role in the Hollywood blockbuster *The Dark Knight* was also reduced.

Chen remained in the public eye during the Yin Earth Luck Cycle (age 30 to 34), even though his acting and singing career had stalled. In 2011 (Yin Metal Rabbit year), there was another photo scandal involving Chen. Pictures of him hugging and kissing 16 year-old model Cammi Tse were posted online after Tse lost her phone. It was revealed that Chen had sent text messages to Tse, asking her to pose in swimsuits and school uniforms. The Annual Rabbit Branch clashed with his Rooster Month Branch, disrupting the Partial Three Harmony Metal Combination.

In 2014 (Yang Wood Horse year), the negative element Fire was present. Chen flashed his middle finger at a fan who was trying to take a picture of him as he was walking on the streets of Paris. The fan posted the photo of Chen online.

The Ox Luck Cycle (age 35 to 39) is favourable for Chen, as the Luck Cycle reinforces the favourable element Metal by combining with the Ox and Rooster Branches present in his chart. However, in 2015 (Yin Wood Sheep year), there was a Clash between the Annual Sheep Branch and the Ox Day Branch and Luck Cycle, disrupting the Partial Three Harmony Metal Combination. Chen made headlines again when he got into a fight with a man who jumped the line at Shanghai Airport. Although they were both taken to the police station, no charges were made as they reached a settlement.

The Ox is also the Animal Branch that is present in Chen's House of Spouse, so there is an increased possibility of him getting married in this Luck Cycle. With the favourable Metal present, there is also the possibility of him returning to the Hong Kong entertainment industry.

The Yang Metal (age 40 to 44) Luck Cycle is also positive, as the most favourable element is present. The Tiger Luck Cycle (age 45 to 49) contains the favourable element Earth but also the negative element Fire, so Chen's fortunes will depend more on the Annual Energies. The Yin Metal (age 50 to 54) Luck Cycle is also favourable. However, there may be issues during the Rabbit Luck Cycle (age 55 to 59) as there is a Clash with the Rooster Month Branch, disrupting the Partial Three Harmony Metal Combination.

Example 2.11 Tori Spelling, American Actress
(born May 16, 1973, 01:13 hours)

Hour	Day	Month	Year
辛	壬	丁	癸
Yin Metal	Yang Water	Yin Fire	Yin Water
丑	子	巳	丑
Ox	Rat	Snake	Ox

7	17	27	37
戊	己	庚	辛
Yang Earth	Yin Earth	Yang Metal	Yin Metal
午	未	申	酉
Horse	Sheep	Monkey	Rooster

47	57	67	77
壬	癸	甲	乙
Yang Water	Yin Water	Yang Wood	Yin Wood
戌	亥	子	丑
Dog	Pig	Rat	Ox

There is a Partial Three Harmony Metal Combination in Spelling's chart. Her Snake Month Branch combines with her Ox Year and Hour Branches to form Metal. While there is a Six Harmony Combination between the Ox Hour Branch and the Rat Day Branch, the Partial Three Harmony Combination takes precedence. There is also a Yin Metal Hour Stem. The prevalent element within Spelling's chart is Metal. As she is a Yang Water Day Master, Metal represents her Resource. Spelling has a Follow the Resource (Metal) chart.

There is a Stem Combination involving the Yin Fire Month Stem and Yang Water Day Master. This indicates that Spelling had a good relationship with her father, producer Aaron Spelling. As there is a Wealth Combination involving the Day Master, it also suggests that Spelling's father provided her with financial support. Spelling inherited a sum of money following his death.

The Rat in the House of Spouse (Day Branch) is able to combine with the Monkey or Dragon year or Luck Cycle to transform Spelling into a Dominant Water chart. The list of favourable elements will then be:

1) Resource element Metal.
2) Self element Water.
3) Output element Wood.
4) Wealth element Fire.
5) Power element Earth.

Spelling is born on a Yang Water Rat day, which indicates that she is sitting on a Rival. The Rat has the Yin Water Stem hidden within it. With the exception of Dominant charts, all other charts where the Day Master sits on the Rival indicate marital issues. Spelling has been married twice and has had her share of marital turmoil, as discussed below.

In the Yin Earth Luck Cycle (age 17 to 21) in 1990 (Yang Metal Horse year), Spelling had her first major professional break when she was cast in the role of Donna Martin in the television series *Beverly Hills, 90210*. The favourable element Metal and negative element Fire were both present that year. While Spelling became a teenage idol and star as a result of the show, there was also criticism that she landed the role as her father's company produced it.

Spelling's success continued in the Sheep Luck Cycle (age 22 to 26). Although the Sheep clashed with the Ox Year Branch, the disruption of the Partial Three Harmony Metal Combination was tempered by the presence of the second favourable element Earth. Spelling remained on *Beverly Hills, 90210* throughout this period, maintaining her public profile. In 1997 (Yin Fire Ox year), Spelling appeared in the independent comedy *The House of Yes*, a critical success. The Annual Ox Branch contained the second favourable element Earth. The Partial Three Harmony Metal Combination between the Annual Ox Branch and the Snake Month Branch was disrupted by the clash from the Sheep Luck Cycle. In 1999 (Yin Earth Rabbit year), Spelling appeared in the cult comedy *Trick*. Her second favourable element Earth was present.

The Yang Metal Luck Cycle (age 27 to 31) contained Spelling's favourable element. Although *Beverly Hills, 90210* had ended its run in 2000 (Yang Metal Dragon year), she continued to appear in television movies. In 2004 (Yang Wood Monkey year), there was a Combination between the Annual Monkey Branch and the Rat in her House of Spouse. This indicated the possibility of romance or marriage. Spelling married actor and writer Charlie Shanian that year. She also transformed into a Dominant Water chart in 2004.

In the Monkey Luck Cycle (age 32 to 36), there was a Partial Three Harmony Water Combination between the Monkey and the Rat in the House of Spouse. Spelling became a Dominant Water chart during this period. The Combination between the Luck Cycle and the House of Spouse also suggested the possibility of romance or marriage. For a single person, this represents the possibility of settling down. However, for a person who is already married, the Combination involving the House of Spouse indicates the possibility of extra-marital affairs. In 2005 (Yin Wood Rooster year), Spelling met actor Dean McDermott on a TV movie set and started an affair with him while still married to Shanian. McDermott was also married at that time.

In 2006 (Yang Fire Dog year), Spelling married McDermott after their divorces were finalized. For a Yang Water Day Master, the Special Stars are the Monkey and the Dog. The Annual Dog Branch in the Monkey Luck Cycle worked together to bring Spelling fulfilment. In March 2007 (Yin Fire Pig year), Spelling had her first child, Liam Aaron McDermott. Her Output or Children element Wood was present that year. In June 2008 (Yang Earth Rat year), Spelling had her second child, Stella Doreen McDermott. Women with Follow the Resource charts tend to have difficulties becoming pregnant as the Resource element attacks the Output or Children element. However, Spelling was able to have her first two children during a Luck Cycle in which she was a Dominant Water chart. In 2008 (Yang Earth Rat year), the Annual Rat Branch reinforced the Water Combination between the Monkey Luck Cycle and the Rat Day Branch. Spelling released her autobiography *sTori Telling*, a *New York Times* bestseller.

The Yin Metal Luck Cycle (age 37 to 41) also contained Spelling's favourable element. She had reverted back to being a Follow the Resource (Metal) chart. In October 2011 (Yin Metal Rabbit year), she had her third child, Hattie Margaret McDermott. Her Children element Wood was present in the Annual Rabbit Branch. In 2012 (Yang Water Dragon year), the Annual Dragon Branch combined with the Rat in her House of Spouse to transform Spelling again into a Dominant Water chart. Spelling had her fourth child Finn Davey McDermott in August 2012. In 2013 (Yin Water Snake year), there was a Yin Water Rival present. McDermott had an affair. However, as the Snake that year reinforced the favourable element Metal by combining with the Snake and Ox Branches present in her chart, Spelling was able to salvage her marriage.

The Rooster Luck Cycle (age 42 to 46) reinforced the favourable element Metal by combining with the Ox and Snake Branches present in Spelling's chart. In 2016 (Yang Fire Monkey year), the Annual Monkey Branch combined with the Rat Day Branch in Spelling's chart to transform her into a Dominant Water chart. She became pregnant as the Resource element Metal supported her Dominant Water status and no longer attacked the Children element Wood. In March 2017 (Yin Fire Rooster year), Spelling gave birth to her fifth child, Beau Dean McDermott.

The Yang Water Luck Cycle (age 47 to 51) indicates the presence of a Water Rival. There may be some issues for Spelling during this period. However, the Dog Luck Cycle (age 52 to 56) contains her second favourable element Earth. The Yin Water Luck Cycle (age 57 to 61) may also create issues due to the presence of a Water Rival. The Pig Luck Cycle (age 62 to 66) clashes with the Snake Month Branch, disrupting the Partial Three Harmony Metal Combination that accounts for Spelling's Follow the Resource (Metal) chart.

Example 2.12 Jose Feliciano, Puerto Rican Singer
(born September 10, 1945, 10:00 hours)

Hour	Day	Month	Year
乙	壬	乙	乙
Yin Wood	Yang Water	Yin Wood	Yin Wood
巳	午	酉	酉
Snake	Horse	Rooster	Rooster

1	11	21	31
甲	癸	壬	辛
Yang	Yin	Yang	Yin
Wood	Water	Water	Metal
申	未	午	巳
Monkey	Sheep	Horse	Snake

41	51	61	71
庚	己	戊	丁
Yang	Yin	Yang	Yin
Metal	Earth	Earth	Fire
辰	卯	寅	丑
Dragon	Rabbit	Tiger	Ox

There is a Partial Three Harmony Metal Combination between the Rooster Month Branch and the Snake Hour Branch in Feliciano's chart. As the Hour Pillar is involved, this Combination will only be felt in the second half of his life, after the age of 40. However, in the first half of his life (i.e. the Day, Month and Year Pillars), there are two Rooster Branches, in the Month and Year. There are no other Combinations. The prevalent element is Metal. For a Yang Water Day Master like Feliciano, Metal represents the Resource. He has a Follow the Resource (Metal) chart.

Feliciano first gained success in the Sheep Luck Cycle (age 16 to 20) when he released his first single *Everybody Do the Click* in 1964 (Yang Wood Dragon year). The second favourable element Earth was present in both the Luck Cycle and the Annual Branch. In 1965 (Yin Wood Snake year), he released his first album *The Voice and Guitar of Jose Feliciano*. The Annual Snake Branch combined with the Rooster Branches in his chart to reinforce his favourable element Metal.

There was a Water Rival present in the Yang Water Luck Cycle (age 21 to 25), which meant that Feliciano required favourable elements for success. In 1967 (Yin Fire Sheep year), there is a Stem Combination between the Annual Yin Fire Stem and his Yang Water Day Master. This indicated opportunities for him to generate Wealth. He toured the United Kingdom and in London, Jimi Hendrix appeared on stage to compliment Feliciano on his guitar work. In 1968 (Yang Earth Monkey year), Feliciano's rendition of the Doors' *Light My Fire* reached Number 3 on the US Singles chart, selling over a million copies. It also won him two Grammys, for Best New Artist and Best Pop Song. The second favourable element Earth was present in the Annual Stem.

In 1970 (Yang Metal Dog year), Feliciano wrote and released an album of Christmas songs, *Feliz Navidad*. The title track became one of the most played Christmas tracks of all time and is in the Grammy Hall of Fame. The favourable elements Metal and Earth were present in the Annual Stem and Branch.

The Horse Luck Cycle (age 26 to 30) contained Feliciano's negative element Fire. However, the Horse is also the animal present in his House of Spouse, indicating romance and marriage. During this period, his chances of finding romance are high. In 1971 (Yin Metal Pig year), Feliciano performed the song *Che Sara* at the Sanremo Music Festival, earning second place. His favourable element Metal was present in the Annual Stem. The same year, he started dating Susan Omillian, an art student. They dated for 11 years before marrying in 1982 (Yang Water Dog year). The Annual Dog Branch formed a Combination with the Horse in the House of Spouse, indicating marriage. When the Annual Branch or Luck Cycle is the House of Spouse animal or forms a Three Harmony or Six Harmony Combination with it, the chances of finding romance or getting married will be higher.

The Yin Metal (age 31 to 35) Luck Cycle contained Feliciano's favourable element Metal. He released the albums *Angela* in 1976 (Yang Fire Dragon year) and *Sweet Soul Music* in 1977 (Yin Fire Snake year). The favourable elements Metal and Earth were present, and the Annual Snake Branch in 1977 combined with the Rooster Branches in his chart to reinforce Metal. In 1979 (Yin Earth Sheep year), the second favourable element was present in the Annual Branch. He recorded a spontaneous duet of *Light My Fire* with rhythm and blues singer Minnie Riperton.

The subsequent Luck Cycles all contained his favourable elements Metal and Earth: Snake (age 36 to 40), Yang Metal (age 41 to 45), Dragon (age 46 to 50) and Yin Earth (age 51 to 55). In 1981 (Yin Metal Rooster year), Feliciano released a self-titled album after being the first artist to be signed to the Latin Division of Motown Records. The Annual Rooster Branch combined with the Snake Luck Cycle and the Rooster Branches in Feliciano's birth chart to reinforce the favourable element Metal. In 1989 (Yin Earth Snake year), Ray Bradbury approached Feliciano and wife Susan to write songs for his new play *The Man in the Ice Cream Suit*. The Annual Snake Branch combined with the Rooster Branches to reinforce the favourable element Metal. In 2000 (Yang Metal Dragon year), Feliciano was presented with a Grammy Legend Award. The favourable elements Metal and Earth were present in the Annual Stem and Branch.

The Rabbit Luck Cycle (age 56 to 60) clashed with the Rooster Month and Year Branch in his chart. Feliciano only released two albums in this period.

Feliciano is currently in the Yin Fire Luck Cycle (age 71 to 75). There is a Stem Combination involving the Luck Cycle and the Yang Water Day Master involving the Wealth element. After the age of 70, a Stem Combination involving Wealth indicates a higher incidence of illness. Fortunately, the Ox Luck Cycle (age 76 to 80) is favourable as it combines with the Rooster Month Branch and Snake Hour Branch to form the Full Three Harmony Metal Combination.

Example 2.13 Prince Christian, Second in Line to the Danish Throne (born October 15, 2005, 01:57 hours)

Hour	Day	Month	Year
辛	壬	丙	乙
Yin Metal	Yang Water	Yang Fire	Yin Wood
丑	申	戌	酉
Ox	Monkey	Dog	Rooster

2	12	22	32
乙	甲	癸	壬
Yin Wood	Yang Wood	Yin Water	Yang Water
酉	申	未	午
Rooster	Monkey	Sheep	Horse

42	52	62	77
辛	庚	己	戊
Yin Metal	Yang Metal	Yin Earth	Yang Earth
巳	辰	卯	寅
Snake ·	Dragon	Rabbit	Tiger

There is a Seasonal Metal Combination in Prince Christian's birth chart. His Monkey Day Branch, Rooster Year Branch and Dog Month Branch combine to form Metal. There are no other Combinations in the chart. As Prince Christian is a Yang Water Day Master, Metal represents his Resource. He has a Follow the Resource (Metal) chart.

For a Yang Water Day Master like Prince Christian, his Special Stars are the Monkey and Dog. Both are present in his chart, suggesting that he will be extremely successful.

The Monkey Luck Cycle (age 17 to 21) has the same animal that is located in Prince Christian's House of Spouse. This suggests that he has a good chance of finding love and romance during this period.

The Yin Water Luck Cycle (age 22 to 26) may be challenging for Prince Christian as there is a Water Rival present. The Sheep Luck Cycle (age 27 to 32) not only contains his second favourable element Earth, it also provides him with a very favourable configuration. Prince Christian has the auspicious Four Branches in a Row during this period: Sheep Luck Cycle, Monkey Day Branch, Rooster Year Branch and Dog Month Branch.

The Yang Water Luck Cycle (age 32 to 36) contains a Water Rival, so this may be another challenging period for Prince Christian. In the Horse Luck Cycle (age 37 to 46), there is a Partial Three Harmony Combination involving the Luck Cycle and the Dog Month Branch. The Seasonal Metal Combination is disrupted. The prevalent element becomes Fire, so the chart transforms into a Follow the Wealth (Fire) chart. The list of favourable elements during this Luck Cycle will be:

1) Wealth element Fire.
2) Output element Wood.
3) Power element Earth.
4) Resource element Metal.
5) Self element Water.

The Yin Metal Luck Cycle (age 42 to 46) contains Prince Christian's favourable element as his chart reverts back to a Follow the Resource (Metal) chart. The Snake Luck Cycle (age 47 to 51) forms a Partial Three Harmony Metal Combination with the Ox Hour Branch. However, it also forms a Six Harmony Combination with the Monkey Day Branch. This may manifest as Prince Christian having to choose between two different paths in his life.

The Yang Metal Luck Cycle (age 52 to 56) has the favourable element Metal. In the Dragon Luck Cycle (age 57 to 61), there is a Clash with the Dog Month Branch. This disrupts the Seasonal Metal Combination that accounts for the Follow the Resource chart. The Dragon combines with the Monkey Day Branch, transforming Prince Christian's chart into a Dominant Water chart. His list of useful elements will be:

1) Resource element Metal.
2) Self element Water.
3) Output element Wood.
4) Wealth element Fire.
5) Power element Earth.

Example 2.14 Nicolae Ceaucescu, General Secretary of the Romanian Communist Party 1965 to 1989 (born January 26, 1918, died December 25, 1989)

Hour	Day	Month	Year
	癸	癸	丁
	Yin Water	Yin Water	Yin Fire
	酉	丑	巳
	Rooster	Ox	Snake

7	17	27	37
壬	辛	庚	己
Yang Water	Yin Metal	Yang Metal	Yin Earth
子	亥	戌	酉
Rat	Pig	Dog	Rooster

47	57	67
戊	丁	丙
Yang Earth	Yin Fire	Yang Fire
申	未	
Monkey	Sheep	

Hour	Day	Month	Year
	己	丙	己
	Yin Earth	Yang Fire	Yin Earth
	未	子	巳
	Sheep	Rat	Snake

80

There is a Full Three Harmony Metal Combination in Ceaucescu's birth chart. His Rooster Day Branch, Ox Month Branch and Snake Year Branch all combine to form Metal. There are no other Combinations. As he is a Yin Water Day Master, Metal represents his Resource. Ceaucescu has a Follow the Resource (Metal) chart.

There were Water Rivals present in the Yang Water (age 7 to 11) and Rat (age 12 to 16) Luck Cycles. This indicated difficult years for Ceaucescu. He was born as one of ten children to a peasant family. At the age of 11 in 1929 (Yin Earth Snake year), he ran away from home to Bucharest, where he became an apprentice shoemaker. In 1933 (Yin Water Rooster year), Ceaucescu was arrested for street fighting during a strike. There was a Water Rival present in the Annual Stem.

In 1943 (Yin Water Sheep year) during the Pig Luck Cycle (age 22 to 26), Ceaucescu shared a cell in Targu Jiu internment camp with Communist Leader Gheorghe Gheorghiu-Dej and became his protégé. The second favourable element Earth was present in the Annual Branch.

In the favourable Yang Metal Luck Cycle (age 27 to 31), Ceaucescu served as secretary of the Union of Communist Youth in 1945 (Yin Wood Rooster year). He was also made Brigadier General in the Romanian army. The Annual Rooster Branch reinforced the favourable element Metal by combining with the Ox, Rooster and Snake Branches present in his chart.

In the Dog (age 32 to 36) Luck Cycle, the second favourable element Earth was present. In 1952 (Yang Water Dragon year), he was brought by Gheorghiu-Dej into the Central Committee. The Annual Branch contained the second favourable element Earth. By the end of this period, Ceaucescu had risen to the second highest position in the Romanian Communist Party hierarchy. He maintained his position in government during the favourable Yin Earth (age 37 to 41) and Rooster (age 42 to 46) Luck Cycles.

In 1965 (Yin Wood Snake year) during the Yang Earth Luck Cycle (age 47 to 51), Ceaucescu was elected General Secretary of the Romanian Communist Party following Gheorghiu-Dej's death. The Annual Snake Branch combined with the Ox, Rooster and Snake Branches present in his chart to reinforce the favourable Metal. In 1968 (Yang Earth Monkey year), there was a Stem Combination with Ceaucescu's Yin Water Day Master. The Power Combination indicated professional success. He stood up to the Soviet Union by condemning the invasion of Czechoslovakia.

The Monkey Luck Cycle (age 52 to 56) had a Yang Water Rival present, indicating issues for Ceaucescu. In 1971 (Yin Metal Pig year), after visiting China and North Korea, he started developing a cult of personality adopted by North Korea's Kim Il Sung. It was also a means to control any political opposition within his country.

In 1977 (Yin Fire Snake year) during the negative Yin Fire Luck Cycle (age 57 to 61), two events threatened Ceaucescu's rule. The first one was natural: the Bucharest earthquake destroyed much of the city and affected his plans to build oil refineries in Romania. The second was a strike by more than 30 000 miners in the Jiu River Valley complaining of low pay and poor working conditions. The negative Fire present in the Luck Cycle and Annual Stem attacked his favourable element Metal. However, the Annual Snake Branch combined with the Rooster, Ox and Snake present in Ceaucescu's chart to reinforce Metal. He was able to negotiate with the miners and maintain his power.

In the Yang Fire Luck Cycle (from age 67), Ceaucescu was overthrown by the Revolution in December 1989 (Yang Fire Rat month in the Yin Earth Snake year). He and his wife Elena were captured by the army and tried by a kangaroo court. After being found guilty of genocide, both were executed on Christmas Day. It was a

Sheep day, which clashed with his Ox Month Branch and disrupted the Three Harmony Metal Combination. There was also a Yin Water Rival present in the Rat Month. While there were Yin Earth Stems present on the day he died, it was not sufficient to protect him against the Yin Water Rival present that month. The Wealth element Fire was also present in the Luck Cycle and Month. When the Wealth element is present after retirement age (i.e. from late 60s), there is an increased possibility of health issues.

Example 2.15 Hank Williams, American Singer
(born September 17, 1923, 01:00 hours,
died January 1, 1953)

Hour	Day	Month	Year
癸	癸	辛	癸
Yin Water	Yin Water	Yin Metal	Yin Water
丑	巳	酉	亥
Ox	Snake	Rooster	Pig

3	13	23	
庚	己	戊	
Yang Metal	Yin Earth	Yang Earth	
申	未	午	
Monkey	Sheep	Horse	

Hour	Day	Month	Year
	壬	壬	壬
	Yang Water	Yang Water	Yang Water
	子	子	辰
	Rat	Rat	Dragon

There is a Full Three Harmony Metal Combination present in Williams' chart. His Snake Day Branch combines with the Rooster Month Branch and the Ox Hour Branch. There is also a Yin Metal Month Stem. In spite of the Yin Water Year and Hour Stems, the prevalent element remains Metal. As Williams is a Yin Water Day Master, Metal represents the Resource. He has a Follow the Resource (Metal) chart.

Note that there are three Yin Water Stems in Williams' chart, including the Day Master. This does not conform to the Three Friends in the Stems Configuration, which states that the Stems all have to occupy consecutive Pillars and involve the Day Master. So this configuration would include three Stems of the same Element and Polarity in the Hour, Day and Month Stems or Day, Month and Year Stems. Those with the Three Friends in the Stems Configuration are very sociable and enjoy life.

Williams' musical ability was first noticed during the favourable Yin Earth Luck Cycle (age 13 to 17). In 1937 (Yin Fire Ox year), Williams won a talent show at the Empire Theatre in Montgomery, Alabama. Known as the singing kid, he started a 15-minute singing show twice a week on local radio. The Annual Ox Branch combined with the Rooster Month Branch and Snake Day Branch to reinforce his favourable element Metal. In 1939 (Yin Earth Rabbit year), the second favourable element Earth was present. Williams dropped out of school to tour full time with his band, the *Drifting Cowboys*. There was also a clash between the Annual Rabbit Branch and the Rooster Month Branch. It was believed that Williams' alcohol problems started at this point during the tours.

The Sheep Luck Cycle (age 18 to 22) did not clash with the Ox Hour Branch as the Hour Pillar only exerts its influence when a person reaches the age of 40. Rather, it combined with the Pig Year Branch to form Wood. Williams' chart experienced a clash between Metal and Wood, which resulted in complications for him during this period. In 1942 (Yang Water Horse year), there was a Water Rival present in the Annual Stem and the negative element Fire in the Annual Branch. Williams was fired from his radio show for "habitual drunkenness". He also lost members of his band as they were drafted for military service. Williams worked for the rest of the war in a shipbuilding company and sang in bars for soldiers.

On a personal note, he married Audrey Shephard in 1944 (Yang Wood Monkey year). The Annual Monkey Branch formed a Six Harmony Combination with the Snake in the House of Spouse, indicating the possibility of romance or marriage. In 1945 (Yin Wood Rooster year), the Annual Rooster Branch combined with the Snake Day Branch and Rooster Month Branch to reinforce the favourable element Metal. Williams started performing again on radio and published his first songbook.

The Yang Earth Cycle (age 23 to 27) was favourable for Williams. Not only did it contain his second favourable element Earth, it also formed a Stem Combination with his Yin Water Day Master. The Combination involves his Power element, indicating professional recognition and success. In 1946 (Yang Fire Dog year), Williams had his first recording session, including the successful tracks *Never Again (Will I Knock on Your Door)* and *Honky Tonkin*. In 1948 (Yang Earth Rat year), there was another Stem Power Combination involving the Annual Stem. Williams moved to Shreveport, Louisiana and joined the highly rated *Louisiana Hayride* radio show. In 1949 (Yin Earth Ox year), the Annual Ox Branch combined with the Rooster Month Branch and the Snake Day Branch to form the Full Three Harmony Metal Combination. Williams' version of the 1922 song *Lovesick Blues* became a huge country hit, staying at number 1 on the Billboard charts for four months.

The Horse Luck Cycle (from age 28) contained Williams' negative element Fire. He started 1951 (Yin Metal Rabbit year) with the hit song *Dear John* and its flipside *Cold, Cold Heart*. However, the Annual Rabbit Branch combined with his Pig Year Branch to form Wood, resulting in a Metal Wood clash within his chart. In November 1951,

Williams injured his back after falling on a hunting trip and required spinal fusion surgery. In the first half of 1952 (Yang Water Dragon year), Audrey Williams divorced him. There is a Water Rival present in the Annual Stem.

Williams was found dead by his driver on New Year's Day 1953 on his way from Montgomery, Alabama to a concert in Canton, Ohio. An autopsy found the cause of death to be heart failure due to the ingestion of alcohol, morphine and chloral hydrate. On the day he died, there was a Partial Three Harmony Water Combination involving the Rat Day and Month Branches and the Dragon Year Branch. There were also three Yang Water Rivals present. Together with the Three Harmony Branch Combination, they formed a Dominant Water Rival chart that a Follow the Resource (Metal) chart was not able to cope with.

Example 2.16 Donny Hathaway, American Singer
(born October 1, 1945, died January 13, 1979)

Hour	Day	Month	Year
	癸	乙	乙
	Yin Water	Yin Wood	Yin Wood
	卯	酉	酉
	Rabbit	Rooster	Rooster

8	18	28	
甲	癸	壬	
Yang	Yin	Yang	
Wood	Water	Water	
申	未	午	
Monkey	Sheep	Horse	

Hour	Day	Month	Year
	庚	乙	戊
	Yang Metal	Yin Wood	Yang Earth
	辰	丑	午
	Dragon	Ox	Horse

86

There are no Branch Combinations in Hathaway's birth chart. However, there are two Rooster Branches which contain only Metal. There is also a Rabbit Day Branch and two Yin Wood Stems. In the absence of a Pig or Sheep year or Luck Cycle, the prevalent element is Metal. For a Yin Water Day Master like Hathaway, Metal represents the Resource. He has a Follow the Resource (Metal) chart.

However, when there is a Pig or Sheep year or Luck Cycle, there is a Partial Three Harmony Wood Combination involving the Rabbit Day Branch. The prevalent element in these years or Luck Cycles will be Wood. Hathaway transforms into a Follow the Output (Wood) chart. His list of favourable elements will be:

1) Output element Wood.
2) Wealth element Fire.
3) Power element Earth.
4) Self element Water.
5) Resource element Metal.

Hathaway's chart has the potential to follow either Metal or Wood, elements which clash with each other. There is a Metal-Wood conflict in his chart. In his case, it manifested as psychological illness. Hathaway had depressive episodes and was diagnosed with paranoid schizophrenia at the height of his success. He was known not to take his medications regularly.

Hathaway is also born on a Yin Water Rabbit day. This is one of the four days where the Day Master sits on a Nobleman. It is also one of the six days where the Day Master sits on an Academic Star. The Yin Water Rabbit day is one of two days where the Day Master sits on both the Nobleman and Academic Star. The other day that conforms to these criteria is the Yin Fire Rooster day. This suggests that Hathaway married a spouse who assisted him. As he is sitting on his Academic Star, it also indicates that he is extremely intelligent. Hathaway married his wife Eulalah in 1967 (Yin Fire Sheep year).

The Annual Sheep Branch combined with his Rabbit Day Branch, indicating the possibility of marriage.

During the Sheep Luck Cycle (age 23 to 27), Hathaway transformed into a Follow the Output (Wood) chart. In 1970 (Yang Metal Dog year), his debut album *Everything Is Everything* was released. The negative element Metal was present in the Annual Stem. He also released the seasonal track *This Christmas*, but both album and single did not achieve much success. However, *This Christmas* became a classic when re-released in 1991. In 1971 (Yin Metal Pig year), there was a Full Three Harmony Combination when the Annual Pig Branch combined with the Rabbit Day Branch and the Sheep Luck Cycle. The self-titled second album *Donny Hathaway* reached the top 10 of the Rhythm and Blues chart.

In the Yang Water Luck Cycle (age 28 to 32), Hathaway reverted back to a Follow the Resource (Metal) chart. The presence of a Water Rival in the Luck Cycle created issues. However, in 1973 (Yin Water Ox year), the Annual Ox Branch combined with the Rooster Branches in his chart to form the favourable element Metal. His third and final studio album *Extension of A Man* was released. It is noted for its classic ballad *Someday We'll All Be Free*. Although Hathaway did not release any more music of his own for the rest of this period, he produced albums for other artists.

The Horse Luck Cycle (from age 33) contained Hathaway's negative element Fire. In the first half of 1978 (Yang Earth Horse year), there was a Stem Combination between the Annual Stem and his Yin Water Day Master. The Combination with the Power element indicated professional success and recognition. Hathaway's duet with Roberta Flack, *The Closer I Get to You*, reached Number 2 on the US Singles chart.

On January 13, 1979 (still the Yang Earth Horse year), Hathaway's body was found on the sidewalk below the window of his room on the 15th floor of the Essex House hotel in New York City. He had been recording hours prior to his death and it was reported that he had been acting irrationally and appeared delusional and paranoid. There were no signs of struggle and it was ruled that he committed suicide by jumping from his balcony. On the day he died, there was a Partial Three Harmony Metal Combination involving the Ox Month and the Rooster Branches in his chart, reinforcing the favourable element Metal. However, the negative element Fire was also present in the Horse Luck Cycle and year. There was a conflict between Metal and Fire.

Example 2.17 Hansie Cronje,
South African Cricket Team Captain
(born September 25, 1969, died June 1, 2002)

Hour	Day	Month	Year
	癸	癸	己
	Yin Water	Yin Water	Yin Earth
	卯	酉	酉
	Rabbit	Rooster	Rooster

6	16	26	
壬	辛	庚	
Yang Water	Yin Metal	Yang Metal	
申	未	午	
Monkey	Sheep	Horse	

Hour	Day	Month	Year
	庚	乙	壬
	Yang Metal	Yin Wood	Yang Water
	子	巳	午
	Rat	Snake	Horse

There are no Combinations in Cronje's birth chart. There are two Rooster Branches which contain only Metal. There is also a Yin Earth Year Stem that further supports the Metal within the Rooster Branches. The prevalent element within his chart is Metal. As Cronje is a Yin Water Day Master, Metal represents his Resource. He has a Follow the Resource (Metal) chart.

Cronje is born on a Yin Water Rabbit day. As discussed in Example 2.16 Donny Hathaway, this is one of the two days in which the Day Master is sitting on his Nobleman and Academic Star. It indicates that Cronje married a spouse who assisted him. It also suggests that Cronje is highly intelligent. He married Bertha Hans in April 1995 (Yin Wood Pig year) during the Sheep Luck Cycle (age 21 to 25). Both the Sheep Luck Cycle and the Annual Pig Branch combined with the Rabbit Branch in the House of Spouse. This indicated that the chances of Cronje getting married in 1995 were very high.

In the favourable Yin Metal Luck Cycle (age 16 to 20), Cronje became a regular player representing Orange Free State in the South African First Class Cricket league in 1989 (Yin Earth Snake year). The Annual Snake Branch combined with the Rooster Branches in his chart to reinforce the favourable element Metal.

The Sheep Luck Cycle (age 21 to 25) formed a Partial Three Harmony Wood Combination with the Rabbit in the House of Spouse. As previously discussed, Cronje got married during this period. However, the presence of Wood also meant that there was a Wood-Metal conflict within his chart, which may manifest as professional or personal issues. In 1990 (Yang Metal Horse year), Cronje became Captain of the Orange Free State team. The Annual Stem contained Metal. In 1993 (Yin Water Rooster year), Cronje scored his first two centuries in Test Cricket while representing South Africa against India and Sri Lanka. The Annual Rooster Branch reinforced the favourable element Metal. In 1994 (Yang Wood Dog year), Cronje was made Captain of the South African Cricket team following Keplar Wessels' retirement. The second favourable element Earth was present in the Annual Branch.

The Yang Metal (age 26 to 30) was a highly favourable period for Cronje. In 1997 (Yin Fire Ox year), he led South Africa to their first series victory over Pakistan. The Annual Ox Branch combined with the Rooster Branches in his chart to reinforce the favourable element Metal. In 1998 (Yang Earth Tiger year), he became only the second South African to pass 3 000 runs. The second favourable element Metal was present in the Annual Stem. In October 1999 (Yin Earth Rabbit year), Cronje became South Africa's highest Test run scorer during their first match against Zimbabwe. Earth was present in the Annual Stem, as well as in the month.

The Horse Luck Cycle (from age 31) contained Cronje's negative element Fire. In 2000 (Yang Metal Dragon year), he was investigated and found guilty of match fixing. As a result, he was banned from cricket for life. Although the favourable elements Metal and Earth were present in the Annual Stem and Branch, the negative Fire from the Luck Cycle was able to exert its influence.

Cronje died on June 1, 2002 (Yang Water Horse year) after the cargo plane that he had hitched a ride on crashed into the Outeniqua Mountains close to the town of George in South Africa. The Snake month combined with the Rooster Branches in Cronje's chart to form the favourable element Metal. However, the negative element Fire was present in the Annual Horse Branch and the Horse Luck Cycle. There was a Fire-Metal conflict that unfortunately in this case, manifested as a plane crash.

Example 2.18 Zayn Malik, British Singer
(born January 12, 1993, 10:00 hours)

Hour	Day	Month	Year
丁	癸	癸	壬
Yin Fire	Yin Water	Yin Water	Yang Water
巳	巳	丑	申
Snake	Snake	Ox	Monkey

8	18	28	38
甲	乙	丙	丁
Yang Wood	Yin Wood	Yang Fire	Yin Fire
寅	卯	辰	巳
Tiger	Rabbit	Dragon	Snake

48	58	68	78
戊	己	庚	辛
Yang Earth	Yin Earth	Yang Metal	Yin Metal
午	未	申	酉
Horse	Sheep	Monkey	Rooster

As Zayn Malik is known professionally as Zayn, he will be referred to as Zayn in our discussion. There is a Partial Three Harmony Metal Combination in Zayn's birth chart. His Snake Day and Hour Branches combine with his Ox Month Branch to form Metal. There are also Water Rivals present in the Month and Year Stems and a Yang Water Rival hidden in the Monkey Year Branch. However, the Combination between the Snake and Ox take precedence as the Combination between the Day and Month Branch persists throughout a person's life. The prevalent element in Zayn's chart is Metal. As he is a Yin Water Day Master, Metal represents his Resource element. Zayn has a Follow the Resource (Metal) chart.

He is born on a Yin Water Snake day, one of four days where the Day Master sits on the Nobleman Star. This indicates that Zayn will marry a spouse who will assist him. Note that the House of Spouse animal is repeated in his chart. The Snake is present is both the Day and Hour Branches. This suggests that Zayn will have a higher chance of being married twice. He was engaged to Perrie Edwards of musical group Little Mix in 2013 (Yin Water Snake year). It was the year of his House of Spouse animal. The engagement was broken off two years later in 2015 (Yin Wood Sheep year) and Zayn started dating model Gigi Hadid in 2016 (Yang Fire Monkey year). The Annual Monkey Branch formed a Six Harmony Combination with the Snake in the House of Spouse.

As Zayn is born in a Monkey year, he has the ability to transform into a Dominant Water chart when there is a Dragon or Rat year or Luck Cycle. In these circumstances, his list of favourable would be:

1) Resource element Metal.
2) Self element Water.
3) Output element Wood.
4) Wealth element Fire.
5) Power element Earth.

In 2010 (Yang Metal Tiger year) during the Tiger Luck Cycle (age 13 to 17), Zayn auditioned for the reality-television singing competition *X Factor*. Judges Simon Cowell and Nicole Scherzinger placed Zayn in a musical group called *One Direction* together with Liam Payne, Lous Tomlinson, Harry Styles and Niall Horan. The group finished third.

During the Yin Wood Luck Cycle (age 18 to 22), *One Direction* achieved significant success. Their debut album *Up All Night* debuted at Number 1 on the US Billboard Album charts. It contained the UK Number 1 single *What Makes You Beautiful* that was released in 2011 (Yin Metal Rabbit year). The favourable element Metal was present in the Annual Stem.

In 2012 (Yang Water Dragon year), Zayn was transformed into a Dominant Water chart when the Annual Dragon Branch combined with his Monkey Year Branch. The Water Rivals in his chart were no longer an issue. *One Direction* released their second album *Take Me Home*, which went to number 1 in 35 countries, including the US. Success continued in 2013 (Yin Water Snake year) as third album *Take Me Home* debuted at Number 1 on the US Billboard Album charts, making them the first group ever to have their first three albums debut in the top spot.

In 2014 (Yang Wood Horse year), the Annual Stem gave Zayn the auspicious 4 in a Row Stem Configuration: Yang Water Year Stem, Yin Water Day Master, Annual Yang Wood Stem and Yin Wood Luck Cycle. *One Direction's* fourth album *Four* made it four successive albums to debut at the Number 1 spot on the US Billboard Album charts.

In 2015 (Yin Wood Sheep year), Zayn quit *One Direction* and signed a record contract with RCA Records. His debut single *Pillowtalk* was released in January 2016 (still Yin Wood Sheep year) and debuted at number 1 in both the US and UK charts. The second favourable element was present in the Annual Branch.

Zayn released his solo album *Mind of Mine* in 2016 (Yang Fire Monkey year) during the Rabbit Luck Cycle (age 23 to 27). There was a Yang Water Rival present in the Annual Monkey Branch. While *Mind of Mine* debuted at Number 1 on the US and UK charts, it remained on the top for just one week and did not yield any more top 10 hits. 2017 (Yin Fire Rooster year) saw Zayn start the year with a US Number 2 duet with Taylor Swift, *I Don't Wanna Live Forever*. It was from the soundtrack to the movie *Fifty Shades Darker*. The Annual Yin Fire Stem formed a Stem Combination with Zayn's Yang Water Year Stem. It was a favourable configuration in which a person uses the Wealth Element to combine away a Yang Rival.

For the remainder of this Luck Cycle, 2018 (Yang Earth Dog year) appears favourable for two reasons. There is a Stem Combination between the Annual Yang Earth Stem and Zayn's Yin Water Day Master. The Combination involving the Power element indicates professional success and recognition. For a Yin Water Day Master like Zayn, the Special Stars are the Dog and Monkey. The Annual Dog Branch will work in conjunction with his Monkey Year Branch to bring him success. 2019 (Yin Earth Pig year) contains his second favourable element Earth. In 2020 (Yang Metal Rat year), Zayn will transform into a Dominant Water chart.

The Yang Fire Luck Cycle (age 28 to 32) contains the negative element Fire, so the individual years need to be considered to determine Zayn's fortune. In the Dragon Luck Cycle (age 33 to 37), he will again transform into a Dominant Water chart due to the Combination between the Dragon Luck Cycle and his Monkey Year Branch. While the Yin Fire Luck Cycle (age 38 to 42) contains his negative element, there is also a Stem Combination involving his Yang Water Year Stem. Any potential problem is removed. The Snake Luck Cycle (age 43 to 47) sees his House of Spouse animal repeated, so this may be a period for him to find romance.

The Yang Earth Luck Cycle (age 48 to 52) involves a Stem Combination involving the Power Element and his Yin Water Day Master, indicating professional success or recognition. The Horse Luck Cycle (age 53 to 57) contains the negative element Fire, so there may be some upheavals.

Conclusion

From the examples covered in this chapter, you can see that the ranking for favourable elements for Follow the Resource (Metal) charts is:

1) Resource element Metal.
2) Power element Earth.
3) Output element Wood.
4) Wealth element Fire.
5) Self element Water.

All 18 examples that were discussed were either Yang Water or Yin Water Day Masters with the Resource Element Metal as the most prominent element. This qualified them as Follow the Resource (Metal) charts. The majority of charts contained either the Full or Partial Three Harmony Metal Combination within its Branches. Dolly Parton, Shonda Rhimes, Nicolae Ceaucescu and Hank Williams had the Full Three Harmony Metal Combination consisting of the Snake, Rooster and Ox in their birth charts.

Madeleine Albright has the Partial Three Harmony Metal Combination consisting of the Snake and Ox. Bill O'Reilly, Anita Baker, Edison Chen and Jim Jarmusch have the Partial Three Harmony Metal Combination consisting of the Ox and Rooster.

Jennifer Hudson has a Partial Three Harmony Metal Combination consisting of a Snake with two Roosters, while Andrew Lincoln has two Oxen combining with a Rooster. Jose Feliciano has two Roosters combining with a Snake in his chart. Tori Spelling has a Snake combining with two Oxen in her chart, while Zayn Malik has two Snakes combining with an Ox in his chart.

Zayn Malik and Edison Chen have a Monkey Year Branch. When there is a Dragon or Rat year or Luck Cycle, they transform into Dominant Water charts. Jim Jarmusch has a Dragon Year Branch. When there is a Monkey or Rat year or Luck Cycle, he transforms into a Dominant Water chart. Tori Spelling is born on a Rat Day. She transforms into a Dominant Water chart when there is a Dragon or Monkey year or Luck Cycle.

Prince Christian has the Seasonal Metal Combination in his chart. As he is born on a Monkey Day, he transforms into a Dominant Water chart in the Rat or Dragon year or Luck Cycle. Prince Christian has a Dog Month Branch that allows him to Follow the Wealth (Fire) when the Tiger or Horse year or Luck Cycle approaches.

Lleyton Hewitt and Hansie Cronje do not have any Three Harmony or Seasonal Combinations in their charts. They have two Rooster Branches in their Day, Month and Year Pillars. This allows them to Follow Metal, their Resource element.

Donny Hathaway also has two Rooster Branches in his Month and Year Pillars. This allows him to Follow Metal, his Resource element. However, he also has two Yin Wood Stems and a Sheep Day Branch. In the Pig or Rabbit year or Luck Cycle, he is able to Follow Wood, the Output element.

Chapter Three Follow the Output (Metal) Charts

Follow the Output charts are those in which the Output element is the most prominent. The Day Master produces the Output element. For women, the Output, or what they produce is Children. In Chinese texts, this type of chart is also known as a Follow the Children chart. For men, the equivalent of the Child element is the Power Element that is produced by the Wealth element that represents the Spouse. Referring to the charts as Follow the Output charts is more universal. For Yang Earth and Yin Earth Day Masters, the Output element is always Metal.

Those with Follow the Output charts are very good at expressing themselves in their personal and professional lives. They are generally sociable with a good network of friends. They tend to have a wide variety of interests, enjoy challenges and are adept at multi tasking. They may have more than one career in their lifetime as they like to be intellectually stimulated.

Their list of favourable elements differs slightly from the other types of charts. For most charts, the second favourable element tends to be the one that produces the most favourable element. What is important to Follow the Output charts is that they have an avenue to channel their energies. For instance, their Children should produce Grandchildren to ensure continuity of the family. The second favourable element is the element that the Output element produces, which is the Wealth element.

For Follow the Output (Metal) charts, the list of favourable elements is as follows:

1) Metal, the Output element.
2) Water, the Wealth element that is produced by Metal.
3) Wood, the Power element controls Earth Rivals and Competitors.
4) Earth, the Self element controls the second favourable element Water.
5) Fire, the Resource element controls the favourable element Metal.

Example 3.1 Justin Timberlake, American Singer
(born January 31, 1981, 18:30 hours)

Hour	Day	Month	Year
癸	己	己	庚
Yin Water	Yin Earth	Yin Earth	Yang Metal
酉	酉	丑	申
Rooster	Rooster	Ox	Monkey

1	11	21	31
庚	辛	壬	癸
Yang Metal	Yin Metal	Yang Water	Yin Water
寅	卯	辰	巳
Tiger	Rabbit	Dragon	Snake

41	51	61	71
甲	乙	丙	丁
Yang Wood	Yin Wood	Yang Fire	Yin Fire
午	未	申	酉
Horse	Sheep	Monkey	Rooster

There is a Partial Three Harmony Metal Combination in Timberlake's birth chart. His Ox Month Branch combines with his Rooster Day and Hour Branches to form Metal. There are no other Combinations within his chart. As Timberlake is a Yin Earth Day Master, Metal represents his Output. He has a Follow the Output (Metal) chart.

For a Yin Earth Day Master, the Special Stars are the Ox and Monkey. Timberlake has both present in his chart. This suggests that he will be able to achieve significant success in his life. He is also born on a Yin Earth Rooster day, one of six days where the Day Master is sitting on an Academic Star. This indicates that Timberlake is highly intelligent and a good student, and not necessarily academically.

During the favourable Yin Metal Luck Cycle (age 11 to 15) in 1993 (Yin Water Rooster year), Timberlake appeared in the children's entertainment show *The Mickey Mouse Club* alongside Britney Spears, Christian Aguilera and Ryan Gosling. The Annual Rooster Branch combined with the Rooster and Ox Branches in his chart to reinforced the favourable element Metal. In 1996 (Yang Fire Rat year), Timberlake became the lead singer of boy band *NSYNC* together with Justin Chasez, starting their career in Europe with their first hit *I Want You Back*. The Annual Rat Branch formed the second favourable element Water by forming a Partial Three Harmony Water Combination with the Monkey Year Branch.

The Rabbit Luck Cycle (age 16 to 20) clashed with his Rooster Day Branch, disrupting the Partial Three Harmony Metal Combination. In 1998 (Yang Earth Tiger year), Earth Rivals were present in the Annual Stem and Branch. *NSYNC* was involved in a legal battle with their manager Lou Perlman for defrauding them over more than fifty per cent of their earnings. The case was settled out of court.

In 2000 (Yang Metal Dragon year), *NSYNC's* second album *No Strings Attached* sold 2.4 million copies in its first week alone in the US. The Annual Dragon Branch combined with the Monkey Year Branch to form the second favourable element Water. In 2001 (Yin Metal Snake year), *NSYNC's* third album *Celebrity* sold more than 1.8 million copies in its first week in the US and was another major success. The Annual Snake Branch combined with the Ox Month Branch to reinforce the favourable element Metal.

In the Yang Water Luck Cycle (age 21 to 25), Timberlake left *NSYNC* to pursue a solo career. In 2002 (Yang Water Horse year), his first solo album *Justified* was a success, selling more than ten million copies worldwide. However, the negative element Fire was also present in the year. His departure from *NSYNC* left some of his band members feeling upset.

In 2004 (Yang Wood Monkey year), there was a Stem Combination with the Annual Stem and his Yin Earth Day Master. The Power Element Combination indicates professional success or recognition. Timberlake won two Grammys, for Best Pop Vocal Album and Best Male Pop Vocal Performance. He was also able to publicly apologize and salvage his career after the Super Bowl halftime performance that year where his duet partner Janet Jackson's breast was exposed following a 'wardrobe malfunction'.

In 2006 (Yang Fire Dog year), the Annual Dog Branch formed the Seasonal Metal Combination with the Monkey Year Branch and Rooster Day Branch in Timberlake's chart. His second solo album *FutureSex/LoveSounds* debuted at Number One on the US Album Charts and the lead single *Sexy Back* was number 1 for seven weeks.

In the Dragon Luck Cycle (age 26 to 30), there was a Partial Three Harmony Water Combination between the Dragon and Timberlake's Monkey Year Branch. The Dragon also forms a Six Harmony Combination with the Rooster in the House of Spouse. This indicates the possibility of romance. Timberlake started dating actress Jessica Biel and became engaged to her during this period.

In 2008 (Yang Earth Rat year), the Annual Rat Branch combined with the Dragon Luck Cycle and the Monkey Year Branch to reinforce the second favourable element Water. Timberlake's duet with Madonna, *4 Minutes*, was an international hit. He also switched his focus to acting, appearing in a string of high profile movie roles in 2010 (Yang Metal Tiger year) and 2011 (Yin Metal Rabbit year). The favourable element Metal was present in both Annual Stems. These roles included portraying Napster founder Sean Parker in *The Social Network*, and the lead character in science fiction thriller *In Time* and romantic comedy *Friends with Benefits*.

The Yin Water Luck Cycle (age 31 to 35) contained his second favourable element Water. In 2012 (Yang Water Dragon year), there was a Six Harmony Combination with the Rooster in the House of Spouse, indicating romance or marriage. Timberlake married Jessica Biel that year.

In 2013 (Yin Water Snake year), the Annual Snake Branch combined with the Rooster and Ox Branches in Timberlake's chart to reinforce the favourable element Metal. He released two best selling albums *The 20/20 Experience 1 of 2* and *2 of 2*, both of which topped the US Album Charts. In 2016 (Yang Fire Monkey year), the Annual Branch contained his favourable elements Metal and Water. He returned to the top of the US Singles charts with *Can't Fight This Feeling*, written for the *Trolls* soundtrack.

The Snake Luck Cycle (age 36 to 40) will be favourable for Timberlake as it combines with the Rooster and Ox Branches in his chart to reinforce Metal. However, there is a Combination with the Rooster in the House of Spouse, so there is the possibility of romance. The Yang Wood Luck Cycle (age 41 to 45) combines with his Yin Earth Day Master, indicating professional success and recognition. The Horse Luck Cycle (age 46 to 50) contains the negative element Fire, so there may be issues depending on the energy present in the Annual Stems and Branches.

Example 3.2. Dame Joan Collins, British Actress
(born May 23, 1933, 03:00 hours)

Hour	Day	Month	Year
丙	己	丁	癸
Yang Fire	Yin Earth	Yin Fire	Yin Water
寅	丑	巳	酉
Tiger	Ox	Snake	Rooster

5	15	25	35	45
戊	己	庚	辛	壬
Yang Earth	Yin Earth	Yang Metal	Yin Metal	Yang Water
午	未	申	酉	戌
Horse	Sheep	Monkey	Rooster	Dog

55	65	75	85
癸	甲	乙	丙
Yin Water	Yang Wood	Yin Wood	Yang Fire
亥	子	丑	寅
Pig	Rat	Ox	Tiger

There is a Full Three Harmony Metal Combination in Dame Joan's chart. Her Ox Day Branch combines with the Snake Month Branch and Rooster Year Branch to form Metal. There are no other Combinations present in the chart. As Dame Joan is a Yin Earth Day Master, Metal represents the Output element. She has a Follow the Output (Metal) chart.

Dame Joan is born on a Yin Earth Ox day, one of the Six Intelligent days. Not only is she an actress, she has also had success as an author and producer. Her chart contains one of the Red Light Pillars, Yang Fire Tiger, in her Hour Pillar. This suggests that she may have relationship issues. Dame Joan has been married five times.

At the age of 17 in 1950 (Yang Metal Tiger year), Dame Joan was signed to the British film studio J. Arthur Rank Film Company. The favourable element Metal was present in the Annual Stem. In 1955 (Yin Wood Sheep year), she was chosen by director Howard Hawks to portray the villainess in the biblical epic *Land of the Pharaohs*. While the movie did not perform well at the box office upon release, it has now acquired cult status. The Annual Sheep Branch clashed with the Ox Day Branch and also contained an Earth Rival. However, Dame Joan's chart was still able to follow Metal as there was still a Partial Three Harmony Combination between the Rooster and Snake Branches. In 1957 (Yin Fire Rooster year), Dame Joan appeared in *Sea Wife* opposite Richard Burton and joined an all-star cast in *Island in the Sun*.

The Yang Metal Luck Cycle (age 25 to 29) saw Dame Joan establish herself in Hollywood movies. In 1958 (Yang Earth Dog year), the Annual Stem gave her the auspicious configuration of 4 Stems in a Row: Yang Fire Hour Stem, Yin Fire Month Stem, Annual Yang Earth Stem and Day Master Yin Earth. She appeared in the Western *The Bravados* opposite Gregory Peck. Dame Joan finished this period on a high, appearing alongside Bob Hope and Bing Crosby in *The Road to Hong Kong*.

The Monkey Luck Cycle (age 30 to 34) was another favourable period for Dame Joan. For a Yin Earth Day Master, the Special Stars are the Ox and Monkey. The Monkey Luck Cycle worked in conjunction with her Ox Day Branch to bring her success. During this period, she appeared in popular television series like *Batman*, *The Man from U.N.C.L.E* and *Star Trek*. For a woman, the Output element also represents her Children. Dame Joan's Children element Metal was also present during this period. She married actor and singer Anthony Newley in 1963 (Yin Water Rabbit year) and had daughter Tara Newley that year and son Alexander Newley in 1965 (Yin Wood Snake year). The Output or Children element Metal was present when the Annual Snake Branch combined with the Snake, Rooster and Ox Branches in her chart.

In the Yin Metal Luck Cycle (age 35 to 39), Dame Joan divorced Newley in 1970 (Yang Metal Dog year). There was a Yang Earth Rival present in the Annual Branch. In 1972 (Yang Water Rat year), she married American businessman Ron Kass. The Annual Rat Branch formed a Six Harmony Combination with Dame Joan's Ox Day Branch, indicating the possibility of love and marriage. Her Output or Children element was also present during this period. Dame Joan gave birth to daughter Katyana Kass in 1972.

The Rooster Luck Cycle (age 40 to 44) was also a favourable period for Dame Joan, as the Rooster reinforced the favourable element Metal by combining with the Snake, Rooster and Ox Branches present within her chart. In Ox and Snake years during this period when Metal was reinforced, she made notable film appearances. In 1973 (Yin Water Ox year), Dame Joan appeared in the horror film *Tales That Witness Madness* alongside Kim Novak. In 1977 (Yin Fire Snake year), she appeared in *Empire of the Ants*.

The Yang Water Luck Cycle (age 45 to 49) saw resurgence in Dame Joan's career. In 1978 (Yang Earth Horse year), there was once again the auspicious Four Stems in a Row Configuration: Yang Fire Hour Stem, Yin Fire Month Stem, Annual Yang Earth Stem and Yin Earth Day Master. She appeared in *The Stud*, the movie adaptation of her sister Jackie Collins' novel. In 1981 (Yin Metal Rooster year), Dame Joan was offered the role of Alexis Carrington in the second season of the television soap opera *Dynasty*. It was the defining role of her career. The Annual Rooster Branch reinforced the favourable element Metal by combining with the Snake, Ox and Rooster Branches present within Dame Joan's chart.

The Dog Luck Cycle (age 50 to 54) proved to be challenging for Dame Joan on a personal level. In 1983 (Yin Water Pig year), she divorced Ron Kass and married Swedish singer Peter Holm in 1985 (Yin Wood Ox year). Her House of Spouse animal Ox was present in the Annual Branch. In 1986 (Yang Fire Tiger year), the negative elements Fire and Earth were present. Dame Joan separated from Holm and received a restraining order against him that year. In 1987 (Yin Fire Rabbit year) with the negative element present in the Annual Stem, Holm contested the pre-nuptial agreement he had with Dame Joan and the legal proceedings became a media circus. He lost his case and the divorce was finalized.

In the Yin Water Luck Cycle (age 55 to 59), Dame Joan took time off after Dynasty finished in 1989 (Yin Earth Snake year). She appeared on stage in a revival of Noel Coward's *Private Lives* in 1990 (Yang Metal Horse year). The favourable element Metal was present in the Annual Stem.

The Pig Luck Cycle (age 60 to 64) clashed with Dame Joan's Snake Month Branch, disrupting the Full Three Harmony Metal Combination. She was embroiled with her publisher Random House in a lawsuit. Dame Joan had signed a two-book deal worth $4 million USD. She had been paid $1.2 million USD in advance but Random House contended that the manuscript she had sent in was of such poor quality they demanded the return of the advance. In 1996 (Yang Fire Rat year), a court ruled that Dame Joan could keep the advance given to her plus a further $1 million USD for the first completed manuscript.

The Luck Cycles of Yang Wood (age 65 to 69), Rat (age 70 to 74), Yin Wood (age 75 to 79) and Ox (age 80 to 84) all contained favourable elements for Dame Joan. At the start of 2015 (still the Yang Wood Horse year), she was made a Dame Commander of the Order of the British Empire (OBE) for her services to charity in the 2015 New Year's Honours. The Annual Yang Wood Stem formed a Stem Combination with her Yin Earth Day Master. The Combination involving the Power element indicated professional success or recognition.

Example 3.3 Eddie Redmayne, British Actor
(born January 6, 1982, 20:00 hours)

Hour	Day	Month	Year
甲	己	辛	辛
Yang Wood	Yin Earth	Yin Metal	Yin Metal
戌	丑	丑	酉
Dog	Ox	Ox	Rooster

0	10	20	30
庚	己	戊	丁
Yang Metal	Yin Earth	Yang Earth	Yin Fire
子	亥	戌	酉
Rat	Pig	Dog	Rooster

40	50	60	70
丙	乙	甲	癸
Yang Fire	Yin Wood	Yang Wood	Yin Water
申	未	午	巳
Monkey	Sheep	Horse	Snake

Note that Redmayne is born on an Agricultural Marker day, specifically the Little Cold day. On the *Ten Thousand Year Almanac*, the changeover time for the Little Cold day is listed as 00:03 hours. As he is born at 20:00 hours, this means that he is born in the Yin Metal Ox Month.

There is a Partial Three Harmony Metal Combination in Redmayne's birth chart. His Ox Day and Month Branches combine with his Rooster Year Branch to form Metal. There are also two Yin Metal Stems. His Dog Hour Branch provides further support to Metal. The prevalent element within Redmayne's chart is Metal. As he is a Yin Earth Day Master, Metal represents the Resource element. Redmayne has a Follow the Output (Metal) chart.

During the Yang Earth (age 20 to 24) and Dog (age 25 to 29) Luck Cycles, Redmayne struggled in supporting roles after graduating from Cambridge in 2003 (Yin Water Sheep year). There were Yang Earth Rivals present during this period. In 2008 (Yang Earth Rat year), he appeared alongside Natalie Portman, Eric Bana and Scarlett Johansson in *The Other Boleyn Girl*. The second favourable element Water was present. In 2011 (Yin Metal Rabbit year), the favourable element was present in the Annual Stem. Redmayne had his first major role in *My Weekend with Marilyn* opposite Michelle Williams.

The Yin Fire Luck Cycle (age 30 to 34) contained Redmayne's negative element Fire. However, he was able to perform well in years with his favourable elements. In 2012 (Yang Water Dragon year), there was a Stem Combination between the Annual Yang Water Stem and the Yin Fire in the Luck Cycle. The negative element was combined away. Redmayne appeared as Marius Pontmercy in the movie adaptation of the musical *Les Misérables*.

In 2014 (Yang Wood Horse year), there was a Stem Combination between the Annual Yang Wood Stem and Redmayne's Yin Earth Day Master. The Power Element Combination indicates professional recognition or success. He won the Best Actor Oscar for his portrayal of Stephen Hawking in *The Theory of Everything*. In 2015 (Yin Wood Sheep year), the negative elements Fire and Earth were present in the Annual Branch. Redmayne portrayed a villain in the science fiction film *Jupiter Ascending*. He won a Golden Raspberry Award for Worst Performance by a Supporting Actor.

In 2016 (Yang Fire Monkey year), the Annual Monkey Branch worked in conjunction with his Ox Day Branch to bring him success. For a Yin Earth Day Master, the Special Stars are the Monkey and Ox. Redmayne received another Best Actor Oscar nomination for his performance as a transgender pioneer in the biographical drama *The Danish Girl*. He finished the year portraying the leading role in *Fantastic Beasts and Where to Find Them*, written by J.K. Rowling.

The Rooster Luck Cycle (age 35 to 39) should be very successful for Redmayne, as the Rooster combines with the Ox and Rooster Branches present in his chart to reinforce the favourable element Metal. The Yang Fire Luck Cycle (age 40 to 44) combines with the Yin Metal Stems present in Redmayne's birth chart. Any negative effects will be reduced.

The Monkey Luck Cycle (age 45 to 49) will also be favourable for Redmayne as it works in conjunction with the Ox Day Branch (as the two Special Stars) to bring him success. The Yin Wood Luck Cycle (age 50 to 54) will control any potential Earth Rivals in the years.

The Sheep Luck Cycle (age 55 to 59) may be problematic for Redmayne, as there is a clash with the Ox Day and Month Branches. This disrupts the Partial Three Harmony Metal Combination that confers upon the chart its Follow Metal status. The Yang Wood Luck Cycle (age 60 to 64) will be favourable as there is a Stem Combination with the Yin Earth Day Master, indicating professional recognition or success. However, the Horse Luck Cycle (age 65 to 69) contains the negative elements Fire and Earth, so there may be problems during this period.

Example 3.4 Frank Oz, American Puppeteer and Film Director (born May 25, 1944)

Hour	Day	Month	Year
	己	己	甲
	Yin Earth	Yin Earth	Yang Wood
	丑	巳	申
	Ox	Snake	Monkey

4	14	24	34
庚	辛	壬	癸
Yang Metal	Yin Metal	Yang Water	Yin Water
午	未	申	酉
Horse	Sheep	Monkey	Rooster

44	54	64	74
甲	乙	丙	丁
Yang Wood	Yin Wood	Yang Fire	Yin Fire
戌	亥	子	丑
Dog	Pig	Rat	Ox

There is a Partial Three Harmony Metal Combination in Oz's birth chart. His Ox Day Branch combines with his Snake Month Branch to form Metal. There are no other Branch Combinations within his chart. The prevalent element in the chart is Metal. Oz is a Yin Earth Day Master, which means that Metal represents his Output. He has a Follow the Output (Metal) chart.

Oz is born on a Yin Earth Ox day, one of the Six Intelligent days. He started his career as a puppeteer and actor before becoming a movie director and screenwriter. For a Yin Earth Day Master, his Special Stars are the Ox and Monkey. Both are present in Oz's birth chart, indicating significant success for him.

111

There is also a Stem Combination involving the Yang Wood Year Stem and Yin Earth Month Stem. The Earth Rival is thereby removed. This indicates a person who is able to solve problems with his Rivals.

During the Yin Metal Luck Cycle (age 14 to 18), Oz met 23 year-old Jim Henson at a puppeteer conference while still in high school in 1959 (Yin Earth Pig year). Two years later in 1961 (Yin Metal Ox year), Oz joined Henson's Muppets team after struggling through his first year of college. The Annual Ox Branch reinforced the favourable element Metal by combining with the Ox and Snake Branches in his chart. The Annual Stem also contained Metal.

In 1969 (Yin Earth Rooster year) during the favourable Yang Water Luck Cycle (age 24 to 28), the Muppets team joined a new public television program for children called *Sesame Street*. Oz provided the voice for the characters Bert, Grover and the Cookie Monster. The Annual Rooster Branch reinforced the favourable element Metal by forming the Full Three Harmony Combination with the Snake and Ox Branches.

The Monkey Luck Cycle (age 29 to 33) was successful for Oz as it contained the favourable elements Metal and Water. In 1976 (Yang Fire Dragon year), the Annual Dragon Branch combined with the Monkey Luck Cycle to form Water, Oz's second favourable element. Henson started the adult variety show *The Muppet Show*. Oz provided the voice for popular characters such as Miss Piggy, Fozzie Bear and Animal.

The Yin Water Luck Cycle (age 34 to 38) was also favourable for Oz. In 1980 (Yang Metal Monkey year), the favourable elements Metal and Water were present in the Annual Stem and Branch. Oz provided the voice of Yoda in *The Empire Strikes Back*. He also appeared as a corrections officer in the comedy *The Blues Brothers*.

In 1981 (Yin Metal Rooster year), the Annual Rooster Branch reinforced the favourable element Metal by forming the Full Three Harmony Combination with the Ox and Rooster Branches in his chart. Oz voiced the characters of Miss Piggy, Fozzie Bear and Animal in *The Great Muppet Caper*. In 1982 (Yang Water Dog year), Oz made his debut as a director, co-directing *The Dark Crystal* with Jim Henson. The second favourable element Water was present in the Annual Stem.

The Rooster Luck Cycle (age 39 to 43) formed the Full Three Harmony Metal Combination with the Snake and Ox Branches in Oz's chart. In 1983 (Yin Water Pig year), he again provided the voice of Yoda in *Return of the Jedi*. In 1984 (Yang Wood Rat year), there is a Stem Combination involving the Annual Stem and the Yin Earth Day Master. The Power Element Combination indicated professional success and recognition. Oz directed, wrote and acted in *The Muppets Take Manhattan*.

In 1986 (Yang Fire Tiger year), Oz directed his first non-Muppets feature, the musical horror comedy *Little Shop of Horrors*. The negative elements Earth and Fire were present in the Annual Stem and Branch. The movie was not a box office success.

The Yang Wood Luck Cycle (age 44 to 48) formed a Stem Combination with Oz's Yin Earth Day Master. This indicated professional success or recognition. In 1988 (Yang Earth Dragon year), Oz directed the hit comedy *Dirty Rotten Scoundrels* starring Michael Caine and Steve Martin. The Annual Dragon Branch combined with his Monkey Year Branch to form the second favourable element Water. In 1992 (Yang Water Monkey year), the favourable elements Metal and Water were present. Oz directed Goldie Hawn and Steve Martin in the comedy *Housesitter*. He also voiced Fozzie Bear, Miss Piggy and Animal for *The Muppets Christmas Carol*.

The Dog Luck Cycle (age 49 to 53) contained a Yang Earth Rival. It was a relatively quiet period for Oz. In 1995 (Yin Wood Pig year), he directed adventure fantasy film *The Indian in the Cupboard*, which performed badly at the box office. In 1997 (Yin Fire Ox year), the Annual Ox Branch combined with the Ox and Snake Branches in his chart to form the favourable element Metal. Oz directed the comedy *In and Out* featuring Kevin Kline, a critical and commercial success.

The Yin Wood Luck Cycle (age 54 to 58) contained the third favourable element Wood, which was able to control Earth Rivals present in the Annual Stems and Branches. In 2001 (Yin Metal Snake year), Oz directed Marlon Brando, Robert de Niro and Edward Norton in the thriller *The Score*. The Annual Snake Branch combined with the Snake and Ox Branches within Oz's chart to reinforce the favourable element Metal. Oz also retired from performing muppets that year.

In the Pig Luck Cycle (age 59 to 63), there was a clash with the Snake Month Branch that disrupted the Metal Combination. Professional recognition came in 2004 (Yang Wood Monkey year) when a Stem Combination involving the Annual Stem and the Yin Earth Day Master gave Oz the responsibility of directing the $90 million USD remake of *The Stepford Wives*, starring Nicole Kidman, Matthew Broderick and Bette Midler. In 2007 (Yin Fire Pig year), the second and third favourable elements Water and Wood were present in the Annual Branch. Oz directed the British comedy *Death at a Funeral*, a critical and commercial success.

In the negative Yang Fire Luck Cycle (age 64 to 68) and the Rat Luck Cycle (age 69 to 73), Oz kept a low profile, only returning to provide the voice of Yoda for *Star Wars: The Force Awakens* towards the end of 2015 (Yin Wood Sheep year).

Example 3.5 Marc Anthony, American Singer-Songwriter (born September 16, 1968)

Hour	Day	Month	Year
	己	辛	戊
	Yin Earth	Yin Metal	Yang Earth
	丑	酉	申
	Ox	Rooster	Monkey

7	17	27	37
壬	癸	甲	乙
Yang Water	Yin Water	Yang Wood	Yin Wood
戌	亥	子	丑
Dog	Pig	Rat	Ox
47	57	67	77
丙	丁	戊	己
Yang Fire	Yin Fire	Yang Earth	Yin Earth
寅	卯	辰	巳
Tiger	Rabbit	Dragon	Snake

There is a Partial Three Harmony Metal Combination in Anthony's chart. His Ox Day Branch combines with his Rooster Month Branch to form Metal. There is also a Yin Metal Month Stem. There are no other Combinations present within the chart. The prevalent element in Anthony's chart is Metal. As he is a Yin Earth Day Master, Metal represents his Output. He has a Follow the Output (Metal) chart.

Anthony is born on a Yin Earth Ox day, one of the Six Intelligent days. Apart from being a singer-songwriter, he has also had success as a record and television producer and actor. For a Yin Earth Day Master, the Special Stars are the Ox and Monkey. Anthony has both Special Stars present in his chart. This suggests that he will achieve a degree of success in his life.

During the Yang Wood Luck Cycle (age 27 to 31), there was a Stem Combination involving the Luck Cycle and Anthony's Yin Earth Day Master. The Power Element Combination indicates professional recognition and success. In 1997 (Yin Fire Ox year), the Annual Ox Branch reinforced the favourable element Metal by combining with the Rooster and Ox Branches within his chart. Anthony released his third album *Contra la Corriente*, a commercial success.

Anthony's success continued in the Rat Luck Cycle (age 32 to 36), which combined with his Monkey Year Branch to form his second favourable element Water. In 2000 (Yang Metal Dragon year), the Annual Dragon Branch combined with his Monkey Year Branch and the Rat Luck Cycle to form the Full Three Harmony Water Combination. His debut English album *Marc Anthony* sold more than three million copies in the US and the song *You Sang to Me* was a Number 2 hit. The Rat Luck Cycle also formed a Six Harmony Combination with the Ox in the House of Spouse. This suggested the possibility of love or marriage during this period. Anthony married former Miss Universe Dayanara Torres in 2000 during this period.

In 2001 (Yin Metal Snake year), the Annual Snake Branch formed the Full Three Harmony Metal Combination with the Ox and Rooster Branches within his chart. Anthony released the salsa album *Libre*, which spent 14 weeks at the top of the Billboard Latin Albums chart.

In 2004 (Yang Wood Monkey year), there was a Stem Combination between the Annual Stem and the Yin Earth Day Master. This Power Element Combination indicated professional success and recognition. Anthony released a Latin pop album *Amar Sin Mentiras* and also appeared in the thriller *Man on Fire* alongside Denzel Washington. On a personal note, his divorce from Torres was finalized and he married actress and singer Jennifer Lopez. He also recorded a duet with wife Lopez *Escapemonos*.

The Yin Wood Luck Cycle (age 37 to 41) was also favourable for Anthony as the Power Element Wood was able to control Earth Rivals present in the years within this period. However, in 2007 (Yin Fire Pig year), the negative Yin Fire threatened the favourable element Metal. Anthony starred with wife Lopez in *El Cantante*, a biopic about salsa legend Hector Lavoe. The movie did not fare well. In 2009 (Yin Earth Ox year), the Ox combined with the Ox Luck Cycle and the Ox and Rooster Branches within the chart to reinforce the favourable element Metal. He received a Lifetime Achievement Award from the Hispanic Caucus Institute in Washington, D.C.

The Ox Luck Cycle (age 42 to 46) was also favourable as it combined with the Ox and Rooster in his chart to reinforce their favourable element Metal. In 2010 (Yang Metal Tiger year) with the favourable element in the Annual Stem, Anthony released another successful Latin album *Iconos*. In 2011 (Yin Metal Rabbit year), there was a clash with the Rooster Month Branch that disrupted the Metal Combination within his chart. Anthony and Lopez announced their separation. In 2013 (Yin Water Snake year), the Annual Snake Branch combined with the Rooster and Ox to form the Full Three Harmony Metal Combination. Anthony released the successful *3.0*, his 11th studio album and 1st salsa album in more than a decade.

In 2014 (Yang Wood Horse year), there was a Stem Combination between the Annual Yang Wood Stem and the Yin Earth Day Master, indicating professional success and recognition. The negative elements Fire and Earth were present in the Annual Horse Branch, but this did not deter his success. His *Vivir Mi Vida* World Tour was extremely successful, and Anthony's divorce from Lopez was finalized. He then married model Shannon de Lima.

The Yang Fire Luck Cycle (age 47 to 51) contained the negative Fire but there was a Stem Combination with the Yin Metal Month Stem, reducing its impact. However, in 2016 (Yang Fire Monkey year), Anthony announced his separation from de Lima. The negative element Fire was present in the Annual Stem. Their divorce was finalized in the first half of 2017 (Yin Fire Rooster year), with the negative element Fire in the Annual Stem. The Annual Rooster Branch also forms a Three Harmony Combination with the Ox in the House of Spouse, so there is a good possibility of Anthony finding romance this year.

Example 3.6 Lara Fabian, Belgian-Canadian Singer
(born January 9, 1970, 19:30 hours)

Hour	Day	Month	Year
甲	己	丁	己
Yang Wood	Yin Earth	Yin Fire	Yin Earth
戌	丑	丑	酉
Dog	Ox	Ox	Rooster

9	19	29	39
戊	己	庚	辛
Yang Earth	Yin Earth	Yang Metal	Yin Metal
寅	卯	辰	巳
Tiger	Rabbit	Dragon	Snake

49	59	69	79
壬	癸	甲	乙
Yang Water	Yin Water	Yang Wood	Yin Wood
午	未	申	酉
Horse	Sheep	Monkey	Rooster

There is a Partial Three Harmony Metal Combination in Fabian's birth chart. Her Ox Day and Month Branches combine with her Rooster Year Branch to form Metal. There are no other Branch Combinations present in the chart. The prevalent element is Metal. As Fabian is a Yin Earth Day Master, Metal represents her Output. She has a Follow the Output (Metal) chart.

The Yang Wood Hour Pillar forms a Stem Combination with the Yin Earth Day Master. This Combination involves the Power Element and exerts its influence after the age of 40. This indicates professional recognition and success in the latter half of life. For a woman, the Power Combination also suggests marriage or romance. In Fabian's case, she has a high chance of finding love in the second half of life. The Hour Stem also indicates the relationship with the son. This Stem Combination suggests that Fabian will have a close relationship with her son.

The House of Spouse Branch Ox is repeated twice in Fabian's chart. This indicates that she has a higher chance of being married more than once. She married Sicilian musician and artist Gabriel di Giorgio in 2013 (Yin Water Snake year). There was a Combination between the Annual Snake Branch and her Ox in the House of Spouse, indicating the possibility of love or romance.

Fabian is born a Yin Earth Ox day, one of the Six Intelligent days. She is multilingual and sings in French, Italian, Spanish and English. Fabian has also sung in German, Russian, Spanish and Turkish.

During the Yin Earth Luck Cycle (age 19 to 23), Fabian moved from Belgium to Montreal and released her first French language album *Lara Fabian* in 1991 (Yin Metal Sheep year). The favourable element was present in her Annual Stem.

In the Rabbit Luck Cycle (age 24 to 28), there was a clash between the Luck Cycle and her Rooster Year Branch, disrupting the Three Harmony Metal Combination. Despite this, Fabian fared well in years with her favourable elements. Her second album *Carpe Diem* went gold within two weeks of its release in 1994 (Yang Wood Dog year). There was a Stem Combination between the Annual Yang Wood Stem and her Yin Earth Day Master, an indication of professional recognition and success. In 1996 (Yang Fire Rat year), Fabian was chosen by Disney to provide the voice of Esmeralda in the cartoon *The Hunchback of Notre Dame*. She also recorded a song for the soundtrack. The Annual Rat Branch formed a Six Harmony Combination with both the Ox Branches in her chart, suggesting the presence of mentors or helpful individuals. It also contained the second favourable element Water.

In the favourable Yang Metal Luck Cycle (age 29 to 33), her first English language album *Lara Fabian* was released in 2000 (Yang Metal Dragon year). The favourable element was present in the Annual Stem. It featured the hit singles *I Will Love Again*. In 2001 (Yin Metal Snake year), there was a Full Three Harmony Metal Combination involving the Annual Snake Branch and the Ox and Rooster Branches in her chart. The single *Love By Grace* was chosen as the theme song for the lead couple in a Brazilian soap opera. Her fourth French album *Nue* was also released that year.

The Dragon Luck Cycle (age 34 to 38) contained a Yang Earth Rival. However, she was able to thrive in years that contained her favourable elements Metal and Wood. In 2005 (Yin Wood Rooster year), the Annual Rooster Branch combined with the Ox and Rooster Branches in her chart to reinforce the favourable element Metal. She released her fifth French album *9*. She took time off towards the end of this period after her daughter Lou (with then fiancé director Gerard Pullicino) was born in 2007 (Yin Fire Pig year).

In the favourable Yin Metal Luck Cycle (age 39 to 43), Fabian made a comeback in 2009 (Yin Earth Ox year) by releasing a French covers album *Toutes Les Femmes en Moi*.

The Annual Ox Branch combined with the Rooster and Ox Branches in her chart reinforced her favourable element Metal. In 2013 (Yin Water Snake year), she released the album *Le Secret*. The Annual Snake Branch combined with the Rooster and Ox Branches in her chart to form the Full Three Harmony Metal Combination.

The Snake Luck Cycle (age 44 to 48) has the Full Three Harmony Metal Combination present for a period of five years. 2017 (Yin Fire Rooster year) should be another successful year as the Annual Rooster Branch combines with the Ox and Rooster Branches in her chart and the Snake Luck Cycle to reinforce the favourable element Metal. Fabian's success should continue in the Yang Water Luck Cycle (age 49 to 53).

Example 3.7 Tippi Hedren, American Actress
(born January 19, 1930)

Hour	Day	Month	Year
	己	丁	己
	Yin Earth	Yin Fire	Yin Earth
	巳	丑	巳
	Snake	Ox	Snake

5	15	25	35	45
戊	己	庚	辛	壬
Yang Earth	Yin Earth	Yang Metal	Yin Metal	Yang Water
寅	卯	辰	巳	午
Tiger	Rabbit	Dragon	Snake	Horse

55	65	75	85
癸	甲	乙	丙
Yin Water	Yang Wood	Yin Wood	Yang Fire
未	申	酉	戌
Sheep	Monkey	Rooster	Dog

There is a Partial Three Harmony Metal Combination in Hedren's birth chart. Her Snake Day and Year Branches combine with her Ox Month Branch to form Metal. There are no other Combinations in her chart. The prevalent element is Metal. As Hedren is a Yin Earth Day Master, Metal represents the Output element. She has a Follow the Output (Metal) chart.

The House of Spouse Animal Snake is present twice in her chart. This suggests that Hedren has a higher chance of being married twice. She was married three times. Hedren divorced her first husband Peter Griffith after nine years of marriage in 1961 (Yin Metal Ox year). Her second marriage was to her then-agent Noel Marshall in 1964 (Yang Wood Dragon year). There was a Stem Combination involving the Annual Stem with her Yin Earth Day Master. The Power Element Combination indicates the possibility of love or marriage for women. Hedren divorced Marshall in 1982 (Yang Water Dog year). The negative elements Fire and Earth were present in the Annual Branch. She married her third husband steel manufacturer Luis Barrenechea in 1985 (Yin Wood Ox year). The Annual Ox Branch combined with the Snake Branch in her House of Spouse, indicating the possibility of romance or marriage. The marriage lasted until 1995 (Yin Wood Pig year). There was a clash with the Snake Branch in the House of Spouse.

In the favourable Yang Metal Luck Cycle (age 25 to 29), Hedren worked as a model, appearing on the cover of magazines such as *Life* and *Glamour*. She also gave birth to daughter, actress Melanie Griffith, in 1957 (Yin Fire Rooster year). Her Output element Metal, which is also her Children element, was present in the Annual Branch that year.

The Dragon Luck Cycle (age 30 to 34) contained a Yang Earth Rival. Nevertheless, Hedren was still able to enjoy success in years with the favourable elements Metal and Water. In 1961 (Yin Metal Ox year), director Alfred Hitchcock approached her after seeing her on a television commercial for a diet drink. The Annual Ox Branch combined with the Snake and Ox Branches in her chart to reinforce the favourable element Metal. In 1963 (Yin Water Rabbit year), Hedren made her film debut in the thriller *The Birds*. In 1964 (Yang Wood Dragon year), there was a Stem Combination between the Annual Stem and her Yin Earth Day Master. The Power Element Combination indicated professional recognition and success. Hedren appeared in her second Hitchcock film *Marnie* opposite Sean Connery. While the movie did not perform well upon release, her performance is now considered one of the finest in a Hitchcock film. However, with the negative Earth element present, she had to contend with Hitchcock's controlling behaviour and her inflexible contract, which stipulated he had the right to turn down other films offered to her.

The Yin Metal Luck Cycle (age 35 to 39) contained Hedren's favourable element Metal. Hitchcock sold her contract to Universal Studios. In 1967 (Yin Fire Sheep year), she appeared alongside Marlon Brando and Sophia Loren in Charlie Chaplin's last film *A Countess from Hong Kong*. The negative elements Fire and Earth were present in the Annual Stem and Branch. Her role amounted to a cameo.

The Snake Luck Cycle (age 40 to 44) combined with the Snake and Ox Branches in her chart to reinforce the favourable element Metal. In 1973 (Yin Water Ox year), Hedren appeared as a teacher in *The Harrad Experiment*, alongside her future son-in-law Don Johnson. The Annual Ox Branch combined with the Snake and Ox Branches in her chart to reinforce Metal. In 1974 (Yang Wood Tiger year), there was a Stem Combination between the Annual Stem and her Yin Earth Day Master, indicating professional recognition or success. She started filming the animal adventure film *Roar*, which starred her daughter Melanie Griffith. Hedren worked on *Roar* throughout the favourable Yang Water Luck Cycle (age 45 to 49).

The Horse Luck Cycle (age 50 to 54) contained the negative elements Fire and Earth. *Roar* was finally released in 1981 (Yin Metal Rooster year), a year with the favourable element Metal in both the Annual Stem and Branch. However, the movie only grossed $2 million USD despite its production cost of $17 million USD. In 1983 (Yin Water Pig year), Hedren started the non-profit Roar Foundation and the animal sanctuary Shambala Preserve. While the Annual Pig Branch clashed with the Snake Branches in her chart and disrupted the Partial Three Harmony Metal Combination, the Yang Wood within the Pig combined with her Yin Earth Day Master. This indicated professional recognition. She appeared in acting assignments mostly on television through the Yin Water (age 55 to 59) and Sheep (age 60 to 64) Luck Cycles to raise money for her foundation.

In the favourable Yang Wood Luck Cycle (age 65 to 69), Hedren played an abortion rights activist in the satire *Citizen Ruth* in 1997 (Yin Fire Ox year). The Annual Ox Branch combined with the Snake and Ox Branches within her chart to reinforce the favourable element Metal. There was also a Stem Combination involving the Yang Wood Luck Cycle and her Yin Earth Day Master, indicating professional recognition.

In the Monkey Luck Cycle (age 70 to 74), the Monkey worked together with her Ox Month Branch as her Special Stars to bring her success. Hedren appeared in David O.Russell's *I Heart Huckabees* alongside Dustin Hoffman, Jude Law and Naomi Watts.

In 2006 (Yang Fire Dog year) during the Yin Wood Luck Cycle (age 75 to 79), there was an onset accident while filming soap opera *Fashion House*. A gallon of water fell from the ceiling onto her head, causing her to have headaches. Hedren was then involved in a legal battle with her lawyer for malpractice after he was blocked from filing suit against the defendants. The negative elements Fire and Earth were present.

In 2016 (Yang Fire Monkey year) during the Yang Fire Luck Cycle (age 85 to 89), Hedren published her biography *Tippi: A Memoir*. The Annual Monkey Branch worked in conjunction with her Ox Month Branch to bring her success.

Example 3. 8 Heather Graham, American Actress
(born January 29, 1970)

Hour	Day	Month	Year
	己	丁	己
	Yin Earth	Yin Fire	Yin Earth
	酉	丑	酉
	Rooster	Ox	Rooster

2	12	22	32
戊	己	庚	辛
Yang Earth	Yin Earth	Yang Metal	Yin Metal
寅	卯	辰	巳
Tiger	Rabbit	Dragon	Snake

42	52	62	72
壬	癸	甲	乙
Yang Water	Yin Water	Yang Wood	Yin Wood
午	未	申	酉
Horse	Sheep	Monkey	Rooster

There is a Partial Three Harmony Metal Combination in Graham's birth chart. Her Rooster Day and Year Branches combine with her Ox Month Branch to form Metal. There are no other Branch Combinations in her chart. As Graham is a Yin Earth Day Master, Metal represents her Output. She has a Follow the Output (Metal) chart.

Graham is born on a Yin Earth Rooster day, one of the six days where the Day Master is sitting on an Academic Stars. It indicates that she is highly intelligent. However, women born on these days may have difficulties settling down and getting married. Even though Graham's House of Spouse Animal is repeated twice in her chart, she has had several high profile relationships yet has never been married (at the time of writing).

The Yin Fire Month Stem destroys the favourable element Metal. It occupies the position associated with the father. Graham is estranged from her father.

She received her first major break portraying an addict in Gus Van Sant's *Drugstore Cowboy* in 1989 (Yin Earth Snake year) during the Rabbit Luck Cycle (age 17 to 21). The Rabbit Luck Cycle clashed with the Rooster Branches in her chart and disrupted the Metal Combination. However, the Annual Snake Branch was able to combine with her Ox Month Branch to form the favourable element Metal.

In the favourable Yang Metal Luck Cycle (age 22 to 26), Graham appeared in David Lynch's movie *Twin Peaks: Fire Walk with Me*. For a Yin Earth Day Master, the Special Stars are the Monkey and Ox. The Annual Monkey Branch worked in conjunction with her Ox Month Branch to bring her success. In 1993 (Yin Water Rooster year), Graham appeared alongside Will Smith and Donald Sutherland in the movie adaptation of the play *Six Degrees of Separation*. The Annual Rooster Branch combined with the Ox and Rooster Branches within her chart to reinforce the favourable element Metal.

The Dragon Luck Cycle (age 27 to 31) contained a Yang Earth Rival. However, Graham fared well in years with the favourable elements Metal and Water. In 1997 (Yin Fire Ox year), the Annual Ox Branch combined with the

Rooster and Ox Branches in her chart to reinforce the favourable element Metal. Graham won an MTV Award for Best Breakthrough Performance for portraying porn star Rollergirl in Paul Thomas Anderson's highly acclaimed *Boogie Nights*. In 2001 (Yin Metal Snake year), Graham appeared alongside Johnny Depp in period thriller *From Hell* about Jack the Ripper. She also starred with Edward Burns in the romance *Sidewalks of New York*. The Annual Snake Branch formed the Full Three Harmony Metal Combination with the Ox and Rooster Branches in her chart.

The Yin Metal (age 32 to 36) and Snake Luck Cycles (age 37 to 41) contained the favourable element. The Snake formed the Full Three Harmony Metal Combination for a period of five years. During this period, Graham performed well in years with Metal and Water. In 2009 (Yin Earth Ox year), she played a stripper with a heart of gold in the box office hit comedy *The Hangover* alongside Bradley Cooper and Zach Galifianakis. The Annual Ox Branch combined with the Snake Luck Cycle and the Ox and Rooster Branches in her chart to reinforce the favourable element Metal.

The Yang Water Luck Cycle (age 42 to 46) was also favourable. Not only did it contain the second favourable element Water, it also combined with the negative Yin Fire Month Stem, reducing its effect. In 2013 (Yin Water Snake year), Graham reprised her role in *The Hangover Part III*. The Annual Snake Branch combined with the Ox and Rooster Branches in her chart to from the Full Three Harmony Metal Combination.

The Horse Luck Cycle (age 47 to 51) may pose some issues for Graham as the negative element Fire is present. However, the Yin Water Luck Cycle (age 52 to 56) will be favourable for her as the second favourable element Water is present.

Example 3.9 Tony Leung Ka Fai,
Hong Kong Actor (born February 1, 1958)

Hour	Day	Month	Year
	己	癸	丁
	Yin Earth	Yin Water	Yin Fire
	酉	丑	酉
	Rooster	Ox	Rooster

9	19	29	39
壬	辛	庚	己
Yang Water	Yin Metal	Yang Metal	Yin Earth
子	亥	戌	酉
Rat	Pig	Dog	Rooster

49	59	69	79
戊	丁	丙	乙
Yang Earth	Yin Fire	Yang Fire	Yin Wood
申	未	午	巳
Monkey	Sheep	Horse	Snake

There is a Partial Three Harmony Metal Combination in Leung's birth chart. His Rooster Day and Year Branches combine with his Ox Month Branch to form Metal. There are no other Combinations within his chart. The prevalent element is Metal. As Leung is a Yin Earth Day Master, Metal represents his Output. He has a Follow the Output (Metal) chart.

Leung is born on one of the six days where the Day Master sits on the Academic Star. This indicates an intelligent person. He is one of the most prominent actors in the Hong Kong Film Industry, winning four Hong Kong Film Awards in a career spanning more than thirty years.

He appeared in his first movie Burning of the Imperial Palace in 1983 (Yin Water Pig year) during the Pig Luck Cycle (age 24 to 28). There was a Yang Wood Stem hidden within the Pig Luck Cycle and Annual Branch that combined with his Yin Earth Day Master. The Power Element Combination indicated professional recognition and success.

Leung's career gained momentum in the favourable Yang Metal Luck Cycle (age 29 to 33). In 1989 (Yin Earth Snake year), the Annual Snake Branch combined with the Rooster and Ox Branches in his chart to form the Full Three Harmony Metal Combination. He appeared in the box office hit *A Better Tomorrow III: Love and Death in Saigon* with Chow Yun-Fat and Anita Mui. In 1990 (Yang Metal Horse year), Leung starred with Jacky Chan in *Island of Fire*. Promotion for the movie magnified Chan's supporting role and diminished Leung's lead role. The negative elements Fire and Earth were present in the Annual Branch.

The Dog Luck Cycle (age 34 to 38) contained a Yang Earth Rival. However, Leung was able to perform well in years with the favourable elements Metal and Water. In 1992 (Yang Water Monkey year), he appeared in the French production *The Lover* opposite Jane March. For a Yin Earth Day Master, the Special Stars are the Monkey and Ox. The Annual Monkey Branch worked in conjunction with Leung's Ox Month Branch to bring him success that year. In 1994 (Yang Wood Dog year), Leung joined an all-star cast including Leslie Cheung, Brigitte Lin and Maggie Cheung for Wong Kar Wai's *Ashes of Time*. The Stem Combination between the Annual Yang Wood Stem and his Yin Earth Day Master brought Leung professional recognition and success. However, there was a Yang Earth Rival in the Annual Dog Branch. The movie did not fare well commercially upon its release.

The Yin Earth Luck Cycle (age 39 to 43) contained another Earth Rival. Once again, Leung had to depend on favourable elements from the years within this period for success. In 1997 (Yin Fire Ox year), the Annual Ox Branch combined with the Rooster and Ox Branches in Leung's chart to reinforce the favourable element Metal. He appeared in action crime thriller *Island of Greed* with Andy Lau and received a nomination for Best Actor in the Hong Kong Film Awards.

The Rooster Luck Cycle (age 44 to 48) combined with the Rooster and Ox Branches within Leung's chart to reinforce the favourable element Metal. In 2002 (Yang Water Horse year), he starred with David Morse and Rene Liu in the police thriller *Double Vision*, which was filmed by the Asian division of Columbia Pictures. Leung received another Hong Kong Film Award nomination for Best Actor. The second favourable element Water was present in the Annual Stem. In 2005 (Yin Wood Rooster year) when the Annual Rooster Branch combined with the Rooster and Ox Branches in his chart, Leung appeared in the Hong Kong crime thriller *Election*, for which he won a Hong Kong Film Award for Best Actor. It was also nominated for a Golden Palm at Cannes.

In the Yang Earth Luck Cycle (age 49 to 53), there was a Stem Combination between the Luck Cycle and Leung's Yin Water Month Stem. The Yang Earth Rival is combined away by the Wealth Element, which is favourable. In 2010 (Yang Metal Tiger year) when the favourable element Metal was present in the Annual Stem, Leung starred in the biopic *Bruce Lee, My Brother*. In 2012 (Yang Water Dragon year) with the second favourable element Water in the Annual Stem, Leung starred in the police thriller *Cold War* with Aaron Kwok, a major box office hit.

The Monkey Luck Cycle (age 54 to 58) was also favourable for Leung as both the Special Stars were present to bring him success: Monkey in the Luck Cycle and his Ox Month Branch. In 2016 (Yang Fire Monkey year), Leung starred in the sequel *Cold War 2*. Not only was the Annual Monkey Branch one of his Special Stars, it also contained his favourable elements Metal and Water.

Example 3.10 James Cromwell, American Actor
(born January 27, 1940)

Hour	Day	Month	Year
	己	丁	己
	Yin Earth	Yin Fire	Yin Earth
	巳	丑	卯
	Snake	Ox	Rabbit

7	17	27	37
丙	乙	甲	癸
Yang Fire	Yin Wood	Yang Wood	Yin Water
子	亥	戌	酉
Rat	Pig	Dog	Rooster

47	57	67	77
壬	辛	庚	己
Yang Water	Yin Metal	Yang Metal	Yin Earth
申	未	午	巳
Monkey	Sheep	Horse	Snake

There is a Partial Three Harmony Metal Combination in Cromwell's birth chart. His Snake Day Branch and Ox Month Branch combine to form Metal. There are no other Combinations present within the chart. The prevalent element is Metal. As Cromwell is a Yin Earth Day Master, Metal represents his Output. He has a Follow the Output (Metal) chart.

In the favourable Yin Water Luck Cycle (age 37 to 41), Cromwell was making guest appearances on television shows such as *Three's Company*, *Eight is Enough*, *Diff'rent Strokes* and *Little House on the Prairie*.

In 1984 (Yang Wood Rat year) during the Rooster Luck Cycle (age 42 to 46), Cromwell appeared in the comedy *The Revenge of the Nerds*, a box office hit. The Rooster in the Luck Cycle formed the Full Three Harmony Metal Combination with the Snake and Ox Branches in his chart. There was also a Stem Combination between the Annual Yang Wood Stem and Cromwell's Yin Earth Day Master. The Power Element Combination indicates professional success and recognition.

Cromwell worked steadily in supporting roles during the Yang Water Luck Cycle (age 47 to 51). In 1995 (Yin Wood Pig year) during the Monkey Luck Cycle (age 52 to 56), Cromwell received his big break, appearing as a farmer in the live-action comedy *Babe*, for which he received an Oscar Nomination for Best Supporting Actor. For a Yin Earth Day Master like Cromwell, his Special Stars are the Monkey and the Ox. The Monkey in the Luck Cycle worked in conjunction with his Ox Month Branch to bring him success. The favourable elements Water and Wood were also present in the Annual Pig Branch. There was also a Yang Wood Stem within the Pig that formed a Stem Combination with Cromwell's Yin Earth Day Master, indicating professional recognition and success.

In the Yin Metal Luck Cycle (age 57 to 61) in 1997 (Yin Fire Ox year), the Annual Ox Branch combined with the Snake and Ox Branches in Cromwell's chart to reinforce the favourable element Metal. Cromwell played a villain in the film noir *L.A. Confidential*, which received an Oscar nomination for Best Picture. In 1999 (Yin Earth Rabbit year), Cromwell appeared as the warden in the prison drama *The Green Mile* alongside Tom Hanks. It was also nominated for a Best Picture Oscar. The third favourable element Wood was present that year.

The Sheep Luck Cycle (age 62 to 66) disrupted the Three Harmony Combination by clashing with the Ox Month Branch. However, Cromwell was able to perform well in years where the favourable elements Wood and Metal were present. In 2004 (Yang Wood Monkey year), there was a Stem Combination between the Annual Yang Wood Stem and his Yin Earth Day Master, indicating professional recognition and success. Cromwell appeared alongside Will Smith in the science fiction thriller *I, Robot*. In 2005 (Yin Wood Rooster year), the Annual Rooster Branch combined with the Snake Day Branch to form the favourable element Metal. Cromwell appeared with Adam Sandler in the comedy remake *The Longest Yard*.

The Yang Metal Luck Cycle (age 67 to 71) contained the favourable element Metal. Cromwell regained his Follow the Output (Metal) status. In 2008 (Yang Earth Rat year), the second favourable element Water was present. Cromwell portrayed George Herbert Walker Bush in the biopic *W.* about George Walker Bush. In 2011 (Yin Metal Rabbit year) with the favourable element Metal in the Annual Stem, Cromwell appeared in the silent comedy *The Artist*, which won the Oscar for Best Picture.

The Horse Luck Cycle (age 72 to 76) contained the negative elements Fire and Earth. Cromwell had several encounters with law enforcement officers during this period. In early February 2013 (still Yang Water Dragon year), Cromwell was arrested for interrupting a University of Wisconsin Board of Regents meeting. He had been brandishing a graphic photo of a cat to protest against the treatment of animals on campus. There was a Yang Earth Rival in the Annual Dragon Branch. In 2015 (Yin Wood Sheep year), the negative elements Fire and Earth were also present in the Annual Branch. Cromwell and five other people were arrested while protesting against a power station in New York State, close to where he lived. In June (Horse month) 2016, Cromwell was among the 19 people arrested for protesting against underground gas storage in salt caverns near Seneca Lake, New York.

The Yin Earth Luck Cycle (age 77 to 81) also has an Earth Rival present, so there may also be issues during this period.

Example 3.11 Alicia Silverstone, American Actress
(born October 4, 1976, 15:44 hours)

Hour	Day	Month	Year
壬	己	丁	丙
Yang Water	Yin Earth	Yin Fire	Yang Fire
申	丑	酉	辰
Monkey	Ox	Rooster	Dragon

9	19	29	39
丙	乙	甲	癸
Yang Fire	Yin Wood	Yang Wood	Yin Water
申	未	午	巳
Monkey	Sheep	Horse	Snake

49	59	69	79
壬	辛	庚	己
Yang Water	Yin Metal	Yang Metal	Yin Earth
辰	卯	寅	丑
Dragon	Rabbit	Tiger	Ox

There is a Partial Three Harmony Combination in Silverstone's chart. Her Ox Day Branch and Rooster Month Branch combine to form Metal. While there is a Six Harmony Combination between the Dragon Year Branch and Rooster Month Branch, the Three Harmony Combination takes precedence. There are no other Combinations present in her chart. The Dragon Year Branch and the Monkey Hour Branch are too far apart to form a Combination. The prevalent element in Silverstone's chart is Metal. As she is a Yin Earth Day Master, Metal represents the Output element. Silverstone has a Follow the Output (Metal) chart.

134

Silverstone is born on a Yin Earth Ox day, one of the Six Intelligent days. She is noted for being an animal rights and environmental activist and has also written two books on nutrition. For a Yin Earth Day Master, the Special Stars are the Monkey and Ox. Silverstone has the Ox Day Branch and the Monkey Hour Branch, indicating that she will be even more successful in the second half of her life.

During the Monkey Luck Cycle (age 14 to 18), Silverstone made her movie debut in 1993 (Yin Water Rooster year), appearing in the thriller *The Crush* with Carey Elwes. She also appeared in the music video for Aerosmith's *Crying*, catching the attention of director Amy Heckerling, who cast her in the coming of age comedy *Clueless*.

When *Clueless* was released in 1995 (Yin Wood Pig year) during the Yin Wood Luck Cycle (age 19 to 23), it was a major box office hit. The Yang Wood present in the Annual Pig Branch formed a Stem Combination with her Yin Earth Day Master, indicating professional recognition and success. In 1997 (Yin Fire Ox year), the Annual Ox Branch combined with the Ox Day Branch and Rooster Month Branch to reinforce the favourable element Metal. Silverstone appeared as Batgirl in the blockbuster *Batman and Robin* alongside George Clooney and Chris O'Donnell and in the comedy *Excess Baggage* with Benicio del Toro. On a personal note, the Ox is also the animal in her House of Spouse. She started dating rock musician and future husband Christopher Jarecki that year after meeting him outside a movie theatre.

The Sheep Luck Cycle (age 24 to 28) clashed with her Ox Day Branch, disrupting the Metal Combination within her chart. It was a challenging period for Silverstone as she struggled to find suitable roles. In 2004 (Yang Wood Monkey year), there was a Stem Combination with her Yin Earth Day Master, indicating professional recognition and success. She appeared in *Scooby-Doo 2: Monsters Unleashed*. Although a box office success, it was critically derided and won a Golden Raspberry Award for Worst Remake or Sequel.

The Yang Wood Luck Cycle (age 29 to 33) formed a Stem Combination with Silverstone's Yin Earth Day Master, representing professional recognition and success. For a woman, it also represents the potential for marriage. In 2005 (Yin Wood Rooster year), Silverstone married Jarecki after 8 years of dating. The Annual Rooster Branch formed a Partial Three Harmony Combination with the Ox in her House of Spouse. That same year, she also appeared with Queen Latifah in the comedy *Beauty Shop*. In 2009 (Yin Earth Ox year), the Annual Ox Branch reinforced the favourable element Metal by combining with the Ox and Rooster Branches in her chart. Silverstone released her first book *The Kind Diet*, about vegan nutrition.

The Horse Luck Cycle (age 34 to 38) contained the negative elements Fire and Earth. Silverstone did not appear in any big mainstream box-office successes in this period. In 2012 (Yang Water Dragon year), the Annual Stem contained the second favourable element Water. Silverstone reunited with Amy Heckerling in the vampire comedy *Vamps*. It only received a limited release in spite of critical acclaim.

The Yin Water Luck Cycle (age 39 to 43) should be more favourable for Silverstone, as her second favourable element Water is present. In 2017 (Yin Fire Rooster year), the Annual Rooster Branch combines with the Rooster and Ox Branches in her chart to reinforce the favourable element Metal. She appeared in the family road movie *Diary of a Wimpy Kid: The Long Haul*.

Silverstone has favourable elements in the subsequent Luck Cycles: the Snake (age 44 to 48), Yang Water (age 49 to 53), Dragon (age 54 to 58) and Yin Metal (age 59 to 63). The Snake Luck Cycle forms the Full Three Harmony Metal Combination with the Ox and Rooster present in her chart. The Dragon Luck Cycle will combine with her Monkey Hour Branch to form the second favourable element Water. It appears the best periods of Silverstone's life are yet to come.

Example 3.12 Nina Dobrev, Bulgarian-Canadian Actress
(born January 9, 1989)

Hour	Day	Month	Year
	己	乙	戊
	Yin Earth	Yin Wood	Yang Earth
	巳	丑	辰
	Snake	Ox	Dragon

1	11	21	31
甲	癸	壬	辛
Yang	Yin	Yang	Yin
Wood	Water	Water	Metal
子	亥	戌	酉
Rat	Pig	Dog	Rooster

41	51	61	71
庚	己	戊	丁
Yang	Yin	Yang	Yin
Metal	Earth	Earth	Fire
申	未	午	巳
Monkey	Sheep	Horse	Snake

There is a Partial Three Harmony Metal Combination in Dobrev's birth chart. Her Snake Day Branch and Ox Month Branch combine to form Metal. There are no other Combinations in her chart. Metal is her prevalent element. As Dobrev is a Yin Earth Day Master, Metal represents her Output element. She has a Follow the Output (Metal) chart.

Dobrev first achieved recognition in the Yang Water Luck Cycle (age 21 to 25). The second favourable element Water was present. In 2010 (Yang Metal Tiger year), Dobrev became known for playing the role of Elena Gilbert in the supernatural drama series *The Vampire Diaries*. That same year, she also had a supporting role in Atom Egoyan's *Chloe* alongside Liam Neeson and Julianne

Moore. The favourable element Metal was present in the Annual Stem.

In 2012 (Yang Water Dragon), Dobrev appeared in coming of age drama *The Perks of Being a Wallflower* alongside Emma Roberts. The second favourable element Water was present in the Annual Stem. In 2014 (Yang Wood Horse year), there was a Stem Combination involving the Annual Stem and Dobrev's Yin Earth Day Master. The Power Element Combination indicated professional success or recognition. Dobrev appeared in the box office hit comedy *Let's Be Cops* with Damon Wayans, Jr. and Jake Johnson.

The Dog Luck Cycle (age 26 to 30) contained the negative elements Fire and Earth. Despite this, Dobrev performed well in years with the favourable elements Metal and Water. In 2017 (Yin Fire Rooster year), the Annual Rooster Branch combined with the Snake and Ox Branches in her chart to form the Full Three Harmony Metal Combination. Dobrev appeared in her first blockbuster *xXx: Return of Xander Cage* alongside Vin Diesel and Samuel Jackson. She also returned for a special guest appearance in the series finale of *The Vampire Diaries* after leaving the series in 2015 (Yin Wood Sheep year). The negative elements Fire and Earth were present in the Annual Branch.

The subsequent Luck Cycles contain the favourable elements Metal and Water: Yin Metal (age 31 to 35), Rooster (age 36 to 40), Yang Metal (age 41 to 45) and Monkey (age 46 to 50). The Rooster Luck Cycle combines with the Snake and Ox Branches in Dobrev's chart to form the Full Three Harmony Metal Combination. With the favourable element Metal reinforced, it should be a successful and fulfilling period for her. There is also a Combination involving the Snake in the House of Spouse, so there is there is the possibility of romance or marriage for Dobrev as well. The Monkey Luck Cycle is one of the Special Stars for a Yin Earth Day Master like Dobrev. The other Special Star, the Ox, is present in Dobrev's Month Branch. The two Special Stars will work together to bring success for Dobrev during this period. There is also a Six Harmony Combination with the Snake in the House of Spouse, giving Dobrev another opportunity to find romance or marriage.

Example 3.13 Riley Keough, American Actress
(born May 29, 1989, 20:15 hours)

Hour	Day	Month	Year
甲	己	己	己
Yang Wood	Yin Earth	Yin Earth	Yin Earth
戌	丑	巳	巳
Dog	Ox	Snake	Snake

3	13	23	33
庚	辛	壬	癸
Yang Metal	Yin Metal	Yang Water	Yin Water
午	未	申	酉
Horse	Sheep	Monkey	Rooster

43	53	63	73
甲	乙	丙	丁
Yang Wood	Yin Wood	Yang Fire	Yin Fire
戌	亥	子	丑
Dog	Pig	Rat	Ox

There is a Partial Three Harmony Metal Combination in Keough's birth chart. Her Snake Month and Year Branches combine with her Ox Day Branch to form Metal. There are no other Branch Combinations within the chart. Metal is the prevalent element. As Keough is a Yin Earth Day Master, Metal represents her Output element. She has a Follow the Output (Metal) chart.

Keough has three Yin Earth Stems in a row in her chart. There is Yin Earth in her Day Master, Month and Year Stems. This configuration is known as Three Friends in the Stems. It indicates someone who enjoys activities that bring her pleasure in life, as well as someone who is extremely sociable with many friends.

Keough's Yang Wood Hour Stem also forms a Stem Combination with her Yin Earth Day Master. The Power Element Combination indicates professional recognition or success later in life, as the Hour Pillar's influence is only felt after the age of 40. As the Hour Stem is also the sector associated with the son, this also suggests a good relationship between Keough and her son. For a woman, the Power Combination with the Day Master also indicates the possibility of marriage.

Keough is born on a Yin Earth Ox day. This is one of the Six Intelligent days. She is the eldest daughter of singer-songwriter Lisa Presley and the eldest grandchild of singer Elvis Presley and actress Priscilla Presley. Keough has already received a Golden Globe nomination for Best Actress for a Performance in a Limited Series or Motion Picture made for Television for her performance in *The Girlfriend Experience* in 2016 (Yang Fire Monkey year). For a Yin Earth Day Master like Keough, her Special Stars are the Monkey and Ox. The Annual Monkey Branch worked in conjunction with her Ox Day Branch to bring her success.

In 2010 (Yang Metal Tiger year) during the Sheep Luck Cycle (age 18 to 22), Keough made her film debut in *The Runaways*, about a 70s all girl rock band. Although Kristen Stewart and Dakota Fanning also starred in the movie, it underperformed at the box office. There was a Yin Earth Rival present in the Luck Cycle and a Yang Earth Rival in the Annual Branch.

In the favourable Yang Water Luck Cycle (age 23 to 27), Keough appeared in *Magic Mike* alongside Channing Tatum and Matthew McConaughey in 2012 (Yang Water Dragon year). It was a major box office success. The favourable element Water was present in the Luck Cycle and the Annual Stem. In 2013 (Yin Water Snake year), the Annual Snake Branch combined with the Ox and Snake Branches within Keough's chart to reinforce the favourable element Metal. The second favourable element Water was also present in the Annual Stem. She was signed as the *Summer 2013 Ambassador* by Australian fashion brand Bonds.

In 2014 (Yang Wood Horse year), there was a Stem Combination involving the Annual Stem and her Yin Earth Day Master. This indicated professional success and recognition. Keough was announced as the lead actress in Steven Soderbergh's TV series *The Girlfriend Experience*, for which she earned a Golden Globe nomination.

On a personal note, Keough got engaged to stuntman Ben Smith-Petersen in August 2014 and married in early February 2015 (still the Yang Wood Horse year). The Power Element Combination involving her Yin Earth Day Master indicated romance or marriage.

As previously discussed, 2016 (Yang Fire Monkey year) was extremely successful for Keough. With her two Special Stars Monkey and Ox working together, she also appeared in the road movie *American Honey*, which won the Jury Prize at the 2016 Cannes Film Festival.

The Monkey Luck Cycle (age 28 to 32) will be favourable for Keough, as both her Special Stars (the Monkey and Ox) will work together in conjunction to bring her success. The Yin Water Luck Cycle (age 33 to 37) has her second favourable element Water and will also be positive. The Rooster Luck Cycle (age 38 to 42) forms the Full Three Harmony Metal Combination by combining with the Snake and Ox Branches in her chart. The favourable element is reinforced. There is also the possibility of another marriage or romance in this period.

The Yang Wood Luck Cycle (age 43 to 47) forms a Stem Combination with the Yin Earth Day Master. The Power Element Combination indicates professional recognition or success. For a woman, there is also the possibility of love or marriage. The Dog Luck Cycle (age 48 to 52) may create issues, as there is a Yang Earth Rival present.

Example 3.14 Zach Galifianakis, American Actor
(born October 1, 1969)

Hour	Day	Month	Year
	己	癸	己
	Yin Earth	Yin Water	Yin Earth
	酉	酉	酉
	Rooster	Rooster	Rooster

8	18	28	38
壬	辛	庚	己
Yang Water	Yin Metal	Yang Metal	Yin Earth
申	未	午	巳
Monkey	Sheep	Horse	Snake

48	58	68	78
戊	丁	丙	乙
Yang Earth	Yin Fire	Yang Fire	Yin Wood
辰	卯	寅	丑
Dragon	Rabbit	Tiger	Ox

There are no Combinations present in Galifianakis' birth chart. There are three Rooster Branches, where the only element present is Metal. The prevalent element in the chart is Metal. As Galifianakis is a Yin Earth Day Master, Metal represents the Output element. He has a Follow the Output (Metal) chart.

Galifianakis is born on a Yin Earth Rooster day. This is one of the six days where the Day Master is sitting on the Academic Star. This indicates a person who is highly intelligent, not necessarily someone who is academic. Galifianakis is famous as a stand up comedian and writer.

The House of Spouse animal Rooster is present three times in the chart. This suggests a higher possibility of being married more than once. Galifianakis married Quinn Lundberg (co-founder of *Growing Voices* charity) in 2012 (Yang Water Dragon year). There was a Six Harmony Combination between the Annual Dragon Branch and the Rooster in the House of Spouse. This indicated the possibility of love or marriage.

In the favourable Yang Metal Luck Cycle (age 28 to 32), he made his television debut in 1997 (Yin Fire Ox year) in the sitcom *Boston Common*. The Annual Ox Branch combined with the three Rooster Branches in his chart to reinforce the favourable element Metal. In 2001 (Yin Metal Snake year), the Annual Snake Branch combined with the three Rooster Branches within his chart. Galifianakis appeared in an episode of *Comedy Central Presents*.

The Horse Luck Cycle (age 33 to 37) contained Galifianakis' negative elements Fire and Earth. He struggled to land any memorable parts apart from the supernatural series *Tru Calling*, which ran from 2003 (Yin Water Sheep year) to 2005 (Yin Wood Rooster year). In 2003, the Sheep formed a Six Harmony Combination with the Horse Luck Cycle. A Six Harmony Combination indicates the presence of mentors or helpful individuals. In 2004 (Yang Wood Monkey year) and 2005 (Yin Wood

Rooster year), the favourable elements Metal and Water were present in the Annual Branches.

Galifianakis' breakthrough finally came in 2009 (Yin Earth Ox year) in the Yin Earth Luck Cycle (age 38 to 42). The Annual Ox Branch reinforced the favourable element Metal by forming a Partial Three Harmony Combination with the three Rooster Branches in his chart. He appeared in the hit comedy *The Hangover* alongside Bradley Cooper. The role also earned him the MTV Award for Best Comedy Performance. In 2010 (Yang Metal Tiger year), Galifianakis appeared with Robert Downey Jr. in the comedy *Due Date* and with Steve Carell in *Dinner with Schmucks*, the US remake of a French comedy. In 2011 (Yin Metal Rabbit year), he appeared in the sequel *The Hangover Part II*. The favourable element Metal was present in the Annual Stem of both years.

The Snake Luck Cycle (age 43 to 47) was very favourable for Galifianakis. The Snake reinforced the favourable element Metal by combining with the Rooster Branches in his chart. Galifianakis appeared in major Hollywood movies. In 2012 (Yang Water Dragon year), he appeared with Will Ferrell in the comedy *The Campaign*. In 2013 (Yin Water Snake year), he was in The Hangover Part III. He finished off this successful period appearing in two more comedies in 2016 (Yang Fire Monkey year), *Keeping Up with the Joneses* (with Jon Hamm) and *Masterminds* (with Owen Wilson and Jason Sudeikis). The favourable elements Water and Metal were present in the Annual Stems and Branches for all three years.

The Yang Earth Luck Cycle (age 48 to 52) contains an Earth Rival. However, there is a Stem Combination with Galifiankis' Yin Water Month Stem. This Combination is known as using the Wealth Element to pay off a Competitor. This suggests that there may be some money spent to solve legal issues. It is considered to be a favourable period. The Dragon Luck Cycle (age 53 to 57) forms a Six Harmony Combination with the Rooster Branches in the birth chart. The Six Harmony

Combination indicates the presence of mentors or helpful individuals. However, the Combination also involves the House of Spouse, so there is the possibility of another relationship or marriage during this period. The Yin Fire Luck Cycle (age 58 to 62) attacks the favourable element Metal, so circumspection is required during these years.

Example 3.15 Jim Henson, American Puppeteer
(born September 24, 1936, 00:10, died May 16, 1990, 01:21 hours)

Hour	Day	Month	Year
甲	己	丁	丙
Yang Wood	Yin Earth	Yin Fire	Yang Fire
子	酉	酉	子
Rat	Rooster	Rooster	Rat

5	15	25	35	45
戊	己	庚	辛	壬
Yang Earth	Yin Earth	Yang Metal	Yin Metal	Yang Water
戌	亥	子	丑	寅
Dog	Pig	Rat	Ox	Tiger

Hour	Day	Month	Year
己	辛	辛	庚
Yin Earth	Yin Metal	Yin Metal	Yang Metal
丑	巳	巳	午
Ox	Snake	Snake	Horse

There are no Branch Combinations present in Henson's birth chart. There are two Rooster Branches in the Day and Month Pillars. These Branches only contain Metal. As the influence of the Day and Month Pillars remain throughout a person's life, this makes Metal the prevalent element within the chart. Henson is a Yin Earth Day Master, which means that Metal represents his Output. He has a Follow the Output (Metal) chart.

145

Henson is born on a Yin Earth Rooster day, one of six days in which the Day Master is sitting on an Academic Star. This indicates that he is very intelligent and a good student. This is not limited to academic subjects but also to practical skills. The second favourable element Water is also present in Henson's chart. Water represents Wealth for an Earth Day Master. This indicates that he is able to use his talent (Output) to generate Wealth for himself.

Towards the end of the Pig Luck Cycle (age 20 to 24) in 1960 (Yang Metal Rat year), Henson graduated from the University of Maryland with a BSc (Bachelor of Science) in Home Economics. The favourable elements Metal and Water were present in the Annual Stem and Branch. While in college, he had been asked to create puppets for a local television puppet show called *Sam and Friends*.

In the favourable Yang Metal Luck Cycle (age 25 to 29), Henson created the first Muppet star Rowlf the piano playing dog. In 1963 (Yin Water Rabbit year), Rowlf became a regular on *The Jimmy Dean Show*. The second favourable element Water was present in the Annual Stem. It was also the year when Henson moved to New York City and formed the company Muppets Inc., which later became the Jim Henson Company.

During the Rat Luck Cycle (age 30 to 34) in 1969 (Yin Earth Rooster year), Henson was asked to work full time on the new public television children's show *Sesame Street*. The Annual Rooster Branch reinforced the favourable element Metal. Henson created the characters Bert and Ernie, Oscar the Grouch, Cookie Monster, Grover and Big Bird. He personally performed the characters of Ernie and Kermit the Frog, the roving reporter. *Sesame Street* remained popular throughout the favourable Yin Metal Luck Cycle (age 35 to 39).

At the start of the favourable Ox Luck Cycle (age 40 to 44), Henson targeted the adult audience with the variety show *The Muppet Show*, which debuted in 1976 (Yang Fire

Dragon year). The Ox formed the Three Harmony Metal Combination with the Rooster Branches in Henson's chart. In 1976, the Annual Dragon Branch combined with his Rat Year Branch, forming the second favourable element Water. Henson provided the voice for Kermit, the host of *The Muppet Show*, who had to manage characters like Miss Piggy, Fozzie Bear, Gonzo the Great and Animal. In 1979 (Yin Earth Sheep year), the Muppets made their big screen debut in *The Muppet Movie*, a commercial and critical success. In 1980 (Yang Metal Monkey year), Kermit's song *The Rainbow Connection* received an Oscar nomination for Best Song.

Henson's success continued in the Yang Water Luck Cycle (age 45 to 49). In 1981 (Yin Metal Rooster year), *The Great Muppet Caper* was another hit. The Annual Rooster Branch reinforced the favourable element Metal. In 1982 (Yang Water Dog year), Henson co-directed another successful film *The Dark Crystal* with Frank Oz. The second favourable element Water was present in the Annual Stem.

The Tiger Luck Cycle (from age 50) contained the negative elements Fire and Earth. In 1986 (Yang Fire Tiger year), Henson directed *Labyrinth*, an adventure musical fantasy film starring David Bowie and Jennifer Connelly. It performed poorly at the box office, and Henson was reportedly depressed about the reception. The film has since become a cult classic. The negative elements Fire and Earth were present in the Annual Branch.

In 1989 (Yin Earth Snake year), Henson started negotiations to sell his company to the Walt Disney Group for $150 million USD. The Annual Snake Branch combined with his Rooster Branches to reinforce the favourable element Metal.

On May 16, 1990 (Yang Metal Horse year), Henson died from organ failure caused by streptococcal toxic shock syndrome. On May 4, he had been experiencing flu-like symptoms and a sore throat. Left untreated, this progressed to a medical emergency on May 15. The streptococcal bacteria that had caused pneumonia had spread throughout his body. On the day he died, the Snake day and month combined with the Rooster Branches in his chart to form Metal. The Horse year combined with the Tiger Luck Cycle to form Fire. There was a Fire-Metal conflict, with Metal being controlled by Fire. In Chinese medicine, Metal represents the lungs.

Example 3.16 Colleen McCullough,
Australian Novelist and Neuroscientist
(born June 1, 1937, 19:30 hours, died January 29, 2015)

Hour	Day	Month	Year
甲	己	乙	丁
Yang Wood	Yin Earth	Yin Wood	Yin Fire
戌	未	巳	丑
Dog	Sheep	Snake	Ox

2	12	22	32
丙	丁	戊	己
Yang Fire	Yin Fire	Yang Earth	Yin Earth
午	未	申	酉
Horse	Sheep	Monkey	Rooster

42	52	62	72
庚	辛	壬	癸
Yang Metal	Yin Metal	Yang Water	Yin Water
戌	亥	子	丑
Dog	Pig	Rat	Ox

Hour	Day	Month	Year
	乙	丁	甲
	Yin Wood	Yin Fire	Yang Wood
	巳	丑	午
	Snake	Ox	Horse

There is a Partial Three Harmony Metal Combination in McCullough's chart. Her Snake Month Branch and Ox Year Branch combine to form Metal. There are no other Branch Combinations present in her chart. The prevalent element in her chart is Metal. As she is a Yin Earth Day Master, Metal represents the Output. McCullough has a Follow the Output (Metal) chart.

McCullough is born on a Yin Earth Sheep day, one of the Six Intelligent days. Although she became a famous author, McCullough earned a Master's degree in Neurophysiology from the University of London.

There is a Stem Combination involving the Yang Wood Hour Stem and Yin Earth Day Master. The Power Element Combination between the Hour and Day Stems indicates professional success and recognition later in life. For a woman, it also signifies a good marriage. McCullough married Ric Newton Ion Robinson in 1984 (Yang Wood Rat year) at the age of 47. There was a Stem Combination between the Annual Yang Wood Stem and her Yin Earth Day Master, indicating the possibility of romance and marriage. She remained married to Robinson until her death.

The Sheep (age 17 to 21) and Yang Earth (age 22 to 26) Luck Cycles contained Earth Rivals, signifying obstacles. McCullough worked as a teacher, librarian and journalist before starting her tertiary education at the University of Sydney. In her first year of medical school, she discovered she had an allergy to surgical soap and switched to study Neuroscience, obtaining a Bachelor's Degree in Neurophysiology. Towards the end of this period in 1963 (Yin Water Rabbit year), McCullough moved to the United Kingdom, where she worked at the Great Ormond Street Hospital in London. The second favourable element Water was present in the Annual Stem.

In the Monkey Luck Cycle (age 27 to 31), McCullough was offered a research associate job at Yale College in

New Haven, Connecticut in 1967 (Yin Earth Sheep year). During this period, she also taught at the Department of Neurology at Yale Medical School. The favourable elements Metal and Water were present in the Luck Cycle. She continued her research and teaching at Yale during the Yin Earth Luck Cycle (age 32 to 36).

In the Rooster Luck Cycle (age 37 to 41), McCullough's first book, *Tim*, was published in 1974 (Yang Wood Tiger year). There was a Stem Combination involving the Power Element between the Annual Yang Wood Stem and her Yin Earth Day Master. This indicated professional recognition and success. *Tim*, the story of a love affair between an older woman and a handyman with learning disabilities, was very well received.

In 1977 (Yin Fire Snake year), McCullough's second book *The Thorn Birds* was published. The story of a love affair between a Catholic priest and a young woman in the Australian Outback sold more than 30 million copies worldwide, earning her $2 million USD in paperback rights. It allowed McCullough to leave her medical scientific career and concentrate on writing full time. The Annual Snake Branch and the Rooster Luck Cycle combined with the Snake and Ox Branches in her chart to reinforce the favourable element Metal.

The Yang Metal Luck Cycle (age 42 to 46) was also favourable for McCullough. In 1980 (Yang Metal Monkey year), she moved to Norfolk Island, an Australian territory in the Pacific Ocean. The Annual Monkey Branch contained her favourable elements Metal and Water. In 1981 (Yin Metal Rooster year), *An Indecent Obsession*, about a psychiatric ward for shell-shocked soldiers during World War II, was released. The Annual Rooster Branch formed the Full Three Harmony Metal Combination with the Ox and Snake in her chart. In 1983 (Yin Water Pig year), *The Thorn Birds* was made into a highly rated television mini series starring Richard Chamberlain and Rachel Ward. Even though McCullough publicly criticized the adaptation, she was paid $5 million USD for the rights. The second favourable element was present in the Annual Stem.

The Dog Luck Cycle (age 47 to 51) contained a Yang Earth Rival but McCullough was able to fare well in years with her favourable elements. In 1985 (Yin Wood Ox year), the Annual Ox Branch combined with the Snake and Ox Branches in her chart to reinforce the favourable element Metal. *An Indecent Obsession* was made into a movie starring Gary Sweet and Wendy Hughes.

In 1990 (Yang Metal Horse year) during the favourable Yin Metal Luck Cycle (age 52 to 56), McCullough published the first book of her seven-book *Masters of Rome* series, *The First Man in Rome*. The favourable Metal was present in the Annual Stem. The second and third books were also published in this period in years with the favourable elements Water and Metal: *The Grass Crown* in 1991 (Yin Metal Sheep year) and *Fortune's Favourites* in 1993 (Yin Water Rooster year). The remaining four books were all published in years containing favourable elements Metal, Water and Wood: *Caesar's Women* (1996 Yang Fire Rat year), *Caesar* (1997 Yin Fire Ox year), *The October Horse* (2002 Yang Water Horse year) and *Anthony and Cleopatra* (2007 Yin Fire Pig year).

McCullough died from kidney failure after suffering a series of small strokes in January 2015 (still the Yang Wood Horse year). On the day she died, there was a Partial Three Harmony Metal Combination between the Snake day, Ox month and her Snake Month Branch. There was also a Partial Three Harmony Fire Combination between the Horse year and her Dog Hour Branch, creating a Metal-Fire conflict.

Example 3.17 Michael Hutchence,

Australian Rock Singer (born January 22, 1960,
05:00 hours, died November 22, 1997)

Hour	Day	Month	Year
丁	己	丁	己
Yin Fire	Yin Earth	Yin Fire	Yin Earth
卯	酉	丑	亥
Rabbit	Rooster	Ox	Pig

5	15	25	35
丙	乙	甲	癸
Yang Fire	Yin Wood	Yang Wood	Yin Water
子	亥	戌	
Rat	Pig	Dog	

Hour	Day	Month	Year
	戊	辛	丁
	Yang Earth	Yin Metal	Yin Fire
	辰	亥	丑
	Dragon	Pig	Ox

There is a Partial Three Harmony Metal Combination in Hutchence's birth chart. His Rooster Day Branch combines with his Ox Month Branch to form Metal. There are no other Combinations present in his chart. The Pig Year Branch is not able to combine with the Rabbit Hour Branch as they are too far apart. The prevalent element is Metal. As Hutchence is a Yin Earth Day Master, Metal represents his Output. He has a Follow the Output (Metal) chart.

Hutchence is born on a Yin Earth Rooster day, one of six days where the Day Master sits on the Academic Star. This indicates that he is highly talented. Hutchence wrote most of the songs for his band *INXS* together with his band mate Andrew Farriss.

In 1977 (Yin Fire Snake year) during the Yin Wood Luck Cycle (age 15 to 19), Hutchence formed the band *The Farriss Brothers*, which later became *INXS*. The Annual Snake Branch formed the Full Three Harmony Metal Combination with the Rooster and Ox present in Hutchence's chart.

During the Pig Luck Cycle (age 20 to 24) in 1980 (Yang Metal Monkey year), the group released their self-titled debut album *INXS* and had their first hit *Just Keep Walking*. The favourable element Metal was present in the Annual Stem. For a Yin Earth Day Master like Hutchence, the Special Stars are the Ox and Monkey. The Annual Monkey Branch worked in conjunction with his Ox Month Branch to bring him success. The follow up album *Underneath the Colours* was released in 1981 (Yin Metal Rooster year). The Annual Rooster Branch reinforced the favourable element Metal by combining with the Rooster and Ox present in Hutchence's chart.

In 1984 (Yang Wood Rat year), the album *The Swing* yielded their first number one hit in Australia *Original Sin*. There was a Stem Combination involving the Annual Yang Wood Stem with his Yin Earth Day Master. The Power Element Combination indicates professional recognition or success.

There was a Power Combination involving the Luck Cycle and the Yin Earth Day Master in the Yang Wood Luck Cycle (age 25 to 29). This was a highly successful period as *INXS* achieved international recognition. In 1985 (Yin Wood Ox year), the album *Listen Like Thieves* yielded a top 5 US hit *What You Need*. The Annual Ox Branch combined with the Rooster and Ox Branches in Hutchence's chart to form Metal.

In 1987 (Yin Fire Rabbit year), there was a clash between the Annual Rabbit Branch and the Rooster Day Branch. This disrupted the Partial Three Harmony Metal Combination. The Annual Rabbit Branch also formed a Partial Three Harmony Wood Combination with the Pig

Year Branch. Hutchence became a Follow the Power (Wood) chart that year. His list of favourable elements became:

1) Power element Wood.
2) Wealth element Water.
3) Resource element Fire.
4) Self element Earth.
5) Output element Metal.

With the favourable Yang Wood Luck Cycle, Hutchence enjoyed international success as the album *KICK* provided four US top 10 hits, including the Number 1 hit *Need You Tonight*.

The Dog Luck Cycle (age 30 to 34) contained a Yang Earth Rival, creating issues for Hutchence. Although the albums *Welcome to Wherever You Are* (1992 Yang Water Monkey year) and *Full Moon, Dirty Hearts* (1993 Yin Water Rooster year) were released in years with favourable elements, they did not fare as well commercially. Towards the end of this Luck Cycle, Hutchence received more media attention for his affair with the television personality Paula Yates (then married to Bob Geldof) than for his music.

The Yin Water Luck Cycle (from age 35) contained his second favourable element Water. In 1996 (Yang Fire Rat year), Yates gave birth to their daughter Heavenly Hiraani Tiger Lily Hutchence. The Annual Branch contained the favourable Water. In 1997 (Yin Fire Ox year), *INXS* released their 10th album *Elegantly Wasted*. The Annual Ox Branch reinforced the favourable element Metal by combining with the Rooster and Ox Branches in Hutchence's chart.

He was found dead at 11:50 hours in his hotel room in Sydney on November 22, 1997. Following a coronial inquest, it was ruled that his death was the result of suicide while depressed and under the influence of alcohol and other drugs. On the day he died, there was a Three

Harmony Combination involving the Annual Ox Branch and the Ox and Rooster Branches in his chart. It was during the Pig month that contained Yang Wood together with his Pig Year Branch. There was a Metal-Wood conflict. Also present was a Yang Earth Rival in both the Stem and Branch of the Yang Earth Dragon day he died. The presence of Rivals would have adversely affected his thinking.

Example 3.18 Harry Styles, British Singer
(born February 1, 1994, 00:06 hours)

Hour	Day	Month	Year
壬	戊	乙	癸
Yang Water	Yang Earth	Yin Wood	Yin Water
子	午	丑	酉
Rat	Horse	Ox	Rooster

9	19	29	39
甲	癸	壬	辛
Yang Wood	Yin Water	Yang Water	Yin Metal
子	亥	戌	酉
Rat	Pig	Dog	Rooster

49	59	69	79
庚	己	戊	丁
Yang Metal	Yin Earth	Yang Earth	Yin Fire
申	未	午	巳
Monkey	Sheep	Horse	Snake

There is a Partial Three Harmony Metal Combination in Styles' chart. His Ox Month Branch and Rooster Year Branch combine to form Metal. There are no other Combinations present within the chart. As Styles is a Yang Earth Day Master, Metal represents his Output. He has a Follow the Output (Metal) chart.

155

As a Yang Earth Day Master like Styles, his Special Stars are the Rat and Ox. Both are present in his chart, in his Hour Branch and Month Branch respectively. This indicates that Styles will be successful later in life, as the Hour Pillar comes into effect from the age of 40.

In the Rat Luck Cycle (age 14 to 18), Styles auditioned for the reality singing competition *The X Factor* in 2010 (Yang Metal Tiger year). Although he did not proceed to the finals, guest judge Nicole Scherzinger suggested that Styles form a singing group with four other contestants: Louis Tomlinson, Liam Payne, Niall Horan and Zayn Malik. Styles came up with the name *One Direction* and the group ranked third. The Special Star Rat was present in the Luck Cycle and worked in conjunction with Styles' Ox Month Branch to bring him success.

In 2011 (Yin Metal Rabbit year), the group released their debut album *Up All Night* with the UK Number 1 single *What Makes You Beautiful*. In 2012 (Yang Water Dragon year), *One Direction* released their second album *Take Me Home*, another bestseller. The Annual Dragon Branch combined with the Rat Luck Cycle to form the second favourable element Water.

The Yin Water Luck Cycle (age 19 to 23) combined with Styles' Yang Earth Day Master. The Wealth Element Combination indicated opportunities to generate wealth. For a man, the Wealth element also represents women so this period is also one in which Styles can find romance. In 2013 (Yin Water Snake year), there was a further Stem Combination involving Styles' Day Master. *One Direction* released their third album *Midnight Memories*. A documentary about the band directed by Morgan Spurlock entitled *One Direction: This is Us* earned more than $30 million USD worldwide over the weekend it was released. Styles also wrote their US Number 6 hit *Story of My Life*.

In 2015 (Yin Wood Sheep year), the negative elements Fire and Earth were present in the Annual Branch. Zayn

Malik announced his departure from the band and they released their album *Made in the A.M.* as a four-piece band. It was announced that the group would take a break following this album. In 2016 (Yang Fire Monkey year), the favourable elements Metal and Water were present in the Annual Branch. Styles signed a recording contract for three solo albums with Columbia, the same label behind *One Direction*.

In 2017 (Yin Fire Rooster year), the Annual Rooster Branch reinforced the favourable element Metal by combining with the Ox and Rooster Branches in Styles' chart. Styles made his acting debut in Christopher Nolan's wartime drama *Dunkirk*. His self titled debut album *Harry Styles* and his single *Sign of the Times* debuted at number 1 on both the US and UK charts.

The Pig Luck Cycle (age 24 to 28) contains his favourable elements Water and Wood, so it should be another successful period for Styles. The Yang Water Luck Cycle (age 29 to 33) is also favourable.

The Dog Luck Cycle (age 34 to 38) contains a Yang Earth Rival and the negative element Fire, as well as a Three Harmony Combination with the Horse in his House of Spouse. This may be the period for Styles to enjoy a relationship or get married. However, the Horse in the House of Spouse contains his negative elements Fire and Earth. This suggests that the person he marries will create some marital issues.

The subsequent Luck Cycles all contain the favourable elements Metal and Water: Yin Metal (age 39 to 43), Rooster (age 44 to 48), Yang Metal (age 49 to 53) and Monkey (age 54 to 58). These fortunate periods indicate that Styles has a long and successful career ahead of him.

Conclusion

From the 18 examples covered in this chapter, you can see that the ranking of favourable elements for Follow the Output (Metal) charts is:

1) Output element Metal.
2) Wealth element Water.
3) Power element Wood.
4) Self element Earth.
5) Resource element Fire.

All examples covered were either Yang Earth or Yin Earth Day Masters that had the Output element Metal as their most prominent element. This qualified them as Follow the Output (Metal) charts. The majority of them had either the Full or Partial Three Harmony Metal Combination within their Branches. Dame Joan Collins has the Full Three Harmony Metal Combination consisting of the Snake, Rooster and Ox in her chart.

Marc Anthony, Alicia Silverstone, Michael Hutchence and Harry Styles have the Partial Three Harmony Metal Combination consisting of the Rooster and Ox. Justin Timberlake, Heather Graham and Tony Leung Ka Fai have the Partial Three Harmony Metal Combination consisting of the Ox and two Roosters, while Eddie Redmayne and Lara Fabian have the Rooster and two Oxen.

Frank Oz, James Cromwell, Nina Dobrev and Colleen McCullough have the Partial Three Harmony Metal Combination consisting of the Snake and Ox, while Tippi Hedren and Riley Keough have two Snakes and one Ox.

Zach Galifianakis and Jim Henson do not have the Full or Partial Three Harmony Metal Combination in their charts. Jim Henson has two Roosters in Day and Month Branches, while Zach Galifianakis has three Roosters in his Day, Month and Year Branches. This allows them to follow Metal, their Output element.

Chapter Four Follow the Wealth (Metal) Charts

Follow the Wealth charts are those in which the Wealth element is the prevalent element. The Wealth element is that which the Day Master controls. For Follow the Wealth (Metal) charts, the Day Master must be Yang Fire or Yin Fire. In the life cycle of the five elements, Fire controls Metal.

Those with Follow the Wealth charts have an innate ability to generate income. They tend to have good financial sense and confidence with an 'easy come, easy go' attitude to money. What they spend they can make back without stress. Men with Follow the Wealth charts enjoy the company of women and prefer not to be alone. Women with Follow the Wealth charts are either capable of providing for themselves financially or receive ample financial support from their spouse or family.

For a Follow the Wealth (Metal) chart, the ranking of the elements is as follows:

1) Metal, the Wealth element.
2) Earth, the Output element. It produces and supports the Wealth element Metal.
3) Water, the Power element. It controls Fire Rivals and Competitors.
4) Wood, the Resource element. It destroys the second favourable element Earth.
5) Fire, the Self element. Fire Rivals and Competitors control Metal, which is the favourable element.

Unlike some of the other types of charts, Follow the Wealth (Metal) charts can benefit from three favourable elements: Metal, Earth and Water.

Example 4.1 Bruce Springsteen,

American Singer-Songwriter
(born September 23, 1949, 22:50 hours)

Hour	Day	Month	Year
己	丙	癸	己
Yin Earth	Yang Fire	Yin Water	Yin Earth
亥	辰	酉	丑
Pig	Dragon	Rooster	Ox

5	15	25	35
壬	辛	庚	己
Yang Water	Yin Metal	Yang Metal	Yin Earth
申	未	午	巳
Monkey	Sheep	Horse	Snake

45	55	65	75
戊	丁	丙	乙
Yang Earth	Yin Fire	Yang Fire	Yin Wood
辰	卯	寅	丑
Dragon	Rabbit	Tiger	Ox

There is a Partial Three Harmony Metal Combination in Springsteen's birth chart. His Rooster Month Branch combines with his Ox Year Branch to form Metal. There is also a Six Harmony Combination between the Dragon Day Branch and the Rooster Month Branch. However, the Three Harmony Combination takes precedence. There are no other Combinations present in the chart. The prevalent element is Metal. As Springsteen is a Yang Fire Day Master, Metal represents his Wealth element. He has a Follow the Wealth (Metal) chart.

As Springsteen is a Yang Fire Day Master, his Nobleman Stars are the Rooster and Pig. Both are present in his chart: the Rooster Month Branch and the Pig Hour Branch flank the Dragon in the House of Spouse. This is a very favourable Configuration known as Flanking Noblemen. It suggests that the person will always receive the assistance of helpful individuals throughout his life. For Springsteen, the Rooster Nobleman is also involved in the Partial Three Harmony Combination that gives him a Follow the Wealth chart.

Springsteen signed a record deal with Columbia Records in 1972 (Yang Water Rat year) during the Sheep Luck Cycle (age 20 to 24). Although the Sheep clashed with his Ox Year Branch and disrupted the Partial Three Harmony Metal Combination, the second favourable element Earth was present to provide support. His debut album *Greetings from Asbury Park, N.J.* was released in January 1973 (still the Yang Water Rat year). The third favourable element Water was present that year and controlled Fire Rivals. In 1973 (Yin Water Ox year), the Annual Ox Branch combined with the Rooster and Ox Branches in his chart to reinforce his favourable element Metal. His second album *The Wild, the Innocent and the E Street Shuffle* was released. Both albums were critically acclaimed but struggled commercially.

During the favourable Yang Metal Luck Cycle (age 25 to 29), Springsteen had his breakthrough with his third album *Born to Run*, which reached Number 3 on the US charts after being released in August 1975 (Yang Wood Monkey month in the Yin Wood Rabbit year). He had the auspicious Configuration of Four Stems in a Row: Yin Water Month Stem from his chart, Month Yang Wood Stem, Annual Yin Wood Stem, Yang Fire Day Master. In 1976 (Yang Fire Dragon year), there was a Yang Fire Rival in the Annual Stem. Springsteen was involved in a legal battle with former manager Mike Appel which settled in 1977 (Yin Fire Snake year). The Annual Snake Branch combined with the Rooster and Ox Branches in his chart to form the Full Three Harmony Metal Combination.

Manfred Mann's Earth Band also had a Number 1 US hit with their cover of a Springsteen song *Blinded by the Light*. This contributed to his growing reputation as a writer of hit songs.

The Horse Luck Cycle (age 30 to 34) contained the negative Self element Fire. Springsteen has stated that he was depressed during this period. However, there were positive developments in years with the favourable element Metal. In 1980 (Yang Metal Monkey year), *The River* was released, containing *Hungry Heart*, his first ever US Top 10 hit as a performer. Metal was present in the Annual Stem and the Annual Monkey Branch combined with his Dragon Day Branch to form his third favourable element Water, which controlled the Fire Rival present in the Luck Cycle. In 1982 (Yang Water Dog year), *Nebraska* was released. The Annual Dog Branch combined with the Horse Luck Cycle to form the negative element Fire. There was a Fire-Metal conflict in Springsteen's chart. *Nebraska* was a commercial disappointment upon release.

Springsteen rebounded in the favourable Yin Earth Luck Cycle (age 35 to 39) with *Born in the U.S.A.* in 1984 (Yang Wood Rat year). It was his most successful album, selling 30 million copies worldwide with 7 US Top 10 Singles including *Dancing in the Dark*. During the *Born in the U.S.A.* tour the same year, Springsteen met actress Julianne Phillips, whom he would marry the following year. The Annual Rat Branch combined with his Dragon in the House of Spouse, indicating romance or marriage. It also formed the third favourable element Water. In 1986 (Yang Fire Tiger year), the five-record box set *Live/1975-1985* became the first box set to debut at Number 1 on the US Album charts. For a Yang Fire Day Master like Springsteen, the Special Stars are the Tiger and Dragon. The Annual Tiger Branch worked in conjunction with his Dragon Day Branch to bring him success. In 1988 (Yang Earth Dragon year), Springsteen filed for divorce from Phillips and started a relationship with backup singer Patti Scialfa. His House of Spouse animal Dragon was present in the Annual Branch that year.

The Snake Luck Cycle (age 40 to 44) was also favourable for Springsteen. The Snake formed the Full Three Harmony Metal Combination with the Rooster and Ox Branches in his chart. In 1991 (Yin Metal Sheep year), he married Scialfa in a private ceremony. There was a Stem Combination involving his Yang Fire Day Master and the Annual Yin Metal Stem. The Wealth Element Combination indicates the possibility of generating income. For a man, the Wealth element also represents his Spouse. In 1992 (Yang Water Monkey year), Springsteen released the albums *Human Touch* and *Lucky Town* on the same day. They debuted at Number 2 and 3 on the US Album charts. The Annual Monkey Branch combined with the Dragon Day Branch to form Water, his third favourable element.

The Yang Earth Luck Cycle (age 45 to 49) contained his second favourable element Earth. In 1994 (Yang Wood Dog year), Springsteen won an Oscar for Best Song for *Streets of Philadelphia*, which he wrote for the movie *Philadelphia*. Earth was present in the Annual Dog Branch. In 1998 (Yang Earth Tiger year), he released a four-disc set of outtakes, *Tracks*. The Annual Tiger Branch worked in conjunction with his Dragon Day Branch to bring him success as the Special Stars for a Yang Fire Day Master.

The Dragon Luck Cycle (age 50 to 54) again contained the second favourable element Earth. In 2002 (Yang Water Horse year), Springsteen released *The Rising*, written in the wake of the September 11 attacks. It debuted at number 1 on the US Album charts, selling 520 000 copies. Springsteen became the oldest person to achieve first week sales of more than half a million copies in the United States.

The Yin Fire Luck Cycle (age 55 to 59) contained his negative Self element Fire. Springsteen's new material released during this period did not receive much airplay but he was still able to perform well in years with the favourable element Metal. In 2005 (Yin Wood Rooster year), *Devils & Dust* reached number 1 on the US Albums chart.

The Rabbit Luck Cycle (age 60 to 64) clashed with the Rooster Month Branch, disrupting the Partial Three Harmony Metal Combination. It also combined with the Pig Hour Branch, forming a Partial Three Harmony Combination. During this period, Springsteen became a Follow the Resource (Wood) chart. His favourable elements became:

1)   Resource element Wood.
2)   Power element Water.
3)   Output element Earth.
4)   Wealth element Metal.
5)   Self element Fire.

In 2012 (Yang Water Dragon year), Springsteen released *Wrecking Ball*, which became his 10th Number 1 Album on the US charts. The *Wrecking Ball* tour was also one of his most successful, being the second most successful tour of 2012. The favourable element Water was present in the Annual Stem.

The Yang Fire Luck Cycle (age 65 to 69) contained a Yang Fire Rival, so Springsteen had to depend on the Annual Stems and Branches. In 2016 (Yang Fire Monkey year), the Annual Monkey Branch combined with his Dragon Day Branch to form the favourable element Water. His 500-page autobiography *Born to Run*, was released and rose to the top of the *New York Times Best Sellers List*.

The Tiger Luck Cycle (age 70 to 74) contains one of his Special Stars, so it should also be another favourable period for him.

Example 4.2 Kate Moss, British Model
(born January 16, 1974, 17:00 hours)

Hour	Day	Month	Year
己	丁	乙	癸
Yin Earth	Yin Fire	Yin Wood	Yin Water
酉	巳	丑	丑
Rooster	Snake	Ox	Ox

6	16	26	36
丙	丁	戊	己
Yang Fire	Yin Fire	Yang Earth	Yin Earth
寅	卯	辰	巳
Tiger	Rabbit	Dragon	Snake

46	56	66	76
庚	辛	壬	癸
Yang Metal	Yin Metal	Yang Water	Yin Water
午	未	申	酉
Horse	Sheep	Monkey	Rooster

There is a Full Three Harmony Metal Combination in Moss' birth chart. Her Snake Day Branch combines with her Ox Month and Year Branches and Rooster Hour Branch to form Metal. There are no other Combinations in her chart. As Moss is a Yin Fire Day Master, Metal represents her Wealth element. She has a Follow the Wealth (Metal) chart.

Moss has a Special Configuration in her chart. There is the Cycle of Production between the Stems and Branches. Her Yin Water Year Stem produces the Yin Wood Month Branch, which then supports the Yin Fire Day Master. This then gives rise to the Yin Earth Hour Stem that produces the Rooster Hour Branch and the Full Three Harmony Combination within the Branches. The Full

Three Harmony Metal Combination then completes the Cycle of Production by producing the Yin Water Year Stem. The Cycle of Production indicates an extremely successful and resourceful individual.

Moss was discovered at the age of 14 at JFK Airport in New York in 1988 (Yang Earth Dragon year) during the Tiger Luck Cycle (age 11 to 15). For a Yin Fire Day Master like Moss, the Special Stars are the Tiger and Dragon. The Annual Dragon Branch worked in conjunction with the Tiger Luck Cycle to bring her success that year. In 1989 (Yin Earth Snake year), Moss launched her career with a photo shoot by Corinne Day that made the cover of *The Face* magazine in the UK. The Annual Snake Branch reinforced her favourable element Metal by combining with the Snake and Ox Branches within her chart. Note that the Rooster Hour Branch will only come into effect at the age of 40.

The Yin Fire Luck Cycle (age 16 to 20) contained a Fire Rival. Moss had to contend with rumours and allegations of having an eating disorder during this period. In 1993 (Yin Water Rooster year), she featured in the campaign for the Calvin Klein perfume *Obsession*. The Annual Rooster Branch combined with the Snake and Ox Branches in Moss' chart to form the Full Three Harmony Metal Combination.

The Rabbit Luck Cycle (age 21 to 25) contained the negative element Wood. In 1996 (Yang Fire Rat year), Moss featured in the fashion look Heroin Chic. While the third favourable element Water was present in the Annual Branch, there was also a Yang Fire Rival. The trend was condemned by then US President Bill Clinton and it was blamed for glamorising drug use. In 1998 (Yang Earth Tiger year), Moss did a stint in a London clinic for alcohol addiction. The negative elements Fire and Wood were present in the Annual Branch.

The Yang Earth Luck Cycle (age 26 to 30) contained Moss' second favourable element. She continued to feature on magazine covers. In 2001 (Yin Metal Snake year), she started dating *Dazed and Confused* magazine founder Jefferson Hack. Her House of Spouse animal Snake was present that year, indicating the possibility of love or marriage. In 2002 (Yang Water Horse year), their daughter Lila Grace was born. Her Output or Child element Earth was present in the Annual Branch.

In 2005 (Yin Wood Rooster year) during the Dragon Luck Cycle (age 31 to 35), Moss started dating musician Pete Doherty, the former lead singer of the *Libertines*. There was a Combination between the Annual Rooster Branch and the Snake in Moss' House of Spouse. However, in September that year, Moss found herself embroiled in a scandal when photos of her using cocaine with Doherty were published in the press. She lost endorsements with sponsors such as Burberry, Chanel and H&M. However, her favourable element Metal was present in the Annual Rooster Branch. Moss was cleared of all charges and was able to resume her modelling career. 2007 (Yin Fire Pig year) contained a Yin Fire Rival in the Annual Stem. Moss ended her relationship with Doherty.

In the favourable Yin Earth Luck Cycle (age 36 to 40), Moss married guitarist Jamie Hince from *The Kills* in 2011 (Yin Metal Rabbit year). It was a very auspicious year for Moss as she received the influence of four different Yin Stems: Yin Wood Month Stem, Yin Fire Day Master, Annual Yin Metal Stem and Yin Water Year Stem.

During the Snake Luck Cycle (age 41 to 45), Moss separated from Hince in 2015 (Yin Wood Sheep year) and settled their divorce out of court in 2016 (Yang Fire Monkey year). The Annual Monkey Branch contained the favourable elements Metal and Water. The House of Spouse animal Snake is present during this period, so Moss' chances of finding love and marriage during this period are good.

The Yang Metal Luck Cycle (age 46 to 50) should be favourable. However, the negative element Fire is present in the Horse Luck Cycle (age 51 to 55), presenting challenges in Moss' life.

Example 4.3 Steve Winwood, British Singer
(born May 12, 1948, 05:00 hours)

Hour	Day	Month	Year
癸	丁	丁	戊
Yin Water	Yin Fire	Yin Fire	Yang Earth
卯	酉	巳	子
Rabbit	Rooster	Snake	Rat

8	18	28	38
戊	己	庚	辛
Yang Earth	Yin Earth	Yang Metal	Yin Metal
午	未	申	酉
Horse	Sheep	Monkey	Rooster

48	58	68	78
壬	癸	甲	乙
Yang Water	Yin Water	Yang Wood	Yin Wood
戌	亥	子	丑
Dog	Pig	Rat	Ox

There is a Partial Three Harmony Metal Combination in Winwood's birth chart. His Yin Fire Rooster Day Branch combines with his Snake Month Branch to form Metal. There are no other Combinations in the chart. As Winwood is a Yin Fire Day Master, Metal represents his Wealth element. He has a Follow the Wealth (Metal) chart.

Winwood is born on a Yin Fire Rooster day. He is born on one of four days where the Day Master is sitting on the Nobleman Star. This indicates that his Spouse will provide assistance. Winwood has been married twice. His first wife Nicole Weir had contributed background vocals to his earlier solo work. Their marriage was from 1978 (Yang Earth Horse year) to 1986 (Yang Fire Tiger year). Winwood married Eugenia Crafton in 1987 (Yin Fire Rabbit year) and they have four children together.

Winwood also has a Special Configuration. He has three of the four Peach Blossom or Peak Branches in his chart: Rat, Rabbit and Rooster. Winwood needs the Horse to complete the sequence of Peach Blossom Branches in his chart. When the Horse year or Luck Cycle appears, he will have the full sequence, a very auspicious Combination even though the Horse contains the negative element Fire.

During the Horse Luck Cycle (age 13 to 17), Winwood joined *The Spencer Davis Group* in 1963 (Yin Water Rabbit year) together with his brother Muff Winwood. The third favourable element Water was present in the Annual Stem. In 1964 (Yang Wood Dragon year), the group signed with Island Records. The Annual Dragon Branch combined with his Rat Year Branch to form the favourable element Water. In 1965 (Yin Wood Snake year), the Annual Snake Branch combined with the Snake and Rooster Branches to reinforce the favourable element Metal. *The Spencer Davis Group* had their first top UK Number 1 hit with *Keep on Running*.

The Yin Earth Luck Cycle (age 18 to 22) contained the second favourable element. In 1966 (Yang Fire Horse year), *The Spencer Davis Group* scored a US Number 1 hit with *Give Me Some Lovin'*. The Annual Horse Branch completed the sequence of four Peach Blossom animals in Winwood's chart. In 1967 (Yin Fire Sheep year), Winwood left *The Spencer Davis Group* to form *Traffic*, who scored UK top 10 hits that same year with *Hole in My Shoe* and *Here We Go Round the Mulberry Bush*. In 1969 (Yin Earth Rooster year), Winwood formed the short-lived supergroup *Blind Faith* with Eric Clapton. The Annual Rooster Branch combined with the Snake and Rooster

Branches in his chart to reinforce the favourable element Metal. In 1970 (Yang Metal Dog year), the favourable elements Metal and Earth were present. Winwood reformed with *Traffic* and they released their most successful album *John Barleycorn Must Die*, which reached Number 5 in the US Album Charts.

The Sheep Luck Cycle (age 23 to 27) contained the favourable element Earth. However, in 1971 (Yin Metal Pig year), Winwood suffered from peritonitis, which forced him to take a break from *Traffic*. The Annual Pig Branch formed a Partial Three Harmony Wood Combination with the Sheep Luck Cycle. As there was already a Partial Three Harmony Metal Combination in Winwood's chart, there was a Metal-Wood clash. However, the favourable element Metal was present in the Annual Stem. *Traffic* released the US Top 10 Album *The Low Spark of High Heeled Boys*. In 1973 (Yin Water Ox year), *Traffic* released another successful album *Shoot Out at the Fantasy Factory*. The Annual Ox Branch combined with the Snake and Rooster Branches in Winwood's chart to reinforce the favourable element Metal. In 1974 (Yang Wood Tiger year), Winwood became weary of the grind of touring and left *Traffic*. There was a Yang Fire Rival hidden within the Annual Tiger Branch.

The Yang Metal Luck Cycle (age 28 to 32) was favourable for Winwood. In 1977 (Yin Fire Snake year), he released his self-titled debut album, *Steve Winwood*. The Annual Snake Branch combined with the Snake and Ox Branches within his chart to reinforce the favourable element Metal. In 1980 (Yang Metal Monkey year), he released his second solo album *Arc of a Diver* that produced his first solo US Top 10 hit *While You See a Chance*. His favourable elements Metal and Water were present in the Annual Stem and Branch.

The Monkey Luck Cycle (age 33 to 37) combined with his Rat Year Branch to form the third favourable element Water. In 1982 (Yang Water Dog year), Winwood's third album *Talking Back to the Night* was released, which contained the top 10 hit *Valerie*. There was a Stem Combination between the Annual Yang Water Stem and his Yin Fire Day Master. The Power Element Combination indicates professional success or recognition.

The Yin Metal Luck Cycle (age 38 to 42) saw Winwood's commercial success at its peak. In 1986 (Yang Fire Tiger year), he released his fourth solo album *Back in the High Life* and scored his first US Number 1 hit with *Higher Love*. In July (Yin Wood Sheep month) that year, Winwood enjoyed the auspicious Four Stems in a Row: Yin Wood Month, Annual Yang Fire Stem, Yin Fire Day Master, Yang Earth Year Branch. In 1988 (Yang Earth Dragon year), he released the US Number 1 album *Roll With It*. The title track was also a US Number 1 for four weeks. The favourable element Earth was present in the Annual Stem, while the Annual Dragon Branch combined with his Rat Year Branch to form the third favourable element Water. In 1990 (Yang Metal Horse year), he released his sixth album *Refugees of the Heart*. The Annual Horse Branch completed the sequence of four Peach Blossom animals in his chart.

The Rooster (age 43 to 47) and Yang Water (age 48 to 52) were favourable for Winwood as he worked consistently. In 1994 (Yang Wood Dog year), *Traffic* re-formed for their eighth album *Far from Home*. The second favourable element Earth was present in the Annual Dog Branch. In 1997 (Yin Fire Ox year), the Ox combined with the Rooster and Ox Branches in Winwood's chart to reinforce the favourable element Metal. He released the album *Junction Seven*.

In 2004 (Yang Wood Monkey year) during the Dog Luck Cycle (age 53 to 57), his 80s hit *Valerie* was sampled by DJ Eric Prydz for the UK Number 1 hit *Call On Me*. The favourable elements Metal and Water were present in the Annual Branch. In 2008 (Yang Earth Rat year) during the

Yin Water Luck Cycle (age 58 to 62), his album *Nine Lives* saw him return to the US Top 20 Albums at Number 12. His favourable elements Earth and Water were present in the Annual Stem and Branch respectively. Winwood was also awarded an honorary doctorate from the Berklee College of Music.

Example 4.4 Mark Owen, British Singer
(born January 27, 1972)

Hour	Day	Month	Year
	丁	辛	辛
	Yin Fire	Yin Metal	Yin Metal
	巳	丑	亥
	Snake	Ox	Pig

7	17	27	37
庚	己	戊	丁
Yang Metal	Yin Earth	Yang Earth	Yin Fire
子	亥	戌	酉
Rat	Pig	Dog	Rooster

47	57	67	77
丙	乙	甲	癸
Yang Fire	Yin Wood	Yang Wood	Yin Water
申	未	午	巳
Monkey	Sheep	Horse	Snake

There is a Partial Three Harmony Metal Combination in Owen's birth chart. His Snake Day Branch and Ox Month Branch combine to form Metal. There are also Yin Metal Month and Year Stems. The prevalent element within his chart is Metal. As Owen is a Yin Fire Day Master, Metal represents his Wealth element. He has a Follow the Wealth (Metal) chart.

During the favourable Yin Earth Luck Cycle (age 17 to 21), Owen successfully auditioned for *Take That* in 1990 (Yang Metal Horse year). The favourable element Metal was present in the Annual Stem. *Take That*'s debut album *Take That & Party* was released in 1992 (Yang Water Monkey year) and yielded three top 10 hits. There was a Stem Combination between the Annual Yang Water Stem and Owen's Yin Fire Day Master. The Power Element Combination indicates professional recognition and success. Their second album *Everything Changes* was even more successful when released in 1993 (Yin Water Rooster year). It sold three million copies worldwide and produced 7 top 10 UK hits. Owen sang lead vocals on their number 1 hit *Babe*. The Annual Rooster Branch combined with the Snake and Ox Branches in Owen's chart to form the Full Three Harmony Metal Combination.

The Pig Luck Cycle (age 22 to 26) clashed with the Snake Day Branch, disrupting the Partial Three Harmony Metal Combination. In 1995 (Yin Wood Pig year), *Take That* released their third album *Nobody Else* with three UK No. 1 singles. However, Robbie Williams announced his departure from the band and *Take That* broke up the following year (Yang Fire Rat year). Owen was able to benefit as the Annual Yang Fire Stem combined with his Yin Metal Month and Year Stems. He was able to use the Wealth element to combine away a Yang Fire Rival effectively. He became the first member of the band to release a solo album *Green Man* that same year, which contained two Number 3 UK hits *Child* and *Clementine*. However, his label BMG Records dropped him in 1997 (Yin Fire Ox year). There was a Yin Fire Rival present in the Annual Stem.

The Yang Earth Luck Cycle (age 27 to 31) contained his second favourable element. In 2002 (Yang Water Horse year), Owen returned to the public eye by winning the second series of *Celebrity Big Brother*. There was a Stem Combination between the Annual Yang Water Stem and his Yin Fire Day Master, indicating professional recognition and success. In 2003 (Yin Water Sheep year), Owen returned to the UK top 5 with *Four Minute Warning* and released his second album *In Your Own Time*. While the third favourable element Water was present in the Annual Stem, there was also a Partial Three Harmony Wood Combination between the Annual Sheep Branch and the Pig Year Branch. This created a Metal-Wood conflict in Owen's chart. Owen's record company Island/Universal dropped him that same year after the second single *Alone Without You* only made it to Number 26.

The Dog Luck Cycle (age 32 to 36) contained the favourable element Earth. In 2004 (Yang Wood Monkey year), Owen started a relationship with actress Emma Ferguson. There was a Six Harmony Combination between the Annual Monkey Branch and his Snake in the House of Spouse. This indicated the possibility of love or marriage. In 2005 (Yin Wood Rooster year), Owen released his third album *How the Mighty Fall* on an independent label. The Annual Rooster Branch combined with the Snake and Ox Branches in his chart to form the Full Three Harmony Metal Combination.

In 2006 (Yang Fire Dog year), *Take That* reformed and toured before releasing their UK Number 1 comeback album *Beautiful World* with the UK Number 1 singles *Patience* and *Shine*. The second favourable element Earth was present in the Annual Dog Branch. In 2008 (Yang Earth Rat year), the favourable elements Earth and Water were present in the Annual Stem and Branch. *Take That* released their fifth album *The Circus*, which sold 2.2 million copies in the UK and produced the UK Number 1 single *Greatest Day*.

The Yin Fire Luck Cycle (age 37 to 41) contained the negative Fire element. In 2009 (Yin Earth Ox year), Owen married Ferguson after having had two children with her. The Annual Ox Branch combined with his Snake Branch in the House of Spouse. This indicated the possibility of love or marriage. In 2010 (Yang Metal Tiger year), Owen confessed publicly to having had extramarital affairs and an alcohol problem. He checked into a private rehabilitation clinic later that year to deal with his alcohol consumption. The Annual Tiger Branch contained a Yang Fire Rival. In 2013 (Yin Water Snake year), Owen released his fourth album *The Art of Doing Nothing*. The Annual Snake Branch combined with the Ox and Snake Branches in his chart to reinforce the favourable element Metal.

The Rooster Luck Cycle (age 42 to 46) formed the Full Three Harmony Metal Combination with the Snake and Ox Branches in Owen's chart. In 2017 (Yin Fire Rooster year), *Take That* released their 8th studio album *Wonderland*, which debuted at number 2 on the UK charts. The Annual Rooster Branch combined with the Rooster Luck Cycle and the Snake and Ox Branches in Owen's chart to reinforce the favourable element Metal.

The Yang Fire Luck Cycle (age 47 to 51) contains a Rival, but Owen should be able to combine away the Rival with his Yin Metal Month Stem. The Monkey Luck Cycle (age 52 to 56) contains the favourable elements Metal and Water.

Example 4.5 Armistead Maupin, American Author
(born May 13, 1944)

Hour	Day	Month	Year
	丁	己	甲
	Yin Fire	Yin Earth	Yang Wood
	丑	巳	申
	Ox	Snake	Monkey

8	18	28	38
庚	辛	壬	癸
Yang Metal	Yin Metal	Yang Water	Yin Water
午	未	申	酉
Horse	Sheep	Monkey	Rooster

48	58	68	78
甲	乙	丙	丁
Yang Wood	Yin Wood	Yang Fire	Yin Fire
戌	亥	子	丑
Dog	Pig	Rat	Ox

There is a Partial Three Harmony Metal Combination in Maupin's birth chart. His Ox Day Branch combines with his Snake Month Branch to form Metal. There is a Six Harmony Combination between the Snake Month Branch and the Monkey Year Branch. However, when it comes to determining the prevalent element, the Three Harmony Combination always takes precedence over the Six Harmony Combination. There are no other Branch Combinations within Maupin's chart. As he is a Yin Fire Day Master, Metal represents his Wealth element. Maupin has a Follow the Wealth (Metal) chart.

There is a Special Configuration in Maupin's chart. His Year and Month Pillars are involved in a Heaven and Earth Combination. His Yang Wood Year Stem forms a

Stem Combination with his Yin Earth Month Stem, while his Monkey Year Branch forms a Six Harmony Combination with his Snake Month Branch. This Heaven and Earth Combination between the Year and Month Pillars suggest success early in life.

During the Sheep Luck Cycle (age 23 to 27), Maupin volunteered for duty in Vietnam, serving as a Lieutenant in the River Patrol Force from 1967 (Yin Fire Sheep year) to 1970 (Yang Metal Dog year). He received the Navy Commendation Medal. In 1971 (Yin Metal Pig year), Maupin accepted a position in the San Francisco bureau of the Associated Press. He had already started working as a journalist in Charleston covering military stories. His favourable element Metal was present in the Annual Stem.

In 1972 (Yang Water Rat year) during the favourable Yang Water Luck Cycle (age 28 to 32), Maupin received a Presidential Commendation from US President Richard Nixon. Following the Vietnam War, he had helped organize the building of homes for disabled Vietnam veterans. The Annual Yang Water Stem and the Yang Water Luck Cycle formed a Stem Combination with his Yin Fire Day Master. The Power Element Combination indicated professional success and recognition. In 1976 (Yang Fire Dragon year), the *San Francisco Chronicle* picked up his *Tales of the City* newspaper series. The Annual Dragon Branch combined with his Monkey Year Branch to form the third favourable element Water.

During the favourable Monkey Luck Cycle (age 33 to 37), Harper Collins (then Harper & Row) published *Tales of the City* in 1978 (Yang Earth Horse year). The second favourable element Earth was present in the Annual Stem. In 1980 (Yang Metal Monkey year), *More Tales of the City* was published. The favourable element Metal was present in the Annual Stem and Branch, as well as the Luck Cycle.

Subsequent titles in the *Tales of the City* series were published in the favourable Yin Water (age 38 to 42) and Rooster (age 43 to 47) Luck Cycles. The Rooster formed the Full Three Harmony Metal Combination with the Ox and Snake Branches present in Maupin's chart. *Further Tales of the City* was published in 1982 (Yang Water Dog year). There was a Stem Combination between the Annual Yang Water Stem and Maupin's Yin Earth Day Master, indicating professional success and recognition. In 1984 (Yang Wood Rat year), *Babycakes* followed. The Annual Rat Branch formed a Partial Three Harmony Water Combination with Maupin's Dragon Year Branch. *Sure of You* was published in 1989 (Yin Earth Snake year). The Annual Snake Branch combined with the Ox and Snake Branches in Maupin's chart to reinforce the favourable element Metal.

The Yang Wood Luck Cycle (age 48 to 52) contained the negative Resource element. Maupin was less prolific during this period. In 1992 (Yang Water Monkey year), *Maybe the Moon* was published, his first novel not part of the *Tales* series. There was a Stem Combination between the Annual Yang Water Stem and his Yin Fire Day Master, indicating professional recognition and success. In 1993 (Yin Water Rooster year), the Annual Rooster Branch combined with the Ox and Snake Branches in Maupin's chart to form the Full Three Harmony Metal Combination. *Tales of the City* was made into a mini-series by the UK's Channel Four.

The Dog Luck Cycle (age 53 to 57) contained the second favourable element Earth. In 1998 (Yang Earth Tiger year) with Earth in the Annual Stem, *More Tales of the City* was produced. In 2000 (Yang Metal Dragon year) with the favourable elements Metal and Earth, *The Night Listener* was published, based on real life events. In 2001 (Yin Metal Snake year), *More Tales of the City* was made into a mini-series. The Annual Snake Branch combined with the Ox and Snake in his chart to reinforce the favourable element Metal.

The Yin Wood Luck Cycle (age 58 to 62) contained the negative Resource element. In 2007 (Yin Fire Pig year), there was a Yang Water Stem hidden in the Annual Pig Branch that formed a Stem Combination with the Yin Fire Day Master. The *Tales of the City* series continued with *Michael Tolliver Lives*.

The Pig Luck Cycle (age 63 to 67) disrupted the Partial Three Harmony Metal Combination within Maupin's chart by clashing with the Snake Month Branch. Maupin was more dependent on the Annual Energies. In 2010 (Yang Metal Tiger year) with the favourable element Metal in the Annual Stem, *Mary Ann in Autumn* was published.

The Yang Fire Luck Cycle (age 68 to 72) contained a Yang Fire Rival but the Rat Luck Cycle (age 73 to 77) has the favourable element Water.

Example 4.6 Brian de Palma, American Film Director
(born September 11, 1940, 18:58 hours)

Hour	Day	Month	Year
己	丁	乙	庚
Yin Earth	Yin Fire	Yin Wood	Yang Metal
酉	巳	酉	辰
Rooster	Snake	Rooster	Dragon

9	19	29	39
丙	丁	戊	己
Yang Fire	Yin Fire	Yang Earth	Yin Earth
戌	亥	子	丑
Dog	Pig	Rat	Ox

49	59	69	79
庚	辛	壬	癸
Yang Metal	Yin Metal	Yang Water	Yin Water
寅	卯	辰	巳
Tiger	Rabbit	Dragon	Snake

There is a Partial Three Harmony Combination in de Palma's birth chart. His Snake Day Branch combines with his Rooster Month and Hour Branches to form Metal. There is also a Six Harmony Combination between the Dragon Year Branch and the Rooster Month Branch. However, for identifying the prevalent element, the Three Harmony Combination takes precedence. The prevalent element within the chart is Metal. For a Yin Fire Day Master like de Palma, Metal represents his Wealth element. He has a Follow the Wealth (Metal) chart.

The Nobleman Stars for a Yin Fire Day Master are the Rooster and Pig. There are two Rooster Branches in de Palma's chart, in the Month and Hour Branch flanking his Day Branch. As this is a very auspicious Configuration, it indicates that he will always receive assistance throughout his life.

The other Special Configuration in de Palma's chart is that there is a Heaven and Earth Combination between his Month and Year Pillars. His Yang Metal Year Stem combines with his Yin Wood Month Stem, and his Dragon Year Branch forms a Six Harmony Combination with his Rooster Month Branch. This indicates success in the first half of life, i.e. before the age of 40. As discussed below, de Palma already achieved success as a film director while in his 30s.

In 1974 (Yang Wood Tiger year) during the Rat Luck Cycle (age 34 to 38), de Palma directed the cult musical *Phantom of the Paradise*. For a Yin Fire Day Master, the Special Stars are the Tiger and the Dragon. The Annual Tiger Branch worked in conjunction with his Dragon Year Branch to bring him success. In 1976 (Yang Fire Dragon year), the Annual Dragon Branch combined with the Rat Luck Cycle and the Dragon Year Branch to form the third favourable element Water. De Palma released two successful movies that year, *Obsession* with Cliff Robertson and horror film *Carrie*, which earned co-stars Sissy Spacek and Piper Laurie Oscar nominations.

The Yin Earth Luck Cycle (age 39 to 43) was also favourable for de Palma. In 1980, (Yang Metal Monkey year), his thriller *Dressed to Kill* with Michael Caine and Angie Dickinson, was a controversial box office hit. The favourable element Metal was present in the Annual Stem and Branch. In 1981 (Yin Metal Rooster year), de Palma directed political thriller *Blow Out* with John Travolta, now considered a classic. The Annual Rooster Branch combined with the Snake and Rooster Branches in his chart to reinforce the favourable element Metal. In 1983 (Yin Water Pig year), *Scarface* with Al Pacino and Michelle Pfeiffer was released. It was a major box office hit. The third favourable element Water was present in the Annual Stem and Branch.

The Ox Luck Cycle (age 44 to 48) formed the Full Three Harmony Metal Combination with the Snake and Rooster Branches in de Palma's chart. In 1987 (Yin Fire Rabbit year), the gangster film *The Untouchables* with Kevin Costner, Robert de Niro and Sean Connery was released. It was a major critical and commercial success and earned Connery an Oscar for Best Supporting Actor. Even though there was a Clash between the Annual Rabbit Branch and the Rooster Branches in de Palma's chart disrupting the Three Harmony Combination, the Ox Luck Cycle and his Snake Day Branch were still able to combine and form Metal.

The Yang Metal Luck Cycle (age 49 to 53) contained the favourable element. In 1989 (Yin Earth Snake year), de Palma directed the critically acclaimed war film *Casualties of War* with Sean Penn and Michael J. Fox. The Annual Snake Branch combined with the Snake and Rooster Branches in de Palma's chart to reinforce the favourable element Metal. In 1990 (Yang Metal Horse year), *Bonfire of the Vanities* with Tom Hanks and Bruce Willis was released. It was a box office flop. The negative element Fire was present in the Annual Branch. In 1993 (Yin Water Rooster year), de Palma made a comeback with the gangster film *Carlito's Way* with Al Pacino and Sean Penn. The Annual Rooster Branch combined with the Snake and Rooster Branches in his chart to reinforce the favourable element Metal.

Although the Tiger Luck Cycle (age 54 to 58) contained a Yang Fire Rival, it was one of the Special Stars for a Yin Fire Day Master like de Palma. It worked in conjunction with his Dragon Year Branch to bring him success. In 1996 (Yang Fire Rat year), de Palma scored another box office hit with *Mission Impossible* starring Tom Cruise. The third favourable element Water was present in the Annual Branch.

The Yin Metal Luck Cycle (age 59 to 63) was again favourable for de Palma. In 2000 (Yang Metal Dragon year), he directed *Mission to Mars* with Gary Sinise and Jerry O'Connell, another box office success. The favourable elements Metal and Earth were present in the Annual Stem and Branch. 2002 (Yang Water Horse year) was a mixed year for de Palma. There was a Stem Combination between the Annual Yang Water Stem and his Yin Fire Day Master. This indicated professional success and recognition. He directed *Femme Fatale* with Antonio Banderas. While it premiered at the Cannes Film Festival, the movie performed badly at the box office. The negative Self element was present in the Annual Branch.

The Rabbit Luck Cycle (age 64 to 68) was a lean period for de Palma. The Rabbit clashed with the Rooster Branches to disrupt the Three Harmony Metal

Combination in his chart. In 2006 (Yang Fire Dog year), de Palma released *The Black Dahlia*, based on a true story. It did not perform well at the box office but was critically praised. The Annual Dog Branch formed a Six Harmony Combination with the Rabbit Luck Cycle, reducing the Clash with the Rooster Branches. In 2007 (Yin Fire Pig year), de Palma's Iraq war film *Redacted* created controversy and was a major box office failure, even though it won the Silver Lion Award for Best Director at the Venice Film Festival. There was a Partial Three Harmony Wood Combination between the Annual Pig Branch and the Rabbit Luck Cycle. This produced a Metal-Wood conflict in de Palma's chart.

The Yang Water Luck Cycle (age 69 to 73) was more favourable for de Palma as there was a Stem Combination between the Luck Cycle and his Yin Fire Day Master. This indicated professional success and recognition. In 2012 (Yang Water Dragon year), the thriller *Passion* with Rachel McAdams and Noomi Rapace was screened at the Venice Film Festival.

The Dragon (age 74 to 78) and Yin Water (age 79 to 83) Luck Cycles should be favourable for de Palma as they contain the favourable elements Earth and Water. In 2015 (Yin Wood Sheep year), Noah Baumbach and Jake Paltrow released their documentary, *De Palma*. The favourable element Earth was present in the Annual Branch.

Example 4.7 Clive James, Australian Broadcaster and
Author (born October 7, 1939)

Hour	Day	Month	Year
	丁	癸	己
	Yin Fire	Yin Water	Yin Earth
	丑	酉	卯
	Ox	Rooster	Rabbit

10	20	30	40
壬	辛	庚	己
Yang Water	Yin Metal	Yang Metal	Yin Earth
申	未	午	巳
Monkey	Sheep	Horse	Snake

50	60	70	80
戊	丁	丙	乙
Yang Earth	Yin Fire	Yang Fire	Yin Wood
辰	卯	寅	丑
Dragon	Rabbit	Tiger	Ox

There is a Partial Three Harmony Metal Combination in
James' chart. His Ox Day Branch and Rooster Month
Branch combine to form Metal. There are no other
Combinations present in his chart. The prevalent element
in his chart is Metal. As James is a Yin Fire Day Master,
Metal represents his Wealth element. He has a Follow the
Wealth (Metal) chart.

In the favourable Yin Metal Luck Cycle (age 20 to 24),
James graduated with a Bachelor of Arts Honours in
English and then worked as an assistant editor with the
Sydney Morning Herald in 1961 (Yin Metal Ox year). The
favourable element Metal was present in the Annual Stem.
The Annual Ox Branch combined with the Rooster and
Ox Branches in his birth chart to reinforce Metal.

In the Sheep Luck Cycle (age 25 to 29), the Sheep Luck Cycle clashed with the Ox Day Branch, disrupting the Partial Three Harmony Metal Combination. It also combined with his Rabbit Year Branch, forming Wood. There was a Metal-Wood conflict in his chart. James worked in a variety of short-term jobs (e.g. sheet metal worker, library assistant, photo archivist) before being accepted by Cambridge to read English Literature in 1965 (Yin Wood Snake year). The Annual Snake Branch formed the Full Three Harmony Metal Combination with the Ox and Rooster Branches in his chart. James graduated with Second Class Honours, Upper Division from Cambridge in 1968 (Yang Earth Monkey year). He also married Prudence Shaw, the author of *Reading Dante: From Here to Eternity*. The favourable elements Metal and Water were present in the Annual Branch.

In the Yang Metal Luck Cycle (age 30 to 34), James collaborated with Pete Atkin on his first music album *Beware of the Beautiful Stranger* in 1970 (Yang Metal Dog year). This was followed by *Driving Through Mythical America* in 1971 (Yin Metal Pig year). The favourable elements Metal, Earth and Water were present in the Annual Stems and Branches. In 1972 (Yang Water Rat year), there was a Stem Combination between the Annual Yang Water Stem and his Yin Fire Day Master. The Power Element Combination indicated professional recognition and success. James became the television critic for *The Observer*.

The Horse Luck Cycle (age 35 to 39) contained James' negative element Fire. However, James fared well in years with his favourable elements. In 1977 (Yin Fire Snake year), *Visions Before Midnight: Television Criticism from the Observer 1972 to 1976* was published. The Annual Snake Branch formed the Full Three Harmony Metal Combination with the Ox and Rooster Branches in his chart.

The Yin Earth Luck Cycle (age 40 to 44) was favourable for James as he became successful as a non-fiction author. In 1980 (Yang Metal Monkey year), James released his first autobiography, *Unreliable Memoirs*. The favourable elements Metal and Water were present in the Annual Stem and Branch. In 1981 (Yin Metal Rooster year), *The Crystal Bucket: Television Criticism from the Observer 1976 to 1979* was published. The Annual Rooster Branch reinforced the favourable element Metal by combining with the Ox and Rooster Branches in James' chart. In 1982 (Yang Water Dog year), there was a Stem Combination between the Annual Stem and his Yin Fire Day Master, indicating professional recognition and success. James left his position at The Observer and hosted *Clive James on Television*, in which he showcased amusing or unusual television programs from around the world.

The Snake Luck Cycle (age 45 to 49) formed the Full Three Harmony Metal Combination with the Ox and Rooster Branches in his chart. In 1985 (Yin Wood Ox year), his second autobiography *Falling Towards England* was published. The Annual Ox Branch combined with the Rooster and Ox Branches in his chart to reinforce the favourable element Metal. In 1988 (Yang Earth Dragon year), he moved from ITV commercial network to BBC where he started *Saturday Night Clive*. The second favourable element Earth was present in the Annual Stem and Branch.

The Yang Earth Luck Cycle (age 50 to 54) was also favourable for James as he continued his television work. In 1989 (Yin Earth Snake year), James started his travel show *Clive James' Postcard from...* The Annual Snake Branch formed the Full Three Harmony Combination with the Ox and Rooster Branches in his chart. In 1992 (Yang Water Monkey year), he was made a member of the Order of Australia (AM). There was a Stem Combination between the Annual Yang Water Stem and his Yin Fire

Day Master, indicating professional recognition and success. In 1993 (Yin Water Rooster year), the Rooster Branch combined with the Ox and Rooster Branches in James' chart. He produced the major documentary series *Fame in the 20th Century*.

While the Dragon Luck Cycle (age 55 to 59) was also favourable for James, the Yin Fire (age 60 to 64) and Rabbit (age 65 to 69) Luck Cycles contained James' negative elements Fire and Wood. The Rabbit also clashed with his Rooster Month Branch to disrupt the Partial Three Harmony Metal Combination in his chart. He was no longer a Follow the Power (Metal) chart and became more dependent on the Annual Stems and Branches. James retired from mainstream television in 2000 (Yang Metal Dragon year). In 2004 (Yang Wood Monkey year), he started his eight-year affair with model Leanne Edelsten. The negative element Wood was present in the Annual Stem.

By the Yang Fire Luck Cycle (age 70 to 74), James had reverted back to being a Follow the Wealth (Metal) chart following the disruption during the Rabbit Luck Cycle. However, the negative element Fire created issues. In 2010 (Yang Metal Tiger year), life long smoker James was diagnosed with emphysema and kidney failure. There was a Yang Fire Rival present in the Annual Tiger Branch. In 2011 (Yin Metal Rabbit year), the Annual Rabbit Branch clashed with his Rooster Month Branch, disrupting the Metal Combination in his chart. James revealed that he had chronic lymphocytic leukaemia and was placed on experimental drug therapy.

The Tiger Luck Cycle (age 75 to 79) contained the negative elements Fire and Wood. In 2016 (Yang Fire Monkey year), James revealed in an interview that his relationship with his wife has improved as she has been visiting him in his Cambridge home. She had thrown him out of the family home previously after his affair with Edelsten was revealed. The favourable elements Metal and Water were present in the Annual Branch.

Example 4.8 Al Stewart, British Singer-Songwriter
(born September 5, 1945)

Hour	Day	Month	Year
	丁	甲	乙
	Yin Fire	Yang Wood	Yin Wood
	丑	申	酉
	Ox	Monkey	Rooster

9	19	29	39
癸	壬	辛	庚
Yin Water	Yang Water	Yin Metal	Yang Metal
未	午	巳	辰
Sheep	Horse	Snake	Dragon

49	59	69	79
己	戊	丁	丙
Yin Earth	Yang Earth	Yin Fire	Yang Fire
卯	寅	丑	子
Rabbit	Tiger	Ox	Rat

There is a Partial Three Harmony Metal Combination in Stewart's birth chart. His Ox Day Branch and Rooster Year Branch combine to form Metal. There are no other Combinations in his chart. The prevalent element is Metal. As Stewart is a Yin Fire Day Master, Metal represents his Wealth. He has a Follow the Wealth (Metal) chart.

The Yang Water Luck Cycle (age 19 to 23) formed a Stem Combination with Stewart's Yin Fire Day Master, indicating professional recognition or success. Stewart signed with Columbia Records and released his debut album *Bedsitter Images* in 1967 (Yin Fire Sheep year). The favourable element Earth was present in the Annual Sheep Branch.

Although the Horse Luck Cycle (age 24 to 28) contained the negative element Fire, Stewart performed well in years with his favourable elements. Note that during this period, Stewart's music was popular with music critics but this did not translate into commercial success. In 1969 (Yin Earth Rooster year), the Annual Rooster Branch combined with the Rooster and Ox Branches in his chart to reinforce the favourable element Metal. His second album *Love Chronicles* was released. In 1970 (Yang Metal Dog year), the Annual Dog Branch combined with the Monkey and Rooster Branches in his chart to form the Seasonal Metal Combination. The favourable element Metal was also present in the Annual Stem. Stewart performed at the first ever Glastonbury Festival. His third album *Zero She Flies* was also released.

In 1972 (Yang Water Rat year), there was a Stem Combination between the Annual Stem and his Yin Fire Day Master, indicating professional success or recognition. The Annual Rat Branch also combined with his Monkey Year Branch to form a Partial Three Harmony Water Combination. As Metal produces Water, Water became the most prominent element in Stewart's chart. Stewart has the potential to become a Follow the Power (Water) chart in Rat or Dragon Luck Cycles or years. As a Follow the Power (Water) chart, his list of favourable elements becomes:

1) Power element Water.
2) Wealth element Metal.
3) Resource element Wood.
4) Self element Fire.
5) Output element Earth.

Stewart released another album, *Orange*. In 1973 (Yin Water Ox year), the Annual Ox Branch combined with the Rooster and Ox Branches in his chart to reinforce the favourable element Metal. His fifth album, *Past, Present and Future*, achieved some success in the US Album charts.

The Yin Metal Luck Cycle (age 29 to 33) contained the favourable element, and Stewart's music achieved mainstream success. In 1976 (Yang Fire Dragon year), he scored a US Top 10 hit with the title track of his platinum-selling album *Year of the Cat*. The Annual Dragon Branch combined with Stewart's Monkey Month Branch to form a Partial Three Harmony Water Combination. Stewart became a Follow the Power (Water) chart that year. In 1978 (Yang Earth Horse year), he had reverted back to a Follow the Wealth (Metal) chart. The favourable element Earth was present in the Annual Stem. Stewart had another US Top 10 hit with another title track, *Time Passages*, from another platinum-selling album.

The Snake Luck Cycle (age 34 to 38) formed the Full Three Harmony Metal Combination with the Rooster and Ox Branches in Stewart's chart. This reinforced his favourable element Metal. In 1980 (Yang Metal Monkey year), the favourable elements Metal and Water were present in the Annual Stem and Branch. Stewart released *24 Carrots*, which contained the US Top 30 single *Midnight Rocks*. In 1981 (Yin Metal Rooster year), the Annual Rooster Branch combined with the Rooster and Ox Branches in Stewart's chart to reinforce his favourable element Metal. Stewart's first live album *Live/Indian Summer* was released.

The Yang Metal Luck Cycle (age 39 to 43) was also favourable for Stewart. In 1984 (Yang Wood Rat year), the Annual Rat Branch combined with his Monkey Month Branch to form Water. He became a Follow the Power (Water) chart. Stewart released his tenth album, *Russians & Americans*. In 1988 (Yang Earth Dragon year), the Annual Dragon Branch combined with Stewart's Monkey Month Branch to form Water. He became a Follow the Power (Water) chart. Stewart released *The Last Days of the Century*.

The Dragon Luck Cycle (age 44 to 48) combined with Stewart's Monkey Month Branch to form Water. During this period, Stewart was a Follow the Power (Water) chart. In 1992 (Yang Water Monkey year), there was a Stem Combination between the Annual Stem and his Yin Fire Day Master, indicating professional recognition and success. The Annual Monkey Branch also combined with the Dragon Luck Cycle and his Monkey Month Branch to reinforce the favourable element Water. Stewart released his second live album, *Rhymes in Rooms*. In 1993 (Yin Water Rooster year), the Annual Rooster Branch combined with the Ox and Rooster Branches in Stewart's chart to reinforce his favourable element Metal. Stewart released *Famous Last Words*, an album dedicated to Peter White, his regular co-writer who died the year of its release.

The Yin Earth Luck Cycle (age 49 to 53) contained the second favourable element Earth, another favourable period for Stewart. However, the Rabbit Luck Cycle (age 54 to 58) clashed with his Rooster Year Branch, disrupting the Partial Three Harmony Metal Combination. This meant that Stewart was more dependent on the influence of the Annual Stems and Branches. In 2000 (Yang Metal Dragon year), the Annual Dragon Branch combined with Stewart's Monkey Month Branch to form Water. With the Partial Three Harmony Metal Combination disrupted, Stewart became a Follow the Power (Water) chart that year. Stewart released *Down in the Cellar*, an album inspired by wine.

As the Hour Pillar is not ascertained, it is not possible to comment with absolute certainty the direction of Stewart's chart in the latter part of his life. However, what is definite is that he continued to prosper in years when the favourable elements Metal Earth and Water were present. In 2005 (Yin Wood Rooster year) during the Yang Earth Luck Cycle (age 59 to 63), the Annual Rooster Branch combined with his Ox Day Branch to form a Partial Three Harmony Metal Combination. Stewart released *A Beach Full of Shells*.

In 2008 (Yang Earth Rat year) during the Tiger Luck Cycle (age 64 to 68), Stewart released his last album to date, *Sparks of Ancient Light*. The Annual Rat Branch combined with his Monkey Month Branch to form Water, transforming him into a Follow the Power (Water) chart. In 2009 (Yin Earth Ox year), the favourable element Earth was present in the Annual Stem and Branch. He released his third live album, *Uncorked*.

Example 4.9 Viola Davis, American Actress
(born August 11, 1965)

Hour	Day	Month	Year
	丁	甲	乙
	Yin Fire	Yang Wood	Yin Wood
	酉	申	巳
	Rooster	Monkey	Snake

9	19	29	39
乙	丙	丁	戊
Yin	Yang	Yin	Yang
Wood	Fire	Fire	Earth
酉	戌	亥	子
Rooster	Dog	Pig	Rat

49	59	69	79
己	庚	辛	壬
Yin	Yang	Yin	Yang
Earth	Metal	Metal	Water
丑	寅	卯	辰
Ox	Tiger	Rabbit	Dragon

There is a Partial Three Harmony Metal Combination in Davis' birth chart. Her Rooster Day Branch combines with her Snake Year Branch to form Metal. There is also a Six Harmony Combination between her Monkey Month Branch and the Snake Year Branch. However, when it comes to determining the prevalent element within the chart, the Three Harmony Combination takes precedence. The prevalent element within Davis' chart is Metal. As she is a Yin Fire Day Master, Metal represents her Wealth element. She has a Follow the Wealth (Metal) chart.

Davis is born on a Yin Fire Rooster day, which is one of the four days where the Day Master is sitting on its Nobleman Star. This suggests that Davis will marry a Spouse who will be of assistance to her. Her husband is actor Julius Tennon, whom she married in 2003 (Yin Water Sheep year).

In the Yang Fire Luck Cycle (age 19 to 23), Davis earned her degree in Theatre in 1988 (Yang Earth Dragon year) from Rhode Island College. The Annual Yang Earth Stem and the Yang Fire Luck Cycle gave her the auspicious sequence of 5 Stems in a Row: Yang Wood Month Stem, Yin Wood Year Stem, Yang Fire Luck Cycle, Yin Fire Day Master, Annual Yang Earth Stem.

In the Dog Luck Cycle (age 24 to 28), the Dog combined with the Rooster Day Branch and Monkey Month Branch to form the Seasonal Metal Combination. Davis remained a Follow the Wealth (Metal) chart. During this period, she attended the New York's Julliard School of Performing Arts.

The Yin Fire Luck Cycle (age 29 to 33) was challenging as the negative Self element Fire was present. Davis made her Broadway debut in the tragic comedy *Seven Guitars* in 1996 (Yang Fire Rat year). The Annual Rat Branch combined with her Monkey Month Branch to form the favourable element Water.

The Pig Luck Cycle (age 34 to 38) disrupted the Partial Three Harmony Metal Combination in Davis' chart as it clashed with her Snake Year Branch. She was more dependent on the Annual Stems and Branches for success. In 2001 (Yin Metal Snake Branch), she won her first Tony Award for her performance in *King Hedley II*. The favourable element Metal was present in the Annual Stem.

2002 (Yang Water Horse year) was a mixed year. There was a Stem Combination involving the Annual Yang Water Stem and her Yin Fire Day Master. This indicated professional success and recognition. Davis was awarded an honorary doctorate in Fine Arts from Rhode Island College. However, the Annual Horse Branch contained the negative element Fire. Davis received only supporting roles in Hollywood productions like *Antwone Fisher* (alongside Denzel Washington) and Steven Soderbergh's *Solaris* (alongside George Clooney).

In the favourable Yang Earth Luck Cycle (age 39 to 43), Davis received a Best Supporting Actress Oscar nomination for her performance in *Doubt*, where her character stands up to the principal Meryl Streep over abuse allegations. The favourable element Earth was present in both the Luck Cycle and the Annual Stem.

The Rat Luck Cycle (age 44 to 48) was also favourable as it combined with her Monkey Month Branch to form Water. In 2010 (Yang Metal Tiger year), Davis received her second Tony Award for her performance in the Broadway play *Fences* opposite Denzel Washington. The favourable element Metal was present in the Annual Stem. In 2011 (Yin Metal Rabbit year), she received her second Oscar nomination, for portraying the maid Abilene in *The Help*. The favourable element Metal was present in the Annual Stem. In 2012 (Yang Water Dragon year), there was a Stem Combination involving the Annual Yang Water Stem and her Yin Fire Day Master, which indicates professional recognition and success. *Time* magazine named Davis as one of the most influential people in the world. In 2013 (Yin Water Snake year), the Annual Snake Branch combined with her Ox Day Branch to form the favourable element Metal. Davis was elected to receive a star on the Hollywood Walk of Fame.

The Yin Earth Luck Cycle (age 49 to 53) contained her second favourable element. In 2015 (Yin Wood Sheep year), Davis became the first black woman of any nationality to win a Primetime Emmy Award for Outstanding Lead Actress in a Drama Series for her performance in *How to Get Away with Murder*. The favourable element Earth was present in the Annual Sheep Branch. In 2017 (Yin Fire Rooster year), she won a Best Supporting Actress Oscar for her performance in the movie adaptation of *Fences*. The Annual Rooster Branch combined with her Ox Day Branch to reinforce her favourable element Metal. Davis became the first black actress to win an Oscar, Emmy and Tony.

The Ox (age 54 to 58) and Yang Metal (age 59 to 63) Luck Cycles contain Davis' favourable elements, so it appears there are still more memorable performances and achievements waiting for her in the near future.

Example 4.10 Kareena Kapoor, Indian Actress
(born September 21, 1980)

Hour	Day	Month	Year
	丁	乙	庚
	Yin Fire	Yin Wood	Yang Metal
	酉	酉	申
	Rooster	Rooster	Monkey

5	15	25	35
甲	癸	壬	辛
Yang Wood	Yin Water	Yang Water	Yin Metal
申	未	午	巳
Monkey	Sheep	Horse	Snake

45	55	65	75
庚	己	戊	丁
Yang Metal	Yin Earth	Yang Earth	Yin Fire
辰	卯	寅	丑
Dragon	Rabbit	Tiger	Ox

There are no Three Harmony Combinations in Kapoor's birth chart. There are two Rooster Branches that contain only Metal. There is also a Yang Metal Year Stem and Yang Metal present within the Monkey Year Branch. The prevalent element in Kapoor's chart is Metal. As she is a Yin Fire Day Master, Metal represents her Wealth element. She has a Follow the Wealth (Metal) chart.

There is a Stem Combination between Kapoor's Yang Metal Year Stem and her Yin Wood Month Stem. The Yin Wood Stem occupies the position associated with the father and is combined away, which suggests that Kapoor did not spend time with her father when she was growing up. Her parents Randhi Kapoor and Babita separated when she was young.

Kapoor is born on a Yin Fire Rooster day, one of four days where the Day Master is sitting on top of its Nobleman Star, which suggests that Kapoor will marry a man who will assist and help her. Kapoor married fellow actor Saif Ali Khan in 2012 (Yang Water Dragon year). There was a Stem Combination with her Yin Fire Day Master. The Power Element Combination not only indicates professional recognition and success for a woman, it also implies the possibility of love or marriage. There was also a Six Harmony Combination between the Annual Dragon Branch and the Rooster in Kapoor's House of Spouse. This improves the possibility of love or marriage that year.

The House of Spouse animal Rooster is repeated in Kapoor's chart, suggesting the possibility of more than one marriage. She also has two Nobleman Stars in her chart. This indicates that she will always receive assistance from helpful individuals throughout her life.

In 2000 (Yang Metal Dragon year) during the Sheep Luck Cycle (age 20 to 24), Kapoor made her film debut alongside Abhishek Bachchan in the war drama *Refugee*. The second favourable element Earth was present in the Luck Cycle, while the favourable element Metal was in her Annual Stem. The Annual Dragon Branch combined with her Monkey Year Branch to form her third favourable element Water. It earned her the Filmfare Award for Best Female Debut.

In 2001 (Yin Metal Snake year), Kapoor appeared in the historical drama *Asoka* opposite Shah Rukh Khan and also in the blockbuster melodrama *Kabhi Kushi Kabhke Gham* alongside an ensemble cast. The Annual Snake Branch formed a Partial Three Harmony Metal Combination with the Rooster Branches in her chart. In 2004 (Yang Wood Monkey year), Kapoor earned critical acclaim for playing a sex worker in *Chameli* (opposite Rahul Bose) and a riot victim in *Dev* (alongside Amitabh Bachchan).

The Yang Water Luck Cycle (age 25 to 29) formed a Stem Combination with Kapoor's Yin Fire Day Master, which indicates professional success and recognition. In 2006 (Yang Fire Dog year), she portrayed the character of Desdemona in *Omkara*, a Hindi version of William Shakespeare's *Othello*. It premiered at the Cannes Festival that year. The second favourable element Earth was present in the Annual Branch. In 2009 (Yin Earth Ox year), the Annual Ox Branch combined with the Rooster Branches in Kapoor's chart to reinforce the favourable element Metal. She appeared as Aamir Khan's love interest in the comedy *3 Idiots*, which became the highest-grossing Bollywood film of all time up till then.

The Horse Luck Cycle (age 30 to 34) contained Kapoor's negative Self element Fire. In 2010 (Yang Metal Tiger year) and 2011 (Yin Metal Rabbit year), she appeared in box office hits that were attacked by the critics: *We Are Family* (remake of Julia Roberts' Stepmom), *Bodyguard* (opposite Salman Khan) and *Ra.One* (with Shah Rukh Khan). The favourable element Metal was present in both Annual Stems. Following her marriage to Saif Ali Khan in 2012 (Yang Water Dragon year), she took on a decreased workload to focus on family. In 2013 (Yin Water Snake year), Kapoor released her autobiography *The Style Diary of a Bollywood Diva*. The Annual Snake Branch combined with the Rooster Branches in her chart to reinforce the favourable element Metal.

The Yin Metal Luck Cycle (age 35 to 39) contained Kapoor's favourable element. In 2016 (Yang Fire Monkey year), Kapoor appeared in the hit comedy *Ki & Ka* with Arjun Kapoor. Later that year, she gave birth to her son Taimur. Her Output or Child element Earth was present in the Annual Monkey Branch.

Kapoor has several Luck Cycles ahead of her with favourable elements. The Snake Luck Cycle (age 40 to 44) combines with the Rooster Branches in her chart to form the Partial Three Harmony Metal Combination. However, as the Rooster in the House of Spouse forms a Combination with the Luck Cycle, there is also the possibility of love and marriage. The Yang Metal Luck Cycle (age 45 to 49) will also be favourable. The Dragon Luck Cycle (age 50 to 54) contains the second favourable element Earth. There is also a Six Harmony Combination with the Rooster in the House of Spouse, indicating the possibility of romance and marriage. The Yin Earth Luck Cycle (age 55 to 59) also contains the second favourable element Earth.

Example 4.11 Alexis Bledel, American Actress
(born September 16, 1981)

Hour	Day	Month	Year
	丁	丁	辛
	Yin Fire	Yin Fire	Yin Metal
	酉	酉	酉
	Rooster	Rooster	Rooster

7	17	27	37
戊	己	庚	辛
Yang	Yin	Yang	Yin
Earth	Earth	Metal	Metal
戌	亥	子	丑
Dog	Pig	Rat	Ox

47	57	67	77
壬	癸	甲	乙
Yang	Yin	Yang	Yin
Water	Water	Wood	Wood
寅	卯	辰	巳
Tiger	Rabbit	Dragon	Snake

There are no Combinations present in Bledel's birth chart. However, there are three Rooster Branches, all of which only contain Metal. There is also a Yin Metal Year Stem. The prevalent element within her chart is Metal. As Bledel is a Yin Fire Day Master, Metal represents her Wealth element. She has a Follow the Wealth (Metal) chart.

Bledel is born on a Yin Fire Rooster day, one of four days where the Day Master is sitting on its Nobleman Star. This suggests that Bledel's Spouse will provide assistance to her. Bledel started dating her husband actor Vincent Kartheiser in 2012 (Yang Water Dragon year) when they both co-starred in the television series *Mad Men*. There was a Stem Combination between the Annual Yang Water Stem and her Yin Fire Day Master. The Power Element Combination indicates professional success and recognition. For women, it also suggests the possibility of love or marriage. There was also a Six Harmony Combination between the Annual Dragon Branch and the Rooster in her House of Spouse, confirming the possibility of a romance that year.

However, note that the House of Spouse animal Rooster is present three times in Bledel's chart. This also suggests that she has a higher possibility of being married more than once. Bledel also has three Nobleman Stars in her chart. This means that she will always receive assistance from mentors throughout her life.

Bledel received her career break in 2000 (Yang Metal Dragon year) during the favourable Yin Earth Luck Cycle (age 17 to 21). Cast as the teenage daughter Rory Gilmore in the comedy-drama *Gilmore Girls*. The favourable elements Metal and Earth were present in the Annual Stem and Branch. In 2002 (Yang Water Horse year), there was a Stem Combination between the Annual Yang Water Stem and her Yin Fire Day Master. This indicated professional success and recognition. Bledel made her big screen debut in fantasy drama *Tuck Everlasting*, appearing alongside Sissy Spacek and Ben Kingsley.

The Pig Luck Cycle (age 22 to 26) contained the negative element Wood. Bledel was able to find success in years with the favourable elements. In 2005 (Yin Wood Rooster year), the Annual Rooster Branch reinforced the favourable element Metal with the other Rooster Branches in her chart. Bledel appeared in the box office hit *Sin City* alongside Bruce Willis, Jessica Alba and Clive Owen. She also starred with America Ferrara, Blake Lively and Amber Tamblyn in the *Sisterhood of the Travelling Pants*. In 2008 (Yang Earth Rat year), Bledel also appeared in the sequel *Sisterhood of the Travelling Pants 2*. The favourable elements Earth and Water were present in the Annual Stem and Branch.

The Yang Metal Luck Cycle (age 27 to 31) was very favourable for Bledel. In 2009 (Yin Earth Ox year), she had her first starring role in the comedy *Post Grad* and also appeared in the series finale of *ER*. The Annual Ox Branch formed a Partial Three Harmony Metal Combination with the Rooster Branches in her chart. In 2012 (Yang Water Dragon year), there was a Stem Combination between the Annual Yang Water Stem and her Yin Fire Day Master, indicating professional success and recognition. She guest starred in the popular television series *Mad Men*. She also met her husband Vincent Kartheiser on the series.

The Rat Luck Cycle (age 32 to 36) contained her third favourable element Water. In 2015 (Yin Wood Sheep year), Bledel gave birth to a son with Kartheiser. They had married the year before. Her Output or Child element Earth was present in the Annual Sheep Branch. In 2016 (Yang Fire Monkey year), she reprised her role for Netflix's *Gilmore Girls: A Year in the Life*. The Annual Monkey Branch combined with the Rat Luck Cycle to form the favourable element Water. In 2017 (Yin Fire Rooster year), Bledel appeared in the television series *The Handmaid's Tale*. The Annual Rooster Branch reinforced the presence of the favourable element Metal.

The Yin Metal Luck Cycle (age 37 to 41) should be favourable for Bledel, as well as the Ox Luck Cycle (age 42 to 46). The Ox will combine with the Rooster Branches in her chart to reinforce the favourable element Metal. However, there is also a Combination with the Rooster in the House of Spouse, indicating the possibility of love or marriage.

The Yang Water Luck Cycle (age 47 to 51) forms a Stem Combination with Bledel's Yin Fire Day Master, indicating professional success and the possibility of romance or marriage. The Tiger Luck Cycle (age 52 to 56) contains a Yang Fire Rival, so there may be some issues during this period. The Yin Water Luck Cycle (age 57 to 61) is once again favourable, but the Rabbit Luck Cycle (age 62 to 66) clashes with the Rooster Branches in Bledel's chart. The effects of the Annual Energies will either alleviate or magnify any complications.

Example 4.12 Steven Soderbergh,
American Film Director (born January 14, 1963)

Hour	Day	Month	Year
	丁	癸	壬
	Yin Fire	Yin Water	Yang Water
	巳	丑	寅
	Snake	Ox	Tiger

7	17	27	37
甲	乙	丙	丁
Yang Wood	Yin Wood	Yang Fire	Yin Fire
寅	卯	辰	巳
Tiger	Rabbit	Dragon	Snake

47	57	67	77
戊	己	庚	辛
Yang Earth	Yin Earth	Yang Metal	Yin Metal
午	未	申	酉
Horse	Sheep	Monkey	Rooster

There is a Partial Three Harmony Metal Combination in Soderbergh's birth chart. His Snake Day Branch combines with his Ox Month Branch to form Metal. There are no other Combinations in his chart. The prevalent element is Metal. As Soderbergh is a Yin Fire Day Master, Metal represents his Wealth element. He has a Follow the Wealth (Metal) chart.

In 1989 (Yin Earth Snake year) during the Rabbit Luck Cycle (age 22 to 26), Soderbergh won the Palme d'Or at the Cannes Film Festival for his independently filmed drama *Sex, Lies, and Videotape*. The Annual Snake Branch combined with the Snake and Ox Branches in his chart to reinforce the favourable element Metal. His House of Spouse animal was also present in the Annual Branch. Soderbergh married actress Betsy Brantley that year.

The Yang Fire Luck Cycle (age 27 to 31) was problematic for Soderbergh as it contained the negative Self element. In 1993 (Yin Water Rooster year), he directed the Depression era drama *King of the Hill*. The film fared badly at the box office. The Annual Rooster Branch formed the Full Three Harmony Metal Combination with the Snake and Ox Branches in his chart. In 1994 (Yang Wood Dog year), the Annual Dog Branch combined with Soderbergh's Tiger Year Branch to form Fire. He became a Dominant Fire chart, but there was a Fire-Metal conflict as the Snake and Rooster Combination was still present. Soderbergh's marriage to Brantley ended in divorce.

The Dragon Luck Cycle (age 32 to 36) saw Soderbergh return to form. For a Yin Fire Day Master, the Special Stars are the Tiger and Dragon. The Dragon Luck Cycle worked in conjunction with his Tiger Year Branch to bring him success. In 1998 (Yang Earth Tiger year), Soderbergh directed the stylish thriller *Out of Sight* starring George Clooney and Jennifer Lopez. The Annual Stem contained the second favourable element Earth.

The Yin Fire Luck Cycle (age 37 to 41) contained the negative Self element Fire. However, Soderbergh's Yang Water Year Stem was able to form a Stem Combination with it and reduce its negative effects. In 2000 (Yang Metal Dragon year), Soderbergh directed two major box office hits: *Erin Brockovich* with Best Actress Oscar winner Julia Robers and *Traffic* with Michael Douglas and Catherine Zeta Jones. He won the Oscar for Best Director for *Traffic*. The Annual Dragon Branch worked in conjunction with his Tiger Year Branch to bring him success. In 2001 (Yin Metal Snake year), the Annual Snake Branch combined with the Snake and Ox Branches in his chart to reinforce the favourable element Metal. Soderbergh directed the successful remake of *Ocean's Eleven* with George Clooney, Brad Pitt, Matt Damon and Julia Roberts. 2002 (Yang Water Horse year) was a mixed year for Soderbergh. There was a Stem Combination between the Annual Yang Water Stem and his Yin Fire Day Master. This indicated professional success and recognition. The Annual Horse Branch also combined with his Tiger Year Branch to transform him into a Dominant Fire chart. His list of favourable elements became:

1) Resource element Wood.
2) Self element Fire.
3) Output element Earth.
4) Wealth element Metal.
5) Power element Water.

However, there is a Metal-Fire conflict present within his chart. Soderbergh directed the science fiction remake *Solaris* and the experimental *Full Frontal*. They were critically acclaimed but performed badly at the box office.

The Snake Luck Cycle (age 42 to 46) combined with the Snake and Ox Branches in Soderbergh's chart to reinforce the favourable element Metal. Soderbergh took more of an interest in producing. In 2005 (Yin Wood Rooster year), the Annual Rooster Branch formed the Full Three Harmony Metal Combination with the Snake Luck Cycle and Day Branch and the Ox Month Branch. He produced two box office hits starring George Clooney, spy thriller *Syriana* and drama *Good Night, and Good Luck*. In 2009 (Yin Earth Ox year), he directed the comedy caper film *The Informant* starring Matt Damon. The Annual Snake Branch combined with the Snake and Ox Branches in Soderbergh's chart, as well as the Snake Luck Cycle to reinforce Metal.

The Yang Earth Luck Cycle (age 47 to 51) contained the second favourable element Earth. In 2012 (Yang Water Dragon year), Soderbergh released two movies: the action packed *Haywire* with Michael Fassbender and the stripper comedy *Magic Mike* with Channing Tatum. There was a Stem Combination between the Annual Yang Water Stem and his Yin Fire Day Master suggesting professional success and recognition. As one of the Special Stars, the Annual Dragon Branch also worked in conjunction with his Tiger Year Branch to bring him success. In 2013 (Yin Water Snake year), Soderbergh directed the Liberace biopic *Behind the Candelabra* starring Michael Douglas and Matt Damon. Released as a television movie in the US, it won a Best Actor Emmy for Michael Douglas. The Annual Snake Branch combined with the Ox and Snake Branches in Soderbergh's chart to reinforce the favourable element Metal. In 2014 (Yang Wood Horse year), Soderbergh announced that he was taking a break. The negative element Fire was present in the Annual Branch.

The Horse Luck Cycle (age 52 to 56) contains the negative Fire element, so there may be some challenges for Soderbergh during this period. By his 50s, the Year Pillar is no longer exerting its influence, so the Horse Luck Cycle is unable to combine with the Tiger Year Branch. In 2017 (Yin Fire Rooster year), Soderbergh returned to direction with the heist film *Logan Lucky*, starring Channing Tatum and Daniel Craig. The Annual Rooster Branch formed the Full Three Harmony Combination with the Snake and Rooster Branches in his chart. However, the negative element Fire was present in the Luck Cycle and Annual Branch. The film struggled at the box office. The Yin Earth Luck Cycle (age 57 to 61) will be more favourable as his second favourable element will be present.

Example 4.13 Vanessa Redgrave, British Actress
(born January 30, 1937, 18:00 hours)

Hour	Day	Month	Year
己	丁	辛	丙
Yin Earth	Yin Fire	Yin Metal	Yang Fire
酉	巳	丑	子
Rooster	Snake	Ox	Rat

8	18	28	38
庚	己	戊	丁
Yang Metal	Yin Earth	Yang Earth	Yin Fire
子	亥	戌	酉
Rat	Pig	Dog	Rooster

48	58	68	78
丙	乙	甲	癸
Yang Fire	Yin Wood	Yang Wood	Yin Water
申	未	午	巳
Monkey	Sheep	Horse	Snake

There is a Full Three Harmony Metal Combination in Redgrave's birth chart. Her Snake Day Branch combines with her Ox Month Branch and Rooster Hour Branch to form Metal. There are no other Branch Combinations in her chart. The prevalent element in her chart is Metal. For a Yin Fire Day Master like Redgrave, Metal represents the Wealth element. She has a Follow the Wealth (Metal) chart.

The Nobleman Stars for a Yin Fire Day Master are the Rooster and Pig. Redgrave has a Rooster Hour Branch, which occupies the sector associated with the daughter. The Rooster Hour Branch is also involved in a Three Harmony Combination that allows Redgrave to Follow the Wealth. This suggests that her daughters will be able to provide assistance to her. Redgrave enjoyed a good relationship with her late daughter Natasha Richardson and is also close to younger daughter Joely Richardson.

During the favourable Yin Earth Luck Cycle (age 18 to 22), Redgrave made her professional debut in the play *A Touch of the Sun* in 1957 (Yin Fire Rooster year). The Annual Rooster Branch combined with the Snake Day Branch and Ox Month Branch in her chart to form the Full Three Harmony Metal Combination. Note that at this stage, the Rooster Hour Branch had yet to exert its effect.

In the Pig Luck Cycle (age 23 to 27), the Pig clashed with the Snake Day Branch, disrupting the Three Harmony Combination. It formed the Seasonal Water Combination with the Rat Year Branch and Ox Month Branch. The prevalent element became Water. Redgrave became a Follow the Power (Water) chart. Her list of favourable elements became:

1) Power element Water.
2) Wealth element Metal.
3) Resource element Wood.
4) Self element Fire.
5) Output element Earth.

In 1960 (Yang Metal Rat year), Redgrave had her first starring role on stage in Robert Bolt's *The Tiger and the Horse*, in which she appeared with her father, Sir Michael Redgrave. The favourable elements Metal and Water were present in the Annual Stem and Branch. On a personal note, she married director Tony Richardson in 1962 (Yang Water Tiger year). There was a Stem Combination between the Annual Yang Water Stem and her Yin Fire Day Master, indicating professional success and recognition. For women, it also suggests the possibility of love or marriage. She also became pregnant and had her daughters Natasha and Joely Richardson in years when the

Output or Child element Earth was present. Redgrave became pregnant in 1962 (Yang Water Tiger year) and Natasha Richardson was born in May 1963 (Yin Water Rabbit year). Joely Richardson was born in January 1965 (still the Yang Wood Dragon year). Earth was present in the both the Annual Tiger and Dragon Branches.

In the favourable Yang Earth Luck Cycle (age 28 to 32), Redgrave had reverted to a Follow the Wealth chart. 1967 (Yin Fire Sheep year) was a mixed year for her. She appeared opposite Richard Harris in the musical *Camelot*, but she also divorced Richardson after he left her for French actress Jeanne Moreau. There was a Yin Fire Rival present in the Annual Stem and also the second favourable element Earth in the Annual Branch. In 1968 (Yang Fire Monkey year), Redgrave received a Best Actress Oscar nomination for portraying dancer Isadora Duncan in the biopic *Isadora*. The Annual Monkey Branch combined with her Rat Year Branch to form Water. The second favourable element Earth was also present in the Annual Stem. In 1969 (Yin Earth Rooster year), Redgrave had son, Carlo Gabriel Nero, from her relationship with Italian actor Franco Nero. Her Child element Earth was present in the Annual Stem.

The Dog Luck Cycle (age 33 to 37) contained the favourable element Earth. In 1973 (Yin Water Ox year), she portrayed New Zealand Katherine Mansfield in the television series *A Picture of Katherine Mansfield*. The Annual Ox Branch combined with the Ox and Snake Branches in her chart to reinforce the favourable element Metal.

The Yin Fire Luck Cycle (age 38 to 42) contained the negative Self element Fire. In 1977 (Yin Fire Snake year), Redgrave was involved in controversy when she produced and narrated *The Palestinian*, a documentary about the Palestinian situation and the Palestinian Liberation Organization (PLO). She also received a Best Supporting Actress Oscar nomination for her performance in *Julia*.

There was a Fire Rival present in the Annual Stem. However, the Annual Snake Branch combined with the Snake, Rooster and Ox Branches in her chart to reinforce the favourable element Metal. In 1978 (Yang Earth Horse year), Redgrave had to contend with protesters outside the auditorium when she won the Best Supporting Actress Oscar. While the favourable Earth was present in the Annual Stem, the Annual Horse Branch contained the negative element Fire.

The Rooster Luck Cycle (age 43 to 47) combined with the Ox, Snake and Rooster Branches in her chart to reinforce the favourable element Metal. In 1984 (Yang Wood Rat year), Redgrave received another Best Actress nomination for her performance in the Merchant Ivory production *The Bostonians*. The Annual Rat Branch combined with her Monkey Year Branch to form the favourable element Water.

The Yang Fire Luck Cycle (age 48 to 52) formed a Stem Combination with her Yin Metal Month Stem, which occupies the sector associated with the Father. While the threat posed by the Yang Fire Rival is reduced, it also removes the favourable Yin Metal Stem. In 1985 (Yin Wood Ox year), Redgrave lost her father, Sir Michael to Parkinson's Disease.

The Monkey Luck Cycle (age 53 to 57) contained the favourable elements Water and Metal. In 1992 (Yang Water Monkey year), Redgrave received a Best Supporting Actress Oscar nomination for her performance in *Howard's End*. There was a Stem Combination with her Yin Fire Day Master, indicating professional success and recognition.

The Yin Wood (age 58 to 62) contained the negative element Wood, while the Sheep Luck Cycle (age 63 to 67) clashed with her Ox Month Branch, disrupting the Three Harmony Metal Combination. However, there was still a Partial Three Harmony Combination between Redgrave's Snake Day Branch and the Rooster Hour Branch, so she remained a Follow the Wealth chart. Redgrave fared well in years with the favourable elements Metal and Earth. In 2000 (Yang Metal Dragon year), Redgrave's performance as a grieving lesbian in the television series *If These Walls Could Talk 2* won her an Emmy Award for Outstanding Supporting Actress in a Television Film or Miniseries. The favourable elements Metal and Earth were present in the Annual Stem and Branch.

The Yang Wood (age 68 to 72) and Horse (age 73 to 77) Luck Cycles contained the negative elements Wood and Fire. Within 14 months in 2009 (Yin Earth Ox year) and 2010 (Yang Metal Tiger year), Redgrave lost her daughter Natasha and siblings Corin and Lynn. Daughter Natasha died after sustaining a traumatic head injury in a skiing accident. Brother Corin had prostate cancer and sister Lynn breast cancer. In April 2015 (Yin Wood Sheep year), Redgrave had a near fatal heart attack. She also revealed that year that her lungs were only at 30 per cent capacity following years of smoking. The Yin Water Luck Cycle (age 78 to 82) contains the favourable element Water, so Redgrave's health issues should improve during this period.

Example 4.14 Joan Lunden,
American Television Journalist (born September 19, 1950)

Hour	Day	Month	Year
	丁	乙	庚
	Yin Fire	Yin Wood	Yang Metal
	巳	酉	寅
	Snake	Rooster	Tiger

4	14	24	34
甲	癸	壬	辛
Yang	Yin	Yang	Yin
Wood	Water	Water	Metal
申	未	午	巳
Monkey	Sheep	Horse	Snake

44	54	64	74
庚	己	戊	丁
Yang	Yin	Yang	Yin
Metal	Earth	Earth	Fire
辰	卯	寅	丑
Dragon	Rabbit	Tiger	Ox

There is a Partial Three Harmony Metal Combination in Lunden's birth chart. Her Snake Day Branch combined with her Rooster Month Branch to form Metal. There are no other Branch Combinations in her chart. Metal is the prevalent element. As Lunden is a Yin Fire Day Master, Metal represents her Wealth element. She has a Follow the Wealth (Metal) chart.

There is a Stem Combination between the Yang Metal Year Stem and Yin Wood Month Stem. The Yin Wood that occupies the position indicating the Father is removed. It suggests that Lunden did not spend time with her father when she was growing up. She lost her father, a surgeon and pilot, in a plane crash when she was 13.

The Sheep Luck Cycle (age 19 to 23) contained the second favourable element Earth. Lunden earned a degree in Liberal Arts from California State University, Sacramento. In 1973 (Yin Water Ox year), she was hired as a trainee at Sacramento station KCRA. The Annual Ox Branch combined with the Snake and Rooster Branches in her chart to form the Full Three Harmony Meal Combination.

The Yang Water Luck Cycle (age 24 to 28) formed a Stem Combination with Lunden's Yin Fire Day Master. The Power Element Combination indicates professional success and recognition. In 1976 (Yang Fire Dragon year), Lunden joined the American Broadcasting Corporation (ABC) national program *Good Morning America (GMA)* as a feature news/consumer reporter. For a Yin Fire Day Master like Lunden, the Special Stars are the Tiger and Dragon. The Annual Dragon Branch worked in conjunction with her Tiger Year Branch to bring her success. For a woman, the Combination with the Power Element can also suggest love or marriage. Lunden married television producer and radio interviewer Michael A. Krauss during this period in 1978 (Yang Earth Horse year).

During the Horse Luck Cycle (age 29 to 33), there was a Combination between her Tiger Year Branch and the Horse Luck Cycle. This transformed Lunden into a Dominant Fire chart. Her list of favourable elements became:

1) Resource element Wood.
2) Self element Fire.
3) Output element Earth.
4) Wealth element Metal.
5) Power element Water.

In 1980 (Yang Metal Monkey year), Lunden was promoted to co-host GMA with David Hartman. There was a clash between the Annual Monkey Branch and the

Tiger Year Branch. This reverted Lunden back to a Follow the Wealth (Metal) chart. Her favourable elements Metal and Water were present in the Annual Stem and Branch. In 1983 (Yin Water Pig year), Lunden was one of three journalists to interview Prince Charles on his visit to the United States. The favourable Resource element Wood was present in the Annual Pig Branch.

Lunden's success continued in the favourable Yin Metal Luck Cycle (age 34 to 38). In 1986 (Yang Fire Tiger year), her autobiography *I'm Joan Lunden, Good Morning* was published, as well as a book on motherhood, *Joan Luden's Mother Minutes*. The Yin Metal Luck Cycle combined with the Yang Fire Rival in the Annual Stem, reducing any complications. In 1988 (Yang Earth Dragon year), she travelled to Calgary to cover the Winter Olympics. The Annual Dragon Branch worked in conjunction with her Tiger Year Branch to bring her success. She also wrote an infant care book, *Your Newborn Baby: Everything You Need to Know*.

The Snake Luck Cycle (age 39 to 43) was favourable as the Snake combined with the Rooster and Ox Branches in her chart to form the Full Three Harmony Metal Combination. From 1989 (Yin Earth Snake year) to 1991 (Yin Metal Sheep year), Lunden hosted ABC's broadcast of the *Rose Parade* in Pasadena, California. The Annual Snake Branch in 1989 combined with the Rooster and Ox Branches and the Snake Luck Cycle to reinforce the favourable element Metal. In 1991, New York Women in Communications honoured Lunden with an award for outstanding contribution to broadcasting. Her favourable elements Metal and Earth were present in the Annual Stem and Branch. In 1992 (Yang Water Monkey year), there was a Six Harmony Combination between the Annual Monkey Branch and her Snake Branch in the House of Spouse. Lunden divorced from her first husband Michael A. Knauss.

The Yang Metal Luck Cycle (age 44 to 48) was also favourable. In 1997 (Yin Fire Ox year), Lunden left GMA in June (Horse month). The negative Self element Fire was present in the Annual Stem and the month. However, the Annual Ox Branch combined with the Rooster and Snake Branches in her chart to form the Full Three Harmony Metal Combination. Lunden continued working in television as an investigative reporter in the series *Behind Closed Doors with Joan Lunden*. In 1998 (Yang Earth Tiger year), the second favourable element Earth was present in the Annual Stem. Lunden's book *A Bend in the Road is not The End of the Road* was published.

The Dragon (age 49 to 53) and Yin Earth (age 54 to 58) Luck Cycles contained Lunden's second favourable element. The Dragon Luck Cycle also worked in conjunction with her Tiger Year Branch to bring her success. During that period, she married summer camp owner Jeff Konigsberg in 2000 (Yang Metal Dragon year). In 2003 (Yin Water Sheep year), she welcomed her first set of twins born through a surrogate. Her second favourable element Earth was present in the Annual Branch. In 2005 (Yin Wood Rooster year), her second set of twins was born through the same surrogate. The Annual Rooster Branch combined with the Snake and Rooster Branches in her chart to reinforce the favourable element Metal.

The Rabbit Luck Cycle (age 59 to 63) clashed with her Rooster Month Branch, disrupting the Three Harmony Metal Combination and her Follow the Metal status. In 2014 (Yang Wood Horse year) during the Yang Earth Luck Cycle (age 64 to 68), Lunden announced that she had breast cancer on *Good Morning America*. The negative Self element Fire was present in the Annual Branch. In 2015 (Yin Wood Sheep year), Lunden announced she was cancer free following nine months of treatment including surgery, radiation and chemotherapy. Her second favourable element Earth was present in the Annual Branch.

Example 4.15 Lindsey Buckingham,
American Musician (born October 3, 1949)

Hour	Day	Month	Year
	丙	癸	己
	Yang Fire	Yin Water	Yin Earth
	寅	酉	丑
	Tiger	Rooster	Ox

8	18	28	38
壬	辛	庚	己
Yang Water	Yin Metal	Yang Metal	Yin Earth
申	未	午	巳
Monkey	Sheep	Horse	Snake

48	58	68	78
戊	丁	丙	乙
Yang Earth	Yin Fire	Yang Fire	Yin Wood
辰	卯	寅	丑
Dragon	Rabbit	Tiger	Ox

There is a Partial Three Harmony Combination in Buckingham's birth chart. His Rooster Month Branch and Ox Year Branch combine to form Metal. There are no other Combinations present in the chart. The prevalent element is Metal. As Buckingham is a Yang Fire Day Master, Metal represents his Wealth element. He has a Follow the Wealth (Metal) chart.

Buckingham is born on a Yang Fire Tiger day, one of the Red Light Pillars. This indicates turbulent personal relationships. There is also a Yang Fire Rival hidden within the Tiger in the House of Spouse, which suggests that his Spouse may cause issues for him. He started his relationship with singer Stevie Nicks in 1970 (Yang Metal Dog year). There was a Combination between the Annual

Dog Branch and the Tiger in his House of Spouse. Their relationship ended in 1975 (Yin Wood Rabbit year), and Buckingham has written about their relationship in their band *Fleetwood Mac*'s and his own songs.

In 1973 (Yin Water Ox year) during the Sheep Luck Cycle (age 23 to 27), Buckingham and girlfriend Nicks released their debut album, *Buckingham Nicks*. The Sheep Luck Cycle clashed with his Ox Year Branch to disrupt the Metal Combination. Their record label dropped them due to poor sales. However, their work gained the attention of Mick Fleetwood, and they joined *Fleetwood Mac*.

The Yang Metal Luck Cycle (age 28 to 32) was favourable for Buckingham. In 1977 (Yin Fire Snake year), *Fleetwood Mac* released *Rumours*, which chronicled the breakup of the relationships between band members. It became the second biggest selling album of all time (40 million copies worldwide) and produced the hits *Go Your Own Way*, *Don't Stop* and *Dreams*. The Annual Snake Branch formed the Full Three Harmony Metal Combination with the Rooster and Ox Branches in Buckingham's chart. In 1979 (Yin Earth Sheep year), follow-up album *Tusk* was released. The second favourable element Earth was present in the Annual Stem and Branch. In 1981 (Yin Metal Rooster year), Buckingham released his first solo album *Law and Order* with the US Top 10 Single *Trouble*. The Annual Rooster Branch combined with the Ox and Rooster Branches in his chart to reinforce the favourable element Metal.

The Horse Luck Cycle (age 33 to 37) combined with the Tiger Day Branch to transform Buckingham into a Dominant Fire chart. His list of favourable elements became:

1) Resource element Wood.
2) Self element Fire.
3) Output element Earth.
4) Wealth element Metal.
5) Power element Water.

However, the Metal Combination was still present in his chart, resulting in a Fire-Metal conflict. Buckingham did not release much material during this period, apart from his second solo album *Go Insane* in 1984 (Yang Wood Rat year). While the favourable Resource element Wood was present in the Annual Stem, the negative Power element Water was present in the Annual Rat Branch. *Go Insane* was not as successful as the first album.

The Yin Earth Luck Cycle (age 38 to 42) was more favourable for Buckingham. *Fleetwood Mac* reunited to release *Tango in the Night* in 1987 (Yin Fire Rabbit year). Although the album was extremely successful with hits like *Big Love*, Buckingham left Fleetwood Mac as he was tired of touring and needed time away from the strained relationships within the band, especially with his ex Stevie Nicks. The negative elements Fire and Wood were present in the Annual Stem and Branch.

The Snake Luck Cycle (age 43 to 47) combined with the Ox and Rooster Branches in Buckingham's chart to form the Full Three Harmony Metal Combination. In 1992 (Yang Water Monkey year), there was a Stem Combination between the Annual Yang Water Stem and his Yin Fire Day Master. This indicated professional success and recognition. Buckingham released his third solo album *Out of the Cradle*. In January 1993 (still Yang Water Monkey year), Buckingham rejoined *Fleetwood Mac* to perform at President Bill Clinton's Inauguration. Clinton had used *Don't Stop* extensively during his campaign.

In the favourable Yang Earth (age 48 to 52) and Dragon (age 53 to 57) Luck Cycles, Buckingham recorded and toured with *Fleetwood Mac*. In 1997 (Yin Fire Ox year), Buckingham officially rejoined *Fleetwood Mac*, and the group released the successful live album *The Dance*, which was another US Number 1 album. The Annual Ox Branch combined with the Rooster and Ox Branches in his chart to reinforce the favourable element Metal. In 1998 (Yang Earth Tiger year), the group was inducted into the Rock and Roll Hall of Fame. The second favourable element Earth was present in the Annual Stem. Buckingham also became a father that year when girlfriend Kristen Messner gave birth to their son William Gregory. On a personal note, Buckingham married Messner in 2000 (Yang Earth Dragon year). She also gave birth to his second child Leelee that year. The Annual Dragon Branch and his Tiger Day Branch worked together to give him happiness and fulfilment.

In 2003 (Yin Water Sheep year), *Say You Will* was released, entering the US Album charts at Number 3. Earth was present in the Annual Sheep Branch. In 2006 (Yang Fire Dog year) with the favourable element Earth in the Annual Branch, Buckingham released his fourth solo album *Under the Skin*.

The Yin Fire (age 58 to 62) and Rabbit (age 63 to 67) contained the negative elements Fire and Wood. The Rabbit also clashed with Buckingham's Rooster Month Branch to disrupt the Metal Combination. He was more dependent on the Annual Stem and Branch. In 2012 (Yang Water Dragon year), Buckingham embarked on a solo US tour. The Annual Yang Water formed a Stem Combination with his Yin Fire Day Master, indicating professional success and recognition. The Annual Dragon Branch also worked in conjunction with his Tiger Day Branch to bring him success. For a Yang Fire Day Master, the Special Stars are the Tiger and Dragon.

The Yang Fire Luck Cycle (age 68 to 72) contains the negative Self element. This may be an unsettling period for him.

Example 4.16 David Copperfield, American Illusionist
(born September 16, 1956, 07:02 hours)

Hour	Day	Month	Year
壬	丙	丁	丙
Yang Water	Yang Fire	Yin Fire	Yang Fire
辰	戌	酉	申
Dragon	Dog	Rooster	Monkey

7	17	27	37
戊	己	庚	辛
Yang Earth	Yin Earth	Yang Metal	Yin Metal
戌	亥	子	丑
Dog	Pig	Rat	Ox

47	57	67	77
壬	癸	甲	乙
Yang Water	Yin Water	Yang Wood	Yin Wood
寅	卯	辰	巳
Tiger	Rabbit	Dragon	Snake

There is a Seasonal Metal Combination present in Copperfield's birth chart. His Dog Day Branch, Rooster Month Branch and Monkey Year Branch combine to form Metal. In spite of the Yin Fire Month Stem and the Yang Fire Year Stem, the prevalent element is Metal. As Copperfield is a Yang Fire Day Master, Metal represents his Wealth element. He has a Follow the Wealth (Metal) chart.

At the age of 12 in 1968 (Yang Earth Monkey year) during the favourable Dog Luck Cycle (age 12 to 16), Copperfield became the youngest person admitted into the Society of American Magicians. The favourable element Earth was present in the Annual Stem.

During the favourable Yin Earth Luck Cycle (age 17 to 21), Copperfield left Fordham University to play the lead role in the musical *The Magic Man* in Chicago in 1974 (Yang Wood Tiger year). The Annual Tiger Branch clashed with his Monkey Year Branch, disrupting the Seasonal Metal Combination. It also combined with the Dog Day Branch, transforming him into a Dominant Fire chart for that year. His list of favourable elements became:

1) Resource element Wood.
2) Self element Fire.
3) Output element Earth.
4) Wealth element Metal.
5) Power element Water.

In 1977 (Yin Fire Snake year), Copperfield had reverted to a Follow the Wealth (Metal) chart. He had his first television special, *The Magic of ABC*. The Annual Snake Branch combined with his Rooster Month Branch to reinforce his favourable element Metal.

The Pig Luck Cycle (age 22 to 26) was also favourable for Copperfield. It gave him the auspicious sequence of four Branches: Monkey Day Branch, Rooster Month Branch, Dog Year Branch, Pig Luck Cycle. In 1980 (Yang Metal Monkey year), he made his movie debut portraying a magician in the horror film *Terror Train* starring Jamie Lee Curtis. The favourable elements Metal and Water were present in the Annual Stem and Branch. In 1981 (Yin Metal Rooster year), Copperfield performed an illusion involving the disappearance of a Learjet. The favourable element Metal was present in the Annual Stem and Branch. In 1982 (Yang Water Dog year), there was a Stem Combination between the Annual Yang Water Stem and Copperfield's Yin Fire Day Master. The Power Element Combination indicates professional recognition and success. Copperfield founded Project Magic, a rehabilitation program that helps patients regain dexterity by using sleight-of-hand magic as a form of physical therapy.

In the favourable Yang Metal Luck Cycle (age 27 to 31), Copperfield made the Statue of Liberty vanish and reappear in 1983 (Yin Water Pig year). The Annual Pig Branch gave Copperfield the favourable sequence of four Branches: Monkey Year Branch, Rooster Month Branch, Dog Day Branch, Annual Pig Branch. In 1986 (Yang Fire Tiger year), the Annual Tiger Branch clashed with the Monkey Year Branch disrupting the Seasonal Metal Combination. It also combined with the Dog Day Branch to transform Copperfield into a Dominant Fire chart. His list of favourable elements became:

1) Resource element Wood.
2) Self element Fire.
3) Output element Earth.
4) Wealth element Metal.
5) Power element Water.

He performed walking through The Great Wall of China.

The Rat Luck Cycle (age 32 to 36) combined with the Monkey Year Branch to form a Partial Three Harmony Water Combination. Copperfield became a Follow the Power (Water) chart. His list of favourable elements became:

1) Power element Water.
2) Wealth element Metal.
3) Resource element Wood.
4) Self element Fire.
5) Output element Earth.

In 1992 (Yang Water Monkey year), Copperfield flew on stage for several minutes. The Annual Monkey Branch combined with the Monkey Year Branch and Rat Luck Cycle to reinforce the favourable element Water.

The Yin Metal Luck Cycle (age 37 to 41) combined with Copperfield's Yang Fire Day Master, indicating wealth or income. For a man, the Wealth element also indicates the Spouse, so the prospect of romance or marriage is 'on the cards'. In 1993 (Yin Water Rooster year), Copperfield met

German model Claudia Schiffer and by January 1994 (still the Yin Water Rooster year), they were engaged. In 1994 (Yang Wood Dog year), the negative Wood element was present. Copperfield unsuccessfully sued magician and author Herbert L. Becker to prevent publication of Becker's book that reveals how magicians perform their illusions. However, the favourable element Earth was present in the Annual Branch. Becker's publisher removed the section on Copperfield as an independent source had found Becker's description of Copperfield's techniques inaccurate. In 1996 (Yang Fire Rat year), Copperfield's Broadway show *Dreams & Nightmares* broke box office records. He also joined forces with Dean Koontz, Ray Bradbury, Joyce Carol Oates and others for *David Copperfield's Tales of the Impossible*, an anthology of fiction set in the world of magic and illusion. The Annual Rat Branch combined with his Monkey Year Branch to transform him into a Follow the Power (Water) chart.

The Ox Luck Cycle (age 42 to 46) combined with Copperfield's Rooster Month Branch to reinforce his Follow the Wealth (Metal) status. In 1999 (Yin Earth Rabbit year), there was a clash between the Annual Rabbit Branch and his Rooster Month Branch, disrupting his Seasonal Metal Combination. He separated from Schiffer. In 2001 (Yin Metal Snake year), Copperfield performed at the White House benefit for UNICEF the illusion of sawing singer and actress Jennifer Lopez into six pieces. The Annual Snake Branch combined with the Ox Luck Cycle and the Rooster Month Branch to form the Full Three Harmony Metal Combination. In 2002 (Yang Water Horse year), there was a Stem Combination between the Annual Yang Water Stem and his Yin Fire Day Master, indicating professional success and recognition. Copperfield was the subject of an hour-long television biography special.

In the Yang Water Luck Cycle (age 47 to 51), there was a Stem Combination between the Yang Water and his Yin Fire Day Master, indicating professional success and recognition. In 2006 (Yang Fire Dog year), Copperfield bought 11 islands in the Bahamas that he named Musha Cay and developed into a private island resort. The second favourable element Earth was present in the Annual Stem and Branch. In 2007 (Yin Fire Pig year), the negative elements Fire and Wood were present. He was involved in legal action regarding his cancelled shows in Jakarta. His Indonesian promoter held onto more than half a million US dollars worth of equipment in lieu of money paid to Copperfield that had not been returned. The case was resolved in 2009 (Yin Earth Ox year). That same year, Copperfield was accused of sexual assault, but a federal grand jury closed the case in January 2010 (still Yin Earth Ox year) without bringing charges against Copperfield.

The Tiger Luck Cycle (age 52 to 56) clashed with his Monkey Year Branch, disrupting the Seasonal Metal Combination. It also combined with Copperfield's Dog Day Branch, transforming him into a Dominant Fire chart. In 2009 (Yin Earth Ox year), lawsuits involved cancelled concerts in Jakarta and alleged sexual assault were resolved. The third favourable element Earth was present in the Annual Stem and Branch. In 2012 (Yang Water Dragon year), there was a Stem Combination with the Yin Fire Day Master, indicating professional success and recognition. The Annual Dragon Branch and the Tiger Luck Cycle also worked together as the Special Stars to bring him success. The Oprah Winfrey Television Network screened a one-hour special about Copperfield as part of the *Oprah's Next Chapter* series.

In the Yin Water Luck Cycle (age 57 to 61), the Monkey Year Branch has already lost its influence. The prevalent element in Copperfield's chart became Earth. He became a Follow the Output (Earth) chart. The list of favourable elements will be:

1) Output element Earth.
2) Wealth element Metal.
3) Power element Water.
4) Self element Fire.
5) Resource element Wood.

The Rabbit (age 62 to 66) and Yang Wood (age 67 to 71) Luck Cycles contain the negative element Wood, so there may be some issues and complications during this period. Copperfield will now be more dependent on the Annual Stem and Branch.

Example 4.17 Carolyn Bessette,
American Publicist and wife of John F. Kennedy Jr.
(born January 7, 1966, 08:45 hours, died July 16, 1999)

Hour	Day	Month	Year
壬	丙	己	乙
Yang Water	Yang Fire	Yin Earth	Yin Wood
辰	寅	丑	巳
Dragon	Tiger	Ox	Snake

9	19	29
庚	辛	壬
Yang Metal	Yin Metal	Yang Water
寅	卯	
Tiger	Rabbit	

Hour	Day	Month	Year
	己	辛	己
	Yin Earth	Yin Metal	Yin Earth
	巳	未	卯
	Snake	Sheep	Rabbit

There is a Partial Three Harmony Metal Combination in Bessette's birth chart. Her Ox Month Branch and Snake Month Branch combine to form Metal. There is also a Yin Earth Month Stem that further supports Metal. There are no other Combinations present within the chart. The prevalent element is Metal. As Bessette is a Yang Fire Day Master, Metal represents her Wealth element. She has a Follow the Wealth chart.

For a Yang Fire Day Master like Bessette, her Special Stars are the Tiger and Dragon. They are both present in her chart as she has a Tiger Day Branch and a Dragon Hour Branch. However, the Hour Pillar only exerts its influence after the age of 40. Bessette would have enjoyed more success if not for her untimely demise.

Bessette is born on a Yang Fire Tiger day, one of the eight Red Light Pillars. This indicated that her marriage and personal relationships tended to be volatile. There is also a Yang Fire Rival and negative Yang Wood hidden within the Tiger in the House of Spouse. This also suggested that her relationship with her Spouse would have been turbulent.

In the Tiger Luck Cycle (age 14 to 18), Bessette's House of Spouse animal was present in the Luck Cycle, indicating the possibility of romance or marriage. After graduating from high school in 1983 (Yin Water Pig year), she went on to study at Boston University School of Education. While an undergraduate, she dated fellow student John Cullen, who would become a professional National Hockey League (NHL) player.

Upon graduation, Bessette worked for American fashion house Calvin Klein. She began as a salesperson in Boston's Chestnut Hill Mall store to being promoted to director of publicity at the flagship store in Manhattan. This was during the favourable Yin Metal (age 19 to 23) and Rabbit (age 24 to 28) Luck Cycles. There was a Stem Combination between the Yin Metal Luck Cycle and Bessette's Yang Fire Day Master. The Wealth Element Combination indicated the possibility of generating wealth and income.

The Rabbit Luck Cycle also gave Bessette success as the favourable 4 Branches in a Row Configuration appeared: Ox Month Branch, Tiger Day Branch, Rabbit Luck Cycle and Dragon Hour Branch. This suggested that the Rabbit Luck Cycle was also successful for Bessette. In 1994 (Yang Wood Dog year), Bessette started dating John F. Kennedy Jr. The Annual Dog Branch combined with her Tiger in the House of Spouse, indicating the possibility of romance or marriage.

In the Yang Water Luck Cycle (from age 29), the engagement between Bessette and John F. Kennedy Jr. was announced in 1995 (Yin Wood Pig year). There was a Six Harmony Combination between the Annual Pig Branch and the Tiger in the House of Spouse. She married John F. Kennedy Jr. in a private ceremony in 1996 (Yang Fire Rat year). On July 16, 1999, Bessette died with her husband and sister Lauren when the private plane her husband was piloting crashed off the coast of Martha's Vineyard, Massachusetts.

On the day of the accident, there was a Partial Three Harmony Metal Combination between the Snake Day and the Snake and Ox Branches within Bessette's chart. There was also a Partial Three Harmony Wood Combination between the Sheep month and the Annual Rabbit Branch, resulting in a Metal-Wood conflict.

Example 4.18 Sarah McLachlan, Canadian Singer
(born January 28, 1968, 04:00 hours)

Hour	Day	Month	Year
壬	丁	癸	丁
Yang Water	Yin Fire	Yin Water	Yin Fire
寅	酉	丑	未
Tiger	Rooster	Ox	Sheep

3	13	23	33
甲	乙	丙	丁
Yang Wood	Yin Wood	Yang Fire	Yin Fire
寅	卯	辰	巳
Tiger	Rabbit	Dragon	Snake

43	53	63	73
戊	己	庚	辛
Yang Earth	Yin Earth	Yang Metal	Yin Metal
午	未	申	酉
Horse	Sheep	Monkey	Rooster

There is a Partial Three Harmony Metal Combination in McLachlan's birth chart. Her Rooster Day Branch combined with her Ox Month Branch to form Metal. There are no other Branch Combinations within her chart. The prevalent element is Metal. As McLachlan is a Yin Fire Day Master, Metal represents her Wealth element. She has a Follow the Wealth (Metal) chart.

There is a Stem Combination between her Yang Water Hour Branch and her Yin Fire Day Master. The Power Element Combination indicates professional success and recognition in the second half of life. The Hour Pillar only exerts its influence after the age of 40.

McLachlan is born on a Yin Fire Rooster day, one of four days where the Day Master is sitting on its Nobleman Star. This indicates that McLachlan's spouse was of assistance to her. She married Ashwin Sood in 1997 (Yin Fire Ox year) during the Dragon Luck Cycle (age 28 to 32). The Dragon Luck Cycle formed a Six Harmony Combination with her Rooster in the House of Spouse, indicating the possibility of love or marriage during this period. The Annual Ox Branch also combined with the Rooster in the House of Spouse, increasing the possibility of McLachlan finding love or marriage.

McLachlan first achieved success in the challenging Yang Fire Luck Cycle (age 23 to 27). In 1991 (Yin Metal Sheep year), her second album *Solace* enjoyed mainstream success in Canada. The Annual Yin Metal Stem formed a Stem Combination with the Yang Fire in the Luck Cycle, reducing its threat. The second favourable element Earth was also present in the Annual Sheep Branch. In 1993 (Yin Water Rooster year), she released *Fumbling Towards Ecstasy*. The Annual Rooster Branch combined with her Rooster Day Branch and Ox Month Branch to reinforce the favourable element Metal. However, the Fire Rival in the Luck Cycle created issues. That same year, there was a lawsuit against McLachlan from Daryl Neudorf, alleging that he was not properly paid for work done on *Solace*. The judge in the suit ruled on his behalf about the payment issue.

The Dragon Luck Cycle (age 28 to 32) was more favourable for McLachlan. In 1997 (Yin Fire Ox year), she released *Surfacing*, her best selling and most successful album, which contained hits like *Adia*, *Angel* and *Building a Mystery*. She also started Lilith Fair, a successful all-female music festival. The Annual Ox Branch combined with the Rooster and Ox Branches in her chart, reinforcing the favourable element Metal. In 1998 (Yang Earth Tiger year), McLachlan won two Grammy Awards, including one for Best Female Vocal Pop Performance for *Building a Mystery*.

The Yin Fire Luck Cycle (age 33 to 37) contained the negative Fire element. In April 2002 (Yang Water Horse year), she gave birth to her first daughter India. She had fallen pregnant in 2001 (Yin Metal Snake year), when her Output or Child Element Earth had been present in the Annual Snake Branch. In 2003 (Yin Water Sheep year), she returned with the album *Afterglow*. Her second favourable element Earth was present in the Annual Sheep Branch.

The favourable Snake Luck Cycle (age 38 to 42) combined with the Rooster and Ox Branches in her chart to form the Full Three Harmony Metal Combination. In 2006 (Yang Fire Dog year), McLachlan released her first Christmas album *Wintersong*. The second favourable element Earth was present in the Annual Dog Branch. In June 2007 (Yin Fire Pig year), she gave birth to second daughter Taja. She had become pregnant the previous year, when her Output or Child element was present in the Annual Dog Branch. In 2008 (Yang Earth Rat year), the favourable elements Metal and Water were present. McLachlan released *Closer: The Best of Sarah McLachlan*. On a personal note, she divorced Sood that year. In 2010 (Yang Metal Tiger year), McLachlan released *Laws of Illusion*, her 4th US Top 10 album.

The Yang Earth Luck Cycle (age 43 to 47) was also favourable for McLachlan. In 2012 (Yang Water Dragon year), there was a Stem Combination involving the Annual Yang Water Stem and her Yin Fire Day Master. This indicated professional recognition and success. McLachlan was inducted into Canada's Walk of Fame. In 2015 (Yin Wood Sheep year), she received Canada's highest award in performing arts, a Governor General's Performing Arts Award for Lifetime Achievement in Performing Arts. The favourable element Earth was present in the Annual Sheep Branch.

The Horse Luck Cycle (age 48 to 52) combines with McLachlan's Tiger Hour Branch to transform her into a Dominant Fire chart. Her list of favourable elements becomes:

1) Resource element Wood.
2) Self element Fire.
3) Output element Earth.
4) Wealth element Metal.
5) Power element Water.

However, by the Yin Earth Luck Cycle (age 53 to 57), she will revert to a Follow the Wealth (Metal) chart.

Conclusion

From the 18 examples that were covered in this chapter, you can see that the ranking of favourable elements for a Follow the Wealth (Metal) chart is:

1) Wealth element Metal.
2) Output element Earth.
3) Power element Water.
4) Resource element Wood.
5) Self element Fire.

All the examples covered were Yang Fire or Yin Fire Day Masters with birth charts where Metal is the most prominent element. This qualified them as Follow the Wealth (Metal) charts.

Vanessa Redgrave has the Full Three Harmony Metal Combination consisting of the Snake, Rooster and Ox, while Kate Moss has the Snake, Rooster and two Oxen in her chart.

Steve Winwood and Viola Davis have the Partial Three Harmony Metal Combination consisting of the Snake and Rooster, while Bruce Springsteen, Clive James and Al Stewart have the Rooster and Ox in their charts. Bruce Springsteen also has the ability change to a Follow the Wealth (Wood) chart in the second half of his life. Al Stewart has a Monkey Month Branch. He has the ability to change into a Follow the Power (Water) chart in Rat or Dragon Luck Cycles or years. Brian de Palma's chart has two Roosters and one Snake.

Mark Owen, Armistead Maupin and Carolyn Bessette have the Partial Three Harmony Metal Combination consisting of the Snake and Ox.

Kareena Kapoor and Alexis Bledel did not have any Combinations in their charts. Kapoor has two Rooster Branches and Bledel three Rooster Branches. This allowed them to qualify as Follow the Wealth (Metal) charts.

Sarah McLachlan and Lindsey Buckingham have the Rooster and Ox Branches in their birth charts. However, as McLachlan has a Tiger Hour Branch and Buckingham a Tiger Day Branch, they also have the potential to change into Dominant Fire charts when the Horse or Dog Luck Cycle or year appears.

Steven Soderbergh has the Snake and Ox Branches in his chart. However, as he also has a Tiger Year Branch, he also has the potential to change into a Dominant Fire chart when the Horse or Dog Luck Cycle or year approaches.

Joan Lunden has the Snake and Rooster Branches in her chart, as well as a Tiger Year Branch. She also has the potential to transform into a Dominant Fire chart during the Horse or Dog Luck Cycle or year.

David Copperfield has the Seasonal Metal Combination in his chart. He is born on a Dog Day. During the Tiger or Horse Luck Cycle or year, he can change into a Dominant Fire chart. During the Rat or Dragon Luck Cycle or year, Copperfield changes into a Follow the Power (Water) chart. In the second half of his life, the Seasonal Metal Combination no longer applies and he becomes a Follow the Output (Earth) chart.

Chapter Five Follow the Power (Metal) Charts

Follow the Power charts are those whereby the Power element is the prevalent element. The Power element is the element that controls the Day Master. For Follow the Power (Metal) charts, the Day Master must be either the Yang Wood or Yin Wood. In the cycle of the five elements, Metal controls Wood.

Those with Follow the Power charts are extremely disciplined, listen to authority and have a strong sense of right and wrong. They make good employees as they are team players who respect others. They are also trustworthy, responsible, reliable and meticulous in their approach.

For women, the Power element represents the Spouse. Women with Follow the Power charts tend to marry successful and powerful men who provide for them.

For men, the Wealth element represents the Spouse. The Spouse produces the Child. In the cycle, Wealth produces Power, so for men, the Power element represents his Children. Men with Follow the Power charts will have successful and high achieving children.

For Follow the Power (Metal) charts, the ranking of favourable elements is as follows:

1) Metal, the Power element.
2) Earth, the Wealth element. It produces and supports the Power element.
3) Water, the Resource element. While it controls the negative element Fire, it also strengthens Wood Rivals and Competitors.
4) Wood, the Self element. The Wood Rivals and Competitors control the second favourable element Earth.
5) Fire, the Output element. It controls Metal, the most favourable element.

Example 5.1 Anne Rice, American Author
(born October 4, 1941)

Hour	Day	Month	Year
	乙	丁	辛
	Yin Wood	Yin Fire	Yin Metal
	酉	酉	巳
	Rooster	Rooster	Snake

2	12	22	32
戊	己	庚	辛
Yang Earth	Yin Earth	Yang Metal	Yin Metal
戌	亥	子	丑
Dog	Pig	Rat	Ox

42	52	62	72
壬	癸	甲	乙
Yang Water	Yin Water	Yang Wood	Yin Wood
寅	卯	辰	巳
Tiger	Rabbit	Dragon	Snake

There is a Partial Three Harmony Metal Combination in Rice's birth chart. Her Rooster Day and Month Branches combine with her Snake Year Branch to form Metal. There are no other Combinations in the chart. The most prominent element is Metal. As Rice is a Yin Wood Day Master, Metal represents her Power element. She has a Follow the Power (Metal) chart.

The Pig Luck Cycle (age 17 to 21) contained a Yang Wood Rival. She dropped out of North Texas State College in her sophomore year and moved to San Francisco to find work. In 1961 (Yin Metal Ox year), she married Stan Rice, whom she had met in journalism class in high school. The Annual Ox Branch combined with the Rooster in her House of Spouse, indicating the possibility of love or marriage.

The Yang Metal Luck Cycle (age 22 to 26) combined with her Yin Wood Day Master. The Power Element Combination indicated the possibility of professional success and recognition. In 1964 (Yang Wood Dragon year), Rice obtained a Bachelor of Arts in Political Science from San Francisco State University. The second favourable element Earth was present in the Annual Dragon Branch. In September 1966 (Yang Fire Horse year), Rice gave birth to her daughter Michelle. Her Output or Child element Fire was present in the Annual Stem and Branch that year and also in the Annual Branch of the previous year (Yin Wood Snake year).

The Rat Luck Cycle (age 27 to 31) contained the negative element Water. In 1972 (Yang Water Rat year), Michelle died of leukaemia at the age of 6. The negative element Water was present in the Annual Stem and Branch.

The Yin Metal Luck Cycle (age 32 to 36) contained the favourable element. In 1973 (Yin Water Ox year), while still dealing with her grief, Rice took a previously written short story and turned it into the novel *Interview with the Vampire*. The Annual Ox Branch combined with the Rooster and Ox Branches in her chart to form the favourable element Metal. In 1976 (Yang Fire Dragon year), *Interview with the Vampire* was published. The second favourable element Earth was present in the Annual Dragon Branch.

The Ox Luck Cycle (age 37 to 41) combined with the Rooster and Snake Branches to form the Full Three Harmony Metal Combination. In March 1978 (Yang Earth Horse year), her son Christopher was born. The Output or Child element Fire was present in the Annual Stem and Branch of the year she became pregnant, 1977 (Yin Fire Snake year). In 1979 (Yin Earth Sheep year), her second book, *The Feast of all Saints*, was published. The second favourable element Earth was present in the Annual Stem and Branch. Even though the Annual Sheep Branch clashed with the Ox Luck Cycle, there was still the Combination between the Snake and Rooster Branches.

The Yang Water Luck Cycle (age 42 to 46) combined with the Yin Fire Month Stem, reducing its negative effect. In 1985 (Yin Wood Ox year), the second volume of the Vampire Chronicles, *The Vampire Lestat*, was published. The Annual Ox Branch formed the Full Three Harmony Metal Combination with the Snake and Rooster Branches in Rice's chart. Under the pseudonym Anne Rampling, Rice also wrote the erotica novel *Exit to Eden* that year.

The Tiger Luck Cycle (age 47 to 51) contained the negative elements Wood and Fire, as well as the favourable element Earth. In 1988 (Yang Earth Dragon year), the Annual Stem and Branch contained the second favourable element Earth. The third book of the Vampire Chronicles, *The Queen of the Damned*, was published. It reached Number 1 on *The New York Times* Bestseller List.

The Yin Water Luck Cycle (age 52 to 56) gave Rice the auspicious Configuration of all four Yin Stems of the different seasons: Yin Wood Day Master, Yin Fire Month Stem, Yin Metal Year Stem, Yin Water Luck Cycle. In 1994 (Yang Wood Dog year), *Interview with the Vampire* was adapted into a top-grossing movie starring Tom Cruise and Brad Pitt. The second favourable element Earth was present in the Annual Dog Branch. In 1998 (Yang Earth Tiger year), Rice nearly died after falling into a diabetic coma. While the Annual Tiger Branch contained the negative elements Wood and Fire, the favourable element Earth was also present.

The Rabbit Luck Cycle (age 57 to 61) contained a Yin Wood Rival and also clashed with the Rooster Branches in Rice's chart. In 2002 (Yang Water Horse year), Queen of the Damned was made into a movie featuring Aaliyah. It was a commercial and critical failure and Rice distanced herself from the film. Her husband Stan also passed away that year. The negative element Fire was present in the Annual Horse Branch.

The Yang Wood Luck Cycle (age 62 to 66) contained a Wood Rival. In 2004 (Yang Wood Monkey year), the Annual Stem also contained a Yang Wood Rival. Rice came close to death once again after developing a blockage of her intestines, a side effect of gastric bypass surgery that she had the previous year. 2006 (Yang Fire Dog year) was a mixed year for Rice. Her negative element Fire and favourable element Earth were both present in the Annual Stem and Branch. *Interview with a Vampire* was made into the musical *Lestat*, featuring songs by Elton John and Bernie Taupin. It closed after one month on Broadway.

The Dragon Luck Cycle (age 67 to 71) contained Rice's favourable element Earth. In 2009 (Yin Earth Ox year), she started the supernatural thriller series Songs of the Seraphim with *Angel Time*. The Annual Ox Branch formed the Full Three Harmony Metal Combination with the Rooster Branches in her chart. In 2012 (Yang Water Dragon year), Rice published *The Wolf Gift*, the first of the Wolf Chronicles. The favourable element Earth was present in the Annual Branch.

The Yin Wood Luck Cycle (age 72 to 76) contained the Wood Rival but the Snake Luck Cycle (age 77 to 81) combines with the Rooster Branches to reinforce the favourable element Metal.

Example 5.2 Julia Gillard, Australian Prime Minister
2010 to 2013 (born September 29, 1961)

Hour	Day	Month	Year
	乙	丁	辛
	Yin Wood	Yin Fire	Yin Metal
	丑	酉	丑
	Ox	Rooster	Ox

3	13	23	33
戊	己	庚	辛
Yang Earth	Yin Earth	Yang Metal	Yin Metal
戌	亥	子	丑
Dog	Pig	Rat	Ox

43	53	63	73
壬	癸	甲	乙
Yang Water	Yin Water	Yang Wood	Yin Wood
寅	卯	辰	巳
Tiger	Rabbit	Dragon	Snake

There is a Partial Three Harmony Metal Combination in Gillard's birth chart. Her Ox Day and Year Branches combine with the Rooster Month Branch to form Metal. There is also a Yin Metal Year Stem. There are no other Combinations in the chart. As Gillard is a Yin Wood Day Master, Metal represents the Power element. She has a Follow the Power (Metal) chart.

The Pig Luck Cycle (age 18 to 22) contained a Yang Wood Rival. In 1982 (Yang Water Dog year), Gillard cut short her studies at the University of Adelaide to move to Melbourne, in order to work with the Australian Union of Students to fight federal budget cuts to education. The negative element Water was present in the Annual Stem and the favourable element Earth in the Annual Dog Branch. She did not complete her tertiary studies during this period.

The Yang Metal Luck Cycle (age 23 to 27) formed a Stem Combination with her Yin Wood Day Master. The Power Element Combination indicates professional recognition and success. In 1985 (Yin Wood Ox year), Gillard became the President of the Carlton Branch of the Australian Labor Party (ALP). The Annual Ox Branch combined with the Rooster and Ox Branches in her chart to reinforce the favourable element Metal. Gillard graduated from the University of Melbourne with a Bachelor of Laws and Arts degree in 1986 (Yang Fire Tiger year). While the Annual Tiger Branch contained the negative elements Wood and Fire, the favourable Yang Earth was also present.

The Rat Luck Cycle (age 28 to 32) contained the negative element Water. However, Gillard fared well in years with her favourable elements. In 1990 (Yang Metal Horse year), there was a Stem Combination between the Annual Yang Metal Stem and her Yin Wood Day Master. This indicated professional success and recognition. Gillard became the youngest partner in the law firm Slater & Gordon where she was practicing industrial law.

The Yin Metal Luck Cycle (age 33 to 37) contained the favourable element. In 1996 (Yang Fire Rat year), Gillard stood unsuccessfully as a Senate candidate for the federal elections. The negative elements Fire and Water were present in the Annual Stem and Branch. She also left Slater & Gordon to become the Chief of Staff for John Brumby, the Leader of the Opposition in Victoria. In 1998 (Yang Earth Tiger year), Gillard was elected to the Australian House of Representatives representing Lalor, a safe Labor seat near Melbourne. The favourable element Earth was present in the Annual Stem.

The Ox Luck Cycle (age 38 to 42) combined with the Rooster and Ox Branches in Gillard's chart to reinforce the favourable element Metal. In 2001 (Yin Metal Snake year), she was elevated to the front bench and given the shadow portfolio of Population and Immigration. The Annual Snake Branch combined with the Rooster and Ox Branches and Luck Cycle to form the Full Three Harmony Metal Combination. In 2003 (Yin Water Sheep year), Gillard was promoted to the shadow portfolio of Health. Although the Annual Sheep Branch clashed with the Ox Branches in her chart to disrupt the Three Harmony Combination, the favourable element Earth was still present.

The Yang Water Luck Cycle (age 43 to 47) combined with her Yin Fire Month Stem, reducing the effects of the negative element Fire. In 2006 (Yang Fire Dog year), Gillard became Deputy Leader of the Opposition to Kevin Rudd. The favourable element Earth was present in the Annual Dog Branch. Following the ALP's election victory in 2007 (Yin Fire Pig year), Gillard was sworn in the first female Deputy Prime Minister of Australia. There was a Yang Water Stem hidden in the Pig Branch that formed a Stem Combination with the Yin Fire Stem.

The Tiger Luck Cycle (age 48 to 52) contained the negative elements Fire and Wood, as well as the favourable element Earth. In 2010 (Yang Metal Tiger year), there was a Stem Combination between the Annual Yang Metal Stem and Gillard's Yin Wood Day Master. This indicated professional recognition and success. She became the first female Prime Minister of Australia after Rudd resigned. After less than a month in office, Gillard then called for an election that ended up in a hung parliament. However, she was able to form a minority government in a coalition with other independent members of parliament. Gillard's tenure as Prime Minister ended on June 26, 2013 (Yin Water Pig day, Yang Earth Horse month, Yin Water Snake year) when she was ousted by Rudd. The negative elements Wood and Fire were present on the day and month of Rudd's leadership challenge. Gillard also announced her retirement from politics.

The Yin Water Luck Cycle (age 53 to 57) is favourable for Gillard as it provides with the auspicious Configuration of four Yin Stems of the different seasons: Yin Wood Day Master, Yin Fire Month Stem, Yin Metal Year Stem, Yin Water Luck Cycle. In 2017 (Yin Fire Rooster year), Gillard became the chair of mental health organization beyondblue after former Victorian Premier Jeff Kennett stepped down. The Annual Rooster Branch combined with the Rooster and Ox Branches in her chart to reinforce the favourable element Metal.

The Rabbit Luck Cycle (age 58 to 62) may pose some challenges for Gillard as it clashes with her Rooster Month Branch to disrupt the Three Harmony Metal Combination. There is also a Yin Wood Rival present. The Yang Wood Luck Cycle (age 63 to 67) may also be challenging due to the presence of the Wood Rival.

Example 5.3 Jana Novotna, Czech Tennis Player
(born October 2, 1968)

Hour	Day	Month	Year
	乙	辛	戊
	Yin Wood	Yin Metal	Yang Earth
	巳	酉	申
	Snake	Rooster	Monkey

8	18	28	38
庚	己	戊	丁
Yang Metal	Yin Earth	Yang Earth	Yin Fire
申	未	午	巳
Monkey	Sheep	Horse	Snake

48	58	68	78
丙	乙	甲	癸
Yang Fire	Yin Wood	Yang Wood	Yin Water
辰	卯	寅	丑
Dragon	Rabbit	Tiger	Ox

There is a Partial Three Harmony Metal Combination in Novotna's birth chart. Her Snake Day Branch combines with her Rooster Month Branch to form Metal. There is also a Yin Metal Month Stem. There are no other Combinations present within the chart. The most prominent element is Metal. As Novotna is a Yin Wood Day Master, Metal represents the Power element. She has a Follow the Power (Metal) chart.

Novotna first achieved success as a singles player in 1990 (Yang Metal Horse year) during the favourable Yin Earth Luck Cycle (age 18 to 22). She reached the semi-finals of the French Open and finished the year ranked No. 13 in the Women's Tennis Association (WTA) rankings. There was a Stem Combination between the Annual Yang Metal Stem and her Yin Wood Day Master. The Power Element Combination indicates professional success and recognition. Novotna also won three Grand Slam women's doubles titles that year with Helena Sukova, the Australian, French and Wimbledon.

The Sheep Luck Cycle (age 23 to 27) contained Novotna's second favourable element Earth. In 1991 (Yin Metal Sheep year), she was runner-up in the Australian Open final to Monica Seles, having beaten then world No. 1 Steffi Graf in the quarterfinals. Novotna ended the year ranked No. 7. The favourable elements Metal and Earth were present in the Annual Stem and Branch.

In 1993 (Yin Water Rooster year), the Annual Rooster Branch combined with the Snake and Rooster Branches in Novotna's chart to reinforce the favourable element Metal. She reached her first Wimbledon final after beating nine times champion Martina Navratilova in the semifinals. Although she lost to Steffi Graf in three sets in the final, she ended the year ranked No. 6.

Novotna's success continued in the favourable Yang Earth Luck Cycle (age 28 to 32). In 1997 (Yin Fire Ox year), the Annual Ox Branch worked in conjunction with her Monkey Year Branch to bring her success. For a Yin Wood Day Master, the Special Stars are the Monkey and Ox. Novotna made her second Wimbledon final, losing to Martina Hingis in three sets. However, she won the end of year WTA Championships, beating Mary Pierce in the final. She achieved her highest year-end ranking of No. 2.

In 1998 (Yang Earth Tiger year), Novotna finally won Wimbledon. She defeated Venus Williams and Martina Hingis on her way to the title. Novotna became the oldest first ever winner of a Grand Slam title at 29 years and nine months. She also became the fifth female player to earn more than $10 million USD in prize money. The favourable element Earth was present in the Annual Stem.

Novotna retired from professional competition in 1999 (Yin Earth Rabbit year). There was a Yin Wood Rival present in the Annual Branch. The Annual Rabbit Branch also clashed with her Rooster Month Branch, disrupting the Three Harmony Metal Combination.

The Horse Luck Cycle (age 33 to 37) contained the negative element Fire. However, in 2005 (Yin Wood Rooster year), Novotna was inducted into the Tennis Hall of Fame. The Annual Rooster Branch reinforced the favourable element Metal by combining with the Rooster and Snake Branches within her chart.

The Yin Fire Luck Cycle (age 38 to 42) also contained the negative element Fire. However, the Snake Luck Cycle (age 43 to 47) was favourable as the Snake combined with the Snake and Rooster Branches within Novotna's chart to reinforce the favourable element Metal. The Yang Fire Luck Cycle (age 48 to 52) formed a Stem Combination with the Yin Metal Month Stem, reducing its negative effect. The Dragon Luck Cycle (age 53 to 57) contains the second favourable element Earth and will be more favourable for Novotna.

Example 5.4 Jay Chou, Taiwanese Singer and Actor
(born January 18, 1979)

Hour	Day	Month	Year
	乙	乙	戊
	Yin Wood	Yin Wood	Yang Earth
	酉	丑	午
	Rooster	Ox	Horse

6	16	26	36
丙	丁	戊	己
Yang Fire	Yin Fire	Yang Earth	Yin Earth
寅	卯	辰	巳
Tiger	Rabbit	Dragon	Snake

46	56	66	76
庚	辛	壬	癸
Yang Metal	Yin Metal	Yang Water	Yin Water
午	未	申	酉
Horse	Sheep	Monkey	Rooster

There is a Partial Three Harmony Metal Combination in Chou's birth chart. His Rooster Day Branch and Ox Month Branch combine to form Metal. There are no other Combinations in the chart. The most prominent element is Metal. As Chou is a Yin Wood Day Master, Metal represents the Power element. He has a Follow the Power (Metal) chart.

In the Rabbit Luck Cycle (age 21 to 25), Chou's debut album *Jay* was released in 2000 (Yang Metal Dragon year). Although the Rabbit Luck Cycle contained a Yin Wood Rival, Chou was able to benefit in years with the Power element Metal, which controlled the Yin Wood Rival. In 2000, the Annual Yang Metal Stem formed a Stem Combination with his Yin Wood Day Master. The Power Element Combination indicated professional recognition or success. In 2001 (Yin Metal Snake year), the Annual Snake Branch combined with the Ox Month Branch to reinforce the favourable element Metal. Chou won a Golden Melody Award for Best Album for *Jay* and also released his follow up album *Fantasy*, another major success. In 2004 (Yang Wood Monkey year), Chou won another Golden Melody Award for his fourth album *Yi Hui Mei*. For a Yin Wood Day Master, the Special Stars are the Ox and Monkey. The Annual Monkey Branch worked in conjunction with his Ox Month Branch to bring him success.

The Yang Earth Luck Cycle (age 26 to 30) contained Chou's second favourable element. In 2005 (Yin Wood Rooster year), the Annual Rooster Branch combined with the Ox and Rooster Branches in his chart to reinforce the favourable element Metal. Chou made his movie debut in *Initial D*, based on a Japanese comic. Chou won the Golden Horse Award and the Hong Kong Film Awards for Best New Actor. In 2008 (Yang Earth Rat year), Chou appeared in *Kung Fu Dunk*, another major box office success. The second favourable element Earth was present in the Annual Stem.

The Dragon Luck Cycle (age 31 to 35) was also favourable as it contained Earth. In January 2011 (still the Yang Metal Tiger year), Chou made his Hollywood film debut portraying Kato in *The Green Hornet* opposite Seth Rogen. There was a Stem Combination between the Annual Yang Metal Stem and his Yin Wood Day Master, indicating professional success and recognition. In 2013 (Yin Water Snake year), Chou directed his musical fantasy film *The Rooftop*, which performed well commercially in China. The Annual Snake Branch formed the Full Three Harmony Metal Combination with the Ox and Rooster Branches in Chou's chart. On a personal note, Chou married model Hannah Quinlivan on his 36th birthday on January 17, 2015 (a Yin Water Snake day). The Snake day also formed the Full Three Harmony Combination with the Ox and Rooster Branches to bring him happiness and fulfillment that day.

The Yin Earth Luck Cycle (age 36 to 41) will also be favourable for Chou. The Snake Luck Cycle (age 42 to 46) forms the Full Three Harmony Metal Combination with the Ox and Rooster Branches in his chart. It will also be another successful period for him. However, there is a Combination involving the Rooster Branch in his House of Spouse, so there is the possibility of him finding love or marriage during this period.

The Yang Metal Luck Cycle (age 47 to 51) forms a Stem Combination with his Yin Wood Day Master, indicating professional success and recognition. However, there may be issues in the Horse Luck Cycle (age 52 to 56) as the negative element Fire is present. However, the Yin Metal Luck Cycle (age 57 to 61) should be favourable.

Example 5.5 Alan Ball, American Television Writer and Producer (born May 13, 1957)

Hour	Day	Month	Year
	乙	乙	丁
	Yin Wood	Yin Wood	Yin Fire
	酉	巳	酉
	Rooster	Snake	Rooster

2	12	22	32
甲	癸	壬	辛
Yang Wood	Yin Water	Yang Water	Yin Metal
辰	卯	寅	丑
Dragon	Rabbit	Tiger	Ox
42	52	62	72
庚	己	戊	丁
Yang Metal	Yin Earth	Yang Earth	Yin Fire
子	亥	戌	酉
Rat	Pig	Dog	Rooster

There is a Partial Three Harmony Metal Combination in Ball's birth chart. His Rooster Day and Year Branches combine with the Snake Month Branch to form Metal. There are no other Combinations present within the chart. As Ball is a Yin Wood Day Master, Metal represents his Power element. He has a Follow the Power (Metal) chart.

Ball first gained attention in the Ox Luck Cycle (age 37 to 41) for his work on the television sitcom *Grace Under Fire* in 1994 (Yang Wood Dog year). The Ox combined with the Snake and Rooster Branches in Ball's chart to form the Full Three Harmony Metal Combination. The Annual Dog Branch also contained the second favourable element Earth. In 1997 (Yin Fire Ox year), Ball received more acclaim for his writing on the sitcom *Cybill* starring Cybill Shepherd. The Annual Ox Branch combined with the Ox Luck Cycle and the Snake and Rooster Branches in his chart to reinforce Metal.

The Yang Metal Luck Cycle (age 42 to 46) formed a Stem Combination with Ball's Yin Wood Day Master. The Power Element Combination indicates professional success and recognition. In 2000 (Yang Metal Dragon year), there was a further Stem Combination between the Annual Yang Metal Stem and his Yin Wood Day Master. Ball won an Oscar for Best Original Screenplay for *American Beauty*, which also won Best Picture. The second favourable element Earth was also present in the Annual Dragon Branch. In 2001 (Yin Metal Snake year), the Annual Snake Branch combined with the Rooster and Snake Branches in Ball's chart to reinforce the favourable element Metal. Ball created, wrote and produced the Home Box Office (HBO) series *Six Feet Under*.

The Rat Luck Cycle (age 47 to 51) contained the negative element Water. In 2007 (Yin Fire Pig year), Ball wrote, produced and directed the coming of age drama *Towelhead*. It was a commercial failure. The negative elements Fire, Wood and Water were present in the Annual Stem and Branch. In 2008 (Yang Earth Rat year), Ball created and produced another successful HBO series, the dark fantasy horror *True Blood*. The second favourable element Earth was present in the Annual Stem.

The Yin Earth Luck Cycle (age 52 to 56) was also favourable for Ball. In 2009 (Yin Earth Ox year), *True Blood* received an American Film Institute Award for one of 10 Best Television Programs. The Annual Ox Branch combined with the Snake and Rooster Branches in Ball's chart to form the Full Three Harmony Metal Combination. *True Blood* was running for the entire period.

The Pig Luck Cycle (age 57 to 61) clashed with Ball's Snake Month Branch to disrupt the Three Harmony Metal Combination. He was no longer a Follow the Power (Metal) chart and became more dependent on the Annual Stems and Branches. Note that there was also a Yang Wood Rival present as a Hidden Stem in the Pig Luck Cycle. In 2014 (Yang Wood Horse year), *True Blood* ended after seven seasons. The negative elements Wood and Fire were present in the Annual Stem and Branch. In 2017 (Yin Fire Rooster year), Ball was one of the executive producers of the television film *The Immortal Life of Henrietta Lacks* starring Oprah Winfrey. The Annual Rooster Branch contained the favourable element Metal.

The Yang Earth Luck Cycle (age 62 to 66) should be favourable for Ball as he reverts back to a Follow the Power (Metal) chart.

Example 5.6 Helena Bonham Carter, British Actress
(born May 26, 1966)

Hour	Day	Month	Year
	乙	癸	丙
	Yin Wood	Yin Water	Yang Fire
	酉	巳	午
	Rooster	Snake	Horse

7	17	27	37
壬	辛	庚	己
Yang Water	Yin Metal	Yang Metal	Yin Earth
辰	卯	寅	丑
Dragon	Rabbit	Tiger	Ox

47	57	67	77
戊	丁	丙	乙
Yang Earth	Yin Fire	Yang Fire	Yin Wood
子	亥	戌	酉
Rat	Pig	Dog	Rooster

There is a Partial Three Harmony Metal Combination in Bonham Carter's birth chart. Her Rooster Day Branch and Snake Month Branch combine to form Metal. There are no other Combinations in the chart. The most prominent element is Metal. As Bonham Carter is a Yin Wood Day Master, Metal represents her Power element. She has a Follow the Power (Metal) chart.

Bonham Carter first came to prominence with her role in the Merchant Ivory production *A Room with a View* in 1985 (Yin Wood Ox year) during the Yin Metal Luck Cycle (age 17 to 21). The Annual Ox Branch combined with the Snake and Rooster Branches in her chart to form the Full Three Harmony Metal Combination.

The Rabbit Luck Cycle (age 22 to 26) contained a Yin Wood Rival, presenting issues for Bonham Carter. She found herself typecast in period dramas. In 1990 (Yang Metal Horse year), there was a Stem Combination between the Annual Stem and her Yin Wood Day Master. The Power Element Combination indicates professional success and recognition. Bonham Cater portrayed Ophelia in *Hamlet* alongside Mel Gibson and Glenn Close.

The Yang Metal Luck Cycle (age 27 to 31) formed a Stem Combination with Bonham Carter's Yin Wood Day Master, indicating professional recognition and success. In 1994 (Yang Wood Dog year), the Annual Yang Wood Stem gave her the auspicious Sequence of Four Stems in a Row: Yin Water Month Stem, Annual Yang Wood Stem, Yin Wood Day Stem, Yang Fire Year Stem. Bonham Carter appeared in *Mary Shelley's Frankenstein* alongside Robert de Niro and Kenneth Branagh. The Annual Dog Branch also combined with her Horse Year Branch to form Fire. There was a Fire-Metal conflict in her chart. Bonham Carter started a relationship with Kenneth Branagh when filming *Mary Shelley's Frankenstein*. Branagh was still married to actress Emma Thompson at that time. In 1997 (Yin Fire Ox year), Bonham Carter received an Oscar nomination for Best Actress in the period drama *The Wings of the Dove*. The Annual Ox Branch combined with the Snake and Rooster Branches in her chart to form the Full Three Harmony Metal Combination.

The Tiger Luck Cycle (age 32 to 36) combined with her Horse Year Branch to form Fire, resulting in a Fire-Metal conflict within Bonham Carter's chart. In 1999 (Yin Earth Rabbit year), there was a Yin Wood Rival within the Annual Branch. Bonham Carter ended her relationship with Branagh after five years. In 2001 (Yin Metal Snake year), Bonham Carter appeared in the remake of *Planet of the Apes* alongside Mark Wahlberg. The Annual Snake Branch combined with the Rooster and Snake Branches in her chart to reinforce the favourable element Metal. She also started a relationship with director Tim Burton. The

Annual Snake Branch combined with her Rooster in her House of Spouse, indicating the possibility of love or marriage.

The Yin Earth Luck Cycle (age 37 to 41) contained Bonham Carter's second favourable element. She reinvented her career as she teamed with Tim Burton on his movies. In 2003 (Yin Water Sheep year), she appeared in *Big Fish*. The favourable element Earth was present in the Annual Sheep Branch. In 2005 (Yin Wood Rooster year), Bonham Carter was in Burton's remake of *Charlie and the Chocolate Factory* alongside Johnny Depp. The Annual Rooster Branch combined with the Snake and Rooster Branches in her chart to reinforce the favourable element Metal. Bonham Carter also had two children with Burton during this period: son Billy Raymond Burton in October 2003 (Yin Water Sheep year) and daughter Nell Burton in December 2007 (Yin Fire Pig year). For a Yin Wood Day Master, the Output or Child element is Fire, which was present in the Annual Sheep Branch and the Annual Yin Fire Stem.

The Ox Luck Cycle (age 42 to 46) combined with the Rooster and Snake Branches in Bonham Carter's chart to form the Full Three Harmony Metal Combination. In 2009 (Yin Earth Ox year), she played Bellatrix Lestrange in *Harry Potter and the Half-Blood Prince*. The Annual Ox Branch combined with the Rooster and Snake Branches in the chart and the Ox Luck Cycle to reinforce the favourable element Metal. In 2010 (Yang Metal Tiger year), there was a Stem Combination between the Annual Yang Metal Stem and her Yin Wood Day Master. She received an Oscar nomination for Best Supporting Actress for her performance in Best Picture Oscar winner *The King's Speech*.

The Yang Earth Luck Cycle (age 47 to 51) contained Bonham Carter's second favourable element Earth. In 2013 (Yin Water Snake year), she appeared in *The Lone Ranger* opposite Johnny Depp and the children's movie *The Young and Prodigious T.S. Spivet*. The Annual Snake

Branch combined with the Rooster and Snake Branches to reinforce the favourable element Metal. In 2014 (Yang Wood Horse year), the negative element Fire was present in the Annual Branch. The Annual Stem also contained a Yang Wood Rival. Bonham Carter split with Burton amicably. In 2015 (Yin Wood Sheep year), she appeared as the Fairy Godmother in *Cinderella*. The favourable element Earth was present in the Annual Branch.

The Rat Luck Cycle (age 52 to 56) contains the negative element Water, while the Yin Fire Luck Cycle (age 57 to 61) also contains a negative element. Bonham Carter will have to depend on the Annual Stem and Branch to see how she fares.

Example 5.7 Zola Budd Pieterse,
South African-American Runner (born May 26, 1966)

Hour	Day	Month	Year
	乙	癸	丙
	Yin Wood	Yin Water	Yang Fire
	酉	巳	午
	Rooster	Snake	Horse

7	17	27	37
壬	辛	庚	己
Yang Water	Yin Metal	Yang Metal	Yin Earth
辰	卯	寅	丑
Dragon	Rabbit	Tiger	Ox

47	57	67	77
戊	丁	丙	乙
Yang Earth	Yin Fire	Yang Fire	Yin Wood
子	亥	戌	酉
Rat	Pig	Dog	Rooster

Zola Budd Pieterse was known professionally as Zola Budd so for the rest of this discussion, she will be referred to as Zola Budd. Budd is born on the same day as Helena Bonham Carter, so they share the same favourable elements and Luck Cycles. However, there are differences in their chart. They were born in different countries (UK and South Africa) to families with different socio-economic backgrounds. They could also have different Hour Pillars. As the Hour Pillar only exerts its influence from the age of 40, by which stage Budd's athletic career had finished, we can use Bonham Carter's and Budd's charts to see how differently their lives developed.

There is a Partial Three Harmony Metal Combination in Budd's birth chart. Her Rooster Day Branch combines with her Snake Month Branch to form Metal. There are no other Combinations in Budd's chart. The most prominent element is Metal. As she is a Yin Wood Day Master, Metal represents the Power element. Budd has a Follow the Power (Metal) chart.

The negative element Water is present in the Month Stem, in the position associated with the father. Budd had a difficult relationship with her father Frank. He stopped talking to her after she requested that he not attend the 1984 Summer Olympics in which she was participating. Frank also did not attend Budd's wedding to Mike Pieterse.

Budd married Pieterse in 1989 (Yin Earth Snake year). The Annual Snake Branch combined with her Rooster in her House of Spouse, indicating the possibility of love or marriage.

During the Yin Metal Luck Cycle (age 17 to 21), Budd first gained attention in 1984 (Yang Wood Rat year) when she broke the women's 5000 metres world record. However, as the run took place in apartheid-era South Africa, the IAAF (International Amateur Athletics Federation) did not recognize it. There was a Yang Wood Rival present in the Annual Stem, as well as the negative element. Budd was able to represent the UK due to her paternal grandfather being British in the 1984 Summer Olympics. In the 3000 metres final, Budd finished seventh following a mid race collision with American favourite Mary Decker. The American media blamed her for the incident.

In 1985 (Yin Wood Ox year), Budd went on to break the UK records for the 1500 metres, mile, 3000 metres and 5000 metres. The Annual Ox combined with the Rooster and Snake Branches in Budd's chart to form the Full Three Harmony Metal Combination. In 1986 (Yang Fire Tiger year), the Annual Tiger Branch combined with the Horse Year Branch to form Fire. There was a Fire-Metal conflict. Budd sustained a leg injury that forced her to rest from competition in 1987 (Yin Fire Rabbit year). Her negative element Fire was present, as well as a Yin Wood Rival in the Annual Branch.

The Rabbit Luck Cycle (age 22 to 26) contained a Yin Wood Rival, creating issues for Budd. In 1989 (Yin Earth Snake year), her father Frank was found dead five months after her wedding. In 1992 (Yang Water Monkey year), Budd was able to represent South Africa at the Barcelona Olympics following its readmission to international competition post-apartheid. However, the negative element Water was present in the Annual Stem and Branch. Budd did not qualify for the 3000 m final. Although the Monkey is one of the Special Stars for a Yin Wood Day Master, it needed to have the other Special Star Ox present to exert its effects.

The Yang Metal Luck Cycle (age 27 to 31) formed a Stem Combination with Budd's Yin Wood Day Master, indicating professional success and recognition. In 1993 (Yin Water Rooster year), Budd finished fourth in the World Cross Country Championships. The Annual Rooster Branch combined with the Snake and Rooster Branches in her chart to reinforce her favourable element Metal.

The Tiger Luck Cycle (age 32 to 36) combined with the Horse Year Branch to form the negative element Fire. This is also Budd's Output or Child element. In 1998 (Yang Earth Tiger year), she gave birth to a set of twins. The Annual Tiger Branch combined with the Tiger Luck Cycle and Horse Year Branch to form Fire.

In 2006 (Yang Fire Dog year) during the favourable Yin Earth Luck Cycle (age 37 to 41), Budd filed for divorce from Pieterse following allegations that he had been having an affair with former Miss South Africa Agatha Pelser. Budd also took out a restraining order against Pelser. The Annual Dog Branch combined with Budd's Horse Year Branch to form Fire, which created a Fire-Metal conflict. Budd and Pieterse later reconciled.

In the favourable Ox Luck Cycle (age 42 to 46), Budd moved with her children to Myrtle Beach, South Carolina in 2008 (Yang Earth Rat year) after receiving a two-year visa to compete on the US Masters' Circuit. The second favourable element Earth was present in the Annual Stem. The Ox also combined with the Snake and Rooster Branches in her chart to form the Full Three Harmony Metal Combination.

As Budd shares the same day, month and year of birth as Helena Bonham Carter, she also shares the same favourable and negative Luck Cycles. The Rat (age 52 to 56) and Yin Fire (age 57 to 61) Luck Cycles may be challenging due to the presence of negative elements Water and Fire.

Example 5.8 Elisabeth Hasselbeck,
American Television Personality (born May 28, 1977)

Hour	Day	Month	Year
	乙	乙	丁
	Yin Wood	Yin Wood	Yin Fire
	酉	巳	巳
	Rooster	Snake	Snake

3	13	23	33
丙	丁	戊	己
Yang Fire	Yin Fire	Yang Earth	Yin Earth
午	未	申	酉
Horse	Sheep	Monkey	Rooster
43	53	63	73
庚	辛	壬	癸
Yang Metal	Yin Metal	Yang Water	Yin Water
戌	亥	子	丑
Dog	Pig	Rat	Ox

There is a Partial Three Harmony Metal Combination in Hasselbeck's birth chart. Her Snake Month and Year Branches combine with her Rooster Day Branch to form Metal. There are no other Combinations present within the chart. The most prominent element is Metal. As Hasselbeck is a Yin Wood Day Master, Metal represents her Power element. She has a Follow the Power (Metal) chart.

During the Yang Earth Luck Cycle (age 23 to 27), Hasselbeck was working as a shoe designer for sportswear company Puma in 2001 (Yin Metal Snake year) when she successfully auditioned for a slot on the reality show *Survivor: The Australian Outback*. She ended up fourth in the competition. In 2002 (Yang Water Horse year), she married professional football quarterback Tim Hasselbeck, whom she had started dating in college in 1997 (Yin Fire Ox year). The Annual Ox Branch combined with her Rooster in the House of Spouse, indicating the possibility of love or marriage. In 2003 (Yin Water Sheep year), Hasselbeck joined the popular daytime television talk show *The View*, alongside Barbara Walters as one of the co-hosts. Her second favourable element Earth was present in the Annual Sheep Branch.

The Monkey Luck Cycle (age 28 to 32) was mixed as it contained the favourable element Metal and the negative element Water. In 2007 (Yin Fire Pig year), Hasselbeck was involved in a heated on-air debate with co-host Rosie O'Donnell over the involvement of the United States in the war against Iraq. Conservative Hasselbeck was pro-intervention, while O'Donnell was not. The negative elements Fire, Wood and Water were present in the Annual Stem and Branch. O'Donnell left *The View* shortly after, and was replaced by Whoopi Goldberg. In 2008 (Yang Earth Rat year), her book *The G-Free Diet: A Gluten Free Survival Guide* was published. Hasselbeck lives with celiac disease. The Annual Rat Branch combined with the Monkey Luck Cycle to form Water. Hasselbeck became a Follow the Resource (Water) chart that year. Her list of favourable elements became:

1) Resource element Water.
2) Power element Metal.
3) Output element Fire.
4) Wealth element Earth.
5) Self element Wood.

In 2009 (Yin Earth Ox year), Hasselbeck had reverted back to a Follow the Power (Metal) chart. Together with her co-hosts Barbara Walters, Whoopi Goldberg, Joy Behar and Sherri Shephard, she won the Daytime Emmy Award for Outstanding Talk Show Host.

The Yin Earth Luck Cycle (age 33 to 37) contains her second favourable element Earth. In 2013 (Yin Water Snake year), Hasselbeck left *The View* to join the Fox Network's morning show *Fox & Friends* as a co-host. The Annual Snake Branch combines with the Rooster and Snake Branches in her chart to reinforce the favourable element Metal. Towards the end of 2015 (Yin Wood Sheep year), Hasselbeck left Fox & Friends to spend more time with her family. The second favourable element Earth was present in the Annual Sheep Branch.

The Rooster Luck Cycle (age 38 to 42) combines with the Snake and Rooster Branches in Hasselbeck's chart to reinforce the favourable element Metal. The Combination involves the Rooster in the House of Spouse, so there is the possibility of love or marriage during this period. The Yang Metal Luck Cycle (age 43 to 47) forms a Stem Combination with her Yin Wood Day Master. This indicates professional success or recognition. For a woman, there is also the possibility of love or marriage as the Power Element Combination also represents a Spouse.

The Dog Luck Cycle (age 48 to 52) contains the second favourable element Earth. The Yin Metal Luck Cycle (age 53 to 57) should also be favourable. The Pig Luck Cycle (age 58 to 62) contains a Yang Wood Rival, so there may be some complications or issues during this period.

Example 5.9 Bill Medley, American Singer
(born September 19, 1940)

Hour	Day	Month	Year
	乙	乙	庚
	Yin Wood	Yin Wood	Yang Metal
	丑	酉	辰
	Ox	Rooster	Dragon

6	16	26	36
丙	丁	戊	己
Yang Fire	Yin Fire	Yang Earth	Yin Earth
戌	亥	子	丑
Dog	Pig	Rat	Ox

46	56	66	76
庚	辛	壬	癸
Yang Metal	Yin Metal	Yang Water	Yin Water
寅	卯	辰	巳
Tiger	Rabbit	Dragon	Snake

There is a Partial Three Harmony Metal Combination in Medley's birth chart. His Ox Day Branch combines with his Rooster Month Branch to form Metal. There is also a Six Harmony Combination between his Rooster Month Branch and Dragon Year Branch. However, when it comes to determining the most prominent element in a chart, the Three Harmony Combination takes precedence. The prevalent element in the chart is Metal. As Medley is a Yin Wood Day Master, Metal represents the Power element. He has a Follow the Power (Metal) chart.

There is also a Stem Combination between the Yin Wood Month Stem and the Yang Metal Year Stem. Medley's Yin Wood Rival is removed by the Combination with the Year Stem. This indicates a person who is very capable and resourceful, as he is able to combine away his Rival.

In 1964 (Yang Wood Dragon year) during the Pig Luck Cycle (age 21 to 25), Medley and Bobby Hatfield were performing as *The Righteous Brothers* when record producer Phil Spector signed them to his label. Although the Luck Cycle contained the negative elements Wood and Water, the Annual Dragon Branch contained the favourable element Earth. In 1965 (Yin Wood Snake year), *The Righteous Brothers* released *You've Lost That Lovin' Feelin*. It reached Number 1 on the US and UK Singles chart and also became the most played song on US radio and television in the 20th century. They also released US Top 10 hits *Unchained Melody* and *For Once in My Life*. The Annual Snake Branch combined with the Rooster and Ox Branches in Medley's chart to form the Full Three Harmony Metal Combination.

In the favourable Yang Earth Luck Cycle (age 26 to 30), *The Righteous Brothers* left Spector and signed with Verve Records in 1966 (Yang Fire Horse year). They enjoyed another Number 1 hit *(You're My) Soul and Inspiration*. The negative element Fire was present in the Annual Stem and Branch. Their subsequent singles released that year were not as successful. In 1968 (Yang Earth Monkey year), Medley left *The Righteous Brothers* for a solo career. The Annual Monkey Branch combined with the Dragon Year Branch to form Water, which became his prevalent element. He became a Follow the Resource (Water) chart with the following list of favourable elements:

1) Resource element Water.
2) Power element Metal.
3) Output element Fire.
4) Wealth element Earth.
5) Self element Wood.

In 1969 (Yin Earth Rooster year), *You've Lost The Lovin' Feelin* was reissued in conjunction with a Greatest Hits set. It reached the UK Top 10 again after five years. By now, Medley had reverted back to being a Follow the Power (Metal) chart. The Annual Rooster Branch combined with the Ox and Rooster Branches in his chart to reinforce the favourable element Metal.

The Rat Luck Cycle (age 31 to 35) combined with Medley's Dragon Year Branch to form Water. He became a Follow the Resource (Water) chart. *The Righteous Brothers* reformed in 1974 (Yang Wood Tiger year) with the US Number 3 hit *Rock and Roll Heaven* but Medley left for family reasons in 1976 (Yang Fire Dragon year). The Annual Dragon Branch combined with the Dragon Year Branch and Rat Luck Cycle to reinforce the favourable element Water.

Medley had reverted back to a Follow the Power (Metal) chart during the favourable Yin Earth Luck Cycle (age 36 to 40), during which he spent time with his family. In the Ox Luck Cycle (age 41 to 45), *The Righteous Brothers* reformed to perform at the American Bandstand 30th Anniversary Special in 1981 (Yin Metal Rooster year). The Annual Rooster Branch combined with the Ox and Rooster Branches in Medley's chart to reinforce the favourable element Metal. *The Righteous Brothers* continued touring during this period.

The Yang Metal Luck Cycle (age 46 to 50) formed a Stem Combination with Medley's Yin Wood Day Master. This indicated professional success and recognition. In 1988 (Yang Earth Dragon year), Medley enjoyed the biggest hit of his solo career when his duet with Jennifer Warnes (*I've Had) The Time of My Life* was featured on the *Dirty Dancing* soundtrack. The Annual Year and Branch contained the second favourable element Earth. In 1990 (Yang Metal Horse year), there was a Stem Combination between the Annual Yang Metal Stem and Medley's Yin Wood Day Master. *The Righteous Brothers* re-recorded their version of *Unchained Melody* on Curb Records after it was featured in the movie *Ghost*. It reached Number 1 in the UK.

Medley continued performing during the Yang Tiger (age 51 to 55) and Yin Metal (age 56 to 60) Luck Cycles. The Rabbit Luck Cycle (age 60 to 65) clashed with his Rooster

Month Branch to disrupt the Three Harmony Metal Combination. There was also a Yin Wood Rival present. In 2003 (Yin Water Sheep year), Hatfield died of cocaine-related heart failure. The Annual Sheep Branch combined with the Rabbit Luck Cycle to form Wood. There was a Metal-Wood conflict in Medley's chart. The loss of his singing partner meant that Medley performed as a solo artist for more than a decade.

In 2016 (Yang Fire Monkey year), Medley revived *The Righteous Brothers* with Bucky Heard and started a residency in Las Vegas. For a Yin Wood Day Master like Medley, the Special Stars are the Ox and Monkey. The Annual Monkey Branch worked in conjunction with his Ox Day Branch to bring him success.

Example 5.10 Michelle Williams, American Actress
(born September 9, 1980, 03:07 hours)

Hour	Day	Month	Year
戊	乙	乙	庚
Yang Earth	Yin Wood	Yin Wood	Yang Metal
寅	酉	酉	申
Tiger	Rooster	Rooster	Monkey

1	11	21	31
甲	癸	壬	辛
Yang Wood	Yin Water	Yang Water	Yin Metal
申	未	午	巳
Monkey	Sheep	Horse	Snake

41	51	61	71
庚	己	戊	丁
Yang Metal	Yin Earth	Yang Earth	Yin Fire
辰	卯	寅	丑
Dragon	Rabbit	Tiger	Ox

There are no Branch Combinations present in Williams' birth chart. There are two Rooster Branches, as well as a Yang Metal Stem. As the only element present in the Rooster is Metal, the most prominent element within the chart is Metal. As Williams is a Yin Metal Day Master, Metal represents her Power. She has a Follow the Power (Metal) chart.

Williams' Rooster in the House of Spouse is present twice in her chart. This indicates that she has a higher incidence of having two marriages or significant relationships. While she has yet to marry (at the time of writing), Williams started a relationship with actor Heath Ledger in 2004 (Yang Wood Monkey year), when she met him on the set of *Brokeback Mountain*. There was a Yang Metal Stem hidden within the annual Monkey Branch that formed a Stem Combination with Williams' Yin Wood Day Master. For a woman, the Power Element Combination indicates the possibility of love or marriage.

During the Sheep Luck Cycle (age 16 to 20), Williams scored her first major career break in 1998 (Yang Earth Tiger year) when she was cast in the teenage television drama *Dawson's Creek* alongside Katie Holmes, James Van Der Beek and Joshua Jackson. The second favourable element earth was present in the Luck Cycle and the Annual Stem.

The Water Luck Cycle (age 21 to 25) contained the negative Water element, so Williams was dependent on the Annual Stem and Branch. In 2003 (Yin Water Sheep year), the second favourable element Earth was present. Williams appeared in the critically acclaimed comedy *The Station Agent* alongside Peter Dinklage and Bobby Cannavale. The cast was nominated for a Screen Actors Guild Award for Best Cast in a Motion Picture. In 2005 (Yin Wood Rooster year), she received an Oscar nomination for Best Supporting Actress for her performance as a gay cowboy's wife in *Brokeback Mountain* opposite then-boyfriend Heath Ledger. The Annual Rooster Branch contained Metal.

The Horse Luck Cycle (age 26 to 30) contained the negative element Fire. In 2007 (Yin Fire Pig year), Ledger and Williams ended their relationship. There was a Yang Wood Rival hidden within the Annual Pig Branch. In January 2008 (still the Yin Wood Pig year), Ledger died from combined drug intoxication. Williams had to cope with her grief and the sudden attention from paparazzi surrounding her and daughter Matilda Rose Ledger.

She confessed in an interview that 2008 (Yang Earth Rat year) was a difficult year, even though she appeared in four movies that year, including the critically acclaimed *Synecdoche, New York*, directed by Charlie Kaufman. The negative element Water was present in the Annual Branch. In the first half of 2010 (Yang Metal Tiger year), Williams appeared in *Shutter Island* alongside Leonardo di Caprio. There was a Stem Combination between the Annual Yang Metal Stem and her Yin Wood Day Master, indicating professional success and recognition. She also appeared in relationship drama *Blue Valentine* opposite Ryan Gosling, for which she received an Oscar nomination for Best Actress.

The Yin Metal Luck Cycle (age 31 to 35) contained her favourable element. In 2011 (Yin Metal Rabbit year), the favourable element Metal was in the Annual Stem. Williams portrayed Marilyn Monroe in *My Weekend with Marilyn* opposite Eddie Redmayne. She received her second Best Actress Oscar nomination. In 2013 (Yin Water Snake year), the Annual Snake Branch combined with the Rooster Branches in her chart to reinforce the favourable element Metal. Williams had a high profile role in Sam Raimi's blockbuster *Oz the Great and Powerful* opposite James Franco.

The Snake Luck Cycle (age 36 to 40) combined with the Rooster Branches in Williams' chart to reinforce Metal. In 2016 (Yang Fire Monkey year), the favourable element Metal was present in the Annual Monkey Branch. Williams received another Best Supporting Actress Oscar nomination for her performance in the drama *Manchester By The Sea*. In 2017 (Yin Fire Rooster year), the Annual Rooster Branch combined with the Snake Luck Cycle and the Rooster Branches in her chart to reinforce Metal. Williams appeared in the biography *The Greatest Showman* opposite Hugh Jackman. There is also a Combination with the Rooster in her House of Spouse during this period, so there is the possibility of Williams finding love or getting married during this time.

The Yang Metal Luck Cycle (age 41 to 45) will also be favourable for Williams. There is a Stem Combination between the Luck Cycle and the Yin Wood Day Master, indicating professional recognition and success, as well as the possibility of love or marriage. The Dragon Luck Cycle (age 46 to 50) contains the second favourable element Earth.

The Yin Earth Luck Cycle (age 51 to 55) will also be favourable. However, there may be issues in the Rabbit Luck Cycle (age 56 to 60). The Rabbit clashes with the two Rooster Branches and the negative Self element Wood is also present.

Example 5.11 Fran Drescher,
American Actress Comedienne
(born September 30, 1957, 07:28 hours)

Hour	Day	Month	Year
庚	乙	己	丁
Yang Metal	Yin Wood	Yin Earth	Yin Fire
辰	巳	酉	酉
Dragon	Snake	Rooster	Rooster

3	13	23	33
庚	辛	壬	癸
Yang Metal	Yin Metal	Yang Water	Yin Water
戌	亥	子	丑
Dog	Pig	Rat	Ox

43	53	63	73
甲	乙	丙	丁
Yang Wood	Yin Wood	Yang Fire	Yin Fire
寅	卯	辰	巳
Tiger	Rabbit	Dragon	Snake

There is a Partial Three Harmony Metal Combination present in Drescher's birth chart. The Snake Day Branch combines with the Rooster Month and Year Branches to form Metal. There is also a Yang Metal Hour Stem. The most prominent element within her chart is Metal. As Drescher is a Yang Wood Day Master, Metal represents her Power element. She has a Follow the Power (Metal) chart.

Drescher first achieved some success in the Yang Water Luck Cycle (age 23 to 27). Even though the Luck Cycle contained the negative element Water, Drescher had favourable elements in the Annual Stems and Branches. In 1981 (Yin Metal Rooster year), she appeared in Milos Forman's *Ragtime*. The Annual Rooster Branch combined with the Rooster and Snake Branches in her chart to reinforce her favourable element Metal.

In the Rat Luck Cycle (age 28 to 32), the negative element Water was present. Drescher appeared in small movie roles and had yet to make a breakthrough. In 1990 (Yang Metal Horse year), she appeared alongside Robin Williams in the comedy *Cadillac Man*. There was a Stem Combination between the Annual Yang Metal Stem and her Yin Wood Day Master. This indicated professional recognition and success. In 1991 (Yin Metal Sheep year), Drescher has her first television sitcom *Princess*. The Annual Stem and Branch contained the favourable elements Metal and Earth.

Although the Yin Water Luck Cycle (age 33 to 37) contained Drescher's negative element Water, she was able to benefit in years with her favourable element Earth. Her second sitcom *The Nanny* became a top 10 hit after it premiered in 1993 (Yin Water Rooster year). The Annual Rooster Branch combined with the Snake and Rooster Branches in her chart to reinforce the favourable element Metal.

Drescher enjoyed significant success during the Ox Luck Cycle (age 38 to 42), as the Ox formed the Full Three Harmony Metal Combination with the Snake and Rooster Branches in her chart. In 1996 (Yang Fire Rat year), she released her memoir *Enter Whining*. There was a Special Configuration for Drescher that year. For a Yin Wood Day Master, the presence of the Yang Fire Rat indicates success associated with writing and expression. In 1997 (Yin Fire Ox year), Drescher had her first starring role in the comedy *The Beautician and the Beast* opposite Timothy

Dalton. The Annual Ox Branch combined with the Ox Luck Cycle and the Snake and Rooster Branches in her chart to reinforce the favourable element Metal.

However, in 1999 (Yin Earth Rabbit), there was a Yin Wood Rival present in the Annual Rabbit Branch. There was also a clash between the Annual Rabbit Branch and the Rooster Month and Year Branches in Drescher's chart. *The Nanny* finished its run and Drescher's divorce from husband Peter Marc Jacobson was finalized. Their marriage had lasted 21 years.

The Yang Wood Luck Cycle (age 43 to 47) contained a Rival that created issues for Drescher. In 2000 (Yang Metal Dragon year), she underwent a hysterectomy and was given a clean bill of health after being diagnosed with stage 1 uterine cancer. No post-operative therapy was required. Her favourable elements Metal and Earth were present in the Annual Stem and Branch. Drescher's experience formed the basis for her second memoir *Cancer Schmancer.*

The Tiger Luck Cycle (age 48 to 52) contained the negative elements Fire and Wood, as well as the second favourable element Earth. In 2005 (Yin Wood Rooster year), she returned with another sitcom *Living with Fran.* The Annual Rooster Branch combined with the Snake and Rooster Branches in her chart to reinforce the favourable element Metal.

The Yin Wood Luck Cycle (age 53 to 57) also contained the negative Self element for Drescher, although she was able to benefit in years with Metal and Earth. In 2011 (Yin Metal Rabbit year), Drescher had another sitcom *Happily Divorced.* The favourable element Metal was present in the Annual Stem. However, there was also a Yin Wood Rival present in the Annual Rabbit Branch. *Happily Divorced* only lasted two seasons.

The Rabbit Luck Cycle (age 58 to 62) clashed with the Rooster Month and Year Branches in Drescher's chart, disrupting the Partial Three Harmony Metal Combination. She was no longer a Follow the Power (Metal) chart and became more dependent on the Annual Stems and Branches. Drescher had a short-lived marriage to scientist and entrepreneur Shiva Ayadurai from 2014 (Yang Wood Horse year) to 2016 (Yang Fire Monkey year).

In the Yang Fire Luck Cycle (age 63 to 66), Drescher would have reverted back to a Follow the Power (Metal) chart and will become less dependent on the Annual Stems and Branches. The Dragon Luck Cycle (age 67 to 72) contains the second favourable element Earth, so this should be another positive period for her.

Example 5.12 Andy Roddick, American Tennis Player
(born August 30, 1982)

Hour	Day	Month	Year
	乙	戊	壬
	Yin Wood	Yang Earth	Yang Water
	酉	申	戌
	Rooster	Monkey	Dog

3	13	23	33
己	庚	辛	壬
Yin Earth	Yang Metal	Yin Metal	Yang Water
酉	戌	亥	子
Rooster	Dog	Pig	Rat

43	53	63	73
癸	甲	乙	丙
Yin Water	Yang Wood	Yin Wood	Yang Fire
丑	寅	卯	辰
Ox	Tiger	Rabbit	Dragon

There is a Seasonal Metal Combination in Roddick's birth chart. His Monkey Month Branch, Rooster Day Branch and Dog Year Branch combine to form Metal. There are no other Combinations in the chart. Metal is his most prominent element. As Roddick is a Yin Wood Day Master, Metal represents his Power element. He has a Follow the Power (Metal) chart.

Roddick enjoyed his initial success during the Dog Luck Cycle (age 18 to 22). In 2000 (Yang Metal Dragon year), there was a Stem Combination between the Annual Yang Metal Stem and Roddick's Yin Wood Day Master. The Power Element Combination indicates professional success or recognition. Roddick finished the year as the No. 1 ranked junior in the world, winning the Australian Open and US Open junior titles. The Annual Dragon Branch also clashed with his Dog Year Branch, disrupting the Seasonal Metal Combination. It combined with his Monkey Month Branch to form Water. Roddick became a Follow the Resource (Water) chart. His list of favourable elements became:

1) Resource element Water.
2) Power element Metal.
3) Output element Fire.
4) Wealth element Earth.
5) Self element Wood.

In 2003 (Yin Water Sheep year), Roddick had his breakthrough. The Annual Sheep Branch gave him the auspicious Sequence of Four Branches: Annual Sheep Branch, Monkey Year Branch, Rooster Day Branch and Dog Month Branch. Roddick reached the semifinals of the Australian Open and Wimbledon before winning the Men's Singles title at the US Open. He ended the year at No. 1 in the Association of Tennis Professionals (ATP) rankings, becoming the youngest American to do so.

In 2004 (Yang Wood Monkey year), Roddick had to contend with a Yang Wood Rival in the Annual Stem. As his Seasonal Metal Combination is already present, the Annual Monkey Branch contained the negative element Water. Roddick lost his US Open title and was runner-up in the Wimbledon final to Roger Federer. He finished the year ranked No. 2.

The Yin Metal Luck Cycle (age 23 to 27) contained the favourable element. In 2005 (Yin Wood Rooster year), the favourable element Metal was present in the Annual Rooster Branch. However, there is also a Yin Wood Rival present in the Annual Stem. Roddick finished the year ranked No. 3. Once again, he was runner up to Roger Federer at Wimbledon.

In 2006 (Yang Fire Dog year), the negative element Fire was present in the Annual Stem but the second favourable element Earth in the Annual Dog Branch. Roddick played poorly in the first half of the year but after hiring Jimmy Connors to be his coach, he was runner up in the US Open final to Roger Federer and finished the year ranked No. 3.

In 2007 (Yin Fire Pig year), the negative element Fire was present in the Annual Stem. In the first half of the year, Roddick once again struggled, failing to reach any Grand Slam finals. However, the Annual Pig Branch gave Roddick the auspicious Sequence of Four Branches: Monkey Month Branch, Rooster Day Branch, Dog Year Branch and Annual Pig Branch. Roddick was part of the US Davis Cup winning team.

In 2008 (Yang Earth Rat year), the Annual Rat Branch combined with his Monkey Month Branch to form Water. Roddick was transformed into a Follow the Resource (Water) chart. Roddick had a very favourable Partial Three Harmony Water Combination that consisted of his Nobleman Stars Monkey and Rat. This is called the Nobleman Harmony. He finally defeated Roger Federer for the first time in five years in Miami. However, the

Annual Yang Earth Stem controlled the flow of Water. Roddick stopped working with Jimmy Connors and had shoulder, neck and ankle injuries that affected his performance.

In 2009 (Yin Earth Ox year), the Annual Ox Branch combined with his Rooster Day Branch to form the favourable element Metal. The Rooster is located in his House of Spouse and the Combination with the Annual Ox indicated the possibility of love or marriage. Roddick married model Brooklyn Decker in April that year. He also reached the Wimbledon final that year, losing once again to Roger Federer in the longest ever final in terms of games played. He finished the year ranked No. 7.

In 2010 (Yang Metal Tiger year), there was a Stem Combination between the Annual Yang Metal Stem and Roddick's Yin Wood Day Master, indicating professional success and recognition. Roddick won the Miami Masters title defeating Rafael Nadal along the way. However, the Annual Tiger Branch clashed with Roddick's Monkey Month Branch and combined with his Dog Year Branch. Fire became the prevalent element. He was transformed into a Follow the Output (Fire) chart. The list of favourable elements became:

1) Output element Fire.
2) Wealth element Earth.
3) Power element Metal.
4) Self element Wood.
5) Resource element Water.

Roddick still ended the year ranked in the top 10 at No. 8. It was his ninth successive year in the top 10.

In the Pig Luck Cycle (age 28 to 32), the Luck Cycle gave Roddick the auspicious Configuration of Four Branches in a row: Monkey Month Branch, Rooster Day Branch, Dog Year Branch and Pig Luck Cycle. In 2011 (Yin Metal Rabbit year), the Annual Rabbit Branch combined with the Pig Luck Cycle to form a Partial Three Harmony

Wood Combination. Roddick was transformed into a Dominant Wood chart. His list of favourable elements became:

1) Resource element Water.
2) Self element Wood.
3) Output element Fire.
4) Wealth element Earth.
5) Power element Metal.

As Roddick's Seasonal Metal Combination was still present, there was a Metal-Wood conflict that year. Roddick suffered a back injury and fell out of the top 10, ending the year at No. 14.

In 2012 (Yang Water Dragon year), the Annual Dragon Branch clashed with Roddick's Dog Year Branch, disrupting the Seasonal Metal Combination. It combined with his Monkey Month Branch to form Water. Roddick became a Follow the Resource (Water) chart that year. Roddick announced his retirement that year on his 30th birthday.

During the Yang Water Luck Cycle (age 33 to 37), Roddick will be dependent on the Annual Stem and Branch to ascertain the nature of his chart. In the Rat Luck Cycle (age 38 to 42), he will transform into a Follow the Resource (Water) chart. In the Yin Water Luck Cycle (age 43 to 47), there will be a Stem Combination with the Yang Earth Month Stem, reducing the effect of Water. Roddick will be dependent on the Annual Stem and Branch to ascertain the flow of his chart. The Ox Luck Cycle (age 48 to 52) forms a Three Harmony Metal Combination with his Rooster Day Branch. As the House of Spouse is involved in a Combination, his chances of finding love or marriage will be higher during this period.

Example 5.13 Rick Springfield, Australian Singer
(born August 23, 1949, 19:00 hours)

Hour	Day	Month	Year
丙	乙	壬	己
Yang Fire	Yin Wood	Yang Water	Yin Earth
戌	酉	申	丑
Dog	Rooster	Monkey	Ox

5	15	25	35
辛	庚	己	戊
Yin Metal	Yang Metal	Yin Earth	Yang Earth
未	午	巳	辰
Sheep	Horse	Snake	Dragon

45	55	65	75
丁	丙	乙	甲
Yin Fire	Yang Fire	Yin Wood	Yang Wood
卯	寅	丑	子
Rabbit	Tiger	Ox	Rat

In the Day, Month and Year Pillars, there is a Partial Three Harmony Metal Combination in Springfield's birth chart. His Rooster Day Branch and Ox Year Branch combine to form Metal. In the Hour, Day and Month Pillars, there is a Seasonal Metal Combination involving the Monkey Month Branch, Rooster Day Branch and Dog Hour Branch. The most prominent element in Springfield's chart is Metal. As he is a Yin Wood Day Master, Metal represents his Power element. He has a Follow the Power (Metal) chart.

For a Yin Wood Day Master, the Special Stars are the Monkey and Ox. Springfield has both Special Stars in his chart: the Monkey Month Branch and the Ox Year Branch. This indicates that Springfield will have success early in life.

Springfield struggled to achieve success as a singer during the Horse Luck Cycle (age 20 to 24), which contained the negative element Fire. In 1969 (Yin Earth Rooster year), Springfield had joined the Australian rock group *Zoot*. The Annual Rooster Branch combined with the Ox and Rooster Branches in his chart to reinforce the favourable element Metal. However, *Zoot* broke up in 1971 (Yin Metal Pig year). The Annual Pig Branch gave Springfield the auspicious Configuration of Four Stems in a Row: Monkey Month Branch, Rooster Day Branch, Dog Hour Branch and Annual Pig Branch. He scored an Australian top 10 hit with *Speak to the Sky*. In 1972 (Yang Water Rat year), there was a Combination between the Annual Rat Branch and his Monkey Month Branch. The prevalent element in his chart became Water. Springfield became a Follow the Resource (Water) chart. His list of favourable elements became:

1) Resource element Water.
2) Power element Metal.
3) Output element Fire.
4) Wealth element Earth.
5) Self element Wood.

Although his debut album *Beginnings* made the US Top 20, Springfield was typecast as a bubblegum teenage pop idol. In the favourable Yin Earth Luck Cycle (age 25 to 29), Springfield branched into acting. In 1977 (Yin Fire Snake year), the Annual Snake Branch combined with his Ox and Rooster Branches to form the Full Three Harmony Metal Combination. He made his acting debut in an episode of the popular television series *The Six Million Dollar Man*.

The Snake Luck Cycle (age 30 to 34) formed the Full Three Harmony Metal Combination with the Ox and Rooster Branches in Springfield's chart. In 1981 (Yin Metal Rooster year), the Annual Rooster Branch combined with the Snake Luck Cycle and the Ox and Rooster Branches in his chart to reinforce the favourable element Metal. Springfield had a US No. 1 hit with *Jessie's Girl* from his US Top 10 album *Working Class Dog*. He also became a soap opera star on *General Hospital*. He also won the Grammy Award for Best Male Rock Vocal Performance. In 1982 (Yang Water Dog year), the second favourable element Earth was present in the Annual Dog Branch. Springfield had a US No. 2 hit with *Don't Talk to Strangers* from the No. 2 album *Success Hasn't Spoiled Me Yet*. Springfield's success continued in 1983 (Yin Water Pig year). The Annual Pig Branch gave him the auspicious Configuration of Four Branches in a Row: Monkey Month Branch, Rooster Day Branch, Dog Hour Branch, Annual Pig Branch. He had another top 10 hit *Affair of the Heart* from the album *Living In Oz*.

In 1984 (Yang Wood Rat year) during the Yang Earth Luck Cycle (age 35 to 39), Springfield starred in his own musical *Hard to Hold* with a US Top 5 hit *Love Somebody*. The Annual Rat Branch combined with his Monkey Month Branch to form Water. He was transformed into a Follow the Resource (Water) chart. He also married girlfriend Barbara Potter that year. They had met in 1981 (Yin Metal Rooster year) when Potter was the recording studio receptionist at the studio where he was recording *Working Class Dog*. It was a Rooster year, his House of Spouse animal. In 1985 (Yin Wood Ox year), Springfield reverted back to a Follow the Power (Metal) chart. The Annual Ox Branch combined with his Rooster and Ox Branches to reinforce the favourable element Metal. He released another album *Tao* with two US Top 30 hits. His first son Liam was also born that year, and Springfield took time off from recording to spend more time with his family.

In the Dragon Luck Cycle (age 40 to 44), the Dragon clashed with his Dog Hour Branch, disrupting the Seasonal Metal Combination. It also combined with his Monkey Month Branch to form Water. Springfield became a Follow the Resource (Water) chart. He spent this period working on television movies and series. The Yin Fire Luck Cycle (age 45 to 49) formed a Stem Combination with his Yang Water Month Stem. This reduced the negative effects of Fire. The Rabbit Luck Cycle (age 50 to 54) was stressful as there was a clash with the Rooster Day Branch, disrupting the Seasonal Metal Combination. It also contained a Yin Wood Rival. Springfield rebounded in the Yang Fire Luck Cycle (age 55 to 59) as he was invited back to *General Hospital* to reprise his role in 2005 (Yin Wood Rooster year). The Annual Rooster Branch contained the favourable element Metal.

The Tiger Luck Cycle (age 60 to 64) clashed with his Monkey Month Branch, disrupting the Seasonal Metal Combination. It also combined with the Dog Hour Branch to form Fire. He transformed into a Follow the Output (Fire) chart. His list of favourable elements became:

1) Output element Fire.
2) Wealth element Earth.
3) Power element Metal.
4) Self element Wood.
5) Resource element Water.

In 2010 (Yang Metal Tiger year), Springfield released his autobiography *Late, Late at Night*. There was a Stem Combination between the Annual Yang Metal Stem and his Yin Wood Day Master. This indicated professional recognition and success. The Annual Tiger Branch also combined with his Dog Hour Branch and his Tiger Luck Cycle to reinforce the favourable element Fire.

In 2015 (Yin Wood Sheep year) in the Yin Wood Luck Cycle (age 65 to 69), Springfield returned to the big screen opposite Meryl Streep in the drama *Ricki and the Flash*. He also appeared in the television series *True Detective*. The Annual Sheep Branch gave him the auspicious Sequence of Four Branches in a Row: Annual Sheep Branch, Monkey Month Branch, Rooster Day Branch and Dog Hour Branch.

Example 5.14 James Gandolfini, American Actor
(born September 18, 1961,
died June 19, 2013, 2200 hours)

Hour	Day	Month	Year
	甲	丁	辛
	Yang Wood	Yin Fire	Yin Metal
	寅	酉	丑
	Tiger	Rooster	Ox

3	13	23	33	43
丙	乙	甲	癸	壬
Yang Fire	Yin Wood	Yang Wood	Yin Water	Yang Water
申	未	午	巳	辰
Monkey	Sheep	Horse	Snake	Dragon

Hour	Day	Month	Year
己	丙	戊	癸
Yin Earth	Yang Fire	Yang Earth	Yin Water
亥	辰	午	巳
Pig	Dragon	Horse	Snake

There is a Partial Three Harmony Metal Combination in Gandolfini's birth chart. His Rooster Month Branch and Ox Year Branch combine to form Metal. There is also a Yin Metal Year Stem. There are no other Combinations in the chart. The prevalent element is Metal. As Gandolfini is a Yang Wood Day Master, Metal is his Power element. He has a Follow the Power (Metal) chart.

During the Sheep Luck Cycle (age 18 to 22), Gandolfini graduated from Park Ridge High School in 1979 (Yin Earth Sheep year). Although the Sheep Luck Cycle and Annual Sheep Branch disrupted the Three Harmony Metal Combination by clashing with the Ox Year Branch, the second favourable element Earth was still present. There was also a Stem Combination between Gandolfini's Yang Wood Day Master and the Annual Yin Earth Stem. The Wealth Element Combination indicates opportunities to generate wealth. In 1982 (Yang Water Dog year), he graduated with a Bachelor of Arts degree in communication studies from Rutgers University. The Annual Yang Water Stem combined with the negative Yin Fire Month Stem, reducing its negative effect.

In the Yin Water Luck Cycle (age 33 to 37), Gandolfini had his first major film role, playing a hit man in the thriller *True Romance* in 1993 (Yin Water Rooster year). The Annual Rooster Branch combined with the Rooster and Ox Branches in his chart to reinforce the favourable element Metal. In 1997 (Yin Fire Ox year), Gandolfini appeared alongside Sean Penn and John Travolta in John Cassavetes' film *She's So Lovely*. The Annual Ox Branch combined with the Rooster and Ox Branches in his chart to reinforce the favourable Metal.

The Snake Luck Cycle (age 38 to 42) combined with the Rooster and Ox Branches in Gandolfini's birth chart to form the Full Three Harmony Metal Combination. In 1999 (Yin Earth Rabbit year), Gandolfini appeared in his most well known role as Tony Soprano, a New Jersey mob boss having a midlife crisis in the series *The Sopranos*. There was a Stem Combination between his Yang Wood Day Master and the Annual Yin Earth Stem, indicating the possibility of generating wealth. For a man, the Wealth element also represents the Spouse. Gandolfini married Marcy Woldarski that year.

He won three Primetime Emmy Awards for Outstanding Lead Actor in a Drama Series in 2000 (Yang Metal Dragon year), 2001 (Yin Metal Snake year) and 2003 (Yin Water Sheep year). The favourable elements Metal and Earth were present in the Annual Stems and Branches. In 2001 (Yin Metal Snake year), the Annual Snake Branch also combined with the Rooster and Ox and the Snake Luck Cycle to reinforce the favourable element Metal. That same year, Gandolfini also appeared alongside Brad Pitt and Julia Roberts in the action comedy *The Mexican*. In 2002 (Yang Water Horse year), the negative element Fire was present in the Annual Branch. Gandolfini divorced his first wife Woldarski.

The Yang Water Luck Cycle (age 43 to 47) was also favourable for Gandolfini. It combined with the negative Yin Fire Month Stem, reducing its negative effect. In 2006 (Yang Fire Dog year), the second favourable element Earth was present. Gandolfini appeared in the remake of the political drama *All The King's Men* alongside Sean Penn and Kate Winslett. On a personal note, Gandolfini started dating former model and actress Deborah Lin. There was a Combination between the Annual Dog Branch and the Tiger in his House of Spouse. This indicated the possibility of romance. Gandolfini would marry Lin two years later. In 2007 (Yin Fire Pig year), there was a Yang Wood Rival present in the Annual Pig Branch. *The Sopranos* ended its run after eight years.

The Dragon Luck Cycle (from age 48) contained the second favourable element Earth. In 2009 (Yin Earth Ox year), the Ox Branch combined with the Rooster and Ox Branches in Gandolfini's chart to reinforce Metal. Gandolfini appeared in the action remake *The Taking of Pelham 123* alongside John Travolta and Denzel Washington. There was a Stem Combination between his Yang Wood Day Master and the Annual Yin Earth Stem, indicating the possibility of generating wealth. In 2012 (Yang Water Dragon year), the second favourable element Earth was present in the Annual Dragon Branch. Gandolfini appeared alongside Brad Pitt in the crime film *Killing Them Softly*.

Gandolfini died at the age of 51 on June 19, 2013 (Yin Water Snake year) in Rome after suffering a heart attack. He had spent the day sightseeing with his family in sweltering heat. His 13 year-old son Michael found him unconscious around 10 pm in his room. On the day he died, there was a Full Three Harmony Metal Combination between the Annual Snake Branch and his Rooster and Ox Branches. There was also a Partial Three Harmony Fire Combination between the Horse month and his Tiger Day Branch. There was a Metal-Fire Conflict.

Example 5.15 Joan Rivers, American Comedienne
(born June 8, 1933, 02:00 hours, died September 4, 2014)

Hour	Day	Month	Year
丁	乙	戊	癸
Yin Fire	Yin Wood	Yang Earth	Yin Water
丑	巳	午	酉
Ox	Snake	Horse	Rooster

10	20	30	40
己	庚	辛	壬
Yin Earth	Yang Metal	Yin Metal	Yang Water
未	申	酉	戌
Sheep	Monkey	Rooster	Dog

50	60	70	80
癸	甲	乙	丙
Yin Water	Yang Wood	Yin Wood	Yang Fire
亥	子	丑	
Pig	Rat	Ox	

Hour	Day	Month	Year
	戊	癸	甲
	Yang Earth	Yin Water	Yang Wood
	寅	酉	午
	Tiger	Rooster	Horse

There is a Full Three Harmony Metal Combination in Rivers' birth chart. Her Snake Day Branch combines with her Rooster Year Branch and Ox Hour Branch to form Metal. The Horse Month Branch does not interfere with the Combination. There are no other Branch Combinations present within the chart. The most prominent element is Metal. As Rivers is a Yin Wood Day Master, Metal represents the Power element. She has a Follow the Power (Metal) chart.

283

In 1955 (Yin Wood Sheep year) during the Yang Metal Luck Cycle (age 20 to 24), Rivers married James Sanger, the son of a Bonds clothing store manager. The Yang Metal in the Luck Cycle formed a Stem Combination with her Yin Wood Day Master, indicating the possibility of professional recognition and success. For a woman, the Power Element Combination also suggests the possibility of love or marriage. The Annual Sheep Branch also combined with her Snake in the House of Spouse and the Horse Month Branch to form the Seasonal Fire Combination. However, as this is not a favourable element for Rivers, her marriage was annulled after six months.

During the Yin Metal Luck Cycle (age 30 to 34), Rivers had her first major career break in 1965 (Yin Wood Snake year) when she appeared on *The Tonight Show* with Johnny Carson. The Luck Cycle provided an auspicious Sequence of the four Yin Stems: Yin Wood Day Master, Yin Fire Hour Stem, Yin Metal Luck Cycle, Yin Water Year Stem. The favourable element Metal was also present. The Annual Snake Branch combined with the Snake and Rooster Branches in Rivers' chart to reinforce the favourable element Metal. On a personal note, Rivers married television producer Ed Rosenberg the same year. Her House of Spouse animal Snake was also present that year. This indicated the possibility of love or marriage. Rivers gave birth to daughter Melissa on January 20, 1968 (still the Yin Fire Sheep year). Her Output or Child element was present in the Annual Stem and Branch.

The Rooster Luck Cycle (age 35 to 39) combined with her Snake and Rooster Branches to reinforce the favourable element Metal. Rivers became a household name during this period as she continued to appear on *The Tonight Show* and also *The Ed Sullivan Show*. In 1969 (Yin Earth Rooster year), Rivers had her own daytime program *The Joan Rivers Show*. The Annual Rooster year combined with the Rooster Luck Cycle and the Rooster and Snake Branches in her chart to reinforce Metal.

In the Yang Water Luck Cycle (age 40 to 44), Rivers wrote the script for the TV movie *The Girl Most Likely to ...*, featuring Stockard Channing in 1973 (Yin Water Ox year). The Annual Ox Branch combined with the Snake, Rooster and Ox Branches in River's chart to reinforce the favourable element Metal. However, the negative element Water is present in the Luck Cycle and Annual Stem, so the movie was not that successful.

The Dog Luck Cycle (age 45 to 49) combined with Rivers' Horse Month Branch to form the negative element Fire. There was a Fire Metal conflict within her chart. In 1978 (Yang Earth Horse year), the Annual Horse Branch combined with he Dog Luck Cycle and Horse Month Branch to reinforce the negative element Fire. Rivers directed her first feature film *Rabbit Test* starring Billy Crystal. The comedy about a pregnant man was not a success.

During the Yin Water Luck Cycle (age 50 to 54), Rivers started her own late night talk show, *The Talk Show Starring Joan Rivers* in 1986 (Yang Fire Tiger year). While she became the first woman to host a late night television talk show, her friendship with Johnny Carson ended as a result. The Annual Tiger Branch combined with her Horse Month Branch to form the negative element Fire. In 1987 (Yin Fire Rabbit year), the show was cancelled and husband Rosenberg committed suicide by overdosing on prescription drugs. There was a Yin Wood Rival present in the Annual Branch.

The Pig Luck Cycle (age 55 to 59) contained a Yang Wood Rival. Rivers revealed that she developed bulimia nervosa as a result of her husband's suicide and had contemplated suicide. She recovered with counselling and the support of her family and in 1989 (Yin Earth Snake year), she started the daytime show *The Joan Rivers Show*. The Annual Snake Branch also combined with the Snake and Ox Branches in her chart to reinforce the favourable element Metal. In 1990 (Yang Metal Horse year), there was a Stem Combination between the Annual Stem and her Yin Wood Day Master. This indicated professional success and recognition. Rivers won an Emmy for Outstanding Talk Show Host and received her star on the Hollywood Walk of Fame. In the Yang Wood (age 60 to 64), Rat (age 65 to 69) and Yin Wood (age 70 to 74) Luck Cycles, Rivers maintained a constant presence on television.

In the Ox Luck Cycle (age 75 to 79), Rivers was going from strength to strength. The Ox combined with the Ox and Snake Branches in her chart to reinforce the favourable element Metal. In 2010 (Yang Metal Tiger year), she was the subject of an acclaimed documentary *Joan Rivers: A Piece of Work*. There was a Stem Combination between the Annual Stem and her Yin Wood Day Master, indicating professional success and recognition.

Rivers died after developing complications during vocal cord surgery in 2014 (Yang Wood Horse year) during the Yang Fire Luck Cycle (from age 80). She had developed cardiac arrest and stopped breathing during the procedure on August 28 (Yin Metal Sheep day). Rivers was then transferred to hospital and placed on life support and died on September 4, having not woken up from her medically induced coma. On the day she died, there was a Partial Three Harmony Fire Combination between the Tiger day and the Annual Horse Branch. The Rooster month combined with her Snake Day Branch and Ox Hour Branch to form the Full Three Harmony Metal Combination. There was a Fire-Metal conflict.

Example 5.16 Allan Carr, American Producer
(born May 27, 1937, died June 29, 1999)

Hour	Day	Month	Year
	甲	乙	丁
	Yang Wood	Yin Wood	Yin Fire
	寅	巳	丑
	Tiger	Snake	Ox

7	17	27	37	47	57
甲	癸	壬	辛	庚	己
Yang Wood	Yin Water	Yang Water	Yin Metal	Yang Metal	Yin Earth
辰	卯	寅	丑	子	亥
Dragon	Rabbit	Tiger	Ox	Rat	Pig

Hour	Day	Month	Year
	壬	庚	己
	Yang Water	Yang Metal	Yin Earth
	子	午	卯
	Rat	Horse	Rabbit

There is a Partial Three Harmony Metal Combination in Carr's birth chart. His Snake Month Branch and Ox Year Branch combine to form Metal. There are no other Combinations in the chart. The prevalent element is Metal. As Carr is a Yang Wood Day Master, Metal represents the Power element. He has a Follow the Power (Metal) chart.

In 1966 (Yang Fire Horse year), during the Yang Water Luck Cycle (age 27 to 31), Carr founded his own talent agency Allan Carr Enterprises. He managed artistes such as Tony Curtis, Peter Sellers, Joan Rivers, Paul Anka and Frankie Valli and the Four Seasons. The Annual Yang Fire Stem gave Carr's chart the auspicious Sequence of Four Stems: Yang Wood Day Master, Yin Wood Month Stem, Annual Yang Fire Stem and Yin Fire Year Stem.

The Yin Metal Luck Cycle (age 37 to 41) contained Carr's favourable element Metal. In 1976 (Yang Fire Dragon year) with the auspicious Sequence of Four Stems, Carr scored a major box office hit with *Survive!* He re-edited and re-dubbed a low-budget foreign film about a real-life disaster. In 1977 (Yin Fire Snake year), producer Robert Stigwood gave Carr the responsibility of marketing *Saturday Night Fever*, who turned the movie premiere into a television special. The Annual Snake Branch combined with the Snake and Ox Branches to reinforce the favourable element Metal. In 1978 (Yang Earth Horse year), Carr produced the musical *Grease* and cast his client Olivia Newton-John opposite John Travolta. It became the highest grossing film of the year.

The Ox Luck Cycle (age 42 to 46) combined with the Snake and Ox Branches in Carr's chart to reinforce the favourable element Metal. In 1980 (Yang Metal Monkey year), Carr produced the Village People musical *Can't Stop the Music*, which was a critical and commercial failure. Although the favourable element Metal was present in the Annual Stem and Branch, the negative element Water was also hidden within the Annual Monkey. In 1982 (Yang Water Dog year), Carr rebounded with the sequel *Grease 2* with Michelle Pfeiffer. While not as successful as *Grease*, it recouped its investment. The second favourable element Earth was present in the Annual Branch.

The Yang Metal Luck Cycle (age 47 to 51) was also favourable for Carr. During this period, Carr produced a musical version of the French play *La Cage aux Folles*, which ran for five years, the entire duration of this Luck Cycle. It won six Tony Awards in 1984 (Yang Wood Rat year), and was later remade as *The Birdcage*. In early 1989 (Yin Earth Snake year), Carr was asked to produce the 61st Annual Academy Awards. There was a Stem Combination between his Yang Wood Day Master and the Annual Yin Earth Stem, indicating the possibility of generating wealth. The Annual Snake Branch also combined with the Snake and Ox Branches to reinforce the favourable element Metal. His decision to change the award announcement from "And the winner is" to "the Oscar goes to" became the industry standard.

Carr died of liver cancer at the age of 62 on June 9, 1999 (Yin Earth Rabbit year) during the Pig Luck Cycle (from age 62). The Pig Luck Cycle clashed with the Snake Month Branch in his chart, disrupting the Three Harmony Metal Combination that allows him to Follow Power. It also combined with the Annual Rabbit Branch to form a Partial Three Harmony Wood Combination, which represents Carr's Wood Rivals. The Horse month also combined with his Tiger Day Branch to form the negative element Fire. Fire attacked his favourable element Metal and the negative element Wood did not help. In Chinese medicine, the organs associated with Wood are the gall bladder and live.

Example 5.17 Cilla Black, British Singer
(born May 27, 1943, 08:00 hours, died August 1, 2015)

Hour	Day	Month	Year
庚	乙	丁	癸
Yang Metal	Yin Wood	Yin Fire	Yin Water
辰	酉	巳	未
Dragon	Rooster	Snake	Sheep

3	13	23	33
戊	己	庚	辛
Yang Earth	Yin Earth	Yang Metal	Yin Metal
午	未	申	酉
Horse	Sheep	Monkey	Rooster

43	53	63
壬	癸	甲
Yang Water	Yin Water	Yang Wood
戌	亥	子
Dog	Pig	Rat

Hour	Day	Month	Year
	己	癸	乙
	Yin Earth	Yin Water	Yin Wood
	酉	未	未
	Rooster	Sheep	Sheep

There is a Partial Three Harmony Metal Combination in Black's birth chart. Her Rooster Day Branch combines with her Snake Month Branch to form Metal. There is also a Yang Metal Hour Stem. The most prominent element is Metal. As Black is a Yin Wood Day Master, Metal represents the Power element. She has a Follow the Power (Metal) chart.

There is a Heaven and Earth Union between the Day and Hour Pillars. The Yang Metal Hour Stem forms a Stem Combination with the Yin Wood Day Master, while the Dragon Hour Branch forms a Six Harmony Combination with the Rooster Day Branch. This indicates success and recognition in the later half of life. Although Black rose to fame as a singer in the 1960s, she became renowned as a television presenter in the second half of her life.

Black first achieved success in 1964 (Yang Wood Dragon year) during the Sheep Luck Cycle (age 18 to 22). She scored two Number 1 UK hits that sold more than a million copies worldwide: *Anyone Who Had a Heart* and *You're My World*. The second favourable element Earth was present in both the Luck Cycle and the Annual Dragon Branch. In 1965 (Yin Wood Snake year), she scored a Number 2 UK hit with her version of the Righteous Brothers' *You've Lost That Lovin' Feelin'*. The Annual Snake Branch combined with the Snake and Rooster Branches in her chart to reinforce the favourable element metal.

The Yang Metal Luck Cycle (age 23 to 27) formed a Stem Combination with Black's Yin Wood Day Master. The Power Element Combination indicates professional success and recognition. For a woman, it also indicates the possibility of love or marriage. In 1969 (Yin Earth Rooster year), Black married her boyfriend and manager Bobby Willis. The House of Spouse animal Rooster was present that year, indicating a higher chance of love or marriage. The Annual Rooster Branch also combined with the Snake and Rooster Branches in her chart to reinforce the favourable element Metal. Black returned to the UK top 10 with *Conversations* and *Surround Yourself with Sorrow*.

The Monkey Luck Cycle (age 28 to 32) contained the favourable element Metal and the negative element Water. In 1971 (Yin Metal Pig year), she scored a UK Number 3 hit with *Something Tells Me (Something's Gonna Happen Tonight)*. The Annual Yin Metal Stem gave her the auspicious Configuration of Four Yin Stems of the different seasons: Yin Wood Day Master, Yin Fire Month Stem, Annual Yin Metal Stem and Yin Water Year Stem. She also hosted her own television programme *Cilla* during this period. It ran from January 1968 (still the Yin Fire Sheep year) to April 1976 (Yang Fire Dragon year).

The favourable element Metal was present in the Yin Metal (age 33 to 37) and Rooster (age 38 to 42) Luck Cycles. The Rooster Luck Cycle combined with the Rooster and Snake Branches in her chart to reinforce the favourable element Metal. Black was mainly performing in concerts and cabarets. In 1983 (Yin Water Pig year), she shot back into public consciousness with her performance on *Wogan* and her own Christmas special, *Cilla Black's Christmas*. There was a Special Configuration that year: when the Yin Fire Snake encounters the Yin Water Pig, there is success. Black has a Yin Fire Snake Month Pillar and it was a Yin Water Pig year. In 1985 (Yin Wood Ox year), she signed a contract with London Television and became the host of two popular and long running television shows: *Blind Date* and *Surprise Surprise*. Throughout the Yang Water (age 43 to 47) and Dog (age 48 to 52) Luck Cycles, Black's programs rated well and she became the highest paid female performer on UK television.

The Yin Water (age 53 to 57) and Pig (age 58 to 62) Luck Cycles were also favourable for Black due to the Special Configuration. Her Yin Fire Snake Month Pillar worked in conjunction with the Yin Water Pig Luck Cycle to bring her success. However, in 1999 (Yin Earth Rabbit year), husband Willis died of lung cancer. The Yin Wood Rival was present in the Annual Branch. On the professional front, although *Blind Date* finished its run in 2001 (Yin Metal Snake year) and *Surprise Surprise* in 2003 (Yin Water Sheep year), Black continued to appear on television specials.

In the Rat Luck Cycle (from age 68), the Rat combined with the Dragon Hour Branch to form a Partial Three Harmony Water Combination. Metal was still present in her chart due to the Rooster and Snake Combination. Water became the most prominent element, so Black became a Follow the Resource (Water) chart. Her list of favourable elements became:

1) Resource element Water.
2) Power element Metal.
3) Output element Fire.
4) Wealth element Earth.
5) Self element Wood.

Black died from a stroke after falling at her holiday home in Spain on August 1, 2015. The Rooster day combined with her Snake and Rooster Branches to form the favourable element Metal. However, as she was now a Follow the Resource (Water) chart, the Earth within the Sheep month and year were damaging to her. It was also a Yin Earth day, causing an Earth-Water conflict.

Example 5.18 Jason Derulo, American Singer
(born September 21, 1989)

Hour	Day	Month	Year
	甲	癸	己
	Yang Wood	Yin Water	Yin Earth
	申	酉	巳
	Monkey	Rooster	Snake

4	14	24	34
壬	辛	庚	己
Yang Water	Yin Metal	Yang Metal	Yin Earth
申	未	午	巳
Monkey	Sheep	Horse	Snake

44	54	64	74
戊	丁	丙	乙
Yang Earth	Yin Fire	Yang Fire	Yin Wood
辰	卯	寅	丑
Dragon	Rabbit	Tiger	Ox

There is a Partial Three Harmony Metal Combination in Derulo's birth chart. His Rooster Month Branch combines with his Snake Year Branch to form Metal. There are no other Combinations within his chart. The most prominent element is Metal. As Derulo is a Yang Wood Day Master, Metal represents the Power element. He has a Follow the Power (Metal) chart.

During the Sheep Luck Cycle (age 19 to 23), Derulo first achieved success in 2009 (Yin Earth Ox year). The Annual Ox Branch formed the Full Three Harmony Metal Combination with the Rooster and Ox Branches within his chart. Derulo's debut single *Whatcha Say* topped the US Singles charts for a week and follow-up *In My Head* was also a US Top 5 hit. His success continued in 2010 (Yang

Metal Tiger year) as he released his debut self titled debut album *Jason Derulo*. The Annual Stem contained the favourable element Metal.

In 2011 (Yin Metal Rabbit year), Derulo released his follow-up album *Future History*, with the UK Top 10 Singles *Don't Wanna Go Home* and *Fight for You*. The favourable element Metal was present in the Annual Stem. However, the Annual Rabbit Branch contained a Yin Wood Rival. Derulo broke one of his neck vertebrae during rehearsal for his *Future History* tour. He had to cancel all tour dates.

Derulo's success continued in the Yang Metal Luck Cycle (age 24 to 28). In 2013 (Yin Water Snake year), he returned to the US and UK Top 10 with *Talk Dirty* from the album *Tattoos*. The Annual Snake Branch combined with the Rooster and Snake Branches in his chart to reinforce the favourable element Metal. In 2015 (Yin Wood Sheep year), Derulo released his fourth album *Everything is 4* with *Want to Want Me*, a US Top 5 and UK Number 1 hit. The second favourable element Earth was present in the Annual Sheep Branch.

The Horse Luck Cycle (age 29 to 33) may be challenging for Derulo as the negative element Fire will be present. The Yin Earth Luck Cycle (age 34 to 38) will be more favourable for Derulo. There will be a Stem Combination between the Yin Earth and his Yang Wood Day Master. The Wealth Element Combination indicates the possibility of generating wealth. For a man, the Wealth element also represents the Spouse, so this will be the period for Derulo to get married.

The Snake Luck Cycle (age 39 to 43) combines with the Rooster and Snake Branches in his chart to reinforce the favourable element Metal. However, there is also a Six Harmony Combination between the Snake and his Monkey in the House of Spouse. This indicates the possibility of finding love or marriage.

The Yang Earth Luck Cycle (age 44 to 48) will also be favourable. In the Dragon Luck Cycle (age 49 to 53), there is a Combination between the Dragon and the Monkey to form Water. As the Metal Combination between the Rooster and Snake will still be present, Water becomes the most prominent element. Derulo becomes a Follow the Resource (Water) chart. The list of favourable elements will be as follows:

1) Resource element Water.
2) Power element Metal.
3) Output element Fire.
4) Wealth element Earth.
5) Self element Wood.

As the Combination involves the Monkey in his House of Spouse, his chances of finding love or marriage during this period will also be increased.

Conclusion

From the 18 examples that have been discussed in this chapter, the ranking of elements for Follow the Power (Metal) charts is:

1) Power element Metal.
2) Wealth element Earth.
3) Resource element Water.
4) Self element Wood.
5) Output element Fire.

All the examples covered were Yang Wood or Yin Wood Day Masters with birth charts where Metal is the most prominent element. This qualified them as Follow the Power (Metal) charts.

Joan Rivers has the Full Three Harmony Metal Combination consisting of the Snake, Rooster and Ox.

Jana Novotna, Helena Bonham Carter, Zola Budd Pieterse and Jason Derulo have the Partial Three Harmony Combination comprising the Snake and Rooster. Anne Rice, Alan Ball and Fran Drescher have a Snake combining with two Roosters, while Elisabeth Hasselbeck has a Rooster combining with two Snakes in her chart.

Jay Chou and James Gandolfini have the Partial Three Harmony Metal Combination consisting of the Rooster and Ox. Julia Gillard has a Rooster combining with two Oxes in her chart.

Alan Carr has the Partial Three Harmony Metal Combination comprising the Snake and Ox.

Michelle Williams does not have any Metal Combinations in their charts. She has two Rooster Branches that allow Metal to be the most prominent element.

Bill Medley has the Partial Three Harmony Metal Combination consisting of the Rooster and Ox. However, as he is born in a Dragon Year, he becomes a Follow the Resource (Water) chart when there is a Monkey or Rat year or Luck Cycle.

Cilla Black has the Snake and Rooster in her chart. As she is born in a Dragon Hour, she can also Follow the Resource (Water) during the Monkey or Rat year or Luck Cycle.

Andy Roddick has the Seasonal Metal Combination in his chart, with the potential to change into a Follow the Resource (Water) or Follow the Output (Fire) chart. Rick Springfield has a Partial Three Harmony Metal Combination consisting of the Rooster and Ox in the first half of his life and a Seasonal Metal Combination in the second half of his life. He also has the potential to change into a Follow the Resource (Water) or Follow the Output (Fire) chart.

Chapter Six Dominant Metal Charts

Dominant charts are defined by the presence of a Full or Partial Three Harmony Combination or Seasonal Combination that forms the same element as the Day Master. For Dominant Metal charts, the Day Masters would be Yang Metal or Yin Metal with a Full or Partial Three Harmony Metal Combination or Seasonal Metal Combination within the Branches. Note that this definition does not apply to charts with Earth Day Masters, as there are no Full or Partial Three Harmony Combinations or Seasonal Earth Combinations. Dominant Earth charts will be discussed in the forthcoming book on Earth charts.

Those with Dominant charts are motivated, industrious, driven, determined and not adverse to hard work. They are intolerant of those whom they perceive to be lazy or lacking in motivation. They take the initiative in whatever project they undertake and rely on themselves for their success. Unlike the Follow charts, they do not wait for opportunities from mentors or friends. As they work harder to achieve success, they are better equipped to deal with adversity.

For Dominant charts, the ranking of elements is as follows:

1) Earth, the Resource element.
2) Metal, the Self element. Unlike the other charts, they are not afraid of Rivals or Competitors. They gain support from the Self element.
3) Water, the Output element. It controls the negative Power element Fire.
4) Wood, the Wealth element. The Wealth element Wood supports the negative Power element Fire.
5) Fire, the Power element. Dominant charts do not like to be controlled. Fire controls Metal.

Dominant Metal charts benefit from the first three elements: Earth, Metal and Water.

Example 6.1 Mary Pierce, French Tennis Player
(born January 15, 1975, 01:07 hours)

Hour	Day	Month	Year
己	辛	丁	甲
Yin Earth	Yin Metal	Yin Fire	Yang Wood
丑	酉	丑	寅
Ox	Rooster	Ox	Tiger

3	13	23	33
丙	乙	甲	癸
Yang Fire	Yin Wood	Yang Wood	Yin Water
子	亥	戌	酉
Rat	Pig	Dog	Rooster

43	53	63	73
壬	辛	庚	己
Yang Water	Yin Metal	Yang Metal	Yin Earth
申	未	午	巳
Monkey	Sheep	Horse	Snake

There is a Partial Three Harmony Metal Combination in Pierce's birth chart. Her Rooster Day Branch combines with her Ox Month and Hour Branches to form Metal. As Pierce is a Yin Metal Day Master, Metal represents her Self element. She has a Dominant Metal chart.

The Yin Fire Month Stem contains the negative element. It also occupies the position represented by the Father. Pierce has a contentious relationship with her father Jim. In 1993 (Yin Water Rooster year), she filed a restraining order to prevent him from attending her tennis matches due to his disruptive behaviour. They were estranged for several years.

300

In 1989 (Yin Earth Snake year) during the Yin Wood Luck Cycle (age 13 to 17), Pierce became one of the youngest players to turn professional. The Annual Snake Branch combined with the Rooster and Ox Branches in her chart to form the Full Three Harmony Metal Combination.

The Pig Luck Cycle (age 18 to 22) formed a Six Harmony Combination with her Tiger Year Branch. This indicated assistance from mentors. In 1994 (Yang Wood Dog year), the Annual Dog Branch combined with her Tiger Year Branch to form Fire, producing a Fire-Metal conflict in her chart. Although Pierce beat Steffi Graf on her way to the French Open final, she lost in straight sets to Aranxta Sanchez-Vicario. However, in January 1995 (Yin Earth Ox month in the Yang Wood Dog year), Pierce won her first Grand Slam Singles title at the Australian Open. The Ox month combined with the Rooster and Ox Branches in her chart to reinforce the favourable element Metal. In January 1997 (still the Yang Fire Rat year), Pierce reached the final of the Australian Open for the second time, where she lost to Martina Hingis. The Annual Yang Fire Stem formed a Stem Combination with Pierce's Yin Metal Day Master. The Power Element Combination indicated the possibility of professional success or recognition.

The Yang Wood Luck Cycle (age 23 to 27) contained the negative element. Pierce struggled during this period. However, in 2000 (Yang Metal Dragon year), the favourable elements Metal and Earth were present. Pierce won her second Grand Slam Singles title at the French Open. She also won the Ladies' Doubles title at the same tournament with Martina Hingis. However, by 2002 (Yang Water Horse year), the Annual Horse Branch combined with her Tiger Year Branch to form Fire, resulting in a Fire-Metal conflict. Her ranking dropped to almost 300.

The Dog Luck Cycle (age 28 to 32) combined with Pierce's Tiger Year Branch to form Fire. There was a Fire-Metal conflict. Pierce struggled with injuries during this period. However, in 2005 (Yin Metal Rooster year), the Annual Rooster Branch combined with the Rooster and Ox Branches in her chart to reinforce the favourable element Metal. Pierce was runner-up in two Grand Slam tournaments that year, at the French Open (to Justine Henin) and the US Open (to Kim Clijsters). She also won the Wimbledon Mixed Doubles Title with Mahesh Bhupathi. In 2006 (Yang Fire Dog year), the Annual Dog Branch combined with Pierce's Tiger Year Branch and the Dog Luck Cycle to reinforce the negative element Fire. Pierce tore one of her knee ligaments playing in Vienna, which effectively ended her playing career.

The Yin Water (age 33 to 37) and Rooster (age 38 to 42) Luck Cycles were favourable for Pierce as they contained her favourable elements Water and Metal. In 2013 (Yin Water Snake year), Pierce moved to Mauritius where she coached younger players. The Annual Snake Branch combined with the Rooster and Ox Branches in her chart to form the Full Three Harmony Metal Combination. The Yang Water (age 43 to 47), Monkey (age 48 to 52) and Yin Metal (age 53 to 57) Luck Cycles are all favourable for Pierce.

Example 6.2 Collette Dinnigan,
Australian Fashion Designer (born September 24, 1965)

Hour	Day	Month	Year
	辛	乙	乙
	Yin Metal	Yin Wood	Yin Wood
	巳	酉	巳
	Snake	Rooster	Snake

5	15	25	35
丙	丁	戊	己
Yang Fire	Yin Fire	Yang Earth	Yin Earth
戌	亥	子	丑
Dog	Pig	Rat	Ox
45	55	65	75
庚	辛	壬	癸
Yang Metal	Yin Metal	Yang Water	Yin Water
寅	卯	辰	巳
Tiger	Rabbit	Dragon	Snake

There is a Partial Three Harmony Metal Combination in Dinnigan's birth chart. Her Snake Day and Year Branches combine with her Rooster Month Branch to form Metal. The most prominent element in the chart is Metal. As Dinnigan is a Yin Metal Day Master, Metal is her Self element. She has a Dominant Metal chart.

Dinnigan's House of Spouse animal Snake is present in her chart twice. This indicated a higher incidence of being married twice. In 1992 (Yang Water Monkey year), Dinnigan married *Eurogliders* frontman Bernie Lynch. The Annual Monkey Branch formed a Six Harmony Combination with her Snake in the House of Spouse. They divorced nine years later in 2001 (Yin Metal Snake year). In 2007 (Yin Fire Pig year) during the Ox Luck Cycle (age 40 to 44), Dinnigan met Canadian hotelier Bradley Cocks. There was a Clash between the Annual Pig Branch and the Snake Branch in her House of Spouse. However, there was a Combination between the Ox Luck Cycle and the Snake in her House of Spouse. This indicated the possibility of love or marriage during this period. Dinnigan married Cocks in 2011 (Yin Metal Rabbit year).

Dinnigan has two children. Daughter Estella was born in 2004 (Yang Wood Monkey year). Her Output or Child element Water was present in the Annual Monkey Branch. Estelle's father, television host Richard Wilkins had left Dinnigan when she was pregnant with Estella. The negative element Wood was present in the Annual Stem. In 2012 (Yang Water Dragon year), Dinnigan had son Hunter. Once again, her Output or Child element Water was present in the Annual Stem.

In 1990 (Yang Metal Horse year) during the favourable Yang Earth Luck Cycle (age 25 to 29), Dinnigan started her own label after there was high demand for her French-inspired lingerie that she was designing for friends. The favourable element Metal was present in the Annual Stem. In 1992 (Yang Water Monkey year), Dinnigan opened her first store in Paddington, Sydney and started exporting her fashion to international department stores like Harvey Nichols in London, Barneys in New York and Joyce in Hong Kong. Her favourable elements Water and Metal were present in the Annual Stem and Branch.

The Rat Luck Cycle (age 30 to 34) contained Dinnigan's favourable element Water. In 1997 (Yin Fire Ox year), the Annual Ox Branch combined with the Rooster and Snake Branches in her chart to form the Full Three Harmony Metal Combination. Dinnigan was appointed advisor to the South Australian Wool Board. She was also presented with the Louis Vuitton Business Award in recognition of her contribution to Australian Business.

Dinnigan's most favourable element was present in the Yin Earth Luck Cycle (age 35 to 39). In 2000 (Yang Metal Dragon year), she opened a store in Chelsea in London. The favourable elements Metal and Earth were present in the Annual Stem and Branch. In 2004 (Yang Wood Monkey year), inspired by the birth of her daughter Estella, Dinnigan launced the *Collette Dinnigan Enfant Collection*. The favourable elements Metal and Water were present in the Annual Monkey Branch.

The Ox Luck Cycle (age 40 to 44) combined with the Rooster and Snake Branches in her chart to form the Full Three Harmony Metal Combination. In 2005 (Yin Wood Rooster year), Australia Post issued a stamp featuring Dinnigan. The Annual Rooster Branch combined with the Ox Luck Cycle and the Rooster and Snake Branches in her chart to reinforce the favourable element Metal.

The Yang Metal Luck Cycle (age 45 to 49) contained the favourable element Metal. In 2013 (Yin Water Snake year), Penguin Australia released her hard cover book *Obsessive Creative*. The Annual Snake Branch combined with the Rooster and Snake Branches in her chart to reinforce the favourable element Metal. In 2014 (Yang Wood Horse year), Dinnigan scaled down her business, closing down her stores in Sydney, Melbourne and London and stopping her bridal and evening wear lines. 80% of her staff lost their jobs. The decision was made to allow her to have more time for family. The negative element Fire was present in the Annual Horse Branch.

The Tiger Luck Cycle (age 50 to 54) contains the negative elements Fire and Wood, as well as the favourable element Earth. The Yin Metal Luck Cycle (age 55 to 59) contains the favourable element. The Rabbit Luck Cycle (age 60 to 64) clashes with her Rooster Month Branch. It disrupts the Three Harmony Metal Combination. She will no longer be a Dominant Metal chart. The exact nature of her chart will depend on the Hour Pillar.

Example 6.3 Alan Cumming, Scottish Actor
(born January 27, 1965, 08:20 hours)

Hour	Day	Month	Year
壬	辛	丁	甲
Yang Water	Yin Metal	Yin Fire	Yang Wood
辰	巳	丑	辰
Dragon	Snake	Ox	Dragon

3	13	23	33
戊	己	庚	辛
Yang Earth	Yin Earth	Yang Metal	Yin Metal
寅	卯	辰	巳
Tiger	Rabbit	Dragon	Snake

43	53	63	73
壬	癸	甲	乙
Yang Water	Yin Water	Yang Wood	Yin Wood
午	未	申	酉
Horse	Sheep	Monkey	Rooster

There is a Partial Three Harmony Metal Combination in Cumming's birth chart. His Snake Day Branch combines with his Ox Month Branch to form Metal. There are no other Combinations within the chart. Metal is the most prominent element. As Cumming is a Yin Metal Day Master, Metal is his Self element. He has a Dominant Metal chart.

The negative element is present in the Yin Fire Month Stem. This is also the sector associated with the father. Cumming had a very troubled relationship with his father. In his autobiography *Not My Father's Son*, Cumming describes the physical and emotional abuse that his father inflicted on him. He even had to get a DNA test to prove that he was biologically related to his father, who had believed that Cumming is not his biological son.

Cumming is born on a Yin Metal Snake day, one of the Six Intelligent Pillars. Apart from acting, he has also written a novel, *Tommy's Tale* and his autobiography. The Yin Metal Snake day is also one of Two Strategist Pillars.

Cumming first impressed audiences with his performance in *Emma* alongside Gwyneth Paltrow in 1996 (Yang Fire Rat year) during the favourable Dragon Luck Cycle (age 28 to 32). There was a Stem Combination between the Annual Yang Fire Stem and Cumming's Yin Metal Day Master. The Power Element Combination indicates professional recognition and success. The Annual Rat Branch also combines with the Dragon Year Branch and Luck Cycle to form the favourable element Water. In 1997 (Yin Fire Ox year), Cumming made his US film debut in the *Romy and Michele's High School Reunion* with Lisa Kudrow and Mira Sorvino. The Annual Ox Branch combined with the Snake and Ox Branches in his chart to reinforce his favourable element Metal.

Cumming's success continued in the favourable Yin Metal Luck Cycle (age 33 to 37). In 2001 (Yin Metal Snake year), the Annual Snake Branch combined with the Ox and Snake Branches in his chart to reinforce the favourable element Metal. Cummings wrote, directed, produced and starred in the ensemble drama *The Anniversary Party* with Jennifer Jason Leigh and also played Mr. Fegan Floop in the children's movie *Spy Kids*.

In 2003 (Yin Water Sheep year) during the Snake Luck Cycle (age 38 to 42), the Annual Sheep Branch clashed with his Ox Month Branch to disrupt the Three Harmony Combination. Cumming became a Competitive Metal chart. His favourable elements became:

1) Power element Fire.
2) Output element Water.
3) Self element Metal. The Rooster Branch transforms him into a Dominant Metal chart.
4) Resource element Earth.
5) Wealth element Wood.

In 2003 (Yin Water Sheep year), Cumming portrayed Nightcrawler in the blockbuster *X-Men 2*. The favourable element Water was present in the Annual Stem.

The Snake Luck Cycle is the same as the Snake Branch in Cumming's House of Spouse. He met his husband, illustrator Grant Sheffer, in 2005 (Yin Wood Rooster year). The Annual Rooster Branch also combined with his Snake Branch in the House of Spouse, increasing the possibility of Cumming finding love or romance. Cumming identifies as bisexual. He was previously married to actress Hilary Lyon in 1985 (Yin Wood Ox year). The Annual Ox Branch also combined with his Snake Branch in the House of Spouse. The marriage lasted eight years.

The Yang Water Luck Cycle (age 43 to 47) was also favourable. In 2009 (Yin Earth Ox year), Cumming appeared as a regular character on the hit television series *The Good Wife*. The Annual Ox Branch combined with his Snake and Ox Branches to reinforce the favourable element Metal. In 2012 (Yang Water Dragon year), the favourable elements Water and Earth were present in the Annual Stem and Branch. Cumming collaborated with the National Theatre of Scotland and director John Tiffany to play all the roles in *Macbeth*. He also won critical acclaim for his performance in the biopic *Any Day Now*.

The Horse Luck Cycle (age 48 to 52) contained the negative element Fire. However, Cumming was still able to fare well in years with favourable elements. In 2015 (Yin Wood Sheep year), he was nominated for a Primetime Emmy Award for Outstanding Supporting Actor in a Series for his performance in *The Good Wife*. The Annual Sheep Year Branch gave him the auspicious Configuration of Four Branches in a Sequence: Dragon Hour Branch, Snake Day Branch, Horse Luck Cycle and Annual Sheep Branch.

The Yin Water Luck Cylce (age 53 to 57) should be favourable for Cumming as it contains his third favourable element.

Example 6.4 Amy Schumer, American Comedienne and Actress (born June 1, 1981)

Hour	Day	Month	Year
	庚	癸	辛
	Yang Metal	Yin Water	Yin Metal
	戌	巳	酉
	Dog	Snake	Rooster

2	12	22	32
甲	乙	丙	丁
Yang Wood	Yin Wood	Yang Fire	Yin Fire
午	未	申	酉
Horse	Sheep	Monkey	Rooster

42	52	62	72
戊	己	庚	辛
Yang Earth	Yin Earth	Yang Metal	Yin Metal
戌	亥	子	丑
Dog	Pig	Rat	Ox

There is a Partial Three Harmony Metal Combination in Schumer's birth chart. Her Snake Month Branch and Rooster Year Branch combine to form Metal. There is also a Yin Metal Year Stem. The most prominent element in her chart is Metal. As Schumer is a Yang Metal Day Master, Metal is her Self element. She has a Dominant Metal chart.

Schumer is born on a Yang Metal Dog day. This qualifies her as a Commanding Pillar chart. When the Commanding Pillar encounters one of the other six Commanding Pillars in the Luck Cycle, year, month, day or hour, there will be more success.

The Horse Luck Cycle (age 7 to 11) contained the negative element Fire. Schumer has revealed in interviews that this was a difficult time for her. Her father was diagnosed with multiple sclerosis, the family went bankrupt and her parents divorced.

Schumer had her first professional break in 2007 (Yin Fire Pig year) during the Yang Fire Luck Cycle (age 22 to 26). The Annual Pig Branch clashed with her Snake Month Branch, disrupting the Partial Three Harmony Metal Combination. She became a Competitive Metal chart that year. Her list of favourable elements became:

1) Power element Fire.
2) Output element Water.
3) Self element Metal. The Ox Branch transforms her into a Dominant Metal chart.
4) Resource element Earth.
5) Wealth element Wood.

With the Power element Fire present in the Luck Cycle and the Annual Yin Fire Stem, Schumer advanced to the finals of the reality television talent show *Last Comic Standing*.

The Monkey Luck Cycle (age 27 to 31) formed a Seasonal Metal Combination with her Rooster Year Branch and Dog Day Branch. Schumer remained a Dominant Metal chart. In 2012 (Yang Water Dragon year), Schumer appeared in the comedy-drama *Seeking a Friend for the End of the World* alongside Steve Carell and Keira Knightley. She also had her first television special on the Comedy Central Network, *Mostly Sex Stuff*. Not only were her favourable element Water present in the Annual Stem and Branch, it was also a Commanding Pillar year, which gave her opportunities for success.

Although the negative element was present in the Yin Fire Luck Cycle (age 32 to 36), Schumer was able to benefit from years with her favourable elements. In 2013 (Yin Water Snake year), the Annual Snake Branch combined with the Snake and Rooster Branches in her chart to form her favourable element Metal. Schumer had her first regular television show on Comedy Central, *Inside Amy Schumer*. In 2015 (Yin Wood Sheep year), she hosted the Music Television (MTV) Awards and had her first leading film role in the comedy *Trainwreck* opposite Bill Hader. *Time* magazine also named Schumer as one of the top 100 influential people. Her favourable element Earth was present in the Annual Sheep Branch.

In 2016 (Yang Fire Monkey year), there was a Stem Combination between the Annual Yang Fire Stem and her Yin Metal Day Master. This indicated professional recognition or success. Schumer's memoir *The Girl with the Lower Back Tattoo* was Number One on the *New York Times* Non-Fiction Bestsellers List for two weeks.

The Rooster Luck Cycle (age 37 to 41) combined with Schumer's Rooster and Ox Branches in the chart to reinforce her favourable element Metal. In 2017 (Yin Metal Rooster year), Schumer starred with Goldie Hawn as daughter and mother in the comedy *Snatched*. The Annual Rooster Branch combined with the Rooster Luck

Cycle and the Rooster and Ox Branches in Schumer's chart to further reinforce her favourable element Metal. 2018 (Yang Earth Dog year) should be another favourable year for Schumer as her favourable element Earth is present in the Annual Stem and Branch. Yang Earth Dog is one of the Six Commanding Pillars, so Schumer will also benefit from having another Commanding Pillar present. The other five Commanding Pillars are Yang Earth Dragon, Yang Metal Dragon, Yang Water Dragon, Yang Metal Dog and Yang Water Dog.

There may be some issues in 2019 (Yin Earth Pig year) as the Annual Pig Branch clashes with Schumer's Snake Month Branch. This disrupts the Partial Three Harmony Combination that accounts for her Dominant Metal chart. She becomes a Competitive Metal chart for that year. Her list of favourable elements becomes:

1) Output Element Water.
2) Power Element Fire.
3) Self Element Metal. The Ox Branch transforms her into a Dominant Metal chart.
4) Resource Element Earth.
5) Wealth Element Wood.

By 2020 (Yang Metal Rat year), Schumer would have reverted to a Dominant Metal chart. Her favourable elements Metal and Water are present in the Annual Stem and Branch. 2021 (Yin Metal Ox year) will also be favourable. Not only is the favourable Self element Metal present in the Annual Stem, the Annual Ox Branch forms the Full Three Harmony Metal Combination with the Snake and Rooster Branches in her chart.

The Yang Earth (age 42 to 46), Dog (age 47 to 51) and Yin Earth (age 52 to 56) Luck Cycles all contain Schumer's most favourable element Earth, so her success will continue.

Example 6.5 Enya, Irish Singer
(born May 17, 1961)

Hour	Day	Month	Year
	庚	癸	辛
	Yang Metal	Yin Water	Yin Metal
	戌	巳	丑
	Dog	Snake	Ox

7	17	27	37
甲	乙	丙	丁
Yang Wood	Yin Wood	Yang Fire	Yin Fire
午	未	申	酉
Horse	Sheep	Monkey	Rooster
47	57	67	77
戊	己	庚	辛
Yang Earth	Yin Earth	Yang Metal	Yin Metal
戌	亥	子	丑
Dog	Pig	Rat	Ox

There is a Partial Three Harmony Metal Combination in Enya's birth chart. Her Snake Month Branch and Ox Year Branch combine to form Metal. There is also a Yin Metal Year Stem. The most prominent element in her chart is Metal. As Enya is a Yang Metal Day Master, Metal is her Self element. She has a Dominant Metal chart.

Enya is born on a Yang Metal Dog day, one of the Six Commanding Pillar days. When the Commanding Pillars are present in the year or Luck Cycle, Enya will enjoy more success.

313

The Yin Wood Luck Cycle (age 17 to 21) formed a Stem Combination with Enya's Yang Metal Day Master. The Wealth Element Combination indicates opportunities for her to generate income or revenue. In 1980 (Yang Metal Monkey year), Enya joined her family's band *Clannad*. The favourable elements Metal and Water were present in the Annual Stem and Branch. 1982 (Yang Water Dog year) was also a Commanding Pillar year. Enya appeared on the *Clannad* album *Fuaim* and also left the group to pursue her solo career.

The Sheep Luck Cycle (age 22 to 26) clashed with her Ox Year Branch to disrupt the Three Harmony Metal Combination. With the Ox and Dog Branches in her chart and the Sheep Luck Cycle, Enya became a Competitive Metal chart. Her list of favourable elements became:

1) Power element Fire.
2) Output element Water.
3) Self element Metal. The Rooster Branch transforms her into a Dominant Metal chart.
4) Resource element Earth.
5) Wealth element Wood.

In 1985 (Yin Wood Ox year), Enya was commissioned to provide music for a BBC2 series called *The Celts*. There was a Stem Combination between the Annual Yin Wood Stem and her Yang Metal Day Master. This indicated the possibility of generating income or revenue. In 1987 (Yin Fire Rabbit year), the music that Enya wrote was packaged and released as her debut album *Enya*. There was a Combination between the Annual Rabbit Branch and the Sheep Luck Cycle to form Wood. There was a Metal-Wood conflict present. *Enya* only reached Number 69 on the UK Albums chart.

The Yang Fire Luck Cycle (age 27 to 31) contained the negative element. 1988 (Yang Earth Dragon year) was a Commanding Pillar year and also contained her favourable element Earth. Her second album *Watermark* was released, with the single *Orinoco Flow (Sail Away)* was Number 1 for three weeks on the UK Singles chart. In 1991 (Yin Metal Sheep year), the Annual Sheep Branch clashed with her Year Branch to transform Enya into a Follow the Resource (Earth) chart. Her favourable elements became:

1) Resource element Earth.
2) Power element Fire.
3) Output element Water.
4) Wealth element Wood.
5) Self element Metal.

Enya released her third album *Shepherd Moons*, which reached Number 1 on the UK Albums chart. The Annual Yin Metal Stem formed a Stem Combination with the Yang Fire Luck Cycle. Its negative effects were reduced.

The Monkey Luck Cycle (age 32 to 36) contained the favourable elements Metal and Water. In 1995 (Yin Wood Pig year), the Annual Pig Branch clashed with her Snake Month Branch to disrupt the Three Harmony Metal Combination. Earth became the most prominent element. Once again, Enya was transformed into a Follow the Resource (Earth) chart. There was also a Stem Combination between the Yang Metal Day Master and the Annual Yin Wood Day Master. This indicated opportunities to generate income. Enya's fourth album *The Memory of Trees* reached both the UK and US Top 10 albums, selling more than ten million copies worldwide. In 1997 (Yin Fire Ox year), the Annual Ox Branch combined with the Snake and Ox Branches in Enya's chart to reinforce the favourable element Metal. She released her first compilation album *Paint the Sky with Stars*, which sold around twelve million copies worldwide.

The Yin Fire Luck Cycle (age 37 to 41) contained the negative element, so Enya had to depend on the Annual Stems and Branches for success. 2000 (Yang Metal Dragon year) was a Commanding Pillar year. The favourable elements Metal and Earth were also present in the Annual Stem and Branch. Enya released her most successful album *A Day Without Rain*. In 2001 (Yin Metal Snake year), Enya recorded *May It Be* for the movie *The Lord of the Rings: The Fellowship of the Rings*, for which she received an Oscar nomination for Best Original Song. The Annual Snake Branch combined with the Ox and Snake Branches in her chart to reinforce the favourable element Metal.

The Rooster Luck Cycle (age 42 to 46) combined with the Ox and Snake Branches in her chart to form the Full Three Harmony Metal Combination. In 2005 (Yin Wood Rooster year), Enya released *Amarantine*, her sixth studio album which reached the Top 10 in both the UK and US Albums chart. The Annual Rooster Branch combined with the Snake and Ox Branches in her chart and the Rooster Luck Cycle to reinforce Metal. There was also a Stem Combination between the Annual Yin Wood Stem and her Yang Metal Day Master, indicating the possibility of generating income or revenue.

The Yang Earth (age 47 to 51) and Dog (age 52 to 56) Luck Cycles composed a Commanding Pillar Luck Cycle. In 2008 (Yang Earth Rat year), Enya released her Christmas album *And Winter Came*. The favourable elements Metal and Water were present in the Annual Stem and Branch. She then took an extended break from writing and recording music before returning to the studio in 2012 (Yang Water Dragon year), another Commanding Pillar year. In 2015 (Yin Wood Sheep year), Enya released her eighth studio album *Dark Sky Island*. There was a Stem Combination between the Annual Yin Wood Stem and her Yang Metal Day Master, indicating the possibility of generating income. The Annual Sheep Branch clashed with the Ox Month Branch to disrupt the Three Harmony Metal Combination and transform her into a Follow the Resource (Earth) chart.

The Yin Earth Luck Cycle (age 57 to 61) contains the favourable element. 2018 (Yang Earth Dog year) is another Commanding Pillar year, so Enya will have further success. However, the Pig Luck Cycle (age 62 to 66) clashes with the Snake Month Branch to disrupt the Three Harmony Metal Combination. There is also Wood present within the Pig that will attack the favourable element Earth, so Enya can expect some uncertainty.

Example 6.6 Markus Feehily, Irish Singer
(born May 28, 1980)

Hour	Day	Month	Year
	辛	辛	庚
	Yin Metal	Yin Metal	Yang Metal
	丑	巳	申
	Ox	Snake	Monkey

3	13	23	33
壬	癸	甲	乙
Yang Water	Yin Water	Yang Wood	Yin Wood
午	未	申	酉
Horse	Sheep	Monkey	Rooster

43	53	63	73
丙	丁	戊	己
Yang Fire	Yin Fire	Yang Earth	Yin Earth
戌	亥	子	丑
Dog	Pig	Rat	Ox

There is a Partial Three Harmony Metal Combination in Feehily's birth chart. His Snake Month Branch and Ox Day Branch combine to form Metal. Feehily also has a Yin Metal Month Stem and a Yang Metal Year Stem. The most prominent element in the chart is Metal. As he is a Yin Metal Day Master, Metal is Feehily's Self element. He is a Dominant Metal chart.

Feehily was one of the founding members of the pop group *Westlife* that was formed in 1998 (Yang Earth Tiger year) during the Sheep Luck Cycle (age 18 to 22). The Sheep clashed with his Ox Day Branch, transforming him into a Competitive Metal chart. The list of favourable elements became:

1) Output element Water.
2) Power element Fire.
3) Self element Metal. The Rooster Branch transforms him into a Dominant Metal chart.
4) Resource element Earth.
5) Wealth element Wood.

In 1998 (Yang Earth Tiger year), the favourable Power element Fire was present in the Annual Tiger Branch. Feehily was one of the five original members of *Westlife* and one of the two lead singers, the other being Shane Filan. *Westlife* had their first success being the opening act for the concerts of other successful boy bands like *Backstreet Boys* and *Boyzone* in Ireland. In 2000 (Yang Metal Dragon year), the Annual Dragon Branch combined with Feehilly's Monkey Year Branch to form the favourable Output element Water. *Westlife* scored their seventh successive UK Number 1 single from their first two albums, the self-titled *Westlife* and *Coast to Coast*.

In 2001 (Yin Metal Snake year), the Annual Snake Branch combined with the Snake and Ox Branches in Feehilly's chart to reinforce his favourable element Metal. *Westlife* released their third album *World of Our Own*, which contained three UK Number 1 singles, including their remake of Billy Joel's *Uptown Girl*. They also embarked on their first world tour *When Dreams Come True*.

In 2002 (Yang Water Horse year), the favourable elements Water and Fire were present in the Annual Stem and Branch. *Westlife* embarked on their second world tour *World of Our Own*. They also released *Unbreakable – The Greatest Hits Vol. 1*, which contained their 11th UK Number 1 hit, the title track *Unbreakable*.

In the Yang Wood Luck Cycle (age 23 to 27), Feehily had reverted to a Dominant Metal chart. However, in 2003 (Yin Water Sheep year), the Annual Sheep Branch clashed with his Ox Day Branch, transforming him into a Competitive Metal chart that year. The favourable Output element Water was present. *Westlife* released their fourth album *Turnaround* with their 12th Number 1 hit, a remake of Barry Manilow's *Mandy*. In 2004 (Yang Wood Monkey year), the first half contained the negative element Wood. Brian McFadden announced his departure from *Westlife* for personal reasons, with the group continuing on with four members. However, the Annual Monkey Branch contained the favourable elements Water and Metal and Westlife released their Rat Pack-inspired album of standards … *Allow Us to Be Frank*.

In 2005 (Yin Wood Rooster year), the Annual Rooster Branch combined with the Snake and Ox Branches within Feehily's chart to form the Full Three Harmony Metal Combination. The favourable element Metal was reinforced. *Westlife* released their sixth album *Face to Face* with another Number 1 hit, *You Raise Me Up*. On a personal note, Feehily came out to the public and announced that he was in a relationship with partner Kevin McDaid. The Annual Rooster Branch combined with the Ox in his House of Spouse, indicating the possibility of romance.

In 2006 (Yang Fire Dog year), there was a Stem Combination involving the Annual Yang Fire Stem and Feehily's Yin Metal Day Master. This indicated

319

professional success and recognition. The favourable element Earth was also present in the Annual Dog Branch. *Westlife* signed a five-record deal with Sony BMG and scored their 14th UK Number 1 single with their version of Bette Midler's *The Rose*. They tied with Cliff Richard as the third act to have the most number of UK Number 1 Singles, behind Elvis Presley and the Beatles.

The Monkey Luck Cycle (age 28 to 32) contained the favourable elements Water and Metal. In 2008 (Yang Earth Rat year), the Annual Rat Branch combined with Feehily's Monkey Year Branch and the Monkey Luck Cycle to form the favourable element Water. *Westlife* celebrated ten years in the music industry with a special concert entitled *10 Years of Westlife* at Dublin's Croke Park stadium. In 2009 (Yin Earth Ox year), the Annual Ox Branch combined with the Snake and Ox Branches in Feehily's chart to reinforce the favourable element Metal. *Westlife* released another hit album *Where We Are* with the UK Number 2 single *What About Now*. In 2010 (Yang Metal Tiger year), their final album *Gravity* was released. The favourable element Metal was present in the Annual Stem.

In 2011 (Yin Metal Rabbit year), the negative element Wood was present in the Annual Branch. *Westlife* announced their breakup after a greatest hits album and a final tour. On a personal note, Feehily also announced his breakup from McDaid.

The Yin Wood Luck Cycle (age 33 to 37) also contained the negative element. Feehily maintained a low profile and re-emerged in 2015 (Yin Wood Sheep year) with his debut solo album *Fire*. The Annual Sheep Branch clashed with his Ox Day Branch, disrupting the Partial Three Harmony Metal Combination. This transformed Feehily into a Competitive Metal chart. *Fire* only reached Number 25 in the UK Albums chart.

The Rooster Luck Cycle (age 38 to 42) will be favourable for Feehily as it combines with the Ox and Snake Branches in his chart to form the Full Three Harmony Metal Combination. As the Ox in the House of Spouse is involved in the Combination, this indicates the possibility of romance for Feehily. The Yang Fire Luck Cycle (age 43 to 47) forms a Stem Combination with his Yin Metal Day Master. This indicates professional recognition and success. The Dog Luck Cycle (age 48 to 52) contains the favourable element Earth.

However, the Yin Fire Luck Cycle (age 53 to 57) contains the negative Power element, so there may be some issues during this period.

Example 6.7 Richard Roxburgh, Australian Actor
(born January 23, 1962)

Hour	Day	Month	Year
	辛	辛	辛
	Yin Metal	Yin Metal	Yin Metal
	酉	丑	丑
	Rooster	Ox	Ox

6	16	26	36
庚	己	戊	丁
Yang Metal	Yin Earth	Yang Earth	Yin Fire
子	亥	戌	酉
Rat	Pig	Dog	Rooster

46	56	66	76
丙	乙	甲	癸
Yang Fire	Yin Wood	Yang Wood	Yin Water
申	未	午	巳
Monkey	Sheep	Horse	Snake

There is a Partial Three Harmony Metal Combination in Roxburgh's birth chart. His Rooster Day Branch combines with his Ox Month and Year Branches to form Metal. There are also Yin Metal Month and Year Stems. The most prominent element in his chart is Metal. As Roxburgh is a Yin Metal Day Master, Metal is his Self element. He has a Dominant Metal chart.

Roxburgh graduated from the Australian National Institute of Dramatic Arts (NIDA) in 1986 (Yang Fire Tiger year). The Annual Yang Fire Stem combined with his Yin Metal Day Master. The Power Element Combination indicates professional recognition and success.

In 1988 (Yang Earth Dragon year) during the favourable Yang Earth Luck Cycle (age 26 to 30), Roxburgh made his television debut in the film *The Riddle of the Stinson*. The favourable element Earth was present in the Annual Stem and Branch. Roxburgh continued to appear on Australian television during this period.

During the favourable Dog Luck Cycle (age 31 to 35), he made his movie debut in *Doing Time for Patsy Cline*, for which he won an Australian Film Institute (AFI) Award for Best Actor. Roxburgh also appeared opposite Cate Blanchett in the romantic comedy *Thank God He Met Lizzie*. The Annual Ox Branch combined with his Rooster and Ox Branches to reinforce the favourable element Metal.

The Yin Fire Luck Cycle (age 36 to 40) contained his negative element but Roxburgh fared well in years with his favourable elements Earth and Metal. In 2000 (Yang Metal Dragon year), Roxburgh became known to international audiences as one of the villains in John Woo's *Mission: Impossible 2* alongside Tom Cruise. The favourable elements Metal and Earth were present in the Annual Stem and Branch. In 2001 (Yin Metal Snake year), Roxburgh had another high profile role as the Duke in the musical *Moulin Rouge* alongside Nicole Kidman and Ewan McGregor. The Annual Snake Branch formed the Full Three Harmony Metal Combination with Rooster and Snake Branches present in his chart. This reinforced his favourable element Metal. In 2002 (Yang Water Horse year), the negative element Fire was present in the Annual Horse Branch. Roxburgh appeared opposite Michelle Yeoh in the critically panned Hong Kong action movie *The Touch*.

The Rooster Luck Cycle (age 41 to 45) combined with the Ox and Rooster Branches in Roxburgh's chart to reinforce the favourable element Metal. It is also the animal that is found in his House of Spouse. This indicated that there is the possibility of Roxburgh finding love or getting married during this period. In 2004 (Yang Wood Monkey year), he married Silvia Colloca, whom he had met while filming *Van Helsing*. Roxburgh portrayed Dracula while Colloca played his wife. In 2005 (Yin Wood Rooster year), the Annual Rooster Branch combined with the Ox and Rooster Branches in Roxburgh's chart to reinforce the favourable element Metal. He appeared in another Hollywood blockbuster *Stealth* alongside Jamie Foxx and Jessica Biel.

The Yang Fire Luck Cycle (age 46 to 50) combined with Roxburgh's Yin Metal Day Master. This indicated professional recognition and success. In 2010 (Yang Metal Tiger year), Roxburgh won another AFI Award for Best Actor for portraying former Prime Minister Bob Hawke in the television movie *Hawke*. The favourable element was present in the Annual Stem. He also appeared in the Australian Broadcasting Corporation (ABC) series *Rake*, portraying self-destructive barrister Cleaver Greene, one of his most famous roles.

The Monkey Luck Cycle (age 51 to 55) contained his favourable elements Water and Metal. In 2016 (Yang Fire Monkey year), Roxburgh appeared in the Oscar-nominated war movie *Hacksaw Ridge* alongside Andrew Garfield and Sam Worthington. There was a Stem Combination between the Annual Yang Fire Stem and his Yin Metal Day Master. This indicated professional recognition and success.

The Yin Wood Luck Cycle (age 56 to 60) contains the negative element, so Roxburgh will be more dependent on the Annual Stem and Branch. The Sheep Luck Cycle (age 61 to 65) clashes with the Ox Month Branch, disrupting the Three Harmony Metal Combination. Roxburgh will become a Competitive Metal chart. His favourable elements will be:

1) Power element Fire.
2) Output element Water.
3) Self element Metal. The Snake Branch transforms him into a Dominant Metal chart.
4) Resource element Earth.
5) Wealth element Wood.

By the Yang Wood Luck Cycle (age 66 to 70), Roxburgh will revert back to a Dominant Metal chart.

Example 6.8 Joanna Newsom, American Cellist and Singer (born January 18, 1982)

Hour	Day	Month	Year
	辛	辛	辛
	Yin Metal	Yin Metal	Yin Metal
	丑	丑	酉
	Ox	Ox	Rooster

6	16	26	36
壬	癸	甲	乙
Yang	Yin	Yang	Yin
Water	Water	Wood	Wood
寅	卯	辰	巳
Tiger	Rabbit	Dragon	Snake

46	56	66	76
丙	丁	戊	己
Yang	Yin	Yang	Yin
Fire	Fire	Earth	Earth
午	未	申	酉
Horse	Sheep	Monkey	Rooster

There is a Partial Three Harmony Metal Combination in Newsom's birth chart. Her Rooster Year Branch combines with her Ox Day and Month Branches. There are also Yin Metal Month and Year Stems. The most prominent element in her chart is Metal. As Newsom is a Yin Metal Day Master, Metal is her Self element. She has a Dominant Metal chart.

The Rabbit Luck Cycle (age 21 to 25) clashed with the Rooster Year Branch, disrupting the Three Harmony Metal Combination. Newsom became a Competitive Metal chart. Her favourable elements became:

1) Power element Fire.
2) Output element Water.
3) Self element Metal. The Snake Branch transforms her into a Dominant Metal chart.
4) Resource element Earth.
5) Wealth element Wood.

In 2002 (Yang Water Horse year), Newsom recorded her first EP at home *Walnut Whales*. The favourable elements Water and Fire were present in the Annual Stem and Branch. This allowed her to sign a contract with the Drag City label and release her debut album *The Milk-Eyed Mender* in 2004 (Yang Wood Monkey year), which sold 200 000 copies. The favourable element Water was present in the Annual Monkey Branch. In 2006 (Yang Fire Dog year), there was a Stem Combination between the Annual Yang Fire Stem and her Yin Metal Day Master. The Power Element Combination indicates professional recognition and success. Newsom released her second album *Ys*. There was a Six Harmony Combination between the Annual Dog Branch and the Rabbit Luck Cycle. This reduced the effects of the clash between the Rabbit Luck Cycle and her Rooster Year Branch.

The Yang Wood Luck Cycle (age 26 to 30) contained Newsom's negative element, so she was dependent on favourable elements in the Annual Stem and Branch. In 2009 (Yin Earth Ox year), she started recording her third album *Have One on Me* in Tokyo. The Annual Ox Branch combined with the Rooster and Ox Branches in her chart to reinforce the favourable element Metal. In 2010 (Yang Metal Tiger year), *Have One on Me* was released, as well as her first book, *Visions of Joanna Newsom*. The favourable element Metal was present in the Annual Stem.

The Dragon Luck Cycle (age 31 to 35) contained the favourable element Earth. In 2013 (Yin Water Snake year), Newsom married actor and comedian Andy Samberg. The Annual Snake Branch combined with the Ox and Rooster Branches in her chart to form the Full Three Harmony Metal Combination. As the Combination involves the Ox in her House of Spouse, there was the possibility of love or marriage.

The Yin Wood Luck Cycle (age 36 to 40) contains the negative element so Newsom will depend on the Annual Stem and Branch for favourable developments. The Snake Luck Cycle (age 41 to 45) forms the Full Three Harmony Metal Combination with the Ox and Rooster Branches in her chart. Note that the Ox in the House of Spouse is involved in the Combination, so there is the possibility of love or marriage during this period. The House of Spouse animal Ox is also present twice in Newsom's chart, so this indicates a higher incidence of having two marriages or personal relationships.

The Yang Fire Luck Cycle (age 46 to 50) forms a Stem Combination with her Yin Metal Day Master. This indicates professional success or recognition. The Horse Luck Cycle (age 51 to 55) contains the negative element Fire, so there may be issues or complications during this period.

Example 6.9 Jools Holland, British Musician and
Television Presenter (born January 24, 1958)

Hour	Day	Month	Year
	辛	癸	丁
	Yin Metal	Yin Water	Yin Fire
	丑	丑	酉
	Ox	Ox	Rooster

6	16	26	36
壬	辛	庚	己
Yang Water	Yin Metal	Yang Metal	Yin Earth
子	亥	戌	酉
Rat	Pig	Dog	Rooster
46	56	66	76
戊	丁	丙	乙
Yang Earth	Yin Fire	Yang Fire	Yin Wood
申	未	午	巳
Monkey	Sheep	Horse	Snake

There is a Partial Three Harmony Metal Combination in
Holland's birth chart. His Ox Day and Month Branches
combine with his Rooster Year Branch to form Metal.
Metal is the most prominent element in his chart. As
Holland is a Yin Metal Day Master, Metal is his Self
element. He has a Dominant Metal chart.

In the favourable Yin Metal Luck Cycle (age 16 to 20),
Holland was the keyboard player for the band *Squeeze*,
who released their debut collection *Packet of Three* in 1977
(Yin Fire Snake year). The Annual Snake Branch
combined with the Rooster and Ox Branches in his chart
to form the Full Three Harmony Metal Combination.

In 1979 (Yin Earth Sheep year) during the Pig Luck Cycle (age 21 to 25), *Squeeze* found success with their second album *Cool for Cats*, with the title track *Up the Junction* both reaching Number 2 in the UK Album charts. Although the Annual Sheep Branch clashed with the Ox Branches in Holland's chart to disrupt the Three Harmony Metal Combination, it is also one of the Special Stars for a Yin Metal Day Master. The Annual Sheep Branch worked in conjunction with the Pig Luck Cycle to bring Holland success. In 1980 (Yang Metal Monkey year), Holland left *Squeeze* to pursue a solo career. The favourable elements Metal and Water were present in the Annual Stem and Branch.

In 1982 (Yang Water Dog year), Holland branched out into television, hosting the Newcastle-based music program *The Tube* with Paula Yates. The favourable elements Water and Earth were present in the Annual Stem and Branch.

The Yang Metal Luck Cycle (age 26 to 30) was also favourable for Holland. In 1985 (Yin Wood Ox year), *Squeeze* regrouped with Holland as the keyboard player, releasing *Cosi Fan Tutti Frutti*. The Annual Ox Branch combined with the Ox and Rooster Branches in Holland's chart to reinforce the favourable element Metal.

The Dog Luck Cycle (age 31 to 35) contained the favourable element Earth. In 1989 (Yin Earth Snake year), the Annual Snake Branch combined with the Rooster and Ox Branches in Holland's chart to form the Full Three Harmony Metal Combination. Holland was host of the television show *Jukebox Jury*. In 1990 (Yang Metal Horse year), Holland parted with *Squeeze* to focus on his solo projects and television work. The Annual Horse Branch combined with the Dog Luck Cycle to form the negative element Fire. There was a Fire-Metal conflict in his chart.

In 1992 (Yang Water Monkey year), Holland started his television series *Later... with Jools Holland*. The favourable elements Water and Metal were present in the Annual Stem and Branch. In 1993 (Yin Water Rooster year), Holland started his annual New Year's Eve show *Hootenanny*. The Annual Rooster Branch combined with the Rooster and Ox Branches in his chart to reinforce the favourable element Metal.

The Yin Earth Luck Cycle (age 36 to 40) also contained Holland's favourable element. In 1996 (Yang Fire Rat year), there was a Stem Combination between the Annual Yang Fire Stem and Holland's Yin Metal Day Master. The Power Element Combination indicates professional success and recognition. Holland signed a recording contract with Warner Bros. Records. In 1997 (Yin Fire Ox year), he appeared as the Musical Director in the movie *Spice World* featuring the *Spice Girls*. The Annual Ox Branch combined with the Rooster and Ox Branches in his chart to reinforce the favourable element Metal.

The Rooster Luck Cycle (age 41 to 45) also contained Holland's favourable element Metal. In 2001 (Yin Metal Snake year), the Annual Snake Branch formed the Full Three Harmony Metal Combination with the Ox and Rooster Branches in Holland's chart. Holland led his big band through an all-star album that included contributions from Steve Winwood, Sting, Mark Knopfler and George Harrison. The album *Small World Big Band* made the Top 10 in the UK Albums Chart. On June 14, 2003 (Yang Earth Horse day in Yang Earth Horse month in Yin Water Sheep year), Holland received an Officer of the British Empire (OBE) on the Queen's Birthday Honours List for services to the British music industry. The Annual Sheep Branch clashed with the Ox Branches in his chart to disrupt the Three Harmony Metal Combination. He became a Competitive Metal chart. The favourable elements became:

1) Power element Fire.
2) Output element Water.
3) Self element Metal. The Snake Branch transforms him into a Dominant Metal chart.
4) Resource element Earth.
5) Wealth element Wood.

The favourable element Fire was present in the Day and Month Branches when he was presented with his OBE. Water, the second favourable element, was present in the Annual Stem.

The Yang Earth Luck Cycle (age 46 to 50) also contained Holland's favourable element. In 2005 (Yin Wood Rooster year), he married his girlfriend of 15 years, Christabel McEwen, the daughter of artist Rory McEwen. The Annual Rooster Branch combined with the Ox in his House of Spouse, indicating the possibility of love and marriage. In 2006 (Yang Fire Dog year), Holland was appointed Deputy Lieutenant of Kent. The Stem Combination between the Annual Yang Fire Stem and his Yin Metal Day Master indicated professional success and recognition.

The Monkey Luck Cycle (age 51 to 55) contained the favourable elements Metal and Water. In 2010 (Yang Metal Tiger year), Holland was presented with the Sony Gold Award for Broadcaster of the Year. The favourable element Metal was present in the Annual Stem. In 2012 (Yang Water Dragon year), Holland was part of the line up for the Queen's Diamond Jubilee concert. The favourable elements Water and Earth were present in the Annual Stem and Branch.

The Yin Fire Luck Cycle (age 56 to 61) contains the negative element. However, Holland is still able to perform well in years with the favourable elements. In 2017 (Yin Fire Rooster year), Holland was touring with Puerto Rican musician Jose Feliciano with an album release planned later that year. The Annual Rooster Branch combined with the Ox and Rooster Branches in Holland's chart to reinforce the favourable element Metal.

The Sheep Luck Cycle (age 62 to 66) clashes with the Ox Branches in Holland's chart to disrupt the Three Harmony Metal Combination, transforming him into a Follow the Resource (Earth) chart. His favourable elements will be:

1) Resource element Earth.
2) Power element Fire.
3) Output element Water.
4) Wealth element Wood.
5) Self element Metal.

The Yang Fire Luck Cycle (age 67 to 71) forms a Stem Combination with Holland's Yin Metal Day Master, indicating that there is further recognition and success for Holland.

Example 6.10 Paul Keating, Australian Prime Minister 1991 to 1996 (born January 18, 1944)

Hour	Day	Month	Year
	辛	乙	癸
	Yin Metal	Yin Wood	Yin Water
	巳	丑	未
	Snake	Ox	Sheep

4	14	24	34
甲	癸	壬	辛
Yang Wood	Yin Water	Yang Water	Yin Metal
子	亥	戌	酉
Rat	Pig	Dog	Rooster

44	54	64	74
庚	己	戊	丁
Yang Metal	Yin Earth	Yang Earth	Yin Fire
申	未	午	巳
Monkey	Sheep	Horse	Snake

There is a Partial Three Harmony Metal Combination in Keating's birth chart. His Snake Day Branch and Ox Month Branch combine to form Metal. The clash between the Ox Month Branch and the Sheep Year Branch does not affect the Three Harmony Combination. The most prominent element in the chart is Metal. As Keating is a Yin Metal Day Master, Metal represents his Self element. He has a Dominant Metal chart.

Keating is born on a Yin Metal Snake day. It is one of the Six Intelligent days and also one of the Two Strategist days. Although Keating lacked formal education in economics, his time as a Treasurer was extremely successful as he deregulated the financial sector, floated the Australian dollar and introduced capital gains taxes.

During the favourable Yang Water Luck Cycle (age 24 to 28), Keating was elected to the Australian House of Representatives representing the seat of Blaxland in 1969 (Yin Earth Rooster year). He was only 25 years old. The Annual Rooster Branch combined with the Snake and Ox Branches in his chart to form the Full Three Harmony Metal Combination.

Keating was briefly the Minister for the Northern Territory in 1975 (Yin Wood Rabbit year) during the Dog Luck Cycle (age 29 to 33), until the Governor General dismissed the Whitlam government. The Annual Rabbit Branch combined with Keating's Sheep Year Branch to form Wood. There was a Metal-Wood conflict in his chart.

In 1981 (Yin Metal Rooster year) during the favourable Yin Metal Luck Cycle (age 34 to 38), Keating was elected President of the New South Wales Labor Party. The Annual Rooster Branch combined with the Snake and Ox Branches in his chart to form the Full Three Harmony Metal Combination. The favourable Self element Metal was also present in the Annual Stem.

The Rooster Luck Cycle (age 39 to 43) combined with the Snake and Ox Branches in his chart to form the Full Three Harmony Metal Combination. In 1983 (Yin Water Pig year), the Annual Pig Branch clashed with Keating's Snake Day Branch to disrupt the Three Harmony Metal Combination. It also combined with the Sheep Year Branch to form Wood. Wood became the most prominent element. Keating became a Follow the Wealth (Wood) chart. His list of favourable elements became:

1) Wealth element Wood.
2) Output element Water.
3) Power element Fire.
4) Resource element Earth.
5) Self element Metal.

The favourable element Water was present in the Annual Stem. For a Yin Metal Day Master, the Special Stars are the Pig and Sheep. The Annual Pig Year Branch worked in conjunction with his Sheep Year Branch to bring him success. Prime Minister Bob Hawke appointed Keating Treasurer of Australia.

In 1991 (Yin Metal Sheep year) during the favourable Yang Metal Luck Cycle (age 44 to 48), the Annual Sheep Branch clashed with Keating's Ox Month Branch to disrupt the Three Harmony Metal Combination. He became a Competitive Metal chart. His list of favourable elements became:

1) Power element Fire.
2) Output element Water.
3) Self element Metal. The Rooster Branch transforms him into a Dominant Metal chart.
4) Resource element Earth.
5) Wealth element Wood.

On December 20 (Yang Wood Rat day in the Yang Metal month), Keating was sworn in as the 24th Prime Minister of Australia after successfully challenging Bob Hawke. The favourable element Water was present in the day and month.

The Monkey Luck Cycle (age 49 to 53) contained the favourable elements Metal and Water. In 1993 (Yin Water Rooster year), the Annual Rooster Branch combined with the Snake and Ox Branches in Keating's chart to from the Full Three Harmony Metal Combination. Keating led the Australian Labor Party (ALP) to a fifth consecutive election victory. On March 2, 1996 (Yang Earth Dog day, Yang Metal Tiger month, Yang Fire Rat year), the Keating government was swept from power in a landslide. The Dog day combined with the Tiger month to form the negative element Fire. The Annual Rat Branch combined with the Monkey Luck Cycle to form Water. There was a Fire-Water conflict. Following his resignation from Parliament, Keating became a senior adviser to Lazard, an investment banking firm.

During the favourable Yin Earth Luck Cycle (age 54 to 58), Keating published his first book since leaving office, *Engagement: Australia Faces the Asia-Pacific* in 2000 (Yang Metal Dragon year). The favourable elements Metal and Earth were present in the Annual Stem and Branch. In 2002 (Yang Water Horse year), the negative element Fire was present. Keating's former speechwriter Don Watson published *Recollections of a Bleeding Heart: A Portrait of Paul Keating PM*. Keating was unhappy with the book and severed his friendship with Watson.

The Sheep Luck Cycle (age 59 to 63) clashed with Keating's Ox Month Branch to disrupt the Three Harmony Metal Combination. He became a Competitive Metal chart. By the favourable Yang Earth Luck Cycle (age 64 to 68), he had reverted back to a Dominant Metal chart. The Horse (age 69 to 73) and Yin Fire (age 74 to 78) Luck Cycles contain the negative element Fire, so there may be some issues and complications.

Example 6.11 Avicii, Swedish Musician
(born September 8, 1989)

Hour	Day	Month	Year
	辛	癸	己
	Yin Metal	Yin Water	Yin Earth
	未	酉	巳
	Sheep	Rooster	Snake

0	10	20	30
壬	辛	庚	己
Yang Water	Yin Metal	Yang Metal	Yin Earth
申	未	午	巳
Monkey	Sheep	Horse	Snake

40	50	60	70
戊	丁	丙	乙
Yang Earth	Yin Fire	Yang Fire	Yin Wood
辰	卯	寅	丑
Dragon	Rabbit	Tiger	Ox

There is a Partial Three Harmony Metal Combination in Avicii's birth chart. His Rooster Month Branch and Snake Year Branch combine to form Metal. There are no other Combinations in the chart. The most prominent element is Metal. As Avicii is a Yin Metal Day Master, Metal represents his Self element. He is a Dominant Metal chart.

The Sheep Luck Cycle (age 15 to 19) contained the favourable Earth element. Avicii started producing music at the age of 16 in 2005 (Yin Wood Rooster year). The Annual Rooster Branch combined with the Snake and Rooster Branches in his chart to reinforce the favourable element Metal.

The Yang Metal Luck Cycle (age 20 to 24) was favourable for Avicii. In 2010 (Yang Metal Tiger year), Avicii released *Seek Bromance*, which reached the UK Top 20 Singles chart. The favourable element Metal was present in the Annual Stem. In 2012 (Yang Water Dragon year), the Annual Yang Water Stem gave Avicii the favourable Sequence of Five Stems: Yin Earth Year Stem, Yang Metal Luck Cycle, Yin Metal Day Master, Annual Yang Water Stem, Yin Water Month Stem. The Annual Dragon Branch also contained the favourable element Earth. He released *I Could Be the One* with Nicky Romero, a UK Number 1 hit.

In 2013 (Yin Water Snake year), the Annual Snake combined with the Rooster and Snake Branches in his chart to reinforce his favourable element Metal. Avicii released his debut album *True*, which reached the US and UK Top 5 Albums. It also contained the hit singles *Wake Me Up* and *Hey Brother*.

The Horse Luck Cycle (age 25 to 29) formed the Seasonal Fire Combination in Avicii's chart with the Snake Year Branch and his Sheep Day Branch. Fire became the most prominent element. Avicii transformed into a Follow the Power (Fire) chart. His list of favourable elements became:

1) Power element Fire.
2) Wealth element Wood.
3) Resource element Earth.
4) Self element Metal.
5) Output element Water.

In 2014 (Yang Wood Horse year), Avicii released *The Days/Nights* EP. However, with the change from a Dominant Metal chart to a Follow the Power (Fire) chart, Avicii had some health issues. He cancelled a series of shows after having his gall bladder and appendix removed. Avicii also suffered from acute pancreatitis related to excessive drinking.

In 2015 (Yin Wood Sheep year), he released his second album *Stories*. The favourable element Wood was present in the Annual Stem. In 2016 (Yang Fire Monkey year), there was a Stem Combination involving the Annual Yang Fire Stem and his Yin Metal Day Master. The Power Element Combination indicates professional success and recognition. Avicii resumed his extremely popular worldwide tours. However, the negative elements Metal and Water were also present. Avicii announced his retirement from touring.

The Yin Earth Luck Cycle (age 30 to 34) will be favourable as Avicii will revert back to a Dominant Metal chart. The Snake Luck Cycle (age 35 to 39) reinforces the favourable element Metal by combining with the Rooster and Snake Branches in his chart. The Yang Earth Luck Cycle (age 40 to 44) will also be favourable, as well as the Dragon Luck Cycle (age 45 to 49), which contains the favourable element Earth. The Yin Fire Luck Cycle (age 50 to 54) contains the negative element, so there may be some issues and complications during this period.

Example 6.12 Josh Hutcherson, American Actor
(born October 12, 1992)

Hour	Day	Month	Year
	辛	庚	壬
	Yin Metal	Yang Metal	Yang Water
	酉	戌	申
	Rooster	Dog	Monkey

9	19	29	39
辛	壬	癸	甲
Yin	Yang	Yin	Yang
Metal	Water	Water	Wood
亥	子	丑	寅
Pig	Rat	Ox	Tiger

49	59	69	79
乙	丙	丁	戊
Yin	Yang	Yin	Yang
Wood	Fire	Fire	Earth
卯	辰	巳	午
Rabbit	Dragon	Snake	Horse

There is a Seasonal Metal Combination in Hutcherson's birth chart. His Monkey Year Branch, Rooster Day Branch and Dog Month Branch combine to form Metal. There are no other Combinations in his chart. The most prominent element is Metal. As Hutcherson is a Yin Metal Day Master, Metal is his Self element. He has a Dominant Metal chart.

During the favourable Yin Metal Luck Cycle (age 9 to 13), Hutcherson had his first major role in the science fiction fantasy *Zathura: A Space Adventure* in 2005 (Yin Wood Rooster year). The favourable element Metal was present in the Annual Rooster Branch.

The Pig Luck Cycle (age 14 to 18) gave Hutcherson the auspicious Sequence of Four Branches: Monkey Year Branch, Rooster Day Branch, Dog Month Branch and Pig Luck Cycle. In 2006 (Yang Fire Dog year), there was a Stem Combination between the Annual Yang Fire Stem and Hutcherson's Yin Metal Day Master. The Power Element Combination indicates professional success and recognition. Hutcherson appeared alongside Robin Williams in the family comedy *RV*.

In 2008 (Yang Earth Rat year), the Annual Rat Branch combined with the Monkey Year Branch to form Water. Water became the most prominent element in his chart. Hutcherson transformed into a Follow the Output (Water) chart. His favourable elements became:

1) Output element Water.
2) Wealth element Wood.
3) Power element Fire.
4) Self element Metal.
5) Resource element Earth.

Hutcherson appeared alongside Brendan Fraser in the box office hit *Journey to the Center of the Earth*.

In 2010 (Yang Metal Tiger year), the Annual Tiger Branch clashed with the Monkey Year Branch to disrupt the Partial Three Harmony Water Combination. It also combined with his Dog Month branch to form Fire. Fire became the most prominent element. Hutcherson became a Follow the Power (Fire) chart. His list of favourable elements became:

1) Power element Fire.
2) Wealth element Wood.
3) Resource element Earth.
4) Self element Metal.
5) Output element Water.

Hutcherson had his first major dramatic role as the son of a lesbian couple played by Julianne Moore and Annette Benning in the Oscar-nominated *The Kids Are All Right*. The Yang Water Luck Cycle (age 19 to 23) contained the favourable element. In 2012 (Yang Water Dragon year), he was transformed again into a Follow the Output (Water) chart. The Annual Dragon Branch formed the Full Three Harmony Water Combination with his Monkey Year Branch. Hutcherson appeared with Vanessa Hudgens and Dwayne Johnson in the sequel *Journey 2: The Mysterious Island*. He also became a teen idol by playing the role of Peeta Mellark in the major box office hit *The Hunger Games*.

In 2013 (Yin Water Snake year), the Annual Snake Branch combined with Hutcherson's Rooster Day Branch to form Metal. He was transformed back into a Dominant Metal chart. He reprised his role as Peeta Mellark in *The Hunger Games: Catching Fire*. In 2014 (Yang Wood Horse year), the Annual Horse Branch combined with his Dog Month Branch to form Fire. As Fire became the most prominent element, Hutcherson became a Follow the Power (Fire) chart. *The Hunger Games: Mockingjay – Part 1* was released.

In 2015 (Yin Wood Sheep Branch), the Annual Sheep Branch gave Hutcherson the auspicious Sequence of Four Branches in a Row: Annual Sheep Branch, Monkey Year Branch, Rooster Day Branch and Dog Month Branch. Hutcherson produced and appeared in the biopic *Escobar: Paradise Lost* before appearing in the final film of the series *The Hunger Games: Mockingjay – Part 2*.

The Rat Luck Cycle (age 24 to 28) combined with his Monkey Year Branch to transform Hutcherson into a Follow the Output (Water) chart. By the favourable Yin Water Luck Cycle (age 29 to 33), Hutcherson will revert back to being a Dominant Metal chart. This period will also give him the auspicious Sequence of Four Stems: Yang Metal Month Stem, Yin Metal Day Master, Yang Water Year Stem, Yin Water Luck Cycle.

The Yang Wood Luck Cycle (age 34 to 38) contains the negative element Wood, so Hutcherson's will be more dependent on the Annual Stems and Branches. The Tiger Luck Cycle (age 39 to 43) clashes with the Monkey Year Branch to disrupt the Seasonal Metal Combination. It also combines with the Dog Month Branch to form Fire and transform Huthcherson into a Follow the Power (Fire) chart.

While the Yin Wood Luck Cycle (age 44 to 48) contains the negative element Wood, there is also a Stem Combination with the Yang Metal Month Branch. This reduces the complications. However, the Rabbit Luck Cycle (age 49 to 53) clashes with the Rooster Day Branch and contains the negative element Wood. There may be some issues or complications.

Example 6.13 Rainer Werner Fassbinder, German Film Director (born May 31, 1945, died June 10, 1982)

Hour	Day	Month	Year
	庚	辛	乙
	Yang Metal	Yin Metal	Yin Wood
	子	巳	酉
	Rat	Snake	Rooster

8	18	28
庚	己	戊
Yang Metal	Yin Earth	Yang Earth
辰	卯	寅
Dragon	Rabbit	Tiger

Hour	Day	Month	Year
	甲	丙	壬
	Yang Wood	Yang Fire	Yang Water
	子	午	戌
	Rat	Horse	Dog

There is a Partial Three Harmony Metal Combination in Fassbinder's birth chart. His Snake Month Branch and Rooster Year Branch combined to form Metal. There is also a Yin Metal Month Stem. Metal is the most prominent element in his chart. As Fassbinder is a Yang Metal Day Master, Metal is his Self element. He has a Dominant Metal chart.

The Rabbit Luck Cycle (age 23 to 27) clashed with Fassbinder's Rooster Year Branch, disrupting his Three Harmony Metal Combination. He became a Competitive Metal chart with the list of favourable elements:

1) Power element Fire.
2) Output element Water.
3) Self element Metal. The Ox Branch transforms him into a Dominant Metal chart.
4) Resource element Earth.
5) Wealth element Wood.

In 1967 (Yin Fire Sheep year), Fassbinder joined and became the leader of the Munich Action-Theatre, where he was active as an actor, scriptwriter and director. The favourable element Fire was present in the Annual Stem.

By the Yang Earth Luck Cycle (age 28 to 32), Fassbinder reverted back to being a Dominant Metal chart. In 1973 (Yin Water Ox year), the Annual Ox Branch formed the Full Three Harmony Metal Combination with the Snake and Rooster Branches in his chart. *Ali: Fear Eats the Soul* gained Fassbinder international acclaim. For a Yang Metal Day Master like Fassbinder, the Special Stars are the Rat and Ox. The Annual Ox Branch also worked in conjunction with his Rat Day Branch to bring him success.

In 1975 (Yin Wood Rabbit year), *Fox and His Friends* was screened at the Cannes Film Festival. The Annual Rabbit Branch clashed with his Rooster Year Branch to disrupt the Three Harmony Metal Combination. Fassbinder became a Competitive Metal chart. However, there was a Stem Combination between the Annual Stem and his Yang Metal Day Master. The Wealth Element Combination indicated the possibility of generating wealth. In 1977 (Yin Fire Snake year), Fassbinder was part of the jury for the 27th Berlin International Film Festival. The Annual Snake Branch combined with the Rooster and Snake Branches in his chart and reinforced his favourable element Metal.

The Tiger Luck Cycle (from age 33) contained the negative elements Fire and Wood, but also the favourable element Earth. In 1979 (Yin Earth Sheep year), *The Marriage of Maria Braun* featuring Hanna Schygulla was a commercial and critical success. The favourable element Earth was present in the Annual Stem and Branch. In 1980 (Yang Metal Monkey year), Fassbinder adapted novel *Berlin Alexanderplatz* for a television series. The Annual Monkey Branch combined with his Rat Day Branch to form the third favourable element Water. The second favourable element Metal was present in the Annual Stem. In 1981 (Yin Metal Rooster year), Fassbinder released the Third Reich drama *Lili Marleen*, as well as *Lola*, his remake of the Marlene Dietrich movie *The Blue Angel*. The Annual Rooster Branch combined with the Snake and Rooster Branches in Fassbinder's chart to reinforce the favourable element Metal.

Fassbinder was found dead from a lethal combination of cocaine and barbiturates on June 10, 1982. There was a Partial Three Harmony Fire Combination between the Horse Month of his death and the Annual Dog Year Branch. The negative Power element Fire was formed, resulting in a Fire-Metal conflict.

Example 6.14 Nicole Brown Simpson,
American Ex-Wife of O.J. Simpson
(born May 19, 1959, 02:00 hours, died June 12, 1994)

Hour	Day	Month	Year
己	辛	己	己
Yin Earth	Yin Metal	Yin Earth	Yin Earth
丑	丑	巳	亥
Ox	Ox	Snake	Pig

6	16	26	
庚	辛	壬	
Yang Metal	Yin Metal	Yang Water	
午	未	申	
Horse	Sheep	Monkey	

Hour	Day	Month	Year
	己	庚	甲
	Yin Earth	Yang Metal	Yang Wood
	巳	午	戌
	Snake	Horse	Dog

There is a Partial Three Harmony Metal Combination in Brown Simpson's birth chart. Her Snake Month Branch combines with her Ox Day and Hour Branches to form Metal. The most prominent element in her chart is Metal. As Brown Simpson is a Yin Metal Day Master, Metal is her Self element. She has a Dominant Metal chart.

At the age of 18 in 1977 (Yin Fire Snake year) during the favourable Yin Metal Luck Cycle (age 16 to 20), Brown Simpson was working as a waitress at the Daisy, an exclusive Beverly Hills club, after having graduated from high school. She met American football player O.J. Simpson and started dating him, even though he was still married at that time. The Annual Snake Branch combined with the Snake and Ox Branches in her chart to reinforce

345

her favourable element Metal. The Ox in her House of Spouse is involved in the Combination, indicating the possibility of romance or marriage.

Although the Sheep Luck Cycle (age 21 to 25) contained her favourable element Earth, it also clashed with her Ox Day Branch, which disrupted the Partial Three Harmony Metal Combination that accounted for her Dominant Metal chart. However, the Sheep was also involved in a Partial Three Harmony Wood Combination with Brown Simpson's Pig Year Branch. This reduced the potential of the Sheep-Ox Clash. On February 2, 1985 (still the Yang Wood Rat year), Brown Simpson married O.J. Simpson. The Annual Rat Branch combined with her Ox Day Branch, indicating the possibility of romance or marriage.

During the favourable Yang Water Luck Cycle (age 26 to 30), Brown Simpson became the mother of two children. In 1985 (Yin Wood Ox year), she had her daughter Sydney. The Output element Water represents her Children. Water is present in the Luck Cycle and is also hidden in the Annual Ox Branch. There was also a Partial Three Harmony Metal Combination between the Annual Ox Branch and the Ox and Rooster Branches within her chart. This reinforced her favourable element Metal. In 1988 (Yang Earth Dragon year), Brown Simpson had son Justin. The Output element Water was hidden in the Annual Dragon Branch. Her favourable Resource element Earth was also present in the Annual Stem and Branch.

In the Monkey Luck Cycle (from age 31), Brown Simpson filed for divorce in 1992 (Yang Water Monkey year) amidst allegations of domestic abuse and infidelity. The favourable element Water was present in the Annual Stem and Branch. In 1993 (Yin Water Rooster year), there was a failed attempt at reconciliation with her former husband. The Annual Rooster Branch combined with the Ox and Snake Branches in her chart to form the Full Three Harmony Metal Combination. This reinforced her favourable element Metal. As the Ox in her House of Spouse is involved in the Combination, it indicated the possibility of romance.

On June 12, 1994, Brown Simpson was found killed outside her home along with restaurant waiter Ron Goldman with multiple stab wounds in her head and neck. There was a Partial Three Harmony Fire Combination between the Horse Month in which she died and the Annual Dog Branch. The negative Power element is formed. The Snake Branch on the day she died combined with the Snake and Ox Branches in her chart to reinforce her favourable element Metal. There was a Fire-Metal conflict.

Example 6.15 Marilyn Monroe, American Actress
(born June 1, 1926, 09:30 hours, died August 4, 1962 as determined by autopsy)

Hour	Day	Month	Year
癸	辛	癸	丙
Yin Water	Yin Metal	Yin Water	Yang Fire
巳	酉	巳	寅
Snake	Rooster	Snake	Tiger

9	19	29	
壬	辛	庚	
Yang Water	Yin Metal	Yang Metal	
辰	卯	寅	
Dragon	Rabbit	Tiger	

Hour	Day	Month	Year
	甲	戊	壬
	Yang Wood	Yang Earth	Yang Water
	戌	申	寅
	Dog	Monkey	Tiger

There is a Partial Three Harmony Metal Combination in Monroe's birth chart. Her Rooster Day Branch and Snake Month Branch combine to form Metal. The most prominent element in her chart is Metal. As Monroe is a Yin Metal Day Master, Metal is her Self element. She has a Dominant Metal chart.

During the Yin Metal Luck Cycle (age 19 to 23), Monroe found success as a model and signed her first movie contract at the age of 20 in 1946 (Yang Fire Dog year). There was a Stem Combination between the Annual Yang Fire Stem and her Yin Metal Day Master. The Power Element Combination indicates professional success and recognition. Monroe also divorced her first husband Jimmy Dougherty that year. The Annual Dog Branch combined with her Tiger Year Branch to form Fire. There was a Fire-Metal conflict in her chart. In 1948 (Yang Earth Rat year), Monroe had her first starring role in *Ladies of the Chorus*. The favourable elements Earth and Water were present in the Annual Stem and Branch.

The Rabbit Luck Cycle (age 24 to 28) clashed with her Rooster Day Branch, disrupting the Three Harmony Metal Combination. She became a Competitive Metal chart. The list of favourable elements became:

1) Power element Fire.
2) Output element Water.
3) Self element Metal. The Ox Branch transforms her into a Dominant Metal chart.
4) Resource element Earth.
5) Wealth element Wood.

In 1952 (Yang Water Dragon year), Monroe appeared in the box office hit thrillers *Clash by Night* and *Don't Bother to Knock*. The favourable element Water was present in the Annual Stem. She also started a romance with retired baseball player Joe DiMaggio that year. The Annual Dragon Branch combined with her Rooster in the House of Spouse. This indicated the possibility of love or marriage. In 1953 (Yin Water Snake year), the favourable element Water was present once again. Monroe appeared in three major films: *Niagara* with Joseph Cotton, *Gentlemen Prefer Blondes* with Jane Russell and *How to Marry a Millionaire* with Lauren Bacall and Betty Grable.

On January 14 1954 (still the Yin Water Snake year), Monroe married Joe DiMaggio. The Annual Snake Branch combined with the Rooster Branch in her House of Spouse. This indicated the possibility of love or marriage. In 1954 (Yang Wood Horse year), the Annual Horse Branch combined with the Tiger year branch to form Fire, which is favourable for a Competitive Metal chart. Monroe appeared in the Western *The River of No Return* with Robert Mitchum and the musical *There's No Business Like Show Business* alongside Ethel Merman and Donald O'Connor.

The favourable Yang Metal Luck Cycle (age 29 to 33) saw Monroe becoming a major movie star. In 1955 (Yin Wood Sheep year), she appeared in the comedy *The Seven Year Itch*, famous for its iconic subway grate scene. Monroe also renegotiated her movie contract to more favourable terms. Her divorce with DiMaggio was also finalized.

In 1956 (Yang Fire Monkey year), there was a Stem Combination with her Yin Metal Day Master, indicating professional success and recognition. Monroe impressed critics and audiences with her performance in the drama *Bus Stop*. For a woman, the Power Element Combination also indicates the possibility of marriage. In 1956, Monroe married playwright Arthur Miller. In 1957 (Yin Fire Rooster year), Monroe starred in *The Prince and the Showgirl* with Sir Laurence Olivier. The Annual Rooster Branch combined with the Rooster and Ox Branches in her chart to reinforce the favourable element Metal.

In 1959 (Yin Earth Pig year), the Annual Pig Branch clashed with her Snake Month Branch to disrupt the Three Harmony Metal Combination. She became a Competitive Metal chart. However, the Annual Pig Branch also formed a Six Harmony Combination with the Tiger Year Branch. This indicated assistance from mentors. Monroe scored one of her biggest hits in Billy Wilder's comedy *Some Like It Hot* with Tony Curtis and Jack Lemmon.

The Tiger Luck Cycle (from age 34) contained the negative elements Wood and Fire and the favourable element Earth. In 1961 (Yin Metal Ox year), Monroe completed her last movie, *The Misfits,* with Clark Gable and Montgomery Clift. The Annual Ox Branch combined with the Rooster and Snake Branches in her chart to form the Full Three Harmony Metal Combination. In June 1962 (Yang Fire Horse month in the Yang Water Tiger year), Monroe was sacked from *Something's Got to Give* after on set disruptions. The Horse month combined with her Tiger Year Branch to form the negative element Fire.

Monroe was found dead by her housekeeper on the morning of August 5, 1962. The cause of death was an overdose of barbiturates. An autopsy determined that she had died the previous evening between 20:30 and 22:30 hours on August 4, 1962, a Yang Wood Dog day. The Dog Day of death would have combined with the Tiger Luck Cycle and her Tiger Year Branch to form the negative element Fire. There was a Metal-Fire conflict.

Example 6.16 Katharine Hepburn, American Actress
(born May 12, 1907, 17:47 hours, died June 29, 2003)

Hour	Day	Month	Year
丁	辛	乙	丁
Yin Fire	Yin Metal	Yin Wood	Yin Fire
酉	酉	巳	未
Rooster	Rooster	Snake	Sheep

8	18	28	38	48
丙	丁	戊	己	庚
Yang Fire	Yin Fire	Yang Earth	Yin Earth	Yang Metal
午	未	申	酉	戌
Horse	Sheep	Monkey	Rooster	Dog

58	68	78	88
辛	壬	癸	甲
Yin Metal	Yang Water	Yin Water	Yang Wood
亥	子	丑	寅
Pig	Rat	Ox	Tiger

Hour	Day	Month	Year
	癸	戊	癸
	Yin Water	Yang Earth	Yin Water
	酉	午	未
	Rooster	Horse	Sheep

There is a Partial Three Harmony Combination in Hepburn's birth chart. Her Snake Month Branch and Rooster Day and Hour Branches combine to form Metal. There are no other Combinations in the chart. The most prominent element is Metal. As Hepburn is a Yin Metal Day Master, Metal represents her Self element. She has a Dominant Metal chart.

351

The Horse Luck Cycle (age 13 to 17) contained the negative element Fire. At the age of 14 in 1921 (Yin Metal Rooster year), Hepburn was devastated to find her brother dead after he had hanged himself. While the Annual Rooster Branch combined with the Rooster and Ox Branches in her chart to reinforce the favourable element Metal, the negative element Fire was present in the Luck Cycle. There was a Fire-Metal conflict.

The Yin Fire Luck Cycle (age 18 to 22) contained the negative element. Hepburn was studying at Bryn Mawr College. She struggled with the academic demands of university and was suspended once for smoking in her room. In 1928 (Yang Earth Dragon year), Hepburn graduated with a degree in History and Philosophy. Her favourable element Earth was present in the Annual Stem and Branch. Hepburn also married Ludlow Ogden Smith that year. There was a Six Harmony Combination with the Rooster in the House of Spouse. This indicated the possibility of love or marriage.

The Sheep Luck Cycle (age 23 to 27) contained the favourable element Earth. After working in theatre, Hepburn made her movie debut opposite John Barrymore in *A Bill of Divorcement* in 1932 (Yang Water Monkey year). The favourable elements Metal and Water were present in the Annual Stem and Branch. In 1933 (Yin Water Rooster year), the Annual Rooster Branch combined with the Rooster and Ox Branches in Hepburn's chart to reinforce the favourable element Metal. Hepburn starred in the box office hit *Little Women* and *Morning Glory*, for which she received her first Oscar for Best Actress. In 1934 (Yang Wood Dog year), the negative element Wood was present in the Annual Stem. Hepburn divorced from Smith that year.

The Yang Earth Luck Cycle (age 28 to 32) contained the favourable element Earth. However, the negative element Wood was present in 1935 (Yin Wood Pig year). Hepburn starred in a series of flops such as *Sylvia Scarlett* opposite Cary Grant. She had a hit in *Stage Door* alongside Ginger Rogers in 1937 (Yin Fire Ox year). The Annual Ox Branch combined with the Rooster and Snake Branches in her chart to form the Full Three Harmony Metal Combination. In 1939 (Yin Earth Rabbit year), the Annual Rabbit Branch clashed with her Rooster Day Branch to disrupt the Three Harmony Metal Combination. Hepburn became a Competitive Metal chart. Her list of favourable elements became:

1) Power element Fire.
2) Output element Water.
3) Self element Metal. The Ox Branch transforms her into a Dominant Metal chart.
4) Resource element Earth.
5) Wealth element Wood.

Hepburn bought out her contract from RKO Pictures after being labeled box-office poison and starred in the play *The Philadelphia Story*, for which she had acquired the rights.

The Monkey Luck Cycle (age 33 to 37) contained the favourable elements Metal and Water. In 1940 (Yang Metal Dragon year), Hepburn made a triumphant return and received an Oscar nomination for Best Actress in the movie version of *The Philadelphia Story* with Cary Grant and James Stewart. The favourable elements Metal and Earth were present in the Annual Stem and Branch. In 1941 (Yin Metal Snake year), Hepburn met and started a relationship with actor Spencer Tracy when they were filming *Woman of the Year*. The Annual Snake Branch combined with the Rooster in her House of Spouse. This indicated the possibility of love or marriage. The relationship was to last 26 years until Tracy's death. Hepburn has the House of Spouse animal Rooster present twice in her chart. This indicated the possibility of two marriages or major personal relationships.

The Yin Earth Luck Cycle (age 38 to 42) also contained her favourable element. In 1948 (Yang Earth Rat year) and 1949 (Yin Earth Ox year), Hepburn starred with Spencer Tracy in the box office hits *State of the Union* and *Adam's Rib*. In 1948, the favourable elements Earth and Water were present in the Annual Stem and Branch. In 1949, the Annual Ox Branch combined with the Rooster and Snake Branches in her chart to form the Full Three Harmony Metal Combination.

The Rooster Luck Cycle (age 43 to 47) combined with the Rooster and Ox Branches in Hepburn's chart to reinforce the favourable element Metal. In 1951 (Yin Metal Rabbit year), the Annual Rabbit Branch clashed with the Rooster Branches in her chart and the Luck Cycle to transform her into a Competitive Metal chart. Hepburn contracted dysentery while filming *The African Queen* with Humphrey Bogart in Belgian Congo. However, in 1952 (Yang Water Dragon year), she was nominated for another Best Actress Oscar for her performance and also had another hit with Spencer Tracy, *Pat and Mike*. The favourable elements Water and Earth were present in the Annual Stem and Branch.

The Yang Metal Luck Cycle (age 48 to 52) contained the favourable element Metal. In 1955 (Yin Wood Sheep year), Hepburn received another Best Actress Oscar nomination for her performance in David Lean's *Summertime*. The favourable element Earth was present in the Annual Sheep Branch. In 1956 (Yang Fire Monkey year), there was a Stem Combination between the Annual Yang Fire Stem and her Yin Metal Day Master. The Power Element Combination indicated professional success and recognition. Hepburn appeared opposite Burt Lancaster in *The Rainmaker*, for which she received another Best Actress Oscar nomination.

The Dog Luck Cycle (age 53 to 57) contained the favourable element Earth. She took time off to care for the ailing Tracy and they appeared together for the last time on screen in *Guess Who's Coming to Dinner* in 1967 (Yin Fire Sheep year) alongside Sidney Poitier during the Yin Metal Luck Cycle (age 58 to 62). Hepburn won her second Best Actress Oscar. The favourable element Earth was present in the Annual Branch. In 1968 (Yang Earth Monkey year), Hepburn won her third Best Actress Oscar for portraying Eleanor of Aquitaine in *The Lion in Winter*. The favourable elements Earth, Metal and Water were present in the Annual Stem and Branch.

The Pig Luck Cycle (age 63 to 67) clashed with Hepburn's Snake Month Branch and disrupted the Three Harmony Combination. She became a Competitive Metal chart. In 1973 (Yin Water Ox year), the Annual Ox Branch combined with the Rooster Branches in her chart to transform her into a Dominant Metal chart. Hepburn received her first Emmy nomination for her performance in the television movie *The Glass Menagerie*.

The Yang Water (age 68 to 72), Rat (age 73 to 77) and Yin Water (age 78 to 82) all contained her favourable element Water. Hepburn had reverted back to a Dominant Metal chart. In 1981 (Yin Metal Rooster year) during the Rat Luck Cycle, Hepburn won her fourth Best Actress Oscar for *On Golden Pond* opposite Henry Fonda. The Annual Rooster Branch combined with the Snake and Rooster Branches to reinforce her favourable element Metal. In 1985 (Yin Wood Ox year), the Annual Ox Branch combined with the Rooster and Snake Branches in Hepburn's chart to form the Full Three Harmony Metal Combination. Hepburn had her final starring role in *Grace Quigley* opposite Nick Nolte.

The Ox Luck Cycle (age 83 to 87) combined with the Rooster and Snake Branches in Hepburn's chart to form the Full Three Harmony Combination. In 1994 (Yang Wood Dog year), Hepburn appeared in her final film *A Love Affair* alongside Warren Beatty and Annette Benning. The favourable element Earth was present in the Annual Dog Branch. She then retired from public life during the Yang Wood Luck Cycle (age 88 to 92) and passed away at the age of 96 from natural causes during the Tiger Luck Cycle (from age 93).

On the day she died, the Dog Month of her death combined with the Tiger Luck Cycle to form the negative Fire element. The Rooster Day of death combined with the Snake and Rooster Branches in her chart to form the favourable element Metal. There was a Fire-Metal conflict.

Example 6.17 Sylvia Plath, American Author (born October 27, 1932, died February 11, 1963, 04:30 hours)

Hour	Day	Month	Year
	辛	庚	壬
	Yin Metal	Yang Metal	Yang Water
	酉	戌	申
	Rooster	Dog	Monkey

6	16	26
己	戊	丁
Yin	Yang	Yin
Earth	Earth	Fire
酉	申	
Rooster	Monkey	

Hour	Day	Month	Year
戊	乙	甲	癸
Yang Earth	Yin Wood	Yang Wood	Yin Water
寅	酉	寅	卯
Tiger	Rooster	Tiger	Rabbit

356

There is a Seasonal Metal Combination in Plath's birth chart. Her Monkey Year Branch, Rooster Day Branch and Dog Month Branch combine to form Metal. There is also a Yang Metal Month Stem. The most prominent element in the chart is Metal. As Plath is a Yin Metal Day Master, Metal is her Self element. She has a Dominant Metal chart.

The Monkey Luck Cycle (age 21 to 25) contained the favourable elements Metal and Water. In 1955 (Yin Wood Sheep year), Plath obtained a Fullbright Scholarship to study at Newnham College, one of only two women's colleges in Cambridge, England. The Annual Sheep Branch gave Plath the auspicious Sequence of Four Stems in a Row: Annual Sheep Branch, Monkey Year Branch, Rooster Day Branch and Dog Year Branch. In 1956 (Yang Fire Monkey year), there was a Stem Combination between the Annual Yang Fire Stem and her Yin Metal Day Master. The Power Element Combination indicated professional recognition and success. For a woman, it can also indicate the possibility of love or marriage. Plath met and married poet Ted Hughes that year.

The Yin Fire Luck Cycle (age 26 to 30) contained the negative Power element. In January 1960 (still the Yin Earth Pig year), Plath had her first child, daughter Frieda. She had become pregnant in a year with her Output or Child element Water. In 1960 (Yang Metal Rat year), the favourable elements Metal and Water were present in the Annual Stem and Branch. Plath published her first collection of poetry *The Colossus*. In 1961 (Yin Metal Ox year), Plath completed the manuscript for her semi-autobiographical novel *The Bell Jar*. The Annual Ox Branch combined with her Rooster Day Branch to form a Partial Three Harmony Metal Combination. This reinforced her favourable element Metal. Plath also became pregnant that year and gave birth to son Nicholas in January 1962. Her Output or Child element Water was present in the Annual Ox Branch.

In 1962 (Yang Water Tiger year), the Annual Tiger Branch clashed with Plath's Monkey Year Branch to disrupt the Seasonal Metal Combination. It also combined with the Dog Month Branch to form the negative element Fire. Plath separated from Hughes, after discovering that he was having an affair with Assia Wevill, the wife of poet David Wevill. She also attempted suicide by driving her car off the road. In January 1963 (still the Yang Water Tiger year), *The Bell Jar* was released to critical indifference.

In 1963 (Yin Water Rabbit year), the Annual Rabbit Branch clashed with her Rooster Day Branch to disrupt the Seasonal Metal Combination. The negative element Wood was also present in the Annual Rabbit Branch. A few days before she died, Plath visited her general practitioner with regard to her depressive episodes and was prescribed medication that required several weeks to work. On February 11, 1963, Plath was found dead of carbon monoxide poisoning, with her head in the oven. The Tiger month and hour of her death clashed with her Monkey Year Branch to further disrupt the Seasonal Metal Combination. They also combined with her Dog Month Branch to form her negative element Fire. The day of death also contained the Rooster. There was a Fire-Metal conflict.

Example 6.18 Azealia Banks, American Rapper
(born May 31, 1991, 04:43 hours)

Hour	Day	Month	Year
庚	辛	癸	辛
Yang Metal	Yin Metal	Yin Water	Yin Metal
寅	丑	巳	未
Tiger	Ox	Snake	Sheep

2	12	22	32
甲	乙	丙	丁
Yang Wood	Yin Wood	Yang Fire	Yin Fire
午	未	申	酉
Horse	Sheep	Monkey	Rooster

42	52	62	72
戊	己	庚	辛
Yang Earth	Yin Earth	Yang Metal	Yin Metal
戌	亥	子	丑
Dog	Pig	Rat	Ox

There is a Partial Three Harmony Metal Combination in Banks' birth chart. Her Ox Day Branch and Snake Month Branch combine to form Metal. There is also a Yin Metal Year Stem and a Yang Metal Hour Stem. Metal is the most prominent element in her chart. As Banks is a Yin Metal Day Master, Metal is her Self element. She has a Dominant Metal chart.

The Sheep Luck Cycle (age 17 to 21) clashed with Banks' Ox Day Branch to disrupt the Partial Three Harmony Metal Combination. Banks became a Competitive Metal chart. Her list of favourable elements became:

1) Output element Water.
2) Power element Fire.

3) Self element Metal. The Rooster Branch transforms her into a Dominant Metal chart.
4) Resource element Earth.
5) Wealth element Wood.

In 2008 (Yang Earth Rat year), the favourable element Water was present. Banks released the self-produced track *Seventeen*, which secured her a development deal with XL Recordings. However, Banks left XL Recording within the year and revealed that she became depressed in 2009 (Yin Earth Ox year). The Annual Ox Branch was not able to combine with the Snake Branch in her chart due to the Clash with the Sheep Luck Cycle. In 2012 (Yang Water Dragon year), the favourable element was present in the Annual Branch. Banks released her first EP (extended play) *1991*, which was critically acclaimed.

The Yang Fire Luck Cycle (age 22 to 26) formed a Stem Combination with Banks' Yin Metal Day Master. The Power Element Combination indicates professional recognition or success. In 2014 (Yang Wood Horse year), the Annual Horse Branch formed a Seasonal Fire Combination with the Snake Month Branch and the Sheep Year Branch. Fire became the most prominent element. Banks became a Follow the Power (Fire) chart. Her list of favourable elements became:

1) Power element Fire.
2) Wealth element Wood.
3) Resource element Earth.
4) Self element Metal.
5) Output element Water.

Banks released her debut album *Broke with Expensive Taste*. In 2015 (Yin Wood Sheep year), Banks became a Competitive Metal chart when the Annual Sheep Branch clashed with her Ox Day Branch. She became involved in a confrontation with a fellow passenger and the flight crew after the Delta Air Lines landed in Los Angeles. Banks was also arrested towards the end of the year after attacking a female security guard. In 2017 (Yin Fire Rooster year), Banks made her movie debut in the musical drama *Coco*. The Annual Rooster combined with the Snake and Ox Branches in her chart to form the Full Three Harmony Combination.

The Monkey Luck Cycle (age 27 to 31) contains the favourable elements Metal and Water. The Yin Fire Luck Cycle (age 32 to 36) has the negative element, so there may be some issues. The Rooster Luck Cycle (age 37 to 41) forms the Full Three Harmony Metal Combination with the Snake and Ox Branches in her chart to reinforce the favourable element Metal. This should be an extremely favourable period in Banks' life.

The Yang Earth Luck Cycle (age 42 to 46) contains the most favourable element, so it should be another positive period. However, the Dog Luck Cycle (age 47 to 51) combines with the Tiger Hour Branch to form Fire. There is a Fire-Metal conflict, which may create some issues.

Conclusion

From the 18 examples that were covered in this chapter, the list of favourable elements for Dominant Metal charts is:

1) Resource element Earth.
2) Self element Metal.
3) Output element Water.
4) Wealth element Wood.
5) Power element Fire.

All the examples in this chapter were Yang Metal or Yin Metal Day Masters with charts with a Full or Partial Three Harmony Metal Combination or Seasonal Metal Combination. As the Combination produced the element that is the same as the Day Master, this qualified them as Dominant Metal charts.

Mary Pierce and Mark Feehily have the Partial Three Harmony Metal Combination consisting of the Rooster and Ox Branches. Richard Roxburgh, Joanna Newsom and Jools Holland have two Ox Branches and one Rooster Branch.

Alan Cumming and Enya have the Partial Three Harmony Metal Combination consisting of the Snake and Ox Branches. Nicole Brown Simpson has a Snake and two Oxen. Paul Keating and Azealia Banks also have the Snake and Ox Branches in their charts but they have the potential to change into a different type of chart. Paul Keating can change into a Follow the Wealth (Wood) chart, while Azealia Banks has the potential to become a Follow the Power (Fire) chart.

Amy Schumer and Rainer Werner Fassbinder have the Partial Three Harmony Metal Combination consisting of the Snake and Rooster Branches. Marilyn Monroe and Collette Dinnigan have two Snake Branches and one Rooster, while Katharine Hepburn has two Rooster Branches and a Snake Branch. Avicii also has the Snake and Rooster Branches in his chart, but he has the potential to change into a Follow the Power (Fire) chart.

Sylvia Plath and Josh Hutcherson have the Seasonal Metal Combination consisting of the Monkey, Rooster and Dog Branches in their charts. Hutcherson also has the potential to become a Follow Output (Water) chart, as well as a Follow the Power (Fire) chart.

Dominant Metal charts can also be transformed into Competitive Metal charts when the Partial Three Harmony Metal Combination within their charts is disrupted. This can be seen in the charts of Alan Cumming, Amy Schumer, Enya, Markus Feehily, Richard Roxburgh, Joanna Newsom, Jools Holland, Paul Keating, Rainer Werner Fassbinder, Marilyn Monroe, Katherine Hepburn and Azealia Banks.

Chapter Seven Competitive Metal Charts

Competitive Metal charts are those in which Stems and Branches of the Self element (Metal) are present throughout the chart but are not involved in any Combinations. The conditions for Competitive Metal charts are as follows:

1) Yang or Yin Metal Day Masters.
2) There should be two or more Metal Branches (i.e. Snake or Rooster) that are not involved in a Full or Partial Three Harmony Metal Combination.
3) Apart from the Yang or Yin Metal Day Master, there may be one or more Metal Stems.

Branches play more of a vital role in determining Competitive charts as they are able to combine with other Branches to transform the chart into a Dominant chart. With Competitive Metal charts, we are concerned with the Snake and Rooster Branches which are the Birth and Peak respectively. While the Ox is able to combine with either the Snake or Rooster to form a Partial Three Harmony Metal Combination, on its own, the main element is Earth. This means that the main element with two or more Ox Branches without any Snake or Rooster Branches present is Earth, as there is no Partial Three Harmony Metal Combination. On the other hand, when there is at least a Snake or Rooster Branch present with the Ox Branch, a Partial Three Harmony Metal Combination is formed. Metal will then be formed.

Within the Stems, there should be one or more Stems of the Self element in addition to the Day Master. This can be the Year, Month or Hour Stem. Here are some examples of what constitutes a Competitive Metal chart, which requires a Yang or Yin Metal Day Master.

1) One Metal Branch and one additional Metal Stem apart from the Day Master.
2) Two, three or four identical Metal Branches and one, two or three other Metal Stems apart from the Day Master.
3) Two, three or four identical Metal Branches without additional Metal Stems.
4) With all these examples listed above, there are no Partial or Full Three Harmony Combinations in the Branches.

If there are one, two or three additional Metal Stems apart from the Day Master but no Metal Branches, then the chart does not qualify as a Competitive Metal chart. The Branches take precedence when it comes to determining the Competitive nature of the chart.

People with Competitive charts are extremely motivated to succeed in life, so they are well suited to performance driven fields like sports, sales and business. They are generally physically attractive and charismatic. They have a tendency to be insecure as they constantly compare themselves to others. Being extremely demanding of themselves and others, they will persevere until they succeed or reach their goals. While they may question authority and the status quo at times, once they are confident in their circumstances, they thrive on their success.

The main issue of Competitive charts is the presence of their Rivals, which can be exhausted by the Output element or controlled by the Power element. For Competitive charts, the ranking of elements is as follows:

1) Water, the Output element. This drains the Rivals.
2) Fire, the Power element. This controls the Rivals.
3) Self element Metal Branches. This refers to the two other Branches that will result in a Partial Three Harmony Metal Combination, thus transforming the chart again. For example, if there are two Rooster Branches in the chart, then the Snake or Ox Branch will transform the chart into a Dominant Metal chart. Note the Self-element Stems represent more Rivals.
4) Earth, the Resource element. The Resource element not only strengthens the Day Master, it also fuels Rivals.
5) Wood, the Wealth element. This becomes a focus of conflict amongst the Rivals. The only exception to the Wealth element being negative is when the Wealth Stem Yin Wood occurs, as it combines with the Yang Metal Day Master, causing no harm.

Competitive Metal charts benefit from two elements: Water and Fire. With regard to the Self element Metal, Competitive Metal charts can only benefit from Metal Branches that permit a Partial Three Harmony Metal Combination.

Competitive Metal charts have the potential to transform into a Dominant Metal chart when there is a Partial Three Harmony Metal Combination involving the Annual Branch or Luck Cycles. In these circumstances, the list of favourable elements will then be:

1) Resource element Earth.
2) Self element Metal.
3) Output element Water.
4) Wealth element Wood.
5) Power element Fire.

Example 7.1 Kelly Rowland, American Singer
(born February 11, 1981, 02:22 hours)

Hour	Day	Month	Year
丁	庚	庚	辛
Yin Fire	Yang Metal	Yang Metal	Yin Metal
丑	申	寅	酉
Ox	Monkey	Tiger	Rooster

8	18	28	38
辛	壬	癸	甲
Yin Metal	Yang Water	Yin Water	Yang Wood
卯	辰	巳	午
Rabbit	Dragon	Snake	Horse

48	58	68	78
乙	丙	丁	戊
Yin Wood	Yang Fire	Yin Fire	Yang Earth
未	申	酉	戌
Sheep	Monkey	Rooster	Dog

There are no Combinations involving the Branches in Rowland's birth chart. She is a Yang Metal Day Master. In her chart, there is also a Rooster Year Branch, a Yang Metal Month Stem and a Yin Metal Year Stem. This qualifies Rowland as a Competitive Metal chart. In Ox or Snake years or Luck Cycles in the first part of life, Rowland is transformed into a Dominant Metal chart. She remains a Competitive chart in Rooster years. The Year Pillar loses its influence when Rowland is in her 40s. In the second part of life, she is transformed into a Dominant Metal chart in Snake or Rooster years or Luck Cycles.

There is a Yang Metal Month Stem occupying the sector associated with the Father. As a Metal Rival is present in the Month Stem, this indicates a problematic relationship between Rowland and her father. When Rowland was seven, her mother took her and left her abusive and alcoholic father.

In the Rabbit Luck Cycle (age 13 to 17), the Wealth element Wood was present in the form of Yin Wood. This Yin Wood formed a Stem Combination with Rowland's Yang Metal Day Master. The Wealth Element Combination indicates the possibility of generating income or wealth. Rowland joined the group *Destiny's Child* with Beyonce Knowles, LaTavia Robertson and LeToya Luckett during this period. In 1996 (Yang Fire Rat year), *Destiny's Child* signed with Columbia Records. The favourable elements Fire and Water were present in the Annual Stem and Branch. In 1997 (Yin Fire Ox year), the Annual Ox Branch combined with Rowland's Rooster Year Branch to transform her into a Dominant Metal chart. *Destiny's Child* released their self-titled debut album with the US Top 10 hit *No, No, No*.

The Yang Water Luck Cycle (age 18 to 22) contained the favourable element. In 1999 (Yin Earth Rabbit year), *Destiny's Child* released their second album *The Writing's on the Wall* with two US Number 1 hits *Bills, Bills, Bill* and *Say My Name*. There was a Yin Wood Stem hidden in the Annual Rabbit Branch. This combined with Rowland's Yang Metal Day Master, indicating the possibility of generating wealth.

In 2000 (Yang Metal Dragon year), there was a Yang Metal Rival present. The line-up of *Destiny's Child* was changed and former members Robertson and Luckett started legal proceedings against Rowland and Knowles and their manager. The Annual Dragon Branch combined with the Rowland's Monkey Day Branch to form the favourable element Water. The lawsuit against Rowland and Knowles was settled. Destiny's Child released

Independent Woman Part 1, the theme song to the movie *Charlie's Angels*. It was Number 1 on the US Singles Charts for 11 weeks. In 2001 (Yin Metal Snake year), the Annual Snake Branch combined with Rowland's Rooster Year Branch to transform her into a Dominant Metal chart. *Destiny's Child* released their third album *Survivor*, with their fourth Number 1 hit *Bootylicious*.

In 2002 (Yang Water Horse year), the favourable elements Water and Fire were present in the Annual Stem and Branch. Rowland released her first solo album *Simply Deep* with her US Number 1 duet with Nelly, *Dilemma*. It also earned her an award for Best Rap/Sung Collaboration.

The Dragon Luck Cycle (age 23 to 27) combined with Rowland's Monkey Day Branch to form the favourable element Water. In 2005 (Yin Wood Rooster year), there was a Stem Combination between the Annual Yin Wood Stem and her Yang Metal Day Master. This indicated the possibility of generating wealth. *Destiny's Child* released their fourth and final album *Destiny Fulfilled* with the US Top 3 hits *Lose My Breath* and *Soldier*.

In 2006 (Yang Fire Dog year), the Annual Dog Branch combined with the Tiger Month Branch to form the favourable element Fire. *Destiny's Child* embarked on a worldwide concert tour and announced the disbanding of the group. They also received a star on the Hollywood Walk of Fame and released their greatest hits album *Number 1's*, which reached Number 1 on the US Albums Chart.

2007 (Yin Fire Pig year) was a mixed year for Rowland. The favourable element Fire was present in the Annual Stem but the Annual Pig Branch contained the negative element Wood. She released her second album *Ms. Kelly*, which did not achieve the same level of success as her first album.

The Yin Water Luck Cycle (age 28 to 32) contained Rowland's favourable element. In 2009 (Yin Earth Ox year), the Annual Ox Branch combined with Rowland's Rooster Year Branch to transform her into a Dominant Metal chart. Her list of favourable elements became:

1) Resource element Earth.
2) Self element Metal.
3) Output element Water.
4) Wealth element Wood.
5) Power element Fire.

Rowland enjoyed a UK Number 1 hit with David Guetta, *When Love Takes Over*. In 2013 (Yin Water Snake year), she announced her engagement to her manager Tim Witherspoon on the *Queen Latifah Show*. The Annual Snake Branch formed a Six Harmony Combination with her Monkey Year Branch, indicating the possibility of love or marriage.

The Snake Luck Cycle (age 33 to 37) was able to form two Combinations resulting in a Competition for Combination. It combined with Rowland's Rooster Year Branch to transform her into a Dominant Metal chart. It also formed a Six Harmony Combination with Rowland's Monkey Day Branch, indicating the possibility of love or marriage. In 2014 (Yang Wood Horse year), Rowland married Witherspoon. The favourable element Fire was present in the Annual Horse Branch. In 2015 (Yin Wood Sheep year), Rowland became part of the recurring cast of the hit television series *Empire*. There was a Stem Combination between the Yin Wood Annual Stem and her Yang Metal Day Master, indicating the possibility of generating wealth. The Yang Wood Luck Cycle (age 38 to 42) contains the negative element, so there may be issues. The Horse Luck Cycle (age 43 to 47) contains the favourable element Fire and should be a positive period for her. The Yin Wood Luck Cycle (age 48 to 52) forms a Stem Combination with Rowland's Yang Metal Day Master, indicating the possibility of generating wealth during this period.

Example 7.2 Mardy Fish, American Tennis Player
(born December 9, 1981)

Hour	Day	Month	Year
	辛	庚	辛
	Yin Metal	Yang Metal	Yin Metal
	酉	子	酉
	Rooster	Rat	Rooster

1	11	21	31
己	戊	丁	丙
Yin Earth	Yang Earth	Yin Fire	Yang Fire
亥	戌	酉	申
Pig	Dog	Rooster	Monkey

41	51	61	71
乙	甲	癸	壬
Yin Wood	Yang Wood	Yin Water	Yang Water
未	午	巳	辰
Sheep	Horse	Snake	Dragon

There are no Branch Combinations in Fish's birth chart. He is a Yin Metal Day Master. There are two Rooster Branches, in the Day and Year Pillars. There is also a Yang Metal Month Stem and a Yin Metal Year Stem. This qualifies Fish as a Competitive Metal chart. In Snake or Ox years or Luck Cycles, Fish is transformed into a Dominant Metal chart. In Rooster years or Luck Cycles, Fish remains a Competitive Metal chart.

Fish turned professional at the age of 18 in 2000 (Yang Metal Dragon year) during the Dog Luck Cycle (age 16 to 20). The Annual Dragon Branch combined with the Rat Month Branch to form the favourable element Water. In 2002 (Yang Water Horse year), the favourable elements Water and Fire were present in the Annual Stem and

Branch. Fish won his first title on the Association of Tennis Professionals (ATP) tour, winning the doubles title at the U.S. Men's Clay Court Championships in Houston, Texas with Andy Roddick.

The Yin Fire Luck Cycle (age 21 to 25) contained the favourable element. In 2004 (Yang Wood Monkey year), the Annual Monkey Branch combined with Fish's Rat Month Branch to form the favourable element Water. He was runner-up in the Summer Olympics in Athens, losing to Chilean Nicolas Massu but earning a silver medal.

In 2005 (Yin Wood Rooster year), there was a Yin Metal Rival present in the Annual Rooster Branch. Fish injured his left wrist, requiring surgery twice. In 2006 (Yang Fire Dog year), there was a Stem Combination between the Annual Yang Fire Stem and Fish's Yin Metal Day Master. The Power Element Combination indicated professional success and recognition. Fish won the singles title at the U.S. Men's Clay Court Championships after being awarded a wild card.

The Rooster Luck Cycle (age 26 to 30) contained a Yin Metal Rival, a negative element for Fish. However, it is also the animal in his House of Spouse. This indicated the possibility of love or marriage during this period. In 2008 (Yang Earth Rat year), Fish married attorney Stacey Gardner. It was a favourable year for Fish, as the Annual Rat Branch contained the favourable element Water.

In 2009 (Yin Earth Ox year), the Annual Ox Branch combined with the Rooster Branches in Fish's chart to transform him into a Dominant Metal chart. His favourable elements became:

1) Resource element Earth.
2) Self element Metal.
3) Output element Water.
4) Wealth element Wood.
5) Power element Fire.

Fish won the Singles title at the Delray Beach International Tennis Championships. In 2012 (Yang Water Dragon year), there was a Competition for Combination involving the Annual Dragon Branch. It combined with the Rat Month Branch to form the favourable element Water. However, there was also a Six Harmony Combination with the Rooster Day and Year Branches and the Luck Cycle. Fish underwent a surgical procedure after he suffered severe cardiac arrhythmia, or irregular beating of his heart.

The Yang Fire Luck Cycle (age 31 to 35) formed a Stem Combination with Fish's Yin Metal Day Master. This indicated professional success and recognition. Fish received a lot of support from fans and his peers during this period after sharing his health problems through the media. The cardiac condition resulted in him developing severe anxiety. In 2015 (Yin Wood Sheep year), the negative elements Wood and Earth were present in the Annual Stem and Branch. Fish retired from the men's tour that year. In 2016 (Yang Fire Monkey year), there was another Stem Combination involving the Annual Yang Fire Stem and his Yin Metal Day Master. Fish became a leading player on the celebrity golfing circuit, winning the Diamond Resorts International in Orlando, Florida. The Annual Monkey Branch also combined with his Rat Month Branch to form the favourable element Water.

The Monkey Luck Cycle (age 36 to 40) will be favourable for Fish as it combines with his Rat Month Branch to form the favourable element Water. The Yin Wood Luck Cycle (age 41 to 45) forms a Stem Combination with the Yang Metal Month Stem. The Yang Metal Rival is removed through this Combination with the Wealth element Wood, indicating that issues will be solved through the use of money. The Sheep Luck Cycle (age 46 to 50) contains the negative element Earth, so there may be some complications and issues.

Example 7.3 Kevin Scott Richardson, American Singer
(born October 3, 1971, 12:15 hours)

Hour	Day	Month	Year
甲	辛	丁	辛
Yang Wood	Yin Metal	Yin Fire	Yin Metal
午	酉	酉	亥
Horse	Rooster	Rooster	Pig

8	18	28	38
丙	乙	甲	癸
Yang Fire	Yin Wood	Yang Wood	Yin Water
申	未	午	巳
Monkey	Sheep	Horse	Snake

48	58	68	78
壬	辛	庚	己
Yang Water	Yin Metal	Yang Metal	Yin Earth
辰	卯	寅	丑
Dragon	Rabbit	Tiger	Ox

There are no Branch Combinations in Richardson's birth chart. He is a Yin Metal Day Master. There is a Rooster Day Branch, a Rooster Month Branch, as well as a Yin Metal Year Stem. This qualifies Richardson as a Competitive Metal chart. In Snake or Ox years or Luck Cycles, there is a Partial Three Harmony Metal Combination that transforms him into a Dominant Metal chart. In Rooster years or Luck Cycles, he remains a Competitive Metal chart.

During the negative Yin Wood Luck Cycle (age 18 to 22), Richardson was working as a performer at Orlando's Disney World, playing characters such as Aladdin and one of the Teenage Mutant Ninja Turtles. In 1991 (Yin Metal Sheep year), Richardson moved back to Kentucky for two months to spend time with his father, who succumbed to cancer. The Annual Stem contained a Rival and the negative element Earth was also present in the Annual Branch. In 1993 (Yin Water Rooster year) towards the end of this period, Richardson and his cousin Brian Littrell joined a musical group called *Backstreet Boys*. Although the Annual Rooster Branch did not transform Richardson into a Dominant Metal chart, the Annual Stem contained his favourable element Water.

The Sheep Luck Cycle (age 23 to 27) contained the negative element Earth, so Richardson was dependent on the Annual Stems and Branches. In 1996 (Yang Fire Rat year), there was a Stem Combination involving the Annual Stem and his Yin Metal Day Master. This indicated professional success and recognition. *Backstreet Boys* released their self-titled debut album in Europe and Canada, selling half a million copies in Germany.

In 1997 (Yin Fire Ox year), the Annual Ox Branch combined with the Rooster Branches in Richardson's chart to transform him into a Dominant Metal chart. His favourable elements became:

1) Resource element Earth.
2) Self element Metal.
3) Output element Water.
4) Wealth element Wood.
5) Power element Fire.

Backstreet Boys released their second album *Backstreet's Back*. They also compiled their first and second international album for the US market, known as *Backstreet Boys*. With the Number 2 hit *Quit Playing Games (with My Heart)*, it sold more than 11 million copies. In 1998 (Yang Earth Tiger year), the negative element Earth was present. Backstreet Boys filed a lawsuit against manager Lou Perlman for royalty payments. Perlman and his company had earned $10 million USD while the band was only paid $300 000 USD. The lawsuit was eventually settled.

The Yang Wood Luck Cycle (age 28 to 32) also contained the negative Wealth element, so Richardson was once again dependent on the Annual Stems and Branches. In 1999 (Yin Earth Rabbit year), there was a Stem Combination between the Yang Wood Luck Cycle and the Annual Yin Earth Stem. This reduced the negative effects of Wood and Earth. *Backstreet Boys* scored a US Number 1 album with *Millennium*, which contained the US Number 6 hit *I Want It That Way*.

In 2000 (Yang Metal Dragon year), there was a Six Harmony Combination between the Annual Dragon Branch and Richardson's Rooster Day and Month Branches. This indicated recognition and good reputation. *Backstreet Boys* released their fourth album *Black & Blue*, with the US Number 9 hit *The Shape of My Heart*. On a personal note, Richardson also married model Kristin Kay Willits that year. The Annual Dragon Branch formed a Six Harmony Combination with Richardson's Rooster Branch in his House of Spouse. This indicated the possibility of romance or marriage.

In 2001 (Yin Metal Snake year), the Annual Snake Branch combined with the Rooster Branches in Richardson's chart to transform him into a Dominant Metal chart. *Backstreet Boys* released *The Hits – Chapter One*, which sold more than 6 million copies worldwide.

In January 2003 (still the Yang Water Horse year), the favourable elements Water and Fire were present in the Annual Stem and Branch respectively. While *Backstreet Boys* had a break, Richardson played the role of smooth talking lawyer Billy Flynn in the musical *Chicago* on Broadway.

The Horse Luck Cycle (age 33 to 37) contained the favourable element Fire. In 2005 (Yin Wood Rooster year), *Backsteet Boys* released their comeback album *Never Gone* with the US Top 20 hit *Incomplete*. The Annual Rooster Branch contained the negative Self element. Although *Never Gone* sold more than ten million copies worldwide, it did not contain any Top 10 hits.

In 2006 (Yang Fire Dog year), there was a Stem Combination involving the Annual Stem and Richardson's Yin Metal Day Master, which indicated professional recognition or success. Richardson left *Backstreet Boys* and performed with the cast of *Chicago* for the 10th anniversary of the show in New York and Chicago.

The Yin Water Luck Cycle (age 38 to 42) contained the favourable Output element. In 2012 (Yang Water Dragon year), Richardson rejoined *Backstreet Boys* permanently. Not only was the favourable element Water present in the Annual Stem, the Annual Dragon Branch also formed a Six Harmony Combination with the Rooster Branches in Richardson's chart, indicating good reputation. In 2013 (Yin Water Snake year), the Annual Snake Branch combined with the Rooster Branches in his chart to form a Partial Three Harmony Metal Combination. This transformed Richardson into a Dominant Metal chart. *Backstreet Boys* released *In a World Like This*, their 9th US Top 10 Album.

The Snake Luck Cycle (age 43 to 47) combined with the Rooster Branches to form a Partial Three Harmony Metal Combination, transforming Richardson into a Dominant Metal chart for this year. In 2017 (Yin Metal Rooster year), *Backstreet Boys* performed a residency in Las Vegas entitled *Backstreet Boys: Larger Than Life*. The Annual Rooster Branch combined with the Snake Luck Cycle and the Rooster Branches in Richardson's chart to reinforce his favourable element Metal.

The Yang Water Luck Cycle (age 48 to 52) contains the favourable Output element, while the Dragon Luck Cycle (age 53 to 57) forms a Six Harmony Combination with the Rooster Branches in Richardson's chart. This indicates that he will enjoy good reputation during this period.

Example 7.4 Nancy Kerrigan, American Ice Skater
(born October 13, 1969, 17:17 hours)

Hour	Day	Month	Year
丁	辛	甲	己
Yin Fire	Yin Metal	Yang Wood	Yin Earth
酉	酉	戌	酉
Rooster	Rooster	Dog	Rooster

8	18	28	38
乙	丙	丁	戊
Yin Wood	Yang Fire	Yin Fire	Yang Earth
亥	子	丑	寅
Pig	Rat	Ox	Tiger

48	58	68	78
己	庚	辛	壬
Yin Earth	Yang Metal	Yin Metal	Yang Water
卯	辰	巳	午
Rabbit	Dragon	Snake	Horse

There are no Branch Combinations within Kerrigan's birth chart. She is a Yin Metal Day Master with three Rooster Branches present in the Year, Day and Hour Pillars. This qualifies her as a Competitive Metal chart. In Snake or Ox years or Luck Cycles, Kerrigan is transformed into a Dominant Metal chart due to the Partial Three Harmony Metal Combination with her Rooster Branches. In the Monkey years or Luck Cycles, the Seasonal Metal Combination is formed with the Rooster and Dog Branches in her chart. In the Rooster years or Luck Cycles, Kerrigan remains a Competitive Metal chart.

There is a Stem Combination between Kerrigan's Yang Wood Month Stem and Yin Earth Year Stem. The Yang Wood Month Stem occupies the sector that is associated with the Father. The Combination suggests that Kerrigan did not spend much time with her father when she was growing up. Her father Daniel worked three jobs in order to support her skating career.

The Yang Fire Luck Cycle (age 18 to 22) formed a Stem Combination with Kerrigan's Yin Metal Day Master. The Power Element Combination indicated professional success and recognition. In 1989 (Yin Earth Snake year), Kerrigan was ranked fifth in the U.S. Figure Skating Rankings. The Annual Snake Branch combined with the Rooster Branches in her chart to transform her into a Dominant Metal chart. In 1990 (Yang Metal Horse year), Kerrigan moved up to fourth in the National Rankings. The Annual Horse Branch combined with her Dog Month Branch to form the favourable element Fire.

The Rat Luck Cycle (age 23 to 27) contained Kerrigan's favourable element Metal. In 1992 (Yang Water Monkey year), the Annual Monkey Branch combined with the Rooster and Dog Branches in Kerrigan's chart. She was transformed into a Dominant Metal chart. Kerrigan won a bronze medal at the 1992 Winter Olympics in Albertville, France. She also earned the silver medal at the 1992 World Championships.

In 1993 (Yin Water Rooster year), there was a Yin Metal Rival present in the Annual Rooster Branch. Kerrigan performed poorly at the World Championships in Prague that saw her slip in the rankings. On January 6, 1994 (still the Yin Water Rooster year), an assailant clubbed Kerrigan on the right knee following a practice session in Detroit. The assault was planned by rival Tonya Harding's ex-husband. In spite of the injury, Kerrigan recovered and was still able to win a silver medal at the Lillehammer

Winter Olympics in 1994 (Yang Wood Dog year). However, the negative elements Wood and Earth were present in the Annual Stem and Branch. Kerrigan lost some endorsements and goodwill following a few controversial comments that were broadcast publicly. She retired from figure skating following the Olympics.

In 1995 (Yin Wood Pig year), the Annual Pig Branch gave Kerrigan the auspicious Configuration of Four Stems in a Row: Rooster Day Branch, Dog Month Branch, Annual Pig Branch, Rat Luck Cycle. Kerrigan married her agent Jerry Solomon.

The Yin Fire Luck Cycle (age 28 to 32) contained Kerrigan's favourable element. In 1997 (Yin Fire Ox year), the Annual Ox Branch combined with the Rooster Branches in her chart to transform her into a Dominant Metal chart. Her favourable elements became:

1) Resource element Earth.
2) Self element Metal.
3) Output element Water.
4) Wealth element Wood.
5) Power element Fire.

Kerrigan gave birth to her son Matthew in December that year. Her Output or Child element Water was present in the Annual Ox Branch.

The Ox Luck Cycle (age 33 to 37) combined with the Rooster Branches in Kerrigan's chart to transform her into a Dominant Metal chart In 2004 (Yang Wood Monkey year), Kerrigan was inducted into the United States Figure Skating Hall of Fame. The Annual Monkey Branch combined with the Rooster and Dog Branches in her chart to form a Seasonal Metal Combination and transform her into a Dominant Metal chart. That same year, Kerrigan also became pregnant. The Child element Water was present in the Annual Monkey Branch. In April 2005 (Yin Wood Rooster year), Kerrigan had her second son Brian. The Annual Rooster Branch combined with the Ox Luck Cycle and the Rooster Branches in her chart to reinforce the favourable element Metal.

The Yang Earth Luck Cycle (age 38 to 42) contained the negative element, so Kerrigan was more dependent on the Annual Stems and Branches. In May 2008 (Yang Earth Rat year), Kerrigan had a daughter, Nicole. She had become pregnant in 2007 (Yin Fire Pig year). The Output or Child element was present in the Annual Pig Branch. In 2011 (Yin Metal Rabbit year), the negative elements Metal and Wood were present. Kerrigan appeared as a witness for her brother Mark after he was charged with manslaughter following an altercation with their father that resulted in his death. Kerrigan and her mother said her father's death was due to a long standing heart condition. Mark was acquitted of manslaughter but found guilty of assault.

The Tiger Luck Cycle (age 43 to 47) combined with her Dog Month Branch to form the favourable element Fire. 2017 (Yin Fire Rooster year) was a mixed year for Kerrigan. The favourable element Metal was present in the Annual Stem but there was a Yin Metal Rival present in the Annual Rooster Branch. Kerrigan competed on *Dancing with the Stars* but was eliminated in the seventh week of competition.

The Yin Earth Luck Cycle (age 48 to 52) forms a Stem Combination with her Yang Wood Month Stem. The negative effects of Earth are reduced.

Example 7.5 Shane Warne, Australian Cricketer
(born September 13, 1969)

Hour	Day	Month	Year
	辛	癸	己
	Yin Metal	Yin Water	Yin Earth
	卯	酉	酉
	Rabbit	Rooster	Rooster

2	12	22	32
壬	辛	庚	己
Yang Water	Yin Metal	Yang Metal	Yin Earth
申	未	午	巳
Monkey	Sheep	Horse	Snake

42	52	62	72
戊	丁	丙	乙
Yang Earth	Yin Fire	Yang Fire	Yin Wood
辰	卯	寅	丑
Dragon	Rabbit	Tiger	Ox

There are no Combinations in Warne's birth chart. He is a Yin Metal Day Master with two Rooster Branches, in the Month and Year Pillars. This qualifies him as a Competitive Metal chart. In Snake or Ox years or Luck Cycles, there is a Partial Three Harmony Metal Combination that transforms him into a Dominant Metal chart. In Rooster years or Luck Cycles, he remains a Competitive Metal chart.

Warne first distinguished himself in Test Cricket during the Yang Metal Luck Cycle (age 22 to 26) in 1992 (Yang Water Monkey year), when he helped Australia to a 16-run victory over Sri Lanka in the Test series. The Annual Yang Water Stem gave Warne the auspicious Sequence of Five Stems in a Row: Yin Earth Year Stem, Yang Metal Luck Cycle, Yin Metal Day Master, Annual Yang Water Stem and Yin Water Month Stem. Note that Four in a Row is sufficient for the auspicious Configuration, Warne's Five in a Row is superlative. In 1995 (Yin Wood Pig year), there was a Combination between the Annual Pig Branch and his Rabbit Branch in the House of Spouse. This indicated the possibility of love or marriage. Warne married Simone Callahan.

The Horse Luck Cycle (age 27 to 31) contained the favourable element Fire. In 1996 (Yang Fire Rat year), there was a Stem Combination between the Annual Yang Fire Stem and his Yin Metal Day Master. This indicated professional recognition and success. Warne distinguished himself in the World Cup that year and also in the Test Series against the West Indies. In 1997 (Yin Fire Ox year), the Annual Ox Branch combined with his Rooster Branches to transform him into a Dominant Metal chart. His favourable elements became:

1) Resource element Earth.
2) Self element Metal.
3) Output element Water.
4) Wealth element Wood.
5) Power element Fire.

Warne became the second Australian cricket player after Dennis Lillee to take 300 Test Wickets. He was named the Wisden Leading Cricketer in the World.

In 2000 (Yang Metal Dragon year), there was a Six Harmony Combination between the Annual Dragon Branch and the Rooster Month and Year Branches. This is known as the Lovebirds Combination, indicating good reputation. Warne was named Vice Captain of the Australian cricket team. Wisden Cricket Almanac named Warne as one of the Five Cricketers of the Century. However, the negative element Earth is also present. Warne was removed from his position for his off-the-field indiscretions including sending inappropriate text messages to an English nurse.

The Yin Earth Luck Cycle (age 32 to 36) contained the negative element. However, Warne performed well in years with favourable elements. In 2001 (Yin Metal Snake year), the Annual Snake Branch combined with the Rooster Branches in his chart to transform him into a Dominant Metal chart. Warne scored his highest Test score of 99 runs in the third test in Perth against New Zealand. In 2002 (Yang Water Horse year), the Annual Horse Branch contained the favourable element Fire. Warne performed well in the test series against Pakistan and in the Ashes against England.

In 2003 (Yin Water Sheep year), the Annual Sheep Branch combined with the Rabbit Day Branch to form the negative element Wood. Warne was banned for a year from cricket after failing a drug test for using a banned diuretic. In 2004 (Yang Wood Monkey year), Warne returned to cricket and became only the second bowler to take 500 crickets. There was a Stem Combination between the Annual Yang Wood Stem and the Yin Earth Luck Cycle. This reduced the negative effects of both elements.

In 2005 (Yin Wood Rooster year), there was a Yin Metal Rival present in the Annual Rooster Branch. Warne announced his split from wife Callahan.

The Snake Luck Cycle (age 37 to 41) combined with his Rooster Month and Year Branch to transform him into a Dominant Metal chart for this period. In 2006 (Yang Fire Dog year), there was a Stem Combination between the Annual Yang Fire Stem and Warne's Yin Metal Day Master. This indicated professional recognition and success. Warne became the first bowler to take 700 Test wickets. In 2007 (Yin Fire Pig year), the Annual Pig Branch clashed with the Snake Luck Cycle to disrupt the Three Harmony Metal Combination. Warne reverted back to a Competitive Metal chart. He announced his retirement from Test cricket and confirmed his separation from Callahan after a failed attempt to reconcile. In 2008 (Yang Earth Rat year), the favourable elements Earth and

Water were present. Warne signed as captain for the Rajasthan Royals in the Indian Premier League.

The Yang Earth Luck Cycle (age 42 to 46) contained the negative element. In 2011 (Yin Metal Rabbit year), the negative elements Metal and Wood were present in the Annual Stem and Branch. Warne retired from the Indian Premier League after four seasons with the Rajasthan Royals. The House of Spouse animal Rabbit was also present in the Annual Branch. Warne announced his engagement to actress and model Liz Hurley. In 2013 (Yin Water Snake year), the Annual Snake Branch combined with the Rooster Month Branch in his chart to transform him into a Dominant Metal chart. Warne announced his retirement from all formats of cricket. The engagement to Hurley was also called off.

The Dragon Luck Cycle (age 47 to 51) formed a Six Harmony Combination with his Rooster Month Branch, indicating assistance from mentors or helpful individuals. The Yin Fire Luck Cycle (age 52 to 56) contains the favourable element, so Warne will still enjoy some good periods to come.

Example 7.6 Ben Carson, American Neurosurgeon and Politician (born September 18, 1951)

Hour	Day	Month	Year
	辛	丁	辛
	Yin Metal	Yin Fire	Yin Metal
	酉	酉	卯
	Rooster	Rooster	Rabbit

3	13	23	33
丙	乙	甲	癸
Yang Fire	Yin Wood	Yang Wood	Yin Water
申	未	午	巳
Monkey	Sheep	Horse	Snake

43	53	63	73
壬	辛	庚	己
Yang Water	Yin Metal	Yang Metal	Yin Earth
辰	卯	寅	丑
Dragon	Rabbit	Tiger	Ox

There are no Combinations present in Carson's birth chart. He is a Yin Metal Day Master with two Rooster Branches in his Day and Month Pillars. There is also a Yin Metal Year Stem. This qualifies him as a Competitive Metal chart. In Snake or Ox years or Luck Cycles, there is a Partial Three Harmony Metal Combination that transforms him into a Dominant Metal chart. In Rooster years or Luck Cycles, he remains a Competitive Metal chart.

In 1973 (Yin Water Ox year) during the Sheep Luck Cycle (age 18 to 22), Carson graduated from Yale with a B.A. (Bachelor of Arts) in Psychology before entering the University of Michigan Medical School. The Annual Ox Branch combined with the Rooster Branches in Carson's chart to transform him into a Dominant Metal chart.

However, there was also a Combination between the Sheep Luck Cycle and his Rabbit Year Branch that formed the negative element Wood. There was a Metal-Wood conflict in his chart. Carson struggled through his first year of medical school before changing his approach and grades. As mentioned in his autobiography, he stopped attending lectures and focused on reading textbooks and notes.

In the Yang Wood Luck Cycle (age 23 to 27), Carson graduated with a Doctor of Medicine (M.D.) in 1977 (Yin Fire Snake year). The Annual Snake Branch combined with the Rooster Branches in Carson's chart to transform him into a Dominant Metal chart. His list of favourable elements became:

1) Resource element Earth.
2) Self element Metal.
3) Output element Water.
4) Wealth element Wood.
5) Power element Fire.

Carson joined the Johns Hopkins School of Medicine Neurosurgery program. On a personal note, he married Candy Rustin in 1975 (Yin Wood Rabbit year). The Annual Rabbit Branch clashed with his Rooster Branch in the House of Spouse, which also indicates the possibility of love or marriage.

The Horse Luck Cycle (age 28 to 32) contained the favourable element Fire. In 1983 (Yin Water Pig year), he spent the last year of his neurosurgery residency program training at the Sir Charles Gardiner Hospital in Perth, Australia. His favourable element Water was present in the Annual Stem and Branch.

In the favourable Yin Water Luck Cycle (age 33 to 37), Carson returned to the US and became the youngest ever Director of Pediatric Neurosurgery in 1985 (Yin Wood Ox year). The Annual Ox Branch combined with his Rooster Branches to transform him into a Dominant

Metal chart. In 1987 (Yin Fire Rabbit year), Carson attracted international attention by leading a 70 member medical team that carried out an operation in Germany to separate a set of conjoined twins who were joined at the head. His favourable element was present in the Annual Stem. The 22-hour operation was considered a success as both twins survived the procedure. However, the Annual Rabbit Branch contained his negative element Wood. Unfortunately, one of the twins ended up in a vegetative state.

The Snake Luck Cycle (age 38 to 42) combined with his Rooster Branches to transform him into a Dominant Metal chart. In 1992 (Yang Water Monkey year), the favourable element Water was present in the Annual Stem and Branch. Carson released his autobiography *Gifted Hands: The Ben Carson Story*.

The Yang Water Luck Cycle (age 43 to 47) also contained the favourable element. In 1994 (Yang Wood Dog year), Carson and his team went to South Africa to separate the Makwaeba twins. The operation was unsuccessful, as both twins died from surgical complications. The negative elements Wood and Earth were present that year. In 1997 (Yin Fire Ox year), the Annual Ox Branch combined with the Rooster Branches in Carson's chart to transform him into a Dominant Metal chart. Carson and his team went to Zambia to carry out separation surgery on Luka and Joseph Banda. After 28 hours of surgery, both boys survived without any brain damage.

The Dragon Luck Cycle (age 48 to 52) contained the negative element Earth. However, there was a Six Harmony Combination between the Rooster Branches and the Dragon Luck Cycle. The Lovebird Combination indicates good reputation. In 2002 (Yang Water Horse year), Carson developed prostate cancer but was cancer free following a successful operation. The favourable elements Water and Fire were present in the Annual Stem and Branch.

The Yin Metal Luck Cycle (age 53 to 57) contained a Rival but Carson fared well in years with favourable elements. In 2006 (Yang Fire Dog year), there was a Stem Combination between the Annual Yang Fire Stem and Carson's Yin Metal Day Master. The Power Element Combination indicated professional success and recognition. Carson received the Spingarn Medal from the National Association for the Advancement of Colored People (NAACP), their highest honour for outstanding achievement. In 2008 (Yang Earth Rat year), the favourable element Water was present in the Annual Rat Branch. The White House presented Carson the Presidential Medal of Freedom, the nation's highest civilian honour.

The Rabbit Luck Cycle (age 58 to 62) contained the negative element Wood. In 2013 (Yin Water Snake year), Carson announced his retirement from neurosurgery. The Annual Snake Branch combined with the Rooster Branches in his chart to transform him into a Dominant Metal chart.

The Yang Metal Luck Cycle (age 63 to 67) contained a Rival. In 2015 (Yin Wood Sheep year), the Annual Yin Wood Stem formed a Stem Combination with the Yang Metal Luck Cycle. This removed the Rival's influence. Carson announced his run for the Republican nomination in the 2016 US Presidential Election. In 2016 (Yang Fire Monkey year), there was a Stem Combination between the Annual Yang Fire Stem and Carson's Yin Metal Day Master. This indicated professional recognition and success. Carson pulled out of the Presidential race and announced his support for Donald Trump. Following Trump's victory, he nominated Carson for the Secretary of Housing and Urban Development. In 2017 (Yin Fire Rooster year), the United States Senate confirmed Carson's nomination. The favourable element Fire was present in the Annual Stem.

To comment accurately on the subsequent Luck Cycles for Carson, the Hour Pillar needs to be confirmed and verified.

Example 7.7 Vanna White, American Television Personality (born February 18, 1957, 14:35 hours)

Hour	Day	Month	Year
乙	辛	壬	丁
Yin Wood	Yin Metal	Yang Water	Yin Fire
未	酉	寅	酉
Sheep	Rooster	Tiger	Rooster

5	15	25	35
癸	甲	乙	丙
Yin Water	Yang Wood	Yin Wood	Yang Fire
卯	辰	巳	午
Rabbit	Dragon	Snake	Horse

45	55	65	75
丁	戊	己	庚
Yin Fire	Yang Earth	Yin Earth	Yang Metal
未	申	酉	戌
Sheep	Monkey	Rooster	Dog

There are no Branch Combinations in White's birth chart. She is a Yin Metal Day Master. There are two Rooster Branches in the Day and Year Pillars. This qualifies her as a Competitive Metal chart. In Snake or Ox years or Luck Cycles, White is transformed into a Dominant Metal chart. In Rooster years or Luck Cycles, White remains a Competitive Metal chart.

There is a Stem Combination between White's Yin Fire Year Stem and Yang Water Month Stem. The Month Stem occupies the sector associated with the Father. The Stem Combination indicates that White's father did not spend time with her when she was growing up. Her biological father Miguel Angel left shortly after White was born. Her mother Joan Marie Rosich married Herbert White, who raised her. White took her stepfather's name.

In 1982 (Yang Water Dog year) during the Yin Wood Luck Cycle (age 25 to 29), White became the regular hostess on the television show *Wheel of Fortune*. The Annual Dog Branch combined with White's Tiger Month Branch to form the favourable element Fire. Before this, White had been waitressing in between minor acting roles. While the Luck Cycle contained the negative element, the Annual Stem and Branch had favourable elements for White. By 1986 (Yang Fire Tiger year), *Wheel of Fortune* had become a major success, with the syndicated program attracting 30 million viewers. The Annual Yang Fire Stem formed a Stem Combination with White's Yin Metal Day Master. This indicated professional recognition and success.

The Snake Luck Cycle (age 30 to 34) combined with the Rooster Branches in White's birth chart. She transformed into a Dominant Metal chart during this period. Her favourable elements became:

1) Resource element Earth.
2) Self element Metal.
3) Output element Water.
4) Wealth element Wood.
5) Power element Fire.

In 1987 (Yin Fire Rabbit year), the Annual Rabbit Branch clashed with the Rooster Branches to disrupt the Three Harmony Combination. White reverted back to being a Competitive Metal chart. The favourable element Fire was present in the Annual Stem. Her autobiography *Vanna Speaks* became a best seller. However, as the negative element Wood was present in the Annual Rabbit Branch, White had to contend with *Playboy* publishing pictures of her in see-through lingerie that were taken by a previous boyfriend before her *Wheel of Fortune* success. In 1988 (Yang Earth Dragon year), White had reverted back to being a Dominant Metal chart. The favourable element Earth was present in the Annual Stem and Branch. She starred in a television movie *Goddess of Love*, in which she played Venus.

The Combination between the Snake Luck Cycle and the Rooster Day Branch also indicated the possibility of love or marriage during this period. On December 31, 1990 (Yang Metal Horse year), White married restaurant owner George Santo Pietro. In 1992 (Yang Water Monkey year), the Annual Stem and Branch contained the favourable element Water. *The Guinness Book of Records* named White as television's most frequent clapper. She clapped an average of 720 claps per show and over 28 000 per season.

The Yang Fire Luck Cycle (age 35 to 39) formed a Stem Combination with White's Yin Metal Day Master. This indicated professional success and recognition. In 1993 (Yin Water Rooster year), there was a Yin Metal Rival present in the Annual Rooster Branch. White was involved in a lawsuit with the Samsung Electronics Corporation. She alleged that a humorous advertisement featuring a robot turning letters on a game show infringed her personality rights. She was ultimately awarded $403 000 USD in damages. In 1994 (Yang Wood Dog year), White appeared as herself in two major Hollywood movies: action thriller *Double Dragon* and the comedy *Naked Gun 33 1/3: The Final Insult*. She had reverted back to being a Competitive Metal chart. The Annual Dog Branch combined with her Tiger Month Branch to form the favourable element Fire. In 1996 (Yang Fire Rat year), there was another Stem Combination between the Annual Yang Fire Stem and her Yin Metal Day Master. There was further professional success and recognition. As *Wheel of Fortune* was one of the sponsors of the Atlanta Olympics, White carried the torch for part of the Olympic Torch Relay.

On a personal note, White had her son Nicholas in June that same year. She had become pregnant in 1993 (Yin Water Rooster year). Her Output or Child element Water was present in the Annual Branch. She also became pregnant towards the end of 1996 (Yang Fire Rat year), giving birth to daughter Giovanna on July 1, 1997. The Child element Water was present in the Annual Rat Branch.

The Horse Luck Cycle (age 40 to 44) combined with her Tiger Month Branch to form the favourable element Fire. In 1997 (Yin Fire Ox year), the Annual Ox Branch combined with White's Rooster Branches to transform her into a Dominant Metal chart. The *Wheel of Fortune* letters became computerised that year, so White no longer had to turn them manually. In 2001 (Yin Metal Snake year), the Annual Snake Branch combined with the Rooster Branches to transform her again into a Dominant Metal chart. There was a Metal-Fire conflict within her chart. White separated from her husband Santo Pietro. The divorce was finalised in 2002 (Yang Water Horse year).

The Yin Fire Luck Cycle (age 45 to 49) contained her favourable element. It also formed a Stem Combination with her Yang Water Month Stem. In 2006 (Yang Fire Dog year), there was a Stem Combination between the Annual Yang Fire Stem and her Yin Metal Day Master, indicating professional success and recognition. White was honored with a Star on the Hollywood Walk of Fame. The Annual Dog Branch also combined with her Tiger Month Branch to form the favourable element Fire.

The Sheep Luck Cycle (age 50 to 54) and Yang Earth (age 55 to 59) Luck Cycles contained the negative element Earth so White was dependent on the Annual Stem and Branch. In 2012 (Yang Water Dragon year), White started dating contractor John Donaldson. The Annual Dragon Branch combined with the Rooster in her House of Spouse, indicating the possibility of love or marriage.

At the start of the Monkey Luck Cycle (age 60 to 64) in 2017 (Yin Fire Rooster year), White was still the letter turner on *Wheel of Fortune*, one of the most successful game shows in history. The favourable elements Water and Fire were present in the Monkey Luck Cycle and the Annual Stem.

Example 7.8 John Lithgow, American Actor
(born October 19, 1945)

Hour	Day	Month	Year
	辛	丙	乙
	Yin Metal	Yang Fire	Yin Wood
	酉	戌	酉
	Rooster	Dog	Rooster

4	14	24	34
乙	甲	癸	壬
Yin	Yang	Yin	Yang
Wood	Wood	Water	Water
酉	申	未	午
Rooster	Monkey	Sheep	Horse

44	54	64	74
辛	庚	己	戊
Yin	Yang	Yin	Yang
Metal	Metal	Earth	Earth
巳	辰	卯	寅
Snake	Dragon	Rabbit	Tiger

There are no Branch Combinations within Lithgow's birth chart. He is a Yin Metal Day Master with two Rooster Branches in the Day and Year Pillars. This qualifies Lithgow as a Competitive Metal chart. In the Snake or Ox years or Luck Cycles, there is a Partial Metal Combination that transforms Lithgow into a Dominant Metal chart. In the Monkey year or Luck Cycle, there is a Seasonal Metal Combination involving the Rooster and Dog Branches in

Lithgow's chart. He is also transformed into a Dominant Metal chart. In Rooster years or Luck Cycles, he remains a Competitive Metal chart.

There is also a Stem Combination between Lithgow's Yang Fire Month Stem and his Yin Metal Day Master. As the Month Stem represents the father, this indicates a close relationship with his father. The Power Element Combination also indicates professional success and recognition.

The Rooster in the House of Spouse is present twice in Lithgow's chart twice. This indicates that there is the possibility of Lithgow being married more than once. In 1966 (Yang Fire Horse year) during the Monkey Luck Cycle (age 19 to 23), Lithgow married Jean Taynton. The Monkey formed a Seasonal Metal Combination with the Rooster in the House of Spouse and the Dog Month Branch. This indicated the possibility of love or marriage during this period. The marriage ended in divorce in 1980 (Yang Metal Monkey year). In 1981 (Yin Metal Rooster year), Lithgow married Mary Yeager. His House of Spouse animal Rooster was present that year.

In 1976 (Yang Fire Dragon year) during the Sheep Luck Cycle (age 29 to 33), Lithgow had his first major film role in Brian de Palma's *Obsession*. There was a Heaven-Earth Combination involving the Annual Yang Fire Stem and Dragon Branch with his Yin Metal Day Master and Rooster Day Branch. The Stem Element Combination indicates professional recognition and success. The Six Harmony Combination between the Dragon and Rooster indicated assistance from mentors and helpful individuals.

In the favourable Yang Water Luck Cycle (age 34 to 38), Lithgow received a Best Supporting Actor Oscar nomination for his performance in *Terms of Endearment* alongside Shirley MacLaine and Jack Nicholson in 1983 (Yin Water Pig year). The favourable element Water was present in the Annual Stem and Branch.

The Horse Luck Cycle (age 39 to 43) combined with Lithgow's Dog Month Branch to form the favourable element Fire. In 1985 (Yin Wood Ox year), the Annual Ox Branch combined with the Rooster Branches in Lithgow's chart to transform him into a Dominant Metal chart. His list of favourable elements became:

1) Resource element Earth.
2) Self element Metal.
3) Output element Water.
4) Wealth element Wood.
5) Power element Fire.

Lithgow appeared as the villain in *Santa Claus: The Movie* opposite Dudley Moore.

The Yin Metal Luck Cycle (age 44 to 48) contained a Rival. However, it also formed a Stem Combination with the Yang Fire Month Stem, reducing its negative influence. In 1992 (Yang Water Monkey year), the Annual Monkey Branch combined with the Rooster and Dog Branches to form the Seasonal Metal Combination. Lithgow was transformed into a Dominant Metal chart. He played the leading role in Brian de Palma's *Raising Cain*.

The Snake Luck Cycle (age 49 to 53) combined with the Rooster Day Branch to transform Lithgow into a Dominant Metal chart. In 1996 (Yang Fire Rat year), there was a Stem Combination between the Annual Yang Fire Stem and his Yin Metal Day Master. This indicated professional success and recognition. Lithgow appeared as the alien Dick Solomon in the television situation comedy *Third Rock from the Sun* for six seasons, winning three Emmy Awards for Outstanding Lead Actor in a Comedy Series.

The Yang Metal Luck Cycle (age 54 to 58) contained a Rival. In 2001 (Yin Metal Snake year), the Annual Snake Branch combined with the Rooster Day Branch to transform Lithgow into a Dominant Metal chart. He voiced Lord Marquand in the animated movie *Shrek*.

The Dragon Luck Cycle (age 59 to 63) formed a Six Harmony Combination with the Rooster Day Branch, indicating assistance from mentors and helpful individuals. In 2006 (Yang Fire Dog year), there was a Stem Combination involving the Annual Yang Fire Stem and Lithgow's Yin Metal Day Master, indicating professional success and recognition. He appeared in the Oscar winning musical *Showgirls* alongside Eddie Murphy and Beyonce.

The Yin Earth Luck Cycle (age 64 to 68) contained the negative Resource element. However, in 2009 (Yin Earth Ox year), the Annual Ox Branch combined with the Rooster Day Branch to transform Lithgow into a Dominant Metal chart. He had a prominent role in the television series *Dexter*. Lithgow won an Emmy Award for Outstanding Guest Actor in a Drama Series.

The Rabbit Luck Cycle (age 69 to 73) contained the negative element Wood. However, there was a Six Harmony Combination with the Dog Month Branch, indicating the presence of mentors or helpful individuals. In 2014 (Yang Wood Horse year), the Annual Horse Branch combined with the Dog Month Branch to form the favourable element Fire. Lithgow appeared in the box office hit *Interstellar* alongside Matthew McConaughey and Anne Hathaway. He also impressed critics with his performance as a gay man in a decaying relationship in *Love Is Strange*. In 2016 (Yang Fire Monkey year), the Annual Monkey Branch formed the Seasonal Metal Combination with the Rooster and Dog Branches. Lithgow became a Dominant Metal chart. He received a Screen Actors Award for portraying Winston Churchill in the television series *The Crown*.

Example 7.9 Anastacia, American Singer
(born September 17, 1968)

Hour	Day	Month	Year
	庚	辛	戊
	Yang Metal	Yin Metal	Yang Earth
	寅	酉	申
	Tiger	Rooster	Monkey

3	13	23	33
庚	己	戊	丁
Yang Metal	Yin Earth	Yang Earth	Yin Fire
申	未	午	巳
Monkey	Sheep	Horse	Snake

43	53	63	73
丙	乙	甲	癸
Yang Fire	Yin Wood	Yang Wood	Yin Water
辰	卯	寅	丑
Dragon	Rabbit	Tiger	Ox

There are no Combinations in Anastacia's birth chart. She is a Yang Metal Day Master, with a Rooster Month Branch and a Yin Metal Month Stem. This qualifies Anastacia as a Competitive Metal chart. In Snake or Ox years or Luck Cycles, there will be a Partial Three Harmony Metal Combination that transforms her into a Dominant Metal chart. In Rooster years, Anastacia remains a Competitive Metal chart.

There is a Yin Metal Rival present in the Month Pillar occupying the position of the Father. As the sector associated with Father contains a negative element, this indicates that Anastacia does not have a good relationship with her father. Her father Robert Newkirk suffered from bipolar disorder and left the family when Anastacia was a teenager.

At the age of 13 in 1981 (Yin Metal Rooster year) during the Yin Earth Luck Cycle (age 13 to 17), Anastacia was diagnosed with Crohn's disease. She required an operation that removed part of her intestines, causing her to be wheelchair bound and learning to walk again. There were Yin Metal Rivals present in the Annual Stem and Branch. However, the Luck Cycle was favourable as it provided her with the auspicious Sequence of Four Stems in a Row: Yang Earth Year Stem, Yin Earth Luck Cycle, Yang Metal Day Master and Yin Metal Month Stem. In 1983 (Yin Water Pig year), the favourable element Water was present in the Annual Stem. Anastacia started her career as a dancer for hire.

At the age of 19 in 1987 (Yin Wood Rabbit year) during the Sheep Luck Cycle (age 18 to 22), Anastacia had a relapse of her Crohn's disease due to a diet. The Annual Rabbit Branch combined with the Sheep Luck Cycle to form the negative element Wood. In 1989 (Yin Earth Snake year), the Annual Snake Branch combined with her Rooster Month Branch, transforming Anastacia into a Dominant Metal chart. Her favourable elements became:

1) Resource element Earth.
2) Self element Metal.
3) Output element Water.
4) Wealth element Wood.
5) Power element Fire.

She appeared in the rap group *Salt n' Pepa*'s video for *Twist and Shout*. In 1990 (Yang Metal Horse year), the favourable element Fire was present in the Annual Horse Branch. Anastacia started her career as a backing vocalist, singing on pop star Tiffany's album *New Inside*.

The Yang Earth Luck Cycle (age 23 to 27) contained the negative Earth element. Anastacia worked as a backing vocalist for artists like Paula Abdul and Jamie Foxx. She was also told that her voice did not fit into any category. On a personal note, she started a seven-year relationship with actor Shawn Woods in 1994 (Yang Wood Dog year). The Annual Dog Branch combined with the Tiger in the House of Spouse to form the favourable element Fire. The House of Spouse Combination also indicates the possibility of love or marriage.

The Horse Luck Cycle (age 28 to 32) contained the favourable element Fire. In 1997 (Yin Fire Ox year), she met her manager Lisa Braunde. The Annual Ox Branch combined with her Rooster Month Branch to transform her into a Dominant Metal chart. In 1998 (Yang Earth Tiger year), she joined the MTV talent show *The Cut*, impressing the judges to the extent that she was offered a recording contract. The Annual Tiger Branch combined with her Horse Luck Cycle to form the favourable element Fire. In 2000 (Yang Metal Dragon year), the Annual Dragon Branch combined with her Monkey Year Branch to form the favourable element Water. Anastacia released her debut album *Not That Kind* with the UK Top 10 hit *I'm Outta Love*.

The Yin Fire Luck Cycle (age 33 to 37) also contained the favourable element. In 2001 (Yin Metal Snake year), the Annual Snake Branch combined with her Rooster Month Branch to transform her into a Dominant Metal chart. She released her second album *Freak of Nature*, which went triple platinum in the UK. It contained top 20 hits *Paid My Dues* and *One Day in Your Life*. In January 2003 (Yin Water Ox month in the Yang Water Horse year), Anastacia discovered that she had breast cancer following a routine mammogram before having breast reduction surgery. The Ox month combined with her Rooster Month Branch to transform her into a Dominant Metal chart that month.

However, Fire was present in the Annual Horse Branch and also the Luck Cycle. There was a Fire-Metal conflict. 2003 (Yin Water Sheep year) was a mixed year. The favourable element Water was present in the Annual Stem but the Annual Branch contained the negative element Earth. While she responded well to surgery and radiotherapy, Anastacia lost her voice and was unable to record for some time.

In 2004 (Yang Wood Monkey year), her self-titled third album *Anastacia* was released. The Annual Monkey Branch contained the favourable element Water. Once again, it went triple platinum in the UK and included the hit *Left Outside Alone*. In 2005 (Yin Wood Rooster year), there was a Stem Combination with her Yang Metal Day Master. The Wealth Element Combination indicated the possibility of generating income. Her first greatest hits compilation *Pieces of a Dream* was released. She also enjoyed a European hit with *I Belong to You (Il Ritmo della Passione)*, a duet with Eros Ramazzotti.

The Snake Luck Cycle (age 38 to 42) combined with her Rooster Month Branch to transform her into a Dominant Metal chart during this period. In 2007 (Yin Fire Pig year), the Annual Snake Branch clashed with her Snake Luck Cycle to disrupt the Three Harmony Metal Combination. She reverted back to a Competitive Metal chart. Anastacia started experiencing heart palpitations. What she thought were panic attacks was in fact a condition called supraventricular tachycardia. The Annual Pig Branch also formed a Six Harmony Combination with the Tiger in the House of Spouse. This indicated the possibility of love or marriage. Anastacia married her bodyguard Wayne Newton.

In 2008 (Yang Earth Rat year), the favourable elements Earth and Water were present. She released her fourth album *Heavy Rotation*. In 2009 (Yin Earth Ox year), the Annual Ox Branch combined with the Snake Luck Cycle and her Rooster Month Branch to reinforce the favourable element Metal. Anastacia embarked on a well-received tour to support her album and also received a World Artist Award from the Women's World Award. In 2010 (Yang Metal Tiger year), the negative element Fire was present in the Annual Tiger Branch as she had been transformed into a Dominant Metal chart. Anastacia filed for divorce from Newton.

The Yang Fire Luck Cycle (age 43 to 47) contained the favourable element. In February 2013 (Yang Wood Tiger month in the Yin Water Snake year), Anastacia announced that she was diagnosed with breast cancer for the second time. The Annual Snake Branch combined with her Rooster Month Branch to transform her into a Dominant Metal chart. The negative elements Wood and Fire were present in the month of diagnosis. Anastacia had a double mastectomy and was given the all clear later that year. In 2014 (Yang Wood Horse year), she had reverted back to being a Competitive Metal chart. The Annual Horse Branch combined with her Tiger Day Branch to form the favourable element Fire. Anastacia returned with the album *Resurrection*, which made the UK Top 10.

The Dragon Luck Cycle (age 48 to 52) formed a Six Harmony Combination with her Rooster Month Branch. This indicated assistance from mentors or helpful individuals. The Year Pillar is not able to exert much influence in Anastacia's chart in her late 40s. The Yin Wood Luck Cycle (age 53 to 57) formed a Stem Combination with her Yang Metal Day Master, indicating the possibility of generating wealth. The Rabbit Luck Cycle (age 58 to 62) contains the negative element Wood, so there may be some issues and complications during this period.

Example 7.10 Sergio Mendes, Brazilian Musician
(born February 11, 1941)

Hour	Day	Month	Year
	庚	庚	辛
	Yang Metal	Yang Metal	Yin Metal
	寅	寅	巳
	Tiger	Tiger	Snake

2	12	22	32
己	戊	丁	丙
Yin	Yang	Yin	Yang
Earth	Earth	Fire	Fire
丑	子	亥	戌
Ox	Rat	Pig	Dog

42	52	62	72
乙	甲	癸	壬
Yin	Yang	Yin	Yang
Wood	Wood	Water	Water
酉	申	未	午
Rooster	Monkey	Sheep	Horse

There are no Combinations in Mendes' birth chart. He is a Yang Metal Day Master with a Snake Year Branch, a Yang Metal Month Stem and Yin Metal Year Stem. This qualifies him as a Competitive Metal chart. In Rooster or Ox years or Luck Cycles, there is a Partial Three Harmony Metal Combination that transforms Mendes into a Dominant Metal chart. In Snake years, he remains a Competitive Metal chart.

During the favourable Rat Luck Cycle (age 17 to 21), Mendes formed the *Sexteto Bossa Rio* and recorded his first album *Dance Moderno* in 1961 (Yin Metal Ox year). The Annual Ox Branch combined with his Snake Year Branch to transform him into a Dominant Metal chart.

The Yin Fire Luck Cycle (age 22 to 26) contained the favourable element Fire. In 1966 (Yang Fire Horse year), Mendes and his band *Brasil '66* were signed to A&M Records. The platinum selling *Herb Alpert Presents: Sergio Mendes & Brasil '66* was released with the hit single *Mas Que Nada*. The Annual Horse Branch combined with the Tiger Branches in his chart to form the favourable element Fire. On a personal note, he met his future wife Gracinha Leporace that year. The Combination that year involved the Tiger in his House of Spouse.

The Pig Luck Cycle (age 27 to 31) formed a Six Harmony Combination with the Tiger Day and Month Branches in Mendes' chart. This is known as the Lovebirds Combination and indicates good reputation. In 1968 (Yang Earth Monkey year), Mendes performed the Oscar-nominated *The Look of Love* on the Academy Awards show. His version made the US Top 10, as did *The Fool on the Hill*. The Annual Monkey Branch gave him the complete set of four Travelling Horse Branches: Tiger Day Branch, Snake Year Branch, Annual Monkey Branch and Pig Luck Cycle. In 1969 (Yin Earth Rooster year), the Annual Rooster Branch combined with his Snake Year Branch to transform him into a Dominant Metal chart. His favourable elements became:

1) Resource element Earth.
2) Self element Metal.
3) Output element Water.
4) Wealth element Wood.
5) Power element Fire.

Mendes enjoyed another hit with his version of *(Sittin' on) The Dock of the Bay*.

The Yang Fire Luck Cycle (age 32 to 36) contained the favourable element. In 1974 (Yang Wood Tiger year), Mendes married Leporace. His House of Spouse animal Tiger was present that year. In 1977 (Yin Fire Snake year), Mendes released *Sergio Mendes and the new Brasil '77* but it failed to make an impression on the charts. There was a Yang Metal Rival present in the Annual Snake Branch.

The Dog Luck Cycle (age 37 to 41) combined with his Tiger Day and Month Branches to form the favourable element Fire. Mendes continued releasing albums during this period, but they did not fare well commercially. His fortunes finally turned round in 1983 (Yin Water Pig year) during the Yin Wood Luck Cycle (age 42 to 46). The Yin Wood formed a Stem Combination with his Yang Metal Day Master. The Wealth Element Combination indicated the possibility of generating income. Mendes scored a US Number 1 Adult Contemporary Hit with *Never Gonna Let You Go* from the self-titled album *Sergio Mendes*. The favourable element Water was present in the Annual Stem. The Annual Pig Branch also formed the Lovebirds Combination with the Tiger Branches in Mendes' chart, indicating good reputation. In 1984 (Yang Wood Rat year), the favourable element Water was present in the Annual Rat Branch. Mendes' song *Olympia* was used as the theme song for the 1984 Los Angeles Olympics.

The Rooster Luck Cycle (age 47 to 51) contained the Yin Metal Rival. The Year Pillar's effect at this stage was waning so the Luck Cycle could not combine with the Snake Year Branch. Mendes was still able to perform well in years with favourable elements. In 1992 (Yang Water Monkey year), Mendes released his Grammy Award winning album *Brasileiro*. The favourable element Water was present in the Annual Stem and Branch.

Mendes returned to the spotlight again during the favourable Yin Water Luck Cycle (age 62 to 66). In 2006 (Yang Fire Dog year), the Annual Dog Branch combined with the Tiger Branches in his chart to form the favourable element Fire. Mendes released *Timeless*, which featured a new version of *Mas Que Nada* recorded with *The Black Eyed Peas*.

In 2012 (Yang Water Dragon year) during the Sheep Luck Cycle (age 67 to 71), Mendes received his first Oscar nomination for Best Song for *Real in Rio* from the animated film *Rio*. The favourable element Water was present in the Annual Yang Water Stem.

In 2014 (Yang Wood Horse year) during the Yang Water Luck Cycle (age 72 to 76), the Annual Horse Branch combined with the Tiger Branches in Mendes' chart to form the favourable element Fire. Mendes released the album *Magic* with the song *One Nation*, recorded with Brazilian Carlinhos Brown, the theme song for the 2014 FIFA World Cup.

Example 7.11 Wyclef Jean, Haitian Rapper and Singer (born October 17, 1972)

Hour	Day	Month	Year
	辛	庚	壬
	Yin Metal	Yang Metal	Yang Water
	巳	戌	子
	Snake	Dog	Rat

7	17	27	37
辛	壬	癸	甲
Yin	Yang	Yin	Yang
Metal	Water	Water	Wood
亥	子	丑	寅
Pig	Rat	Ox	Tiger

47	57	67	77
乙	丙	丁	戊
Yin	Yang	Yin	Yang
Wood	Fire	Fire	Earth
卯	辰	巳	午
Rabbit	Dragon	Snake	Horse

There are no Combinations in Jean's birth chart. He is a Yin Metal Day Master with a Snake Day Branch and a Yang Metal Month Stem. This qualifies him as a

Competitive Metal chart. In Rooster or Ox years or Luck Cycles, there is a Partial Three Harmony Metal Combination that transforms Jean into a Dominant Metal chart. In Snake years or Luck Cycles, Jean remains a Competitive Metal chart.

In the favourable Yang Water Luck Cycle (age 17 to 21), Jean joined his cousin Pras Michel and Lauryn Hill to form a group called *Tranzlator Crew* in 1990 (Yang Metal Horse year). The Annual Horse Branch combined with his Dog Month Branch to form the favourable element Fire. In 1993 (Yin Water Rooster year), the Annual Rooster Branch combined with Jean's Snake Day Branch to transform him into a Dominant Metal chart. His favourable elements became:

1) Resource element Earth.
2) Self element Metal.
3) Output element Water.
4) Wealth element Wood.
5) Power element Fire.

Tranzlator Crew changed its name to *Fugees*, a reference to Haitian immigrants. They also signed a record deal.

In the Rat Luck Cycle (age 22 to 26), *Fugees* released their debut album *Blunted on Reality* in 1994 (Yang Wood Dog year). The negative elements Wood and Earth were present in the Annual Stem and Branch. The album had limited success. In 1996 (Yang Fire Rat year), *Fugees* released their second album *The Score*. There was a Stem Combination between the Annual Yang Fire Stem and Jean's Yin Metal Day Master. The Power Element Combination indicates professional recognition and success. *The Score* sold six million copies alone in the US and contained the UK Number 1 hits *Killing Me Softly* and *Ready or Not*.

In 1997 (Yin Fire Ox year), the Annual Ox Branch combined with Jean's Snake Day Branch to transform him into a Dominant Metal chart. *Fugees* won two Grammy

Awards, Best Rap Album and Best Rhythm and Blues Performance by a Duo or Group. Jean also released his debut solo album *Wyclef Jean Presents the Carnival* with the US Top 10 hit *Gone till November*.

The Yin Water Luck Cycle (age 27 to 31) was also favourable for Jean. In 2000 (Yang Metal Dragon year), he released his second album *The Ecleftic: II Sides 2 a Book*. The Annual Dragon Branch combined with his Rat Year Branch to form the favourable element Water. In 2002 (Yang Water Horse year), the Annual Horse Branch combined with his Dog Month Branch to form the favourable element Fire. Jean released his third album *Masquerade*.

The Ox Luck Cycle (age 32 to 36) combined with Jean's Snake Day Branch to transform him into a Dominant Metal chart. In 2006 (Yang Fire Dog year), there was a Stem Combination between the Annual Yang Fire Stem and his Yin Metal Day Master. This indicated professional recognition and success. Jean's collaboration with Shakira *Hips Don't Lie* was a US Number 1 hit and one of the biggest selling singles of the 21st century.

The Yang Wood Luck Cycle (age 37 to 41) contained the negative element. In 2010 (Yang Metal Tiger year), questions were raised about the management of his charity organisation *Yele Haiti*. *The New York Times* reported that the charity had not filed its tax returns for several years. There was a Yang Metal Rival present in the Annual Stem. However, there was a Combination between the Annual Tiger Branch and Jean's Dog Month Branch to form the favourable element Fire. In August 2010 (Yang Wood Monkey month), there was a Clash between the Monkey month and the Annual Tiger Branch disrupting the favourable Fire combination. Jean filed papers to run as a candidate for the 2010 Haitian Presidential Election. However, Haiti's Provisional Electoral Council turned him down as Jean had not fulfilled the constitutional requirement of having lived in Haiti for five years before the November 28 election. In 2012 (Yang Water Dragon year), the Annual Dragon Branch combined with his Rat Year Branch to form the favourable element Water. Jean released his memoir *Purpose: An Immigrant's Story*.

The Tiger Luck Cycle (age 42 to 46) combined with his Dog Month Branch to form the favourable element Fire. The Yin Wood Luck Cycle (age 47 to 51) forms a Stem Combination with the Yang Metal Month Stem. The Metal Rival is removed. While the Rabbit Luck Cycle (age 52 to 56) contains the negative element Wood, it forms a Six Harmony Combination with the Dog Month Branch, indicating the possibility of assistance from mentors or helpful individuals. The Yang Fire Luck Cycle (age 57 to 61) forms a Stem Combination with Jean's Yin Metal Day Master, indicating the potential for professional recognition or success during this period.

Example 7.12 Tarkan, Turkish Singer
(born October 17, 1972)

Hour	Day	Month	Year
	辛	庚	壬
	Yin Metal	Yang Metal	Yang Water
	巳	戌	子
	Snake	Dog	Rat

7	17	27	37
辛	壬	癸	甲
Yin Metal	Yang Water	Yin Water	Yang Wood
亥	子	丑	寅
Pig	Rat	Ox	Tiger

47	57	67	77
乙	丙	丁	戊
Yin Wood	Yang Fire	Yin Fire	Yang Earth
卯	辰	巳	午
Rabbit	Dragon	Snake	Horse

There are no Combinations in Tarkan's birth chart. He is a Yin Metal Day Master with a Snake Day Branch and a Yang Metal Month Stem. This qualifies him as a Competitive Metal chart. In the Rooster or Ox years or Luck Cycles, there is a Partial Three Harmony Metal Combination that transforms Tarkan into a Dominant Metal chart. In Snake years or Luck Cycles, he remains a Competitive Metal chart.

Tarkan shares the same three pillars as Wyclef Jean, as they share the same day, month and year of birth. As they are both males, they also have the same Luck Cycles. The difference between their charts could be the Hour Pillar if the time of birth of both singers can be verified.

Tarkan first achieved success in the favourable Yang Water Luck Cycle (age 17 to 21) when his debut album *Without You Again* was released in 1992 (Yang Water Monkey year). The Annual Monkey Branch combined with his Rat Year Branch to form the favourable element Water.

His career success continued in the Rat Luck Cycle (age 22 to 26), which contained the favourable element Water. In 1994 (Yang Wood Dog year), the negative elements Wood and Earth were present in the Annual Stem and Branch. Tarkan's popularity dipped when he said he needed to urinate during a live interview on Turkish television. In 1997 (Yin Fire Ox year), the Annual Ox Branch combined with his Snake Day Branch to transform him into a Dominant Metal chart. His favourable elements became:

1) Resource element Earth.
2) Self element Metal.
3) Output element Water.
4) Wealth element Wood.
5) Power element Fire.

Tarkan released the album *I'd Die for You* with the hit single *Kiss Kiss*. In 1998 (Yang Earth Tiger year), the Annual Tiger Branch combined with the Dog Month Branch to form the favourable element Fire. *Kiss Kiss* was released in France and throughout Europe, as well as the compilation album *Tarkan*.

The Yin Water Luck Cycle (age 27 to 31) also contained the favourable element. However, in 1999 (Yin Earth Rabbit year), the negative elements Earth and Wood were present in the Annual Stem and Branch. Tarkan was embroiled in a controversy, as he had still not performed military service after deferring it due to his studies in the US. Following the earthquake that year, legislation was passed to allow those who donated $16,000 USD to earthquake relief to serve only 28 days of military service. Tarkan returned to Turkey from the US in January 2000 (still the Yin Earth Rabbit year), to take advantage of the legislative change.

In January 2001 (still the Yang Metal Dragon year), Tarkan became the first Pepsi spokesperson in Turkey. The Annual Dragon Branch combined with his Rat Year Branch to form the favourable element Water. In 2001 (Yin Metal Snake year), his album *Karma* was released. While the album sold well, there were Metal Rivals present in the Annual Stem and Branch. That same year, Tarkan's lawyer sued the writer of the book *Tarkan – Anatomy of a Star* for violating Tarkan's reputation by publishing personal information and copyrighted photos. The book was withdrawn. On a personal note, the House of Spouse animal Snake was present in the Annual Branch. Tarkan started a seven-year relationship with lawyer Bilge Ozturk that year.

In 2002 (Yang Water Horse year), the favourable elements Water and Fire were present in the Annual Stem and Branch. Tarkan became the official mascot of the Turkish national football team for the 2002 World Cup. He also recorded the song *United for You*.

The Ox Luck Cycle (age 32 to 36) combined with his Snake Day Branch to transform him into a Dominant Metal chart. In 2006 (Yang Fire Dog year), there was a Stem Combination between the Annual Yang Fire Stem and Tarkan's Yin Metal Day Master. The Power Element Combination indicated professional success and recognition. He released his debut English album *Come Closer* with the single *Bounce*. In 2008 (Yang Earth Rat year), he released another Turkish album *Metamorphosis*. The favourable element Water was present in the Annual Branch.

The Yang Wood Luck Cycle (age 37 to 41) contained the negative element. Tarkan released *Adimi Kalbine Yaz* in 2010 (Yang Metal Tiger year). The Annual Tiger Branch combined with his Dog Month Branch to form the favourable element Fire. He did not release any music during this period.

The Tiger Luck Cycle (age 42 to 46) combined with his Dog Month Branch to form the favourable element Fire. In 2016 (Yang Fire Monkey year), Tarkan married his longtime girlfriend Pinar Dilek. The Annual Monkey Branch combined with the Snake in his House of Spouse. This indicated the possibility of love or marriage.

The Yin Wood Luck Cycle (age 47 to 51) forms a Stem Combination with the Yang Metal Month Stem. The Metal Rival is removed. While the Rabbit Luck Cycle (age 52 to 56) contains the negative element Wood, it forms a Six Harmony Combination with the Dog Month Branch, indicating the possibility of assistance from mentors or helpful individuals. The Yang Fire Luck Cycle (age 57 to 61) forms a Stem Combination with Tarkan's Yin Metal Day Master, indicating the potential for professional recognition or success during this period.

Example 7.13 Jacqueline McKenzie, Australian Actress
(born October 24, 1967)

Hour	Day	Month	Year
	辛	庚	丁
	Yin Metal	Yang Metal	Yin Fire
	酉	戌	未
	Rooster	Dog	Sheep

5	15	25	35
辛	壬	癸	甲
Yin Metal	Yang Water	Yin Water	Yang Wood
亥	子	丑	寅
Pig	Rat	Ox	Tiger

45	55	65	75
乙	丙	丁	戊
Yin Wood	Yang Fire	Yin Fire	Yang Earth
卯	辰	巳	午
Rabbit	Dragon	Snake	Horse

There are no Branch Combinations in McKenzie's birth chart. She is a Yin Metal Day Master with a Rooster Day Branch and a Yang Metal Month Stem. This qualifies her as a Competitive Metal chart. In Snake or Ox years or Luck Cycles, there is a Partial Three Harmony Metal Combination. McKenzie will be transformed into a Dominant Metal chart. In Monkey years or Luck Cycles, there is a Seasonal Metal Combination with the Rooster and Dog Branches. McKenzie is once again transformed into a Dominant Metal chart. In Rooster years or Luck Cycles, she remains a Competitive Metal chart.

In the favourable Rat Luck Cycle (age 20 to 24), McKenzie successfully auditioned for Australia's *National Institute of Dramatic Arts* (NIDA) in 1988 (Yang Earth Dragon year). The Annual Dragon Branch combined with the Rat Luck Cycle to form the favourable element Water. She graduated in 1990 (Yang Metal Horse year). The Annual Horse Branch combined with her Dog Month Branch to form the favourable element Fire.

The Yin Water Luck Cycle (age 25 to 29) also contained the favourable element. In 1992 (Yang Water Monkey year), the Annual Monkey Branch combined with the Rooster and Dog Branches in her chart. She was transformed into a Dominant Metal chart. There was also the auspicious Sequence of Four Branches in a Row: Sheep Year Branch, Annual Monkey Branch, Rooster Day Branch and Dog Month Branch. McKenzie made her film debut in the highly acclaimed drama *Romper Stomper* opposite Russell Crowe. She won Best Actress at the Stockholm International Film Festival for her performance.

In 1995 (Yin Wood Pig year), there was a Stem Combination between the Annual Yin Wood Stem and her Yang Metal Month Stem. This removed her Yang Metal Rival. McKenzie made Australian Film Institute (AFI) history by winning Best Actress in a Leading Role for *Angel Baby* and Best Actress in a TV Drama for *Halifax f.p.* In 1996 (Yang Fire Rat year), there was a Stem Combination between the Annual Yang Fire Stem and her Yin Metal Day Master. The Power Element Combination indicated professional success and recognition. She was awarded Australian Star of the Year at the Australian Movie Convention. For a woman, the Power Element Combination also indicates marriage. McKenzie married high school sweetheart, Bill Walter, an orthopaedic surgeon that year.

The Ox Luck Cycle (age 30 to 34) combined with her Rooster Year Branch to transform her into a Dominant Metal chart. Her list of favourable elements became:

1) Resource element Earth.
2) Self element Metal.
3) Output element Water.
4) Wealth element Wood.
5) Power element Fire.

In 2000 (Yang Metal Dragon year), there was a Six Harmony Combination between the Annual Dragon Branch and her Rooster in the House of Spouse. The Rooster Branch was involved in a Competition for Combination as it also formed a Partial Three Harmony Metal Combination with the Ox Luck Cycle. McKenzie divorced Walter after four years of marriage. In 2001 (Yin Metal Snake year), the Annual Snake Branch combined with the Ox Luck Cycle and her Rooster Day Branch to reinforce the favourable element Metal. McKenzie portrayed tennis legend Margaret Court in the television movie *When Billie Beat Bobby* alongside Holly Hunter.

The Yang Wood Luck Cycle (age 35 to 39) contained the negative element, so McKenzie was dependent on the Annual Stems and Branches. In 2002 (Yang Water Horse year), the Annual Horse Branch combined with McKenzie's Dog Branch to form the favourable element Fire. McKenzie appeared in *Divine Secrets of the Ya-Ya Sisterhood* alongside Sandra Bullock and Ashley Judd. In 2004 (Yang Wood Monkey year), the Annual Monkey Branch combined with the Rooster and Dog Branches in McKenzie's chart to transform her into a Dominant Meal chart. She landed a leading role in the science fiction television series *The 4400*. In 2006 (Yang Fire Dog year), there was a Stem Combination between the Annual Yang Fire Stem and her Yin Metal Day Master. This indicated professional success and recognition. McKenzie had a significant role in the television series *Nightmares & Dreamscapes: From The Stories of Stephen King*.

The Tiger Luck Cycle (age 40 to 44) combined with the Dog Month Branch to form the favourable element Fire. In 2009 (Yin Earth Ox year), McKenzie had a daughter. She had become pregnant in 2008 (Yang Earth Rat year). Her Output or Child element Water was present in the Annual Rat Branch. In 2010 (Yang Metal Tiger year), McKenzie appeared in the Australian war drama *Beneath Hill 60*. The Annual Tiger Branch combined with the Dog Month Branch and the Tiger Luck Cycle to reinforce the favourable element Fire.

The Yin Wood Luck Cycle (age 45 to 49) formed a Stem Combination with the Yang Metal Month Stem. This removed the Yang Metal Rival. In 2013 (Yin Water Snake year), the Annual Snake Branch combined with her Rooster Day Branch to transform McKenzie into a Dominant Metal chart. She appeared as Maggie the cat in *Cat on a Hot Tin Roof* in the Theatre Royal in Sydney. In 2014 (Yang Wood Horse year), the Annual Horse Branch combined with McKenzie's Dog Month Branch to form the favourable element Fire. She appeared with Russell Crowe in his feature film directing debut *The Water Diviner*.

The Rabbit Luck Cycle (age 50 to 54) contains the negative element Wood but it also forms a Six Harmony Combination with McKenzie's Dog Month Branch. This indicates assistance from mentors and helpful individuals. The Yang Fire Luck Cycle (age 55 to 59) forms a Stem Combination with her Yin Metal Day Master, indicating professional success and recognition. The Dragon Luck Cycle (age 60 to 64) forms a Six Harmony Combination with the Rooster in the House of Spouse. This indicates the possibility of love or marriage for McKenzie during this period.

Example 7.14 Toni Tennille, American Singer
(born May 8, 1940, 18:15 hours)

Hour	Day	Month	Year
丁	辛	辛	庚
Yin Fire	Yin Metal	Yin Metal	Yang Metal
酉	亥	巳	辰
Rooster	Pig	Snake	Dragon

1	11	21	31
庚	己	戊	丁
Yang Metal	Yin Earth	Yang Earth	Yin Fire
辰	卯	寅	丑
Dragon	Rabbit	Tiger	Ox

41	51	61	71
丙	乙	甲	癸
Yang Fire	Yin Wood	Yang Wood	Yin Water
子	亥	戌	酉
Rat	Pig	Dog	Rooster

There are no Branch Combinations in the first three pillars of Tennille's birth chart. She is a Yin Metal Day Master with a Snake Month Branch. There is a Yang Metal Year Stem and a Yin Metal Month Stem. This qualifies her as a Competitive Metal chart in the first half of her life, i.e. before the age of 40. In Ox or Rooster years or Luck Cycles, Tennille is transformed into a Dominant Metal chart. In Snake years or Luck Cycles, she remains a Competitive Metal chart.

In the second half of her life, there is a Partial Three Harmony Metal Combination between the Snake Month Branch and the Rooster Hour Branch. This qualifies Tennille as a Dominant Metal chart. It should be noted that the Pig in the House of Spouse sits between the Combination of the Snake and the Rooster. This indicates potential marital issues, as the Spouse is an obstacle in the path of the Combination.

At the age of 22 during the Yang Earth Luck Cycle (age 21 to 25), Tennille married her first husband Kenneth Shearer in 1962 (Yang Water Tiger year). The Annual Tiger Branch formed a Six Harmony Combination with the Pig Branch in her House of Spouse. This indicated the possibility of love or marriage.

The Tiger Luck Cycle (age 26 to 30) formed a Six Harmony Combination with her Pig Day Branch. This indicated assistance from mentors or helpful individuals. At this time, Tennille was a member of the South Coast Repertory Theatre company. In 1969 (Yin Earth Rooster year), the Annual Rooster Branch combined with Tennille's Rooster Month Branch. She was transformed into a Dominant Metal chart. Her favourable elements became:

1) Resource element Earth.
2) Self element Metal.
3) Output element Water.
4) Wealth element Wood.
5) Power element Fire.

Tennille was asked by one of the directors of the repertory to write the music for *Mother Earth*, a rock musical.

The Yin Fire Luck Cycle (age 31 to 35) contained the favourable element. In 1971 (Yin Metal Pig year), Tennille met her future husband, studio musician Daryl Dragon during auditions for *Mother Earth*. Her House of Spouse animal Pig was present in the Annual Branch. This indicated the possibility of love or marriage. In 1972 (Yang Water Rat year), the favourable element Water was present. Tennille played electric piano with *The Beach Boys* during their tour and *Mother Earth* opened on Broadway. She also finalised her divorce from Shearer.

In 1973 (Yin Water Ox year), Dragon and Tennille formed *Captain & Tennille*. The Annual Ox Branch combined with her Snake Month Branch to transform her into a Dominant Metal chart. *Captain & Tennille* signed a recording contract after their song *The Way I Want to Touch You* became popular on a local radio station. In 1975 (Yin Wood Rabbit year), Tennille married Dragon. The Annual Rabbit Branch combined with the Pig Day Branch to form Wood. As the Pig in the House of Spouse is involved in a Combination, this indicated the possibility of love or marriage. The Annual Yin Wood Stem also formed a Stem Combination with Tennille's Yang Metal Year Stem. This effectively removed the Yang Metal Rival. *Captain & Tennille* scored a US Number 1 hit with *Love Will Keep Us Together*.

The Ox Luck Cycle (age 36 to 40) combined with Tennille's Snake Month Branch to transform her into a Dominant Metal chart. In 1976 (Yang Fire Dragon year), the Annual Yang Fire Stem formed a Stem Combination with her Yin Metal Day Master. The Power Element Combination indicated professional recognition and success. Captain & Tennille had three US Top 10 hits: *Shop Around*, *Muskrat Love* and *Lonely Night (Angel Face)*. They also had their own television show *The Captain & Tennille Show*.

1978 (Yang Earth Horse year) was a mixed year as the favourable element Earth was present in the Annual Stem and the negative element Fire in the Annual Branch. Captain & Tennille released the album *Dream*, which did not fare as well as their previous releases. In 1979 (Yin Earth Sheep year), *Captain & Tennille* signed a new contract with Casablanca Records and released the album *Make Your Move*. The favourable element Earth was present in the Annual Stem and Branch. In 1980 (Yang Metal Monkey year), *Captain & Tennille* scored their second Number 1 US hit with *Do That to Me One More Time*.

By the Yang Fire Luck Cycle (age 41 to 45), Tennille had become a Dominant Metal chart. There was also a Stem Combination between the Yang Fire Luck Cycle and her Yin Metal Day Master, indicating professional success. Tennille found another career singing and touring with big bands and symphonies, releasing the solo album *More Than You Know* in 1984 (Yang Wood Rat year). The Rat Luck Cycle (age 46 to 50) contained the favourable element Water. Tennille continued touring with classic jazz bands during this period.

In the Yin Water Luck Cycle (age 71 to 75), Tenille returned to the media spotlight when she filed for divorce from Dragon in January 2014 (still the Yin Water Snake year). After 39 years of marriage, the divorce was finalised in July 2014 (Yang Wood Horse year). The negative elements Wood and Fire were present in the Annual Stem and Branch. In 2016 (Yang Fire Monkey year), there was a Stem Combination between the Annual Yang Fire Stem and her Yin Metal Day Master. This indicated professional success and recognition. *Toni Tennille: A Memoir* was released.

Example 7.15 Gwen Stefani, American Singer
(born October 3, 1969, 10:23 hours)

Hour	Day	Month	Year
癸	辛	癸	己
Yin Water	Yin Metal	Yin Water	Yin Earth
巳	亥	酉	酉
Snake	Pig	Rooster	Rooster

2	12	22	32
甲	乙	丙	丁
Yang	Yin	Yang	Yin
Wood	Wood	Fire	Fire
戌	亥	子	丑
Dog	Pig	Rat	Ox

42	52	62	72
戊	己	庚	辛
Yang	Yin	Yang	Yin
Earth	Earth	Metal	Metal
寅	卯	辰	巳
Tiger	Rabbit	Dragon	Snake

There are no Branch Combinations in the first three pillars of Stefani's birth chart. She is a Yin Metal Day Master, with two Rooster Branches, in the Month and Year Pillar. This qualifies her as a Competitive Metal chart in the first half of life. In the Snake or Ox years or Luck Cycles, there is a Partial Three Harmony Combination that will transform Stefani into a Dominant Metal chart. In Rooster years or Luck Cycles, Stefani remains a Competitive Metal chart.

The Hour Pillar exerts its influence in the second half of life, after the age of 40. There is a Partial Three Harmony Combination between the Snake Hour Branch and the Rooster Month Branch. This transforms Stefani into a Dominant Metal chart. However, note that the Pig in the House of Spouse is in the way of the Combination of the Snake and Rooster Branches. This indicates potential marital issues.

The Pig Luck Cycle (age 17 to 21) contains the negative element Wood, as well as the favourable element Water. In 1986 (Yang Fire Tiger year), there was a Stem Combination between the Annual Yang Fire Stem and Stefani's Yin Metal Day Master. The Power Element Combination indicated professional success and recognition. Stefani joined her brother's band *No Doubt* as a vocalist. In 1987 (Yin Fire Rabbit year), there was a Combination involving the Pig in the House of Spouse and the Annual Rabbit Branch. Stefani started a seven-year relationship with bassist Tony Kanal that year.

There was a Stem Combination between the Yang Fire Luck Cycle (age 22 to 26) and Stefani's Yin Metal Day Master. This indicated professional recognition and success. In 1995 (Yin Wood Pig year), *No Doubt's* third album *Tragic Kingdom* was released. The House of Spouse animal Pig was present in the Annual Branch. Stefani started a relationship with *Bush* guitarist and lead singer Gavin Rossdale. *Tragic Kingdom* became popular in 1996 (Yang Fire Rat year) during the favourable Rat Luck Cycle (age 27 to 31). There was a Stem Combination between the Annual Yang Fire Stem and Stefani's Yin Metal Day Master. *No Doubt* scored a US Number 1 Airplay hit with *Don't Speak*. In 2000 (Yang Metal Dragon year), the Annual Dragon Branch combined with the Rat Luck Cycle to form the favourable element Water. *No Doubt* released the follow-up album *Return of Saturn*.

The Yin Fire Luck Cycle (age 32 to 36) contained the favourable element. In 2001 (Yin Metal Snake year), the Annual Snake Branch combined with the Rooster Branches in Stefani's chart to transform her into a Dominant Metal chart. Her favourable elements became:

1) Resource element Earth.
2) Self element Metal.
3) Output element Water.
4) Wealth element Wood.
5) Power element Fire.

No Doubt released another hit album *Rock Steady* with the US Top 10 singles *Hey Baby* and *Underneath It All*. Stefani also carved herself a career as a singer outside of the band, enjoying a US Number 2 hit with *Let Me Blow Ya Mind*, a duet with Eve. In 2002 (Yang Water Horse year), the favourable elements Water and Fire were present. Stefani married Gavin Rossdale.

In 2004 (Yang Wood Monkey year), Stefani released her debut solo album *Love. Angel. Music. Baby.* with the top US Top 10 hits *Rich Girl* and *Hollaback Girl*. The favourable element Water was present in the Annual Monkey Branch. She also made her acting debut in Martin Scorsese's *The Aviator* playing Jean Harlow.

The Ox Luck Cycle (age 37 to 41) combined with Stefani's Rooster Branches, transforming her into a Dominant Metal chart. In 2006 (Yang Fire Dog year), there was a Stem Combination between the Annual Yang Fire Stem and her Yin Metal Day Master. This indicated professional recognition and success. Stefani released her second album *The Sweet Escape* with the top 10 hits *Wind It Up* and the title track. On May 26 that year, she gave birth to son Kingston. Stefani had become pregnant in August (Yang Wood Monkey month) the previous year. Her Output or Child element Water was present in the month she became pregnant. On August 21, 2008 (Yang Earth Rat year), Stefani gave birth to second son Zuma. The Child element Water was present in the Annual Pig Branch in 2007 (Yin Fire Pig year), the year she became pregnant.

By the Yang Earth Luck Cycle (age 42 to 46), Stefani had become a Dominant Metal chart. In 2012 (Yang Water Dragon year), the favourable elements Water and Earth were present in the Annual Stem and Branch. *No Doubt* released another US Top 10 album *Push and Shove*. On February 24, 2014 (Yang Wood Horse year), Stefani gave birth to her third son Apollo. She had become pregnant in 2013 (Yin Water Snake year), a year in which her Child element was present. In 2015 (Yin Wood Sheep year), Stefani filed for divorce from Rossdale. There was a Combination between the Annual Sheep Branch and the Pig Day Branch to form Wood. There was a Metal-Wood conflict in Stefani's chart. However, the Combination involved the Pig Branch in the House of Spouse, indicating the possibility of love. In November that year, Stefani announced her relationship with country singer Blake Shelton. The Pig Branch in the House of Spouse indicates the possibility of love or marriage.

The Tiger Luck Cycle (age 47 to 51) contained the negative elements Fire and Wood and the favourable element Earth. In 2016 (Yang Fire Monkey year), there was a Stem Combination between the Annual Yang Fire Stem and Stefani's Yin Metal Day Master. This indicated professional success and recognition. She had her first US Number 1 solo album *This Is What the Truth Feels Like*.

The Yin Earth Luck Cycle (age 52 to 56) contains the favourable element Earth. The Rabbit Luck Cycle (age 57 to 61) clashes with the Rooster Month Branch, disrupting the Three Harmony Metal Combination. Stefani reverts back to being a Competitive Metal chart. There is also a Combination between the Rabbit Luck Cycle and her Pig Day Branch, forming Wood. There is the possibility of love or marriage as the House of Spouse is involved in a Combination.

Example 7.16 Richard Dreyfuss, American Actor
(born October 29, 1947, 18:07 hours)

Hour	Day	Month	Year
丁	辛	庚	丁
Yin Fire	Yin Metal	Yang Metal	Yin Fire
酉	巳	戌	亥
Rooster	Snake	Dog	Pig

7	17	27	37
己	戊	丁	丙
Yin Earth	Yang Earth	Yin Fire	Yang Fire
酉	申	未	午
Rooster	Monkey	Sheep	Horse

47	57	67	77
乙	甲	癸	壬
Yin Wood	Yang Wood	Yin Water	Yang Water
巳	辰	卯	寅
Snake	Dragon	Rabbit	Tiger

There are no Branch Combinations in the first three pillars of Dreyfuss' birth chart. He is a Yin Metal Day Master with a Snake Day Branch and a Yang Metal Month Stem. This qualifies him as a Competitive Metal chart in the first half of his life. In Rooster or Ox years or Luck Cycles, there is a Partial Three Harmony Metal Combination that transforms Dreyfuss into a Dominant Metal chart. In the Snake years or Luck Cycles, he remains a Competitive Metal chart.

The Hour Pillar exerts its influence in the second half of life after the age of 40. The Rooster Hour Branch forms a Partial Three Harmony Metal Combination with the Snake Day Branch. Dreyfuss is transformed into a Dominant Metal chart.

In the favourable Monkey Luck Cycle (age 22 to 26), Dreyfuss had his first major film role as a college bound young man in *American Graffiti* alongside Ron Howard in 1973 (Yin Water Ox year). The Annual Ox Branch combined with his Snake Day Branch to transform him into a Dominant Metal chart. His favourable elements became:

1) Resource element Earth.
2) Self element Metal.
3) Output element Water.
4) Wealth element Wood.
5) Power element Fire.

The Monkey Luck Cycle also contained the favourable element Water.

The Yin Fire Luck Cycle (age 27 to 31) also included Dreyfuss' favourable element. In 1974 (Yang Wood Tiger year), he appeared in the highest grossing Canadian film at that time, the comedy *The Apprenticeship of Duddy Kravitz*. The Annual Tiger Branch combined with his Dog Month Branch to form the favourable element Fire. In 1975 (Yin Wood Rabbit year), there was a Stem Combination between the Annual Yin Wood Stem and his Yang Metal Month Stem. The Yang Metal Rival was removed. Dreyfuss starred in Steven Spielberg's blockbuster *Jaws*. In 1978 (Yang Earth Horse year), the Annual Horse Branch combined with Dreyfuss' Dog Month Branch to form the favourable element Fire. He became the youngest ever winner of the Best Actor Oscar for his performance as a struggling young actor in the romantic comedy *The Goodbye Girl*. Dreyfuss also appeared in Steven Spielberg's science fiction hit *Close Encounters of the Third Kind*.

The Sheep Luck Cycle (age 32 to 36) combined with his Pig Year Branch to form the negative element Wood. Although Dreyfuss was an in demand actor during this period, he also had substance abuse issues involving alcohol and cocaine. In 1982 (Yang Water Dog year), Dreyfuss was arrested for cocaine possession after he blacked out while driving and crashed his car into a tree. The negative element Earth was present in the Annual Dog Branch. He entered rehabilitation.

The Yang Fire Luck Cycle (age 37 to 41) combined with Dreyfuss' Yin Metal Day Master. The Power Element Combination indicates professional recognition and success. In 1986 (Yang Fire Tiger year), there was another Stem Combination involving the Annual Yang Fire Stem and his Yin Metal Day Master. He made his comeback in the comedy *Down and Out in Beverly Hills* alongside Bette Midler and Nick Nolte. Dreyfuss also appeared as the narrator in the coming of age drama *Stand by Me*.

By the Horse Luck Cycle (age 42 to 46), Dreyfuss had become a Dominant Metal chart. The Horse Luck Cycle combined with the Dog Month Branch to form the negative element Fire. There was a Fire-Metal conflict in Dreyfuss' chart. Although he appeared in some notable films in years with favourable elements, they were not major box office successes. In 1989 (Yin Earth Snake year), the Annual Snake Branch combined with the Rooster and Snake Branches in his chart to reinforce the favourable element Metal. Dreyfuss appeared in the romantic comedy *Always* with Holly Hunter. In 1991 (Yin Metal Sheep year), the favourable elements Metal and Earth were present. Dreyfuss starred opposite Bill Murray in the comedy *What About Bob?* In 1993 (Yin Water Rooster year), the Annual Rooster Branch combined with the Snake and Rooster Branches in his chart to reinforce the favourable element Metal. Dreyfuss appeared in the movie adaptation of Neil Simon's Pulitzer Prize winning play *Lost in Yonkers*.

The Yin Wood Luck Cycle (age 47 to 51) formed a Stem Combination with his Yang Metal Month Stem. Any negative effects were reduced. In 1996 (Yang Fire Rat year), there was a Stem Combination between the Annual Yang Fire Stem and his Yin Metal Day Master. This indicated professional recognition and success. Dreyfuss received another Best Actor Oscar nomination for his performance in *Mr. Holland's Opus*.

The Snake Luck Cycle (age 52 to 56) combined with the Rooster and Snake Branches to reinforce the favourable element Metal. The Snake is also Dreyfuss' House of Spouse animal, indicating the possibility of love or marriage. Dreyfuss married Janelle Lacey during this period in 1999 (Yin Earth Rabbit year).

The Yang Wood Luck Cycle (age 57 to 61) contained the negative element Wood. However, Dreyfuss fared well in years with his favourable elements. In 2006 (Yang Fire Dog year), there was a Stem Combination between the Annual Yang Fire Stem and his Yin Metal Day Master, indicating professional recognition and success. Dreyfuss appeared in the remake *Poseidon* alongside Josh Lucas and Kurt Russell. In 2008 (Yang Earth Rat year), the favourable element Earth and Water were present in the Annual Stem and Branch. Dreyfuss portrayed Dick Cheney in Oliver Stone's biopic of George W. Bush *W.*

The Dragon (age 62 to 66) and Yin Water (age 67 to 71) Luck Cycles contained the favourable elements. In 2016 (Yang Fire Monkey year), Dreyfuss portrayed fraudster Bernie Madoff in the television series *Madoff* opposite Michelle Pfeiffer. There was a Stem Combination between the Annual Yang Fire Stem and his Yin Metal Day Master.

The Rabbit Luck Cycle (age 72 to 76) clashes with his Rooster Hour Branch to disrupt the Three Harmony Metal Combination. Dreyfuss reverts back to a Competitive Metal chart. The negative element Wood is also present. There may be some issues or complications, especially in years with the negative elements.

Example 7.17 Peter Benchley, American Author
(born May 8, 1940, died February 11, 2006)

Hour	Day	Month	Year
	辛	辛	庚
	Yin Metal	Yin Metal	Yang Metal
	亥	巳	辰
	Pig	Snake	Dragon

10	20	30	40	50	60
壬	癸	甲	乙	丙	丁
Yang Water	Yin Water	Yang Wood	Yin Wood	Yang Fire	Yin Fire
午	未	申	酉	戌	亥
Horse	Sheep	Monkey	Rooster	Dog	Pig

Hour	Day	Month	Year
	辛	庚	丙
	Yin Metal	Yang Metal	Yang Fire
	未	寅	戌
	Sheep	Tiger	Dog

There are no Combinations in Benchley's birth chart. He is a Yin Metal Day Master with a Snake Month Branch, Yin Metal Month Stem and Yang Metal Month Stem. This qualifies him as a Competitive Metal chart. In Rooster or Ox years or Luck Cycles, there is a Partial Three Harmony Metal Combination that transforms Benchley into a Dominant Metal chart. In Snake years or Luck Cycles, he remains a Competitive Metal chart.

In the favourable Yin Water Luck Cycle (age 20 to 24), Benchley graduated from Harvard University in 1961 (Yin Metal Ox year). The Annual Ox Branch combined with his Snake Month Branch to transform him into a Dominant Metal chart. His favourable elements became:

1) Resource element Earth.
2) Self element Metal.
3) Output element Water.
4) Wealth element Wood.
5) Power element Fire.

In 1963 (Yin Water Rabbit year), Benchley met Wendy Wesson while dining at an inn in Nantucket. They started dating. There was a Combination between the Annual Rabbit Branch and the Pig in the House of Spouse. This indicated the possibility of love or marriage. He also married Wesson the following year, 1964 (Yang Wood Dragon year). In the same year, Benchley also published his first book *Time and a Ticket*, a travel memoir.

The Sheep Luck Cycle (age 25 to 29) combined with the Pig Day Branch to form the negative element Wood. However, for a Yin Metal Day Master, the Special Stars are the Pig and Sheep. The Sheep Luck Cycle worked in conjunction with Benchley's Pig Day Branch to bring him success. In 1967 (Yin Fire Sheep year), he became the speechwriter for President Lyndon B. Johnson in the White House. The favourable element Fire was present in the Annual Stem.

The Yang Wood Luck Cycle (age 30 to 34) contained the negative element. By 1971 (Yin Metal Pig year), the negative elements Metal and Wood were present in the Annual Stem and Branch. Benchley was working various freelance jobs in his struggle to support his family. His first novel *Jaws*, was published in 1974 (Yang Wood Tiger year), staying on the bestseller lists for 44 weeks. The Annual Tiger Branch formed a Six Harmony Combination with his Pig Day Branch, indicating assistance from mentors.

The Monkey Luck Cycle (age 35 to 39) contained the favourable element Water. *Jaws* was adapted into a major hit movie in 1975 (Yin Wood Rabbit year) starring Richard Dreyfuss and Roy Scheider. There was a Stem Combination between the Annual Yin Wood Stem and his Yang Metal Year Stem. This removed the Yang Metal Rival. In 1976 (Yang Fire Dragon year), there was a Stem Combination involving the Annual Yang Fire Stem and Benchley's Yin Metal Day Master. The Power Element Combination indicated professional recognition and success. Benchley published *The Deep*, which was made into a successful movie in 1977 (Yin Fire Snake year) with Nick Nolte and Jacqueline Bisset. The favourable elmement Fire was present in the Annual Stem. In 1979 (Yin Earth Sheep year), the Annual Sheep Branch worked in conjunction with his Pig Day Branch to bring him success. Benchley published *The Island*.

The Yin Wood Luck Cycle (age 40 to 44) combined with the Yang Metal Year Stem. This removed the Yang Metal Rival. In 1980 (Yang Metal Monkey year), *The Island* was made into a movie starring Michael Caine. The Annual Yang Stem also formed a Stem Combination with the Yin Wood Luck Cycle. Potential negative effects were reduced.

The Rooster Luck Cycle (age 45 to 49) combined with Benchley's Snake Month Branch to transform him into a Dominant Metal chart. In 1986 (Yang Fire Tiger year), there was a Stem Combination between the Annual Yang Fire Stem and his Yin Metal Day Master. This indicated professional success and recognition. Benchley published *Q Clearance*, a novel about a political speechwriter.

The Yang Fire Luck Cycle (age 50 to 54) formed a Stem Combination with Benchley's Yin Metal Day Master. This indicated professional recognition and success. In 1991

(Yin Metal Sheep year), Benchley published *Beast*. The Annual Sheep Branch worked in conjunction with his Pig Day Branch to bring him success as the Special Stars.

The Dog Luck Cycle (age 55 to 59) contained the negative element Earth. In 1996 (Yang Fire Rat year), there was a Stem Combination between the Annual Yang Fire Stem and Benchley's Yin Metal Day Master indicating professional success or recognition. *The Beast* was made into a television movie. In 1997 (Yin Fire Ox year), his novel *White Shark* was republished as *Creature*. The Annual Ox Branch combined with his Snake Month Branch to transform him into a Dominant Metal chart. In 1998 (Yang Earth Tiger year), the television movie *Creature* with Craig T. Nelson and Kim Cattrall was released. The Annual Tiger Branch combined with the Dog Luck Cycle to form the favourable element Fire.

The Yin Fire Luck Cycle (age 60 to 64) contained the favourable element. Benchley published non-fiction books such as *Shark: True Stories and Lessons from the Deep* in 2002 (Yang Water Horse year). The favourable elements Water and Fire were present in the Annual Stem and Branch.

Benchley died of pulmonary fibrosis on February 11, 2006 during the Pig Luck Cycle (from age 65). On the day he died, the Tiger month of death combined with the Dog year to form the favourable element Fire. The Sheep day of death also combined with the Pig Luck Cycle and Pig Day Branch to form the negative element Wood. It was also a Yin Metal day during a Yang Metal month. Metal Rivals created issues for him.

Example 7.18 Alicia Vikander, Swedish Actress
(born October 3, 1988)

Hour	Day	Month	Year
	辛	辛	戊
	Yin Metal	Yin Metal	Yang Earth
	卯	酉	辰
	Rabbit	Rooster	Dragon

9	19	29	39
庚	己	戊	丁
Yang Metal	Yin Earth	Yang Earth	Yin Fire
申	未	午	巳
Monkey	Sheep	Horse	Snake

49	59	69	79
丙	乙	甲	癸
Yang Fire	Yin Wood	Yang Wood	Yin Water
辰	卯	寅	丑
Dragon	Rabbit	Tiger	Ox

There are no Full or Partial Three Harmony or Seasonal Combinations within Vikander's birth chart. She is a Yin Metal Day Master. There is a Rooster Month Branch and a Yin Metal Month Branch. This qualifies Vikander as a Competitive Metal chart. In the Snake or Ox years or Luck Cycles, she is transformed into a Dominant Metal chart. In Rooster years or Luck Cycles, she remains a Competitive Metal chart.

There is a Six Harmony Combination between Vikander's Rooster Month Branch and Dragon Year Branch. This indicates the presence of mentors and helpful individuals in her life.

Although the Yin Earth Luck Cycle (age 19 to 23) contained the negative element, Vikander fared well in

432

years with her favourable elements. In 2008 (Yang Earth Rat year), the Annual Rat Branch combined with her Monkey Year Branch to form the favourable element Water. Vikander gained the attention of Northern European audiences with her performance in the television series *Andra Avenyn*. In 2009 (Yin Earth Ox year), the Annual Ox Branch combined with her Rooster Month Branch to transform her into a Dominant Metal chart. Her list of favourable elements became:

1) Resource element Earth.
2) Self element Metal.
3) Output element Water.
4) Wealth element Wood.
5) Power element Fire.

Vikander made her film debut in the Swedish movie *Pure*, which was first shown at the Pusan Film Festival.

In 2012 (Yang Water Dragon year), the Annual Dragon Branch formed a Six Harmony Combination with the Rooster Month Branch. There are two Six Harmony Combinations, as there is already a Six Harmony Combination between the Rooster Month Branch and the Dragon Year Branch. This is known as a Lovebirds Combination and indicates that the person enjoys a good reputation. Apart from this Combination, the favourable element Water is also present in the Annual Stem. Vikander appeared in the update of *Anna Karenina* alongside Keira Knightley. She also had the leading role in the Danish film *A Royal Affair*, which received an Oscar nomination for Best Foreign Film.

The Sheep Luck Cycle (age 24 to 28) combined with Vikander's Rabbit Day Branch to form the negative element Wood. However, the Combination involves the Rabbit in the House of Spouse. This indicated the possibility of love or marriage during this period.

In 2013 (Yin Water Snake year), the Annual Snake Branch combined with her Rooster Month Branch to form Metal.

Vikander was transformed into a Dominant Metal chart. However, there was also a Wood Combination present between the Sheep Luck Cycle and the Rabbit Day Branch. There was a Metal-Wood conflict. Vikander appeared in *The Fifth Estate*, about the news website WikiLeaks, opposite Benedict Cumberbatch. The movie was not a success.

In 2014 (Yang Wood Horse year), the favourable element Fire was present in the Annual Branch. Vikander appeared in two critically acclaimed films, the romance *Testament of Youth* and Alex Garland's science fiction thriller *Ex Machina*. In 2015 (Yin Wood Sheep year), the Annual Sheep Branch combined with the Rabbit Day Branch in the House of Spouse, indicating the possibility of romance. Vikander started a relationship with actor Michael Fassbender.

In 2016 (Yang Fire Monkey year), there was a Stem Combination involving the Annual Yang Fire Stem and her Yin Metal Day Master. This indicated professional recognition and success. Vikander won the Best Supporting Actress Oscar for her performance in the biopic *The Danish Girl* opposite Eddie Redmayne. The Power Element Combination also indicates the possibility of romance. As previously mentioned, Vikander was involved with Michael Fassbender, her co-star from the romantic drama *The Light Between Oceans*. The Annual Monkey Branch combined with her Dragon Year Branch to form the favourable element Water.

The Yang Earth Luck Cycle (age 29 to 33) contains the negative element Earth, so the influence of the Annual Stems and Branches will be important for Vikander. The Horse (age 34 to 38) and Yin Fire (age 39 to 43) Luck Cycles contain the favourable element Fire. The Snake Luck Cycle (age 44 to 48) combines with Vikander's Rooster Month Branch. She is transformed into a Dominant Metal chart. The Yang Fire Luck Cycle (age 49 to 53) forms a Stem Combination with her Yin Metal Day Master. There will be professional recognition and success during this period. The Dragon Luck Cycle (age 54 to 58) forms a Six Harmony Combination with the Rooster Month Branch, indicating assistance from mentors. The Yin Wood Luck Cycle (age 59 to 63) contains the negative element, so the influence of the Annual Stems and Branches will be significant.

Conclusion

From the 18 examples covered in this chapter, this list of favourable elements for Competitive Metal charts is:

1) Output element Water.
2) Power element Fire.
3) Self element Metal in the Branches.
4) Resource element Earth.
5) Wealth element Wood.

All the examples were Yang or Yin Metal Day Masters without any Partial or Full Three Harmony Metal Combinations or Seasonal Metal Combinations in their Branches. There were either two or more Metal Branches present in their charts or at least one Metal Branch and one Metal Stem in their charts. However, they were able to transform into Dominant Metal charts as a result of the Luck Cycles or the Annual Branch.

Shane Warne, Kevin Scott Richardson, Vanna White and John Lithgow are Yin Metal Day Masters with two Rooster Branches in their birth charts. Kevin Scott Richardson and Ben Carson are Yin Metal Day Masters with two Rooster Branches and another Yin Metal Stem in their charts. Nancy Kerrigan is a Yin Metal Day Master with three Rooster Branches in her chart.

Anastacia is Yang Metal Day Master with a Rooster Branch and a Yin Metal Stem in her chart. Sergio Mendes is a Yang Metal Day Master with a Snake Branch, a Yang Metal Stem and a Yin Metal Stem in his chart.

Wyclef Jean and Tarkan are Yin Metal Day Masters with a Snake Branch and a Yang Metal Stem in their charts. Jacqueline McKenzie is a Yin Metal Day Master with a Rooster Branch and a Yang Metal Stem in her chart, while Alicia Vikander is a Yin Metal Day Master with a Rooster Branch and a Yin Metal Stem in her chart.

Peter Benchley is a Yin Metal Day Master with a Snake Branch, a Yang Metal Stem and a Yin Metal Stem in his chart, while Mardy Fish is a Yin Metal Day Master with two Rooster Branches, a Yang Metal Stem and a Yin Metal Stem.

Kelly Rowland is a Yang Metal Day Master with a Rooster Branch, a Yang Metal Stem and a Yin Metal Stem in her chart.

Gwen Stefani, Toni Tennille and Richard Dreyfuss have charts that are Competitive Metal charts in the first half of their lives before transforming into Dominant Metal charts in the second half of their lives.

Gwen Stefani is a Yin Metal Day Master with two Rooster Branches in her chart. However, her Rooster Month Branch combines with her Snake Hour Branch to transform her into a Dominant Metal chart in the latter part of her life.

Toni Tennille is a Yin Metal Day Master with a Snake Branch, a Yin Metal Stem and a Yang Metal Stem in her chart. In the latter part of her life, her Snake Month Branch combines with her Rooster Hour Branch to transform her into a Dominant Metal chart.

Richard Dreyfuss is a Yin Metal Day Master with a Snake Branch and a Yang Metal Stem in his chart. In the latter half of his life, his Snake Day Branch combines with his Rooster Hour Branch to transform him into a Dominant Metal chart.

Chapter Eight Conclusion

From the 108 examples covered in the previous six chapters, you would have noticed similar principles applied to all these Metal charts. They are known as Metal charts not because Metal is the most favourable element for all, but because Metal is the most prominent element most of the time.

Here are the steps to ascertain a Metal chart and the favourable elements:

Step 1: Look for Metal Combinations within the Branches:

a) Seasonal Metal Combination: all three Branches have to be present, i.e. the Monkey, Rooster and Dog. The Year Pillar's effects are present in the first half of life, while the Hour Pillar only exerts its influence in the latter part of life. This means that the Branches of the Seasonal Water Combination have to be present either in the Day, Month and Year Pillars or the Hour, Day and Month Pillars.

b) The Full Three Harmony Combination: when all three Branches (the Snake, Rooster and Ox) of the Three Harmony Water Combination are present. Even if the Branches are not in a sequence in the chart, e.g. Hour, Month and Year Pillars, it does not affect the Metal Combination within the chart. A Partial Three Harmony Metal Combination is still able to create Metal. If an additional Three Harmony Metal Branch (Snake, Rooster or Ox) is present, it reinforces the formation of Metal.

c) Partial Three Harmony Combination: when two out of the three Branches are present in the chart. These Pairs include the Snake and Rooster, the Rooster and Ox and the Snake and Ox. If an additional Three Harmony Branch is present: two Snakes and a Rooster or two Roosters and a Snake, it also contributes to the formation of Metal. The Partial Three Harmony Metal Combination can still occur when the Branches are separated by one Branch. So if the Branches are in the Day and Year Pillars or in the Hour and Month Pillars, then the Partial Three Harmony Metal Combination still occurs. However, there is no Partial Three Harmony Metal Combination if two other Branches separate the Branches of the Combination. For example, there cannot be a Partial Three Harmony Combination between the Hour Branch and the Year Branch.

Step 2: If there are no Metal Combinations within the Branches but there are two or more Snakes and Roosters, then the Day Master needs to be considered relative to this Metal. If there are Branch Combinations belonging to another element (i.e. Wood, Fire or Metal), then the chart is not a Metal chart. Note that there are no Seasonal or Three Harmony Combinations involving Earth, so different criteria are employed to classify Earth charts.

Step 3: Next consider the Day Master.

    a)   If the Day Master is Yang Water or Yin Water, then Metal is the Resource element. The chart is then classified as a Follow the Resource (Metal) chart with the following ranking of elements:
- i)   Resource element Metal.
- ii)   Power element Earth.
- iii)   Output element Wood.
- iv)   Wealth element Fire.
- v)   Self element Water.

    b)   If the Day Master is Yang Earth or Yin Earth, then Metal is the Output element. The chart is classified as a Follow the Output (Metal) chart with the following ranking of elements:
- i)   Output element Metal.
- ii)   Wealth element Water.
- iii)   Power element Wood.
- iv)   Self element Earth.
- v)   Resource element Fire.

    c)   If the Day Master is Yang Fire or Yin Fire, then Metal is the Wealth element. The chart is classified as a Follow the Wealth (Metal) chart with the following ranking of elements:

i)   Wealth element Metal.
ii)   Output element Earth.
iii)   Power element Water.
iv)   Resource element Wood.
v)   Self element Fire.

d)   If the Day Master is Yang Wood or Yin Wood, then Metal is the Power element. The chart is classified as a Follow the Power (Metal) chart with the following ranking of elements:
i)   Power element Metal.
ii)   Wealth element Earth.
iii)   Resource element Water.
iv)   Self element Wood.
v)   Output element Fire.

e)   If the Day Master is Yang Metal or Yin Metal and Step 1 is met, then there is a Combination within the Branches forming the Self element. The chart is classified as a Dominant Metal chart with the following ranking of elements:
i)   Resource element Earth.
ii)   Self element Metal.
iii)   Output element Water.
iv)   Wealth element Wood.
v)   Power element Fire.

f)   If the Day Master is Yang Metal or Yin Metal and Step 2 is fulfilled and there are Self element Branches scattered throughout the chart without a Combination. The chart is classified as a Competitive Metal chart. If there is only one Metal Branch (i.e. Snake or Rooster), then you need to consider if there are other Metal Stem(s). If there is one or more, then the chart is also classified as a Competitive Metal chart with the following ranking of elements:
i)   Output element Water.
ii)   Power element Fire.
iii)   Self element Metal Branches.
iv)   Resource element Earth.
v)   Wealth element Wood.

You now have the criteria for the six different types of Metal charts and their respective list of favourable elements. What is more important is that you go with the flow of the prevalent element of your chart as demonstrated by the 108 examples that were discussed. There are four other elements (i.e. Metal, Wood, Fire and Earth). As the Water book is already available, Fire, Wood and Earth charts will be discussed in forthcoming books.

Made in the USA
San Bernardino, CA
24 November 2018